# Han

*To the memory of Jean Bayet, to whom I owe my first initiation into classical philology*

# HANNIBAL

Serge Lancel

Translated by *Antonia Nevill*

Originally published in French by Librarie Arthème Fayard, Paris, 1995 and 
First published in English by Blackwell Publishers Ltd 1998, 1999

Reprinted 1999
First published in paperback 1999

Blackwell Publishers Ltd
108 Cowley Road
Oxford OX4 1JF
UK

Blackwell Publishers Inc.
350 Main St
Malden, Massachusetts 02148
USA



*British Library Cataloguing in Publication Data*

A CIP catalogue record for this book is available from the
British Library.

*Library of Congress Cataloging-in-Publication Data*

Lancel, Serge.
[Hannibal. English]
Hannibal / Serge Lancel; translated by Antonia Nevill.
p. cm.
Includes bibliographical references and index.
ISBN 0-631-20631-0 (hbk)
ISBN 0-631-21848-3 (pbk)
1. Hannibal, 247–182 B.C. 2. Generals—Tunisia—Carthage (Extinct city)—Biography. 3. Carthage (Extinct city)—History, Millitary.
4. Rome—History—Republic, 265–30 B.C. I. Title.
DG249.L3513 1998
937'.04'092—dc21 97-37371
[B] CIP

Typeset in Ehrhardt on 10/12 pt by Pure Tech India Ltd, Pondicherry
Printed in Great Britain by T. J. International Ltd., Padstow, Cornwall

This book is printed on acid-free paper

# Contents

# Figures

# Foreword

*Expende Hannibalem: quot libras in duce summo Invenies?*
(Weigh the ashes of Hannibal: how many pounds of this famous general will you find?)

(Juvenal, X, 147–8)

Hostile towards all establishment grandeur, and above all probably towards his own emperor, Trajan – himself a born leader of men – Juvenal ironically weighed up that handful of ashes, the last, pathetic remains of Hannibal. But how heavy these are when weighed in the scales of history! A *momentum*, as they then said in Rome, capable of tipping the balance in decisive fashion. Yet we know what became of this formidable 'weight' – the final failure of the Carthaginian general, harbinger of the fall and the destruction of the country half a century later.

Carthage dragged down the image of its most glorious son into its own ruin. Antiquity did not deal kindly with the vanquished. The kind of *damnatio memoriae* that overcame Rome's rival, already physically annihilated, cast its shadow over the great figure of Hannibal, which did not attain its full historical richness and coherence. Apart from a few rather mediocre pages in Cornelius Nepos, there is no 'Life of Hannibal' that can be placed in the portrait gallery of the mighty leaders of the ancient world, between Alexander and Caesar. Nor has any marble or bronze reliably recorded his features. Nothing remains to us of so great a destiny but partial reflections, glimpsed in the shards of a broken mirror.

Legend feeds on the gaps in history. Perhaps it was from this historical flaw that the personality of Hannibal derived part of the fascination which it exerted from a very early time, first of all in Rome itself. In a powerful summary of some twenty lines, the text of the Latin satirist mentioned above retraces that extraordinary 'career', which became much prized as a subject to be declaimed by Roman adolescents in the schools of rhetoric; and another allusion (*Satires*, VII, 160–4) suggests that by the end of the first century AD the teachers had become heartily tired of it. Later, although Hannibal's exploits did little to inspire poets and dramatists in European literature – though can a great military leader without friends or lovers, at least as far as we know, be a subject of great literature? – painters and engravers, workers in bronze and illuminators of manuscripts and majolica seized upon him, even before the neoclassical period, to the extent of forming a treasury of imaginary iconography into which we must delve for want of a genuine one.

Historians continue to weigh Hannibal's ashes. Not that it is the easiest of tasks, for the reasons mentioned; but it will always be undertaken by those who seek to understand the change which, in the space of 100 years, from the middle of the third to the middle of the second century BC, began to establish the shape of the western Mediterranean region on all levels – political, economic and cultural – for a long time to come. At first Hannibal was one of the principal actors in this great struggle, before becoming more of a spectator than a participant, after his enforced exile in the East.

When the eldest son of Hamilcar Barca was born in 247 BC, Rome was poised, at the end of a long conflict, to oust the Carthaginians from Sicily, the Sicily that was shortly afterwards to become its first 'province', its first extension outside Italy, and the pivot of all its future undertakings in the Mediterranean West. A little over sixty years later, one day in 183, betrayed by his host, Prusias of Bithynia, and about to be handed over to his lifelong enemy, Hannibal took the poison that he always carried with him. Perhaps he had the premonition that after the defeat of Philip of Macedon, and the eviction from Asia Minor of Antiochus of Syria, whom he had sought to use rather than serve, the final barriers that still contained Roman imperialism in Greece and the East would soon fall. And that the way would then be wide open for Rome to proceed to the destruction of the Carthage which he himself, thirty years earlier, had dreamed of restoring to full power and dominance in the western Mediterranean basin.

# Glossary

**aedile** the office of a higher Roman magistrate, entitled to a curule chair

**circumcellions** a group of a schismatic party of Christians, composed of runaway slaves, ruined peasants, and the non-Roman population of North Africa who, combining social with ecclesiastical revolt and courting martyrdom, were suppressed by the government

***comitia centuriata*** one of the three people's assemblies in Rome, presided over by a consul or **praetor** and open to all citizens. It was concerned with declarations of war and peace, the election of consuls and praetors and the trial of some capital crimes

**Council of the Hundred/Council of the Hundred and Four** a select body, called the Gerusia, within the Carthaginian senate, whose chief office was to control the magistrates, and especially the generals returning from foreign service, who might be suspected of attempts to establish a tyranny

**djebel** in Arab countries, a hill or mountain

**eparchy** province or territory of an eparch, governor of a Greek province

**fasces** the bundle of rods, with or without an axe, borne before an ancient Roman magistrate of high grade

**latifundia** large estates owned by the elite and worked by slaves

**penteconter** ancient Greek ship with fifty oars

**Pontifex Maximus** the head of the pontifical college, which advised the Senate and magistrates on all matters relating to the state cult and supervised the calendar of festivals. He was the most important figure in the priestly hierarchy

**praetor** magistrate of ancient Rome next in line to a consul

**praetor peregrinus** an important magistrate who superintended cases involving foreigners, as opposed to the *praetor urbanus*, who dealt with those between Roman citizens

**propraetor** magistrate of ancient Rome who, after acting as **praetor** in Rome, was appointed to the government of a province

**quadrireme** ship with four sets of oars

**quaestor** Roman magistrate

**quinquereme** an ancient ship with five banks of oars

**suffect** additional (of Roman consul), i.e. elected during the official year

**suffete** one of the chief administrative officials of ancient Carthage

**tributum** originally an emergency property tax levied on Roman citizens, this later became the term generally applied to direct taxes raised in the provinces

**trireme** a Greek galley, especially a war-galley, with three banks of rowers

**velites** lightly armed soldiers; skirmishers

# 1

# Hamilcar Barca

The chief protagonist in a struggle he was to wage for nearly twenty years, more often than not forcing his foes to play his own game, Hannibal burst upon history before the walls of Saguntum, in Spain, in the spring of 219 BC. In that place, indeed, and at that moment occurred the event which decided his personal destiny and at the same time marked the start of the second Punic War, which the Romans, who were in no doubt as to the instigator of the enterprise, often referred to as 'Hannibal's War'. In the following pages we shall see on more than one occasion that if, in fact, Hannibal frequently took the initiative, using policies and strategies that appeared novel and original, he always did so on behalf of his city-state, even if only *a posteriori*. Most of all, there is a danger of seeing this fabulous venture as no more than a gratuitous exploit unless we connect it, historically, with the first developments of the decisive confrontation which began in 264, when the Romans gained a foothold in Sicily by bringing help to the Mamertine mercenaries, the protracted first act being ended in 241 by the signing of a treaty that set the seal on Carthage's loss of its Sicilian possessions. An 'entre deux guerres' period was to follow, some twenty years of armed peace which appears as a kind of interlude in the 'longue durée' of the wars. Nowadays, following Arnold Toynbee, the conflict that set Carthage and Rome battling it out from 264 until the peace concluded in 201 (to the great disadvantage of the Carthaginians after their defeat at Zama), is commonly accepted as no more than one and the same 'double Punic War'. And in Carthage, from 247, one family – the Barcids – bore the principal, soon to be exclusive, burden of responsibility.

## The loss of Sicily and the rise of Hamilcar Barca

In Sicily, the first theatre of operations in what, adopting the Roman perspective, is conveniently termed the 'first Punic War', the fighting which pitted Carthaginians against Romans on both land and sea had already lasted eighteen years when an important command was entrusted to a general named Hamilcar Barca. Already the father of three daughters, the new war leader had just seen the birth of his first male offspring, Hannibal.

With one retreat after another, over the years the Carthaginians had lost nearly all their positions in western Sicily. After the capture of Panormos (Palermo) in 254, they were reduced to their fortresses in the extreme west of Sicily, Lilybaeum (Marsala), where they had settled following the destruction of Motya in 397, and Drepanum (Trapani), which was their naval base, as its excellent natural harbour had always made it one of the Italian fleet's best western anchorages.

On this last line of defence, their backs to the sea, the Carthaginian forces organized their resistance. First at Lilybaeum in 249, where the garrison, under the command of a fine general named Himilco, foiled the blockade set up by the Roman consul P. Claudius Pulcher (Polybius, I, 48). The latter fared no better at Drepanum, where his ignorance of the harbour and the ponderous manoeuvrability of his fleet caused him to lose ninety-three vessels in confrontation with the Punic admiral Adherbal. At the same time, the second consul, L. Junius Pullus, suffered defeat at Lilybaeum at the hands of another Carthaginian admiral, Carthalo, and to crown his misfortune his squadron was caught in a storm and sank off Camarina (Polybius, I, 51–4). In Rome, this twofold and grave failure on the part of the consuls of 249 made a bad impression. They were blamed for their rash impiety; disobeying the auspices supposedly cost Junius Pullus the loss of his fleet at Cape Pachynum (Valerius Maximus, I, 54). As for P. Claudius Pulcher, we know that Cicero, who was scarcely given to excessive prejudice, seized on his impiety, aggravated by an insolent mockery, in *De natura deorum* (II, 7); he had well and truly brought upon himself the naval disaster at Drepanum. Enraged to see the sacred chickens refuse the corn when they came out of their cage, he had had them thrown into the water 'so that they might drink, since they don't want to eat' (*ut biberent, quoniam esse nollent!*). At the time, this pleasantry had failed to cause amusement in Rome, and one may suspect that the rival faction of the Claudii in the Senate, that of the Fabii, turned such levity to their own profit. Indeed, from 247 to 245, at the head of the Roman power-structure, the advantage went to the Fabii. Faced with the Carthaginians, the Romans slackened their war effort, and historians are always surprised that Carthage did not profit from that relaxation to regain the upper hand in Sicily. It was as if the Carthaginian senate had already written off its Sicilian 'Land's End'.

Nevertheless, in the same period Hamilcar Barca effectively harassed the Roman troops, with his fleet bringing destruction along the coastline of southern Italy, particularly in Bruttium. Then, returning to the north coast of Sicily, he attacked the territory of Panormos (Palermo) and in the end seized a stronghold, that of *Heirkte*, in Greek the 'enclosure' or 'prison'. Polybius (I, 56) gave a precise description of this height, an escarpment overhanging the coast, the plateau on its summit being capped by a kind of natural keep. In contrast, he is much less precise in giving its location, somewhere between Panormos and Eryx (Erice). Preference should probably be given to Monte Castellaccio, rising to approximately 900 metres some ten kilometres to the north-west of Palermo, rather than to the discouraging barrenness of Monte Pellegrino, which looms directly over the city to the north. Hamilcar made it his base for carrying out carefully planned operations against the Romans holding Panormos, and he also made use of the port defended by Heirkte as a jumping-off point for attacking the Italian coast as far as Cumae.

Hamilcar kept this stronghold for three years. In 244 a bold manoeuvre enabled him to gain control of the town of Eryx (Erice), and thus to occupy a midway position between the Roman garrison at the foot of the mountain and the guard which the consul Junius Pullus had managed to place at its summit in 248 by seizing the temple of the Erycinian Venus. In the north-east, Eryx (Monte San Giuliano) commanded access to Drepanum: with a reduced number of men Hamilcar was thus able to pin down the Roman troops and prevent them from increasing pressure on the Punic naval base, which was still besieged, as was Lilybaeum farther south.

At this point Rome, forced by the disasters it had suffered to refrain from any naval operation for the past five years, decided to rearm in order to break the impasse. For want of money in the public coffers, the Senate resorted to the personal resources of those who had the greatest interest in victory, and thus the conquest of Sicily. Men of the ruling class, as Polybius says (I, 59), in other words the Campanian aristocrats who had been at the origin of the conflict (Nicolet, 1978, p. 608), supplied fully equipped vessels at their own expense, either individually or by forming companies. All they asked was to be reimbursed in the event of victory. In the early summer of 242, a fleet of 200 quinqueremes, under the command of the consul C. Lutatius Catulus, arrived to drop anchor off Drepanum and Lilybaeum. In the spring of 241, out to sea from Lilybaeum, off the Aegates (Goat Islands), this fleet intercepted the provisioning and reinforcement convoy sent by Carthage. The Roman ships, with no cargo on board and more manoeuvrable, easily gained the upper hand; fifty Punic ships were sent to the bottom and seventy others captured with their crews and equipment.

The garrisons at Lilybaeum, Drepanum and Eryx were still firmly holding their positions, but from then on they were more or less left to themselves after Rome regained mastery of the seas. From Carthage Hamilcar received the order to negotiate a peace settlement with the Roman consul. The conditions of an initial draft treaty were worsened in Rome itself by the people, very probably in the setting of a meeting of the *comitia centuriata*. To the evacuation of the whole of Sicily was added the withdrawal of the Carthaginians from all the islands situated between Sicily and Italy, that is to say, the Aeolian Islands, one of the traditional lairs of Carthage's squadrons. In future the Carthaginians would have to give up any intervention against Syracuse and the Syracusans' allies. The financial clauses, especially, were made noticeably more burdensome. The period for payment of the war indemnity, settled between Hamilcar and Lutatius at 2,200 Euboic talents, was cut from twenty to ten years, and Carthage had to pay immediately an additional 1,000 talents (Polybius, I, 63). Considerable though they were, these sums were far from balancing the cost of the war for Rome, which had great fortunes lying at the bottom of the sea in the shape of hundreds of lost ships; 700, according to Polybius, as against 400 for the Carthaginians. Part of this indemnity was probably used to compensate the private ship-owners approached by the Senate in 243 (Nicolet, 1978, p. 609).

So ended, for the time being, a war that had lasted over twenty years and had apparently been unleashed somewhat by chance, through a chain of circumstances in which Rome might seem to have allowed itself to become involved without defining a long-term external policy (Lancel, 1995a, p. 362). The Senate, in fact, had taken no decision. When, in 264, by means of the *comitia centuriata* convened and manipulated by the consuls, notably Appius Claudius Caudex, the Roman people agreed to go to the aid of bands of Campanian mercenaries – the Mamertines – who, in Messina, were turning to Rome against the Carthaginians whose protection they had sought originally, it was apparently more a matter of pretext than political strategy. But a political strategy may assume an air of inconsistency, and what might have passed for a simple policing operation at Messina in 264 could have had a carefully conceived purpose. There is an aspect of automatism in the Roman imperialism of that period, of which it has been said that 'it was dragged ever onwards by the mechanism of its conquests' (Heurgon, 1969, p. 338). Moreover, behind that mechanism and the stimulus lay an ultimate goal that was highlighted not so long ago by Paul Veyne: the need felt at that time by Rome 'to distance Carthage from Italy, by taking away from it the staging-point provided by Sicily' (Veyne, 1975, p. 827). Worried by the knowledge that the Carthaginians were on its doorstep, on the other side of the Straits of Messina, only a few miles from Italian shores, Rome could have ensured its safety by means of a war confined to the Sicilian stakes alone. It was a kind of preventive fight that, by neutralizing the buffer of Sicily – which in fact became a Roman province very soon afterwards – ended by strengthening the 'sanctuary' character of Italian soil. And it must be emphasized that in the years immediately preceding the Romano-Punic war in Sicily, families of Campanian origin became predominant in Rome, and they were obviously more alert to the danger represented by such proximity, which was aggravated by that of Punic naval bases in the Aeolian Islands (Heurgon, 1969, p. 344). Indeed, the Atilii, who were Campanian, held the consulship seven times between 267 and 245; this first Punic war was *their* war, as the wars against the Etruscans in the early third century had been the concern of the Fabii. The annexation of Sardinia that followed shortly, as we shall see, owing to Carthage's difficulties with its mercenaries, succeeded in keeping the Carthaginians away from Italy. Viewed from this perspective, such a geopolitical balance seemed likely to last, had it not been for Hannibal's unfortunate decision to attack Saguntum. And that was by and large the opinion of Hanno, the leader of the pacifist – or rather, 'African' – clan in Carthage's senate. But we shall always lack historical proof.

It would be wrong, however, to neglect other motives, of an economic kind, which seem to have prompted certain people in Rome, and which are adequately documented. Recently, and with reason, emphasis has been placed on the growing importance of Campania, in the early and mid-third century, its men, as we have just seen, controlling the Senate in that period; a Campania whose agricultural richness was established, whose wines were increasingly exported and whose pottery production had recently eclipsed that of Apulia and Tarentum (Picard and Picard, 1970, pp. 183–4). Analyses made over the last twenty or so years of pottery remains collected on the north African sites, especially at Carthage, reveal a flow of exports to these regions from the potters of central Italy, and chiefly from the workshop known as that 'of the little stamps', established in Latium (Morel, 1969, pp. 101–3; 1983, p. 739). The annexation of Sicily, an obligatory staging-post for the coastal shipping transporting these goods, could only make the routes easier for this traffic, as we shall see even more at the very end of the third century, when 'Campanian A pottery' flooded into Carthage.

Although Rome's war aims, which were rather indistinct at the start of the conflict, subsequently appeared quite clear in the light of events, it may seem surprising that the Carthaginians resigned themselves to abandoning Sicily, for possession of which they had vied with the Greeks for centuries. Portraying the bitterness of Hamilcar, so often a victorious and long-lasting master of the terrain in his Sicilian 'Land's End', but whom Carthage's senate had compelled to negotiate the end of the fighting, Livy (XXI, 1, 5) recalled that *nimis celeris desperatio rerum* which had led the Carthaginians, perhaps prematurely, to throw in the towel. It is possible, however, to see in this a fair assessment of the situation. Insignificant in terms of territorial possession, the maintenance of a Carthaginian presence in the bridgeheads of the far west of Sicily made sense only if the naval bases held by the Carthaginians (at Lilybaeum and, chiefly, Drepanum) remained operational, if the western tip of Sicily could in fact retain for Carthage's maritime trade its centuries-old function of port of call and relay-point. The end of the Sicilian war had clearly shown that, owing to Rome's naval development, this function was no longer assured. Political realism compelled inferences to be drawn.

As may be expected, classical sources – in this instance Diodorus and Polybius – are silent about the debates taking place in Carthage at that time. But it cannot be mere coincidence that, during these very years when their eviction from Sicily appeared inevitable, the Carthaginians considerably expanded their African territory. A date of between 247 – the year in which Hamilcar was sent to Sicily – and 243 is ascribed to Hanno's capture of the town of Thevesta (present-day Tebessa, on the borders of Algeria and Tunisia), which brought about a considerable extension of Punic territorial control southwestwards to the extreme southern limits of the old Numidian kingdoms (Lancel, 1995, p. 259). Carthage's desire to strengthen and increase its hold over its hinterland must also be seen in relation to the episode of the expedition carried out by Regulus in 256–255; a failure for Rome, in the end, but it had exposed the Carthaginian mother-city to grave danger, as at the time of Agathocles' incursion fifty years earlier (Lancel, 1995, pp. 367–9). To the 'conservative' clan in Carthage, the expansion and consolidation of its African empire may well have seemed the best response to the 'new deal' in relations with Rome. Throughout the half-century that would end disastrously at Zama, this was to be the constant policy of the faction mobilized by Hanno in the Carthaginian senate.

Such was the situation when Hamilcar returned from Sicily in 241. He left the island with war honours, after bringing back his troops from Eryx to Lilybaeum (Polybius, I, 66, 1) and arranging that his own soldiers, together with those of Gisco, the general in command at Lilybaeum, should keep their liberty without being disarmed. Gisco was burdened with the heavy responsibility of repatriating some 20,000 men to Africa. Concluding his account of almost a quarter of a century of combat, and reviewing the leaders who had been in confrontation, Polybius (I, 64, 6) could not refrain from declaring that, of all those generals, 'the one who, for his intelligence and daring, must be regarded as the best was Hamilcar Barca'.

## Hamilcar Barca and the Barcid family

Like the majority of Punic names, Hamilcar is one of those 'theophoric' names denoting a relationship of dependence or protection between the recipient and the relevant deity in the Semitic pantheon. In this instance, Hamilcar (sometimes more correctly transcribed by Latin writers as Admicar) represents *bdmlqrt* in Punic-Phoenician, that is, the 'Servant of Melqart', the great god of Tyre and divine patron of Phoenician expansion in the West. There will be no surprise that in our sources Hamilcar is one of the commonest names, its earliest and most famous attested bearer, together with the personage we are studying, being the Hamilcar who fell before the Greeks at Himera in Sicily, in 480 BC (Lancel, 1995a, pp. 90–1).

In official records the mention of forebears runs the risk of confusion because of these homonyms. On votive stelae (stone tablets), together with the identity of the dedicant, there is usually an indication of at least the father, often of the preceding generation and sometimes, in exceptional cases, the outline of a real genealogy may be found. In practice, as also in Rome with the *cognomina* and *agnomina*, a surname enabled these homonyms to be distinguished from one another. In the case of Hamilcar, classical sources popularized the surname Barca, through the transcription of which one may hesitate between two Semitic roots. On the one hand, 'blessing', from which the Arabic *baraka* comes, a divine favour which Hamilcar certainly did not lack; on the other, and more probably, the three-letter root *brq*, meaning 'lightning', no less applicable to this general who had made his mark in Sicily by his hit-and-run attacks and 'strong-arm' operations. It would seem to be the equivalent of the Greek *Keraunos*, 'thunderbolt', a surname that was well represented in the names of the military caste of Alexander's epigones. Though there is general agreement in favouring this second meaning of Barca, the debate remains open as to whether it is a matter of a *cognomen ex virtute*, personally gained by our Hamilcar and passed on by him to his sons, notably Hannibal, or whether it has an earlier origin.

At the same time this raises the probably insoluble question of the background of the family, of whom it may confidently be said that its historic emergence in the middle of the third century presupposes more ancient roots in its mother-city of Carthage. But can we go further? People have tried, attributing a probably excessive importance to a few lines of Silius Italicus, a distinguished Roman senator – one of the eponymous consuls of AD 68, the year that witnessed Nero's death – who is more remarkable for his reverence towards Cicero and Virgil, from whom he had purchased property at Tusculum and near Naples, than for his vast epic work in seventeen cantos, the *Punica*, a poetic and baroque version of Livy's third decade, devoted to the second Punic War. At the beginning of this epic – keeping to classical tradition, as we shall see – when introducing the young Hannibal as the instrument of his father's hatred of the Romans, Silius Italicus in fact makes him a descendant of a mythical Belus, through the intermediary of the 'old Barca'. At the time when Dido fled from Tyre, he says, at the start of her wanderings which ended with the founding of Carthage, a young son of this Belus joined her to share her adventures (*Punica*, I, 71–3). The author of the *Punica* obviously found this Belus in the work of his master, Virgil, since the *Aeneid* presents him as the father of Dido. According to Silius, enlightened by his Virgilian source, Hannibal's distant ancestor was none other than Dido's brother. The temptation was indeed strong – and it is understandable that Silius should have yielded to it – to link the greatest man in Carthage's history with its legendary foundress by ties of a mythical genealogy. Certainly, a king of Tyre named Baal existed historically in the second quarter of the seventh century BC, and, as Gilbert Picard wrote (1967, p. 18), it is not impossible that the heavy-handed protectorate exerted at that time over the Phoenician cities by the Assyrian kings (Assarhaddon, then Assurbanipal) was at the root of a fresh exodus of oriental emigrants who came in this period to reinforce the colony founded in Africa at the end of the ninth century, that is to say almost a century and a half earlier, according to textual sources. As we know, recent archaeological discoveries made on the site of Carthage tend to reduce even further the gap that still exists between the date of 814 given by the texts and the first material attestations (Lancel, 1995a, pp. 32–4). There is no longer any question of affording the slightest credence to the romantic proposition of one Emil Forrer (1953), who not long ago had his moment of fame, according to which Carthage was founded circa 666 by two daughters of this Baal, Dido and Anna, who fled from Tyre to escape Assurbanipal.

To return to Virgil's (and Silius') Belus, who could seriously believe that the Latin poet had got wind of the existence of the Baal of Tyre, who was known only through oriental sources? On the other hand, he was certainly acquainted with the interpretation of the word *baal* – a title of eminent significance ('the lord', 'the husband') and a prime element of the great theonyms of the Semitic pantheon – well enough for him to make Belus Dido's mythical father, and all the more so since the Latin transcription of the Punic term, *Belus* (a spondee or a trochee, as the case may be), is a conveniently usable word in a hexameter, to the point where the author of the *Aeneid* allowed himself the luxury of putting it twice in the same line, already mentioned (I, 621). 'The language of the *epos* is the daughter of the hexameter', as Antoine Meillet said; up to and including the choice of proper nouns! Silius had only to place Hannibal at the end of this prestigious line.

However, as I have already suggested, there is scarcely any doubt that Hamilcar and his family belonged to the Punic aristocracy. Various indications have been pinpointed. First, the very fact that Hamilcar was given the command in Sicily. It was not customary in Carthage for the Council of Elders to entrust such responsibilities outside the ruling class. Conscription does not appear to have existed in the Punic state and, apart from contingents of mercenaries, enlistment affected only Libyan subjects, who were commanded by young Carthaginian nobles (Picard, 1967, p. 20). Of course, we shall see that Hamilcar and his eldest son subsequently developed a movement that tended to make public life in Carthage evolve in a direction that has been termed 'democratic'; but there was nothing at all 'revolutionary' about this movement, nothing that revealed any solidarity whatsoever between its instigators and a lower social class. Moreover, from the Barcid standpoint, gaining the support of the army and the people served both to consolidate their personal ambitions and to balance or counter the influence in Carthage's senate of the clan that was hostile to their overseas policy and strategy.

The surest indication that the Barcids belonged to the Carthaginian aristocracy is given by what we know of them as wealthy property-owners. Here again, the data are limited but clear. When Hannibal returned from Italy in the autumn of 203, he landed on African shores not at Carthage, nor at nearby Cape Bon, but at Leptis Minus (Lemta, in the present-day Tunisian Sahel), where he stayed for several months before facing Scipio at Zama. His concern to put some distance between himself and the Roman forces, who had already gained a foothold in the region of Utica and the lower Medjerda basin, is not enough to explain his choice. The fact that, according to a legend worthy of some credence (as we shall see later, p. 180), he set his soldiers to planting olive groves – which he was able to do while awaiting his battle against Scipio at the end of 202, and still more so in the years that elapsed between the peace imposed on Carthage in 201 and his suffetate in 196 – is clear enough testimony to his personal involvement in the *latifundia* of Byzacium. Last, and most important, when during the summer of 195 he was forced precipitately into exile from Carthage, it was on one of his estates in this region, a *turris*, between Thapsus and Acholla (Livy, XXXIII, 47), that he chose to break his journey, in safe surroundings, before leaving Africa for ever. It must have been a family possession, since he had hardly had the opportunity, given that he had left Africa when still a child and had been absent for some thirty-five years, to build up his own landed property. He must therefore have inherited it from his father Hamilcar, who himself had had little time available, between Sicily where he had first fought and Spain where he had gone for a long 'proconsulship' after the Mercenaries' War, to lead the profitable life of a property-owner residing on his estates, following the precepts of Mago the agronomist. The wealth of the Barcids, though perhaps not attaining the splendour described by Flaubert in the introductory pages of *Salammbô*, was thus in all probability inherited.

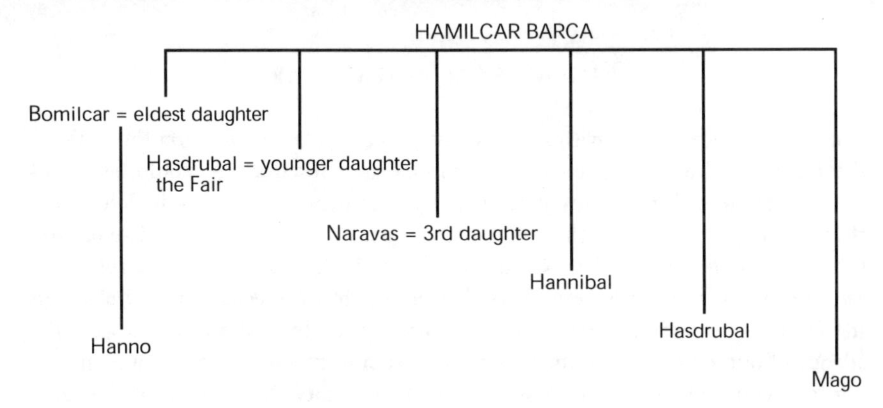


**Figure 1** The Barcid family

If Hamilcar's antecedents are not discernible, the first generation of his descendants is well known (Figure 1). In all likelihood he was born about 275 BC – he was still very young (*admodum adulescentulus*, says Cornelius Nepos, though the diminutive seems somewhat overdone) when he took command in Sicily in 247. By his first wife, whose name has not come down to us, he had three equally anonymous daughters. The eldest married one Bomilcar, who was later to play a far from negligible role as admiral of the Carthaginian fleet between 215 and 212. This couple produced a son named Hanno who, when barely an adult, served efficiently under the command of his uncle Hannibal; we shall see that he was one of the architects of the victory of Cannae in 216. Hamilcar's second daughter married Hasdrubal – known as Hasdrubal the Fair – probably between 241 and 237, before father-in-law and son-in-law left together for Spain. She must have disappeared fairly soon, as Hasdrubal took an Iberian princess as his second wife. Hamilcar's third daughter is indebted to Flaubert for having come down the centuries under the prestigious borrowed name of Salammbô, springing fully armed – or rather, fully adorned – from the novelist's imagination, for all we know of her is that she was promised to the Numidian chief Naravas (Polybius, I, 78).

A first son was born to Hamilcar in 247, the year when he was sent to Sicily. He called him Hannibal (in Punic *Hnb'l*: 'he who finds favour with Baal') after his own father's name. Two other boys followed: Hasdrubal (in Punic *Zrb'l*: 'Baal is my help'), who was to command the troops left in Spain during Hannibal's expedition to Italy and was killed on the Metaurus in 207 while trying to go to his brother's assistance. Then we have Mago (Punic *Mgn*, 'the gift'), whom we shall see fighting in Liguria in the last throes of the campaign in Italy and who, according to Livy (XXX, 19, 5) died at sea on the return voyage in 203. The three boys were born within a few years of one another. There is no doubt that Hamilcar Barca counted greatly upon them for the accomplishment of his plans. And for its likelihood we remember the anecdote recounted by the Latin historian Valerius Maximus (IX, 3, 2), that Hamilcar, watching his three children playing, exclaimed: 'These are the lion cubs I am rearing for the destruction of Rome!'

## The Mercenaries' War

While he was negotiating with Lutatius the peace that ended the 'first Punic War', did Hamilcar already suspect what the immediate consequences would be for his homeland? He had in fact resigned from his command even before he left Sicily, thus handing it over, together with his troops, to the governor of Lilybaeum, Gisco. Then he returned to Carthage. There is endless conjecture about his attitude at that time. It is very likely that he sought to re-establish his links with the circles who were hostile to the clan already led by Hanno; but despite the silence of our sources there must be no question of specifying, or even mentioning, any collusion with a 'king' Bomilcar II, in reality the navarch of the same name who in fact married Barca's eldest daughter at that time (Picard, 1967, p. 68). What we do know, at least, is that a little later the rebellious mercenaries who had served under him at Eryx blamed him for a resignation they considered deliberate (Polybius, I, 68, 12). Unbeaten but bitter about his enforced withdrawal, Hamilcar himself probably wanted some breathing space, at the time gauging the risks of repatriation to Africa with the arrears of pay to be provided, though the state's coffers were empty. If such were his fears, events were soon to prove that they were not idle.

The clauses of the treaty signed with Rome obviously prohibited him from demobilizing on the spot the thousands of men gathered around Lilybaeum; mercenaries from various parts, and Libyans who were subjects of Carthage. Repatriating them was Gisco's task. He carried it out wisely and, to avoid a concentration in the Punic metropolis of a multitude that was all the more dangerous because it was still armed, he organized staggered departures, in small groups, in order to give Carthage's government the time to settle its debts with each arrival, and then to send the dismissed mercenaries back to their country of origin. But financial problems were great, and the senate miscalculated: it allowed the demobilized mercenaries to mass in the city, reckoning that once they were all together it would be easier to make them accept a reduction in the sums owing (Polybius, I, 66, 5). What happened was inevitable; idleness and impatience prompted these hordes of frustrated and hotheaded men to excesses soberly alluded to by Polybius, but which inspired Flaubert to highly coloured descriptions of the 'goings-on' in 'Hamilcar's Gardens'.

The situation became awkward. By means of a payment of a gold stater to each of them, as a kind of deposit, the Council of Elders persuaded the commanding officers to empty the town of these undesirable guests (together with their families and baggage, which increased the mercenaries' resentment, according to Polybius), and reassemble them at Sicca, whose 'rock' ('Le Kef', in Arabic) rears its 800 metres over the western edge of the Tunisian ridge. Why Sicca? The matter of distance must have had some bearing. By the most direct route, which at first ran parallel to the lower course of the Medjerda and then passed through Thugga (Dougga) and Musti (Le Krib), it would put almost 200 kilometres between

Carthage and its soon-to-disappear soldiers. And on the south-western marches of Carthage's African territory, stuck like a wedge in Massylian Numidian country, Sicca had been a camp-town at least since the time, not so long before, when Hanno had seized Thevesta (Tebessa). Polybius describes these men in Sicca, more idle than ever, building castles in Spain, swelling their hopes by calculating and recalculating the pay they expected. Flaubert adds what he calls 'the priestesses of Tanit' (or rather, of Astarte), evoking the temple of Venus which later made the town's reputation (in the Roman era it received the name *Veneria*); but we do not know whether there was at that time the sacred prostitution which Hamilcar's soldiers had already encountered in Sicily when they were holding Eryx, in the neighbourhood of the famous Erycinian Venus. Reputed to have been introduced to Sicca by the Elymi of Sicily, she must have been there for a long time.

It was Hanno himself, the victor of Thevesta, who, in his role of military governor and commander of Carthage's land forces, came to address the troops assembled at Sicca. At the end of his speech, in which he emphasized Carthage's financial embarrassment, he proposed to settle the balance of what was owing to them at a lower rate than had been agreed by contract. This speech was not well received, and went down all the worse because the camp at Sicca comprised a mosaic of nations and languages. Besides a majority of Libyans (Africans), to whom we will return, Polybius (I, 67, 7) says there were Iberians, Gauls, Ligurians, Baleares and some whom the Greek historian calls 'semi-Greeks' (*mixhellenes*, as he writes, using a rare term), adding that they were mostly deserters and fugitive slaves. It was impossible to be understood by all of them at once. In his parleys with each group, therefore, Hanno was reduced to relying on their officers as intermediaries, and they, either through lack of understanding or pure malice, misrepresented his proposals or rendered them unacceptable. Also, the men had nothing but distrust for this Hanno, under whom they had not served and whose very mission, in the place of leaders who were known to them, was suspect. In the end, they rebelled openly against their own company commanders and marched on Carthage, setting up their camp on the other side of the lake, near Tunis, some twenty kilometres from the Punic metropolis.

The break had been made, and those in Carthage could now see more clearly what a mistake it had been to let such a mass of mercenaries gather without being able to hold the slightest threat of reprisals over them, as they had been allowed to leave for Sicca complete with their families and even their possessions. Once again, at Carthage's gates, the mercenaries became aware of their strength. Their claims, says Polybius (I, 68, 6), increased with the terror they inspired among the Carthaginians. Constantly raising the stakes, after receiving satisfaction regarding their back pay, they then demanded reimbursement for their equipment, their horses and their dead, and that they should be paid in cash, and at the highest rate, for the corn rations which had been owing to them for years. To conduct this negotiation with them they rejected Hamilcar Barca, whom they accused of having betrayed them, or at the least of abandoning them, but accepted the arbitration of

Gisco, their leader at Lilybaeum, who had made such a good job of organizing their return from Sicily.

Gisco began to settle their back pay, but deferred payment of the sums representing the estimated value of corn rations and horses. This was the pretext seized upon by two men, among the ringleaders of the rebel mercenaries, who stood for the groups with the most to lose by a conciliation and were thus tempted to adopt the policy of painting matters as black as possible. The more formidable was Spendios, a 'semi-Greek' of Campanian origin, a fugitive slave and therefore renegade, as such without a future and without hope. Spendios, says Polybius (I, 69, 4), was strong and brave, and not the cringing creature Flaubert made him, in contrast with the virile Matho. In addition, he had a genuine tactical skill, ease of manner and linguistic abilities generally lacking in the barbarians around him. He had no difficulty in persuading Matho, one of the ringleaders of the Libyans, to make common cause with him. For other reasons, Matho had no less than Spendios to fear from a negotiated peace. As an African, he did not have the resources to flee far enough from the resentment of Carthage's senate. He found it easy to convince his compatriots that the Carthaginians would seek revenge on them once the foreign mercenaries had returned to their own countries. Gisco's reluctance to satisfy all their demands *en bloc* provoked some stormy meetings, where Spendios and Matho set up a real reign of terror to discourage any potential opponents; whoever tried to speak was immediately stoned even before anyone knew what he was going to say, to the point, says Polybius, where the word 'strike' – the historian uses the Greek imperative *balle* (I, 69, 12), but what was the word used by the soldiers? – was soon the only one to be understood by all. Gisco still came to terms with this mutinous army, but when it was the Africans' turn to come to him to claim their dues, he replied that they should address themselves to their 'general', Matho. This response unleashed their fury. They rushed off to pillage the coffers of the Carthaginians, and with Spendios and Matho fanning the flames of their anger, seized Gisco and his retinue and held them captive.

## The 'inexpiable' war and the Africans' rebellion

By taking this irrevocable step, the mercenaries committed themselves to an implacable war (*polemos aspondos*, says Polybius I, 65, 6: literally, 'a war that admits no truce'), a savage war. The ever-perceptive Greek historian clearly saw what fuelled the fire of this combat. Almost everywhere in the territory controlled by Carthage exasperation was so great that the rebel mercenaries, and especially the Libyans, were in their element. During the war in Sicily, in order to meet the expenses of a very costly conflict, Carthage's senate had put pressure on the inhabitants of its African territories. Polybius (I, 72, 2) states that during those years the amount of tribute demanded from the city-states was doubled, and all rural inhabitants had to render half of their harvests. To appreciate the full value of this confiscation, we must place it in the context of what we are able to learn about the status of these African Libyan peasants under Carthaginian rule.

We must resist the temptation, however great, to imagine that status by drawing inferences from what is known of the African lands and farmers in the time of the Roman empire. The situation, although complex, is well known, notably in the second and third centuries AD, owing to the great regulations carved in stone which were found in the region of the middle basin of the Medjerda, which provide us with information especially about the organization of sharecropping in imperial domains. 'Rome's juridical ingenuity had conceived a quadruple superimposition of rights to be exercised over the same land: the first, immanent and imprescriptible, of the Roman people; then that of the *dominus*, emperor or great capitalist; that of the farmer general and, lastly, that of the *colonus*, who kept two-thirds of the product of his labour' (Picard, 1990, p. 64). By means of handing over one-third of his harvests and giving a certain number of days' enforced service on the part of the estate directly operated by the farmer, the 'colonist' or settler was able to enjoy over his plot of land and its adjoining house a right of use that was potentially transmissible by sale or inheritance. Whether for imperial domains or *latifundia* belonging to the large-scale private property-owners, Rome had opted for this mainly indirect method of control instead of direct control, which involved the inherently unreliable participation of thousands of slaves or farm labourers. Experience of the great slave revolts of the last two centuries of the Roman Republic, which had placed Rome in danger, had served as a lesson. Some sixty years ago, the celebrated historian of ancient Africa, Stéphane Gsell, published an article which translates as 'Rural slaves in Roman Africa' precisely to demonstrate that there were none (Gsell, 1932).

As far as we can see it clearly, for many shadowy areas remain, the situation was perceptibly different in Punic Africa. With Polybius (I, 71, 1), we must set aside the *chora*, the territory directly under Carthage's administration – basically Cape Bon and the neighbouring regions of north Tunisia and the middle basin of the Medjerda — from which the city derived its fundamental agricultural resources, broadly to the point of self-sufficiency, by the exploitation of lands managed in the way that was common in the Hellenistic period, thanks to an abundance of slave labour. This massive use of rural slaves, procured by piracy and more reliably through war, is well attested by our sources. In 310, when Agathocles, the tyrant of Syracuse, conquered the Carthaginians near Tunis, in their camp he found thousands of handcuffs intended for the prisoners that the Carthaginians expected to capture; and in fact, in the following year when the tables of war had been turned, the Greeks from Sicily who had been taken prisoner were put to work to restore to cultivation lands that had lain fallow or been devastated by the fighting (Diodorus Siculus, XX, 13, 2; 69, 5). Half a century later, when Regulus made his expedition in the same region of Cape Bon, the Roman soldiers led over 20,000 slaves off to their ships (Polybius, I, 29, 7).

However, it was not those slaves working on the rich lands of the nearest *chora* to Carthage who grew restive at that time. The thousands of men who came to join the mercenaries – 70,000 according to Polybius (I, 73, 3), though it is hard to believe such an apparently exaggerated number – were 'Libyans', in other words, Africans, and more especially inhabitants of rural states in the interior which had remained free, but from which Carthage exacted taxes to be paid in kind by the peasants. These payments in kind, says Polybius (I, 71, 1), together with the tributes imposed on the cities, supplied the essential part of the resources intended to subsidize the public (notably military) expenditure of the Carthaginian state, and had been increased in the latter years of the war in Sicily to the point where they represented one-half of the harvests. Hanno, the victor of Thevesta, had been one of the architects of these confiscations, and it is understandable that the mercenaries were loth to accept him as negotiator.

The word 'revolution' has sometimes been used to describe the vast uprising that was so helpful to the rebel mercenaries at that time (Picard, 1967, p. 70). The concept is probably too intense and too significant politically to be used in this instance. There is no 'revolution' without a political end, whether that end appears or is proclaimed after the event. And there is nothing to indicate that the insurgents had worked out the slightest political strategy. Among the facts known to us we cannot even discern those classic manifestations of social upheaval that characterize all peasant revolts, and in particular, in Africa itself some centuries later, the movement of the 'circumcellions'. In negative parody of a celebrated phrase, the movement provoked by the mercenaries was a revolt, but it was not a revolution. At least the groundswell that shook the country at the time was revealed by a genuine, almost automatic, solidarity between the despoiled Africans and the men-at-arms rising against Carthage. In such circumstances, the collective solidarity of the women often figures as a cliché in Hellenistic historiography. However, we should have little hesitation in following Polybius when he states (I, 72, 5–6) that, city by city, the African women *en masse* gave up their personal possessions and jewellery to feed the rebels' war funds. Matho and Spendios extracted enough to give the mercenaries the back pay still owed to them and even had funds available to finance their rebellion. If we accept the obviously unverifiable figure of 70,000 men suggested by Polybius for the Libyan back-up, the mercenaries' leaders had a manoeuvrable force of some 100,000 men at their disposal. Matho divided them into several corps: some were to reinforce the troops besieging Utica, to the north-west of Carthage, and farther off, in the same direction, Bizerta; others were to swell the forces already encamped near Tunis, a short distance to the south-west of the Punic metropolis, whose isthmus was caught in a pincer movement, and was thus cut off from its hinterland.

Carthage rallied. An army was raised, composed of mercenaries hastily recruited overseas and citizens old enough to bear arms, some of whom formed cavalry units. Some hundred elephants were added as reinforcement. At the same time, squadrons were formed from the ships that had escaped the naval disasters of the Sicilian War, triremes and penteconters, and a few smaller vessels. It is probably thanks to these methods – the elephants could be loaded on to rafts – that this army under Hanno's command was able to take up a position near Utica (Figure 2). For

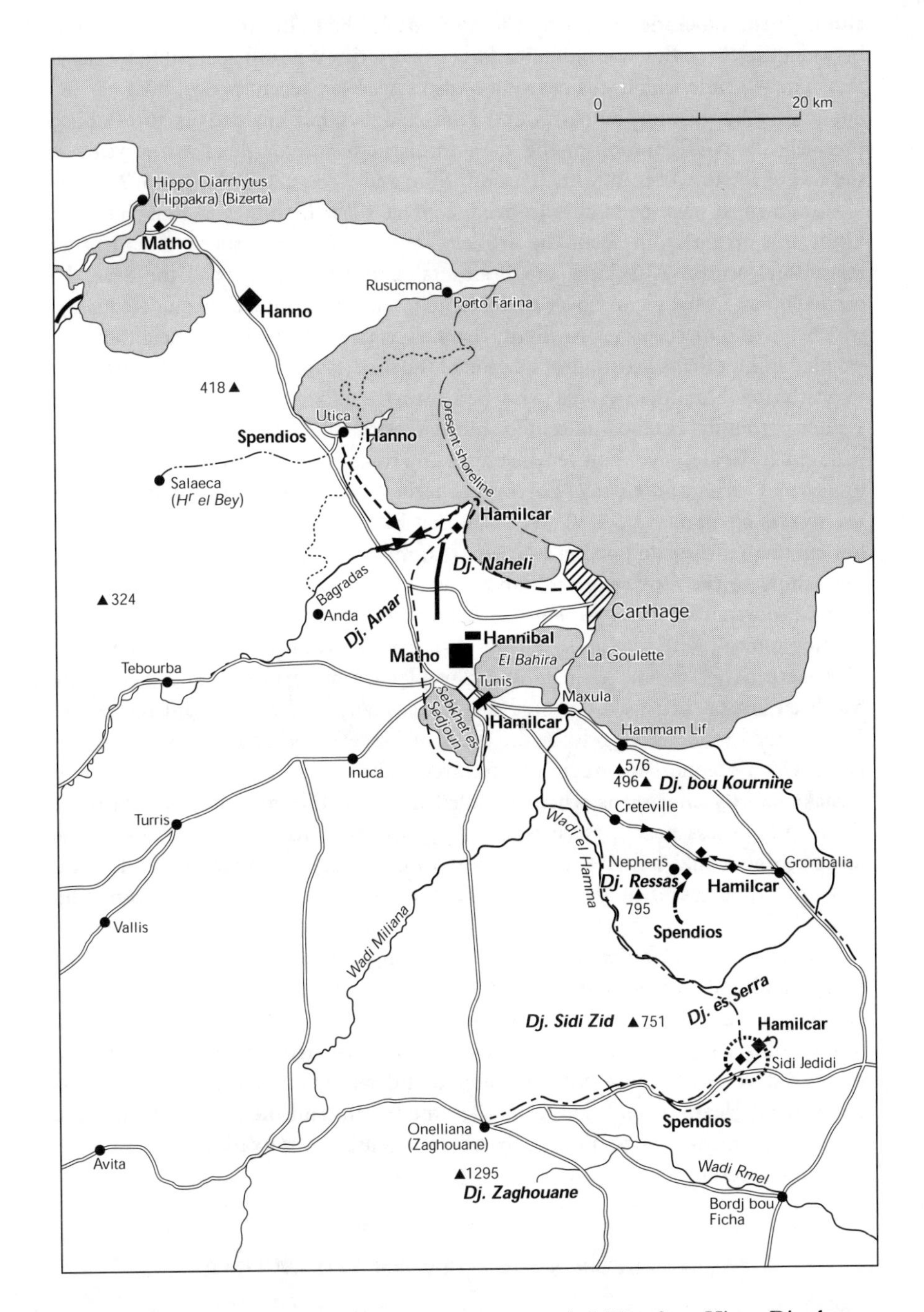


**Figure 2** The theatre of operations in the Mercenaries' War, from Hippo Diarrhytus (Bizerta) in the north to the djebel Zaghouane in the south (from Kromayer, 1912)

although the blockade set up by the mercenaries had cut land communications between the two cities, we must not forget that Utica was still accessible by sea at that time – a time which was drawing to its close. Very recent prospecting carried out jointly by geomorphologists and archaeologists has enabled us to establish precisely the configuration of the site and of the Medjerda delta in the years at the end of the third century BC (Paskoff, Slim and Trousset, 1991, pp. 522–4).

Hanno must have been able to make contact with the besieged inhabitants of Utica and obtain from them the artillery items of the era, catapults and other missile-projectors. Attacking the besiegers' entrenchments from the rear, he carried off an initial victory over them, largely achieved by the charging elephants, which put the mercenaries to flight; the survivors regrouped on a neighbouring wooded hill, perhaps the modest heights of the djebel Menzel Ghoul. Accustomed to scattering Numidian bands who fled into the distance as soon as they had yielded ground, Hanno contented himself with this engagement, which he believed to be decisive, and leaving his camp and troops where they were went to nearby Utica in order, says Polybius soberly, 'to take care of his body' (*peri ten tou somatos therapeian*: I, 74, 9). We know that Flaubert needed no more than these few enigmatic words to portray a picture that must have pleased Thomas Couture, the painter of the *Decline of the Romans*, the star attraction of the 1847 Salon. It was the portrait of an obese suffete, bathing his ulcers in cinammon oil while stuffing himself with rare and gourmet dishes amid exotic young bath attendants. The mercenaries took advantage of his negligence to surprise his soldiers, who had been left to their own devices, kill a great many of them and put the rest to flight – they took refuge within the walls of Utica – and seize the siege equipment which Hanno had previously received. The Punic general made a second mistake shortly afterwards when he failed to attack the mercenaries with some chance of success near a place which Polybius calls Gorza; but in view of the distance one would hesitate to identify it with the city of Gurza (Kalaa-Kebira) subsequently attested in the Roman era, some dozen miles from Hadrumetum (Sousse).

It was here that Hamilcar Barca made his reappearance, having remained in the background and, it would seem, in disgrace since his return from Sicily in 241. Carthage's senate drew its own inferences from Hanno's blunders and entrusted to the unfortunate hero of Eryx command of a small army of some 10,000 men, reinforced by seventy elephants. Recounted in detail by Polybius, Hamilcar's first engagement clearly reveals his feeling for the terrain and the tactical genius that his son Hannibal was to inherit, based on accurate observation and speed in subsequent action.

## Hamilcar's victory on the Macar

We know that the isthmus linking Carthage to the mainland was cut by the mercenaries, who had barricaded the passage between the hills of the djebel

Ammar and the heights of the djebel Nahli, which command the isthmus to the west. Polybius (I, 75, 5) adds that the rebels firmly held the only bridge over the Medjerda (the Greek historian's *Macar*), which had to be crossed to get to Utica. Today, it is difficult to place this bridge that was thrown across the old bed of the Medjerda: either on the arm which in that time ran into the sea – much farther back then in relation to the present shoreline – at the northern extremity of the heights of the djebel Ammar, near the site of today's La Sebala; or, less probably, a little farther upstream, near Djedeida, at a point where the river-bed remained stable throughout historical times. At all events, Hamilcar had noticed that when the wind blew from a certain direction – probably the east – a tongue of sand was formed at the river mouth, alongside the sea, making it fordable. It is all the easier to give credence to Polybius' account since, through a similar phenomenon, a sandy bar now separates the sea, on another shoreline, from the salt-plain of er-Riana and, beyond, the marshy stretches of the old Gulf of Utica.

Hamilcar seized the first opportunity that presented itself, and under cover of night crossed the river mouth over the dike thus formed to attack the bridge guarded by the mercenaries. Caught between the small army holding the bridge and the larger body coming from Utica as reinforcement, the Punic general pretended to give way, then made the bulk of his massed rearguard forces turn to confront the enemy, who were attacking in disorder (Polybius, I, 76, 5; on details of the manoeuvre, see Thompson, 1986, pp. 110–17). The engagement ended in a heavy defeat for the mercenaries, who lost 8,000 men, including 2,000 prisoners. The survivors fled, some to Utica, others to Tunis. Hamilcar occupied the bridge and mopped up all the surrounding region.

In Carthage, this first real success renewed confidence; but the situation was still worrying. A little later, while Matho was still besieging Bizerta, the troops commanded by Spendios, in conjunction with a large part of the Gaulish mercenaries led by a chief named Autharitus, placed Hamilcar in grave danger when he was encircled in a small plain surrounded by mountains, sometimes identified as the cirque of Khanguet-el-Hadjhadj, south-east of Tunis, not far from the ancient Nepheris (Gsell, 1921, III, p. 112, note 3). The presence of a contingent of Numidian horsemen at the Carthaginians' rear was aggravating their situation even further, when the Numidian chief rallied to their side and resolved it. Naravas, whose family had long-standing ties with Carthage, placed his troop of about 2,000 horsemen at the disposal of Hamilcar, who promised him his daughter's hand in marriage if he stayed loyal to Carthage. Of this maiden, history recalls only that she was the Carthaginian general's third daughter (see above, p. 9). Flaubert endowed her with the hieratic poses and bewitching seduction of the most 'sophisticated' heroine in a historical novel, Salammbô. Thanks to Naravas and his cavalry, Hamilcar managed to escape from this tight spot. After a difficult battle, the Punic leader acted astutely. He invited those mercenaries who had been taken prisoner – 4,000 according to Polybius (I, 78, 13) – to serve under him, and armed them with the weapons captured from the enemy. As for those who rejected his offer, he left them free to return to their homes.

Hamilcar's leniency and diplomacy threatened the mercenaries' leaders' policy of painting things in the worst possible light. The immunity offered might tempt the majority of the rebels and prompt massive defections. To guard against this, a brutal retort, which would irrevocably compromise everyone, was proposed in a mass meeting by the Gaulish leader Autharitus, whose knowledge of Punic enabled him to be understood by nearly all the mercenaries. Gisco, the former governor of Lilybaeum, who had conducted the first negotiations with them at Sicca, was still in their hands. Autharitus proposed to torture him to death. Terror soon got the better of the few opponents who stood up to recommend mercy and were immediately stoned. Gisco and several hundred of his companions were massacred.

Emotions ran high in Carthage, which seemed to be the target of all misfortunes at once. The mercenaries of Sardinia had rebelled in their turn and gained mastery of the island; as we shall see later, they did not keep control of it, but their uprising was at the root of Carthage's loss of Sardinia soon afterwards. The towns of Utica and Bizerta which until then had been loyal to the Punic mother-city now defected. To cap it all, a large convoy of provisions and equipment coming from the *Emporia*, or trading-posts controlled by Carthage on the Syrtis Minor, was destroyed by storms.

Carthage's external enemies could have profited from its difficulties, but we find that they did nothing. When asked to provide food aid, Hieron, the tyrant of Syracuse, hastened to satisfy Carthaginian requests. Certainly, at the beginning of the war in Sicily, in 263, he had given allegiance to Rome; but, as Polybius observes (I, 83, 3), he was not anxious to remain on close terms. Helping Carthage to survive seemed to him the best means of preserving his own kingdom, faced with its burdensome protector. As for the Romans themselves, it clearly appears that, far from taking advantage of the situation to overcome the vanquished enemy, they adopted a wait-and-see attitude, and respected the terms of the 'treaty of Lutatius'. They thus rejected the proposal of Utica's inhabitants, who offered to hand over the town; to accept would have been a violation of the treaty. Furthermore – at least for the time being – they made no response to the invitations of the rebel mercenaries on Sardinia, who tried to draw them to the island. With regard to the rebel mercenaries in Africa itself, Rome was extremely reserved. There was, of course, a period of upset with Carthage's government, when the Carthaginians arrested and threw into prison the Italian traders who had come to bring provisions to the rebels. Rome sent ambassadors to demand the release of the captives, who numbered about 500. Carthage yielded, and in return obtained the liberation of the prisoners of war who had been detained since the end of the Sicilian war (Polybius, I, 83, 5–8). Subsequently, Rome gave Carthage a free hand to raise mercenaries in Italy by waiving certain of the clauses in the treaty of Lutatius (Appian, *Libyca*, 5), and we have seen (above, p. 14) that these recruitments had enabled Hanno rapidly to form an initial armed force against the rebels. Moreover, the Roman Senate allowed merchants to export to Carthage everything that the Punic city needed, at the same time prohibiting them from provisioning its enemies inland. We thus find a *de facto* solidarity, if not specifically between the Roman *patres* and the aristocracy of the Elders of Carthage, as Gilbert Picard has written (1967, p. 72), at least between the two great rival city-states. The danger which the mercenaries represented for Carthage was not peculiar to that city alone; it was an international danger. Subversion could be contagious; Rome had fully grasped that fact in 265, faced with the rebel slaves of Volsinii (Bolsena), when it had just gained control of southern Etruria.

## Hanno is Ejected

To increase the chances of overcoming the mercenaries more swiftly by doubling the forces opposing them, Hamilcar had asked Hanno to join him with his own army. But the ill-feeling between the two generals fast reached the stage where in Carthage it became the real turning-point in the conduct of military matters. The Carthaginians decided that one of the generals should give up his command, leaving the choice of the one who should remain sole commander-in-chief to the army itself. The words used by Polybius (I, 82, 5) seem to indicate clearly that it was the people's assembly which took this decision, fraught with consequences, as we shall see from what follows. The episode confirms the growing political importance of the people's assembly in that period, and again, Polybius did not fail to view it as an ill-fated deviation from the constitution that we know through Aristotle (Sznycer, 1978, pp. 581–3; Lancel, 1995a, pp. 117–19). Nevertheless, Hanno was relieved of his command by the soldiers themselves, and Hamilcar was assigned another general as second-in-command, named Hannibal – not to be confused with Hamilcar's own son, who was still a child – himself the son (to round off one of those frequent homonymities that are so awkward for historians) of yet another Hamilcar, sometimes known as Hamilcar of Paropos, from the name of a town in Sicily where this general had distinguished himself at the start of the first Punic War, between 261 and 255. In any case, it seems that this Hannibal was not chosen by the army itself to help Hamilcar, but rather by the people's assembly, if we are to believe Polybius (I, 82, 12), who ascribes the choice to the citizens (*politai*).

Emboldened by Carthage's difficulties, Matho and Spendios had meanwhile undertaken to lay siege to the city itself: *poliorkein auten ten Charchedona*, says Polybius (I, 82, 11) who, versed in siegecraft himself, cannot have used the term thoughtlessly. If we are to assess what may actually have happened, we need to ask whether those formidable entrenchments described by Appian (Lancel, 1995a, pp. 415–19) were already in place; that triple line of ramparts cutting the isthmus, whose effectiveness the Greek historian had plenty of opportunity to judge for himself when he was at Scipio Aemilianus' side in 147–146 and had witnessed the assaults of a powerful army, though fully equipped with all the material necessary for a siege, founder for a long time against these defences. With Stéphane Gsell we may concede that it was the great danger which Carthage encountered at the hands of the mercenaries that prompted it to strengthen its defences soon afterwards. But the town was not an open town; a defence wall (*teichos*) existed, which at the start of the rebellion, when they were holding Tunis and blockading Utica, Matho's men would sometimes approach, to cause the Carthaginians greater terror (Polybius, I, 73, 7). However, neither then nor earlier did the mercenaries attempt to force the defences and enter the town. But the defection of Utica, which in the north-west commanded the approaches to the isthmus, left them completely free to lay siege to Carthage, totally sever its communications with the hinterland, and exert the strongest possible pressure on it.

## The 'Gorge of the Saw'

Carthage's ability to obtain supplies by sea and, above all, the restored cohesion of its military command, foiled the threat of strangulation. By cutting off from the rear the troops who were camped before Carthage, and driving them to a state of famine through lack of provisions, Hamilcar reversed the situation. Besiegers become besieged, the mercenaries were forced to lift their stranglehold. At that point the rebellion entered its final phase, a war of movement which was to hasten to its solution. Calling on African contingents commanded by a Libyan chief named Zarzas, Matho and Spendios formed the best of the mercenaries into a large army – 50,000 men, says Polybius (I, 84, 3), who probably exaggerated the figure in order to increase the merits of Hamilcar, whom he admired: he likens him to a good backgammon player or, as we would say, a good chess player – and pursued the tactics that had succeeded for them before (above, p. 17): marching, with the bulk of their troops, parallel to those of Hamilcar, continually harassing him and avoiding the plains where the elephants and Naravas' cavalry could place them in difficulties. Reading Polybius, we can see that these parallel movements, punctuated by skirmishes and raids in which Hamilcar's experience and skill in manoeuvring gave him the upper hand, led the two armies in a southerly direction, in almost continual contact, towards the region amid whose heights lies the base of the promontory of Cape Bon. There, Hamilcar managed to attract the greater part of the rebels, nearly 40,000 men, in a natural amphitheatre or gorge which, says Polybius (I, 85, 7), 'is known as the Saw, because of its resemblance to the tool of that name'. Flaubert preferred to call it the 'Gorge of the Axe', certainly a more noble instrument, and more evocative of such dramatic episodes. Naturally, people have tried to find this sierra outline in the terrain and identify the site, drawing on the meagre topographical data in the Greek historian's account; ranges of heights that could possibly provide the elements of a 'hoop-net', but confining flat stretches ample enough for the movements of several tens of thousands of men and, chiefly, those of the elephants, the protagonists in the last act of the drama. One of the great German specialists in researching the battlefields of Antiquity believed he had found the site not far from the Gulf of Hammamet, in a spot where the jagged crests of the djebel el-Jedidi and the djebel Menzel Moussa (*Atlas Archéologique Tunisien*,

1/50 000th, p. xxxvi) may have formed the crenellated walls that imprisoned the mercenaries (Veith, 1912, p. 550). But there is no lack of saw-toothed crests in these old reliefs of North Africa, and this site, which is rather surprisingly close to the sea, does not win total support.

At all events, the trap was sprung on the rebels who, having run out of food, were forced to eat the flesh of their prisoners and then of their slaves. Their leaders, Spendios, Autharitus the Gaul and the Libyan Zarras, soon had no alternative but to come to terms with Hamilcar. With seven other negotiators, they came to the Carthaginian camp, where the Punic general dictated his conditions. He would keep ten men, of his own choosing, and would disarm the rest and let them go. When these conditions were accepted, Hamilcar revealed that he would keep the ten plenipotentiaries. *O fides Punica!* The Carthaginian leader could not have foreseen what would happen: learning that their principal leaders were in the hands of the enemy, the Africans, who were not privy to the pact that had been concluded, says Polybius (I, 85, 6), and believed they had been betrayed, rushed to take up arms. Hamilcar had them trampled to death by his elephants.

## The outcome

Matho, however, still held Tunis. Hamilcar and his second-in-command Hannibal came to lay siege to it, the latter taking up his position in the direction of Carthage, perhaps on the heights of the present-day Belvedere district, while his leader established himself on the other side, south of the town. Spendios and the other ringleaders who had been captured at the Gorge of the Saw were brought out in full view of the walls of Tunis and crucified where all eyes could see them. As Polybius, who was always inclined to see the hand of Tyche behind everything, comments, 'one would have said that Fortune deliberately offered each of the adversaries in turn the opportunity to inflict the most appalling tortures on the other' (I, 86, 7). For Matho, grasping the chance of a moment's carelessness by Hannibal, made a sortie and, having seized him, had Spendios taken down from the cross and the Punic general nailed up in his place.

It will be remembered that this Hannibal had been appointed as aide to Hamilcar at the instigation of the people's assembly, after Hanno's eviction by the soldiers themselves (above, p. 19). At the time, attempts were made by a commission of the Council of Elders (Carthage's senate), comprising some thirty members, to reconcile Hamilcar and Hanno and oblige them henceforth to act in concert. In line with the proposition advanced by Gilbert Picard (1967, pp. 73–4), should we regard this as a return to strength of the Carthaginian oligarchy, which had been temporarily dispossessed of its prerogatives? Polybius (I, 87, 3) seems to see it as a purely circumstantial event; yet we meet these Thirty again in 203, shortly before Zama, in a context where their intervention, in the role of a limited council, or permanent committee, belongs in a clearly institutional framework (Livy, XXX, 16, 3). By means of this mission entrusted to the Thirty, and under the flag of 'national unity', the Carthaginian senate replaced in the saddle the hard-wearing Hanno, who was to remain for a further thirty-five years in Carthage as the leader of the anti-Barcid faction.

For the moment, the reconciliation had already forced Matho, who had been beaten by the two generals in several partial engagements, to enter into a decisive battle at a location unknown to us – perhaps not far from Leptis Minus (Lemta, on the coast of the Tunisian Sahel) – but which witnessed his defeat and ended in his capture. In his novel, Flaubert did not invent the blood-drenched parade through the streets of Carthage that was the epilogue to this endless competition in the exercise of cruelty. What escaped the author of *Salammbô* (not that he cared) was that the protagonists in this triumphal march – a *via crucis* for Matho – were the *neoi* of the city, acting as a body, the ancestors of those *juvenes* who were to perpetrate real human sacrifices until the Late Roman Empire (Lepelley, 1980).

Expiatory victims, through their spectacular sufferings, Matho and his companions symbolized the revenge of the Carthaginian master over his African subjects who had enjoyed a momentary emancipation. The whole of Africa, says Polybius, submitted to Carthage. Only Hippou Acra (Bizerta) and Utica, who could look for no clemency from the victor, continued to offer resistance. The two towns were captured, one by Hanno and the other by Hamilcar, and what we know of their subsequent status and their attitude in regard to the mother-city does not suggest that the conditions of their capitulation were draconian. Nevertheless, in the aftermath, things did not return to normal everywhere. Though Naravas and his cavalry had been invaluable auxiliaries for Hamilcar, other Numidian tribes, by contrast, had sided with the rebel mercenaries. Such was the case of the Mikatani – an obscure tribe, that one hesitates to identify with the Muxitani, whose name runs through the history of Carthage (Lancel, 1995a, p. 261) – of whom we know, solely through Diodorus (XXVI, 33), that at the end of the 'Libyan War' they were harshly punished. Still in this period, other Numidian tribes were fought jointly by Hanno and Hamilcar (Appian, *Iberica*, 4). According to certain sources, Hamilcar on this occasion not only re-established peace throughout Africa, but also extended the boundaries of Carthage's empire (Appian, *Hannibalica*, 2; Cornelius Nepos, *Hamilcar*, II, 5). We do not know by exactly how much he extended these boundaries; but whatever the expansion, it would have been nothing but a territorial compensation. For at that time – 237 BC – the consequence of the mercenaries' revolt was the very grievous loss for Carthage of land where its influence, and even its sovereignty, had been exerted for over three centuries.

## The loss of Sardinia

The danger threatening Punic Sardinia had been building since the time – probably 239 – when Hamilcar, placed in a difficult situation by Spendios and Autharitus, had been opportunely aided by Naravas (above, p. 17). The mercenaries then serving in Sardinia, encouraged by the initial success of their brothers-in-arms in Africa, attacked the Carthaginians who were on the island; in particular, they besieged in a citadel (Polybius, I, 79, 2: he unfortunately does not make clear which *akropolis*) the captain of auxiliaries commanding them, named Bostar, and put him to death, together with his compatriots. The same fate was meted out to another general – one of the numerous Hannos to be found in Carthaginian prosopography of that period – who hastened from Carthage with fresh troops, who immediately mutinied. If we are to believe Polybius, who passes rather swiftly over this episode, the mercenaries soon gained mastery over the whole island, before arousing the animosity of the Sardinians against them and having to take refuge in Italy. Rome had turned a deaf ear on the first occasion when the rebel mercenaries on the island had appealed to it, but this time it changed its attitude.

How can one explain the volte-face which, from a scrupulous observance of the 'peace of Lutatius', signed in 241, that left Sardinia outside the stipulations of the treaty, led the Roman Senate to a real bid for power? The strategic value of the island comes to mind; a glance at the map is enough to show that Rome could ill afford that 'long vessel moored alongside its west flank' to remain in the hands of a redoubtable enemy. But why not have included Sardinia in the conditions imposed in 241? Perhaps it was thought in Rome that Sardinia, cut off from the Punic metropolis after the annexation of the Sicilian eparchy, would sooner or later fall like a ripe fruit. And in fact, deserted by the rebel mercenaries, the island in 238 could well have been considered a candidate for forfeit by the Roman Senate. This explanation is probably preferable to the one reported by Polybius (III, 28, 3), although he did not give it credence. This, in order to put a better complexion on the bid for power, consisted in the claim among Roman historiographers that Sardinia had been conquered in compensation for the Carthaginians' capture of Italian traders at the time of the Mercenaries' War (above, p. 18). In addition, as Gilbert Picard said (1967, pp. 74–6), Rome was probably worried by Hamilcar Barca's rise in Carthage at the expense of the oligarchic party represented by Hanno and his faction, and not altogether displeased at inflicting this loss of prestige on him.

Probably at the end of the winter of 238–237 – according to the wavering chronology of our sources (cf. Walbank, 1957, pp. 149–50; Huss, 1985, p. 267) – the Roman Senate made ready an expedition to gain a foothold in Sardinia. Carthage reacted by sending an embassy to Rome with the task of emphasizing its rights over the island and announcing its intention to recover an old possession. Rome let it be known that it would regard any action taken by Carthage on the island as a hostile act against the Romans themselves, and held the threat of a declaration of war over the Carthaginian ambassadors (Polybius, I, 88, 10–11; III, 10, 1–2). Weakened by more than three years of struggle with the mercenaries, Carthage had to yield; it ceded Sardinia – the consul Ti. Sempronius Gracchus took possession of it, and also seized Corsica – and over and above this, had to agree to pay an extra indemnity of 1,200 talents; this was stipulated in additional clauses to the treaty of 241 (Polybius, III, 27, 7). Usually full of understanding for the deeds of the Roman Senate, the Greek historian disapproved of this *Anschluss*, in which – next to the effects of Hamilcar's personal resentment towards the Romans – he recognized the 'second and most important cause' of the second Punic War (III, 10, 4). In fact, this brutal annexation relaunched the cycle of mutual rancour and shattered the dream, nurtured in Carthage by Hanno and his followers, and perhaps by others in Rome as well, of a peaceful coexistence for the two republics on either side of the Straits of Sicily.

# 2

# Time for Spain

Sated with the factual history, of the most warlike nature, in the preceding pages, the reader may perhaps be glad of a breathing space before following Hamilcar to Spain and, from there, launching out with Hannibal towards Gaul and Italy. Trying to untangle the context of Carthaginian internal policy in which the chief of the Barcid clan left for a 'proconsulate' that was unprecedented in Carthage's annals may well provide the opportunity. A chance, also, to take one's bearings from the mainly textual sources which form the basis of this epic.

## Polybius, Livy, Fabius Pictor and others

The historian of this period soon has all his cards on the table. The best, sometimes the only, one is the Polybius whom I have already quoted so frequently. To reject his testimony, on the basis that it is often exclusive of any other, would be to condemn oneself to shutting up shop. The old adage *testis unus, testis nullus* cannot have the same absolute value for the historian of Antiquity as for the lawyer; the more so because, in this instance, the sole witness is a wonderful companion.

Polybius was born at the very end of the third century at Megalopolis in the Peloponnese, to a rich Arcadian family connected with Philopoemen, the last hero of Greece in decline. Caught between Macedonian militarism and Roman imperialism, the Greeks at that time were living through a difficult situation, especially those who, like Polybius and his relatives, had responsibilities in their country – the Achaean Confederation had made the historian their master of cavalry (hipparch) in 170 – and were trying to maintain at least a policy of independence *vis-à-vis* Rome. The defeat of Perseus at Pydna in 168 and the definitive collapse of Macedonian power resulted in a terrible purge in Achaea. A thousand hostages were deported to Italy, Polybius among them. He was fortunate enough – he himself recounted (XXXI, 23, 4) the birth of this friendship – to attract the attention of the young Scipio Aemilianus and, at the age of thirty-five, to become his adviser, almost his mentor. In the twenty years that followed, his close contact with the Roman ruling class, his journeys to Spain, Gaul and Africa (André and Baslez, 1993, pp. 46–7) – where he met Massinissa in 151 – and his physical presence in Carthage during the final phases of the siege of the city in 147–146 gave him an exceptional experience. His 'ethnographic curiosity' has been rightly praised (Momigliano, 1979, p. 40), but he was no less passionate about geography – to the point of setting off in Hanno's tracks for a voyage along the coasts of present-day Morocco and Mauritania during the summer of 146 (Desanges, 1978a, pp. 121–47). In this way he visited the theatres of operations that he describes, questioned survivors – for instance in the Alps (III, 48, 12) – saw with his own eyes famous documents, like the bronze table of Cape Lacinium (below, p. 156) in southern Italy, whose numerical data he preferred to those of other historians when it was a matter of the numbers of troops brought by Hannibal (III, 33, 18). Although he had direct access to the documents in Roman archives – such as the series of treaties between Rome and Carthage (III, 22–7) – Polybius by no means neglected his predecessors, the historians who were contemporary with the events. For his account of the first Punic War, he consulted Philinos of Agrigentum, who had probably witnessed this conflict and championed the Punic cause, and Fabius Pictor, who also wrote in Greek but from the Roman viewpoint. The last-named is to be found again in Polybius' sources for the account of the second Punic War, compared with the Lacedaemonian Sosylos, who had lived in Hannibal's camp (he had been his tutor in Greek literature), and another Greek, Silenos, from Kale Akte in Sicily, who had also been among the Carthaginian leader's entourage (Cornelius Nepos, *Hannibal*, 13, 3).

Polybius, who set great store by his profession of historian, was concerned above all with the 'aetiology' of events: in the following pages we shall see him ponder at length over the deep-seated causes of the second Punic War, making careful distinction between true causality (*aitia*), pretexts (*prophaseis*) and beginnings (*archai*). Fascinated by Rome, whose political prisoner he had at first been but to which he was indebted for the dazzling fulfilment of a second career, he recognized in its institutions and form of government the motivating force behind its conquests and irresistible success (Pédech, 1964, pp. 303–30; Ferrary, 1988, pp. 265–72).

The second great witness to this history, Livy, was a contemporary of Augustus, whose name alone symbolizes Roman success on the brink of the Christian era. Like Polybius, Livy has left us an unbroken account of the second Punic War: it is the famous 'third decade', which posterity's unflagging interest in Hannibal's war has managed to preserve for us complete and intact – books with the patina of long use, like the ivoried vellum covers of the copies read by students in the classical age. European humanist tradition turned Livy's *History* into an oft-translated and commentated text, in which one comes straight to the point; this familiarity would be deceptive and dangerous if it caused the reader to take it as gospel. The brilliance of the style, the success of the dramatic effects and the beauty of the rhetorical elaboration must not make us forget that Livy's account is often unconfirmed; the text must be decoded in the light of the Paduan historian's pro-Roman bias. Sir Ronald Syme's disenchanted maxim, 'Historians are selective, dramatic, impressionistic' (1964), is as applicable to Livy as it is to Sallust. Moreover, Livy did not share the Greek's surprising curiosity about things and people; he did not make on-the-spot inquiries. True, at a distance of two centuries any attempt at direct documentation had little chance of being productive. So, drawing a parallel between the two historians, which is possible over a long narrative episode that they have in common – as regards Hannibal's war, Polybius becomes fragmentary only after the battle of Cannae (216) – and making the inevitable comparison between them only rarely favours the Latin writer. Their paths are often so close, with points that are sometimes so obviously common that they might almost be called carbon copies. For example, the account of the descent of the Italian side of the Alps by Hannibal and his army (Polybius, III, 54, 4–55; Livy, XXI, 35, 10–37): up to this point the two texts are so superimposable, even down to details – Livy, however, is distinct for his allusion to the use of sour wine or vinegar, as we shall see – that many critics, and by no means minor ones, have concluded that Livy made direct use of Polybius, not to say 'plagiarized' him (Jal, 1988, pp. XVI–XVII). It may not be ruled out, however, that the Greek and the Latin both used a common source, which may have been Fabius Pictor. For although the points of contact between Polybius and Livy are evident, their points of divergence are no less so. And since I have just mentioned an episode from the crossing of the Alps, I must swiftly add that the two historians, as we shall see farther on, gave radically different itineraries for that crossing.

Naturally, Livy also delved into other sources, which he sometimes quotes: C. Acilius, Claudius Quadrigarius, Valerius Antias, and chiefly Coelius Antipater, who in the late second century BC had written a history of the second Punic War in seven books, unfortunately now lost, of which only a few rare *membra disiecta* survive, also known from quotations by Cicero. The loss of Coelius' history is the more regrettable since he seems to have followed Silenos, one of Hannibal's historiographers whom we have already seen used by Polybius.

The reader has had, and will have again, occasion to find reference to other early writers, very secondary sources in comparison with our two chief witnesses. Perhaps we should set apart Cornelius Nepos, first because he was a generation earlier than Livy and, more importantly, because without trying to be a historian he concluded his 'treatise on the great generals of foreign nations' with a short 'life of Hamilcar' and a rather fuller biography of Hannibal. From the same period – the second half of the first century BC – surviving fragments of books XXV, XXVI and XXVII of Diodorus are sometimes invaluable, notably for events that took place in Sicily. It should not be surprising that we sometimes resort to a poet, Silius Italicus (above, p. 7); according to Pliny the Younger (*Ep.*, III, 7), who knew him well, the author of the *Punica*, the last consul appointed by Nero in AD 68, was a glutton for work, endowed with a rich library containing Livy, of course, but also Valerius Antias (Devallet and Miniconi, 1979, pp. XLVII–L). There is little to be gained from Cassius Dio and his Byzantine abbreviator Zonaras, but we know that another Greek who was writing in the middle of the second century AD, Appian, is our basic source for the third Punic War and the dramatic end of

Carthage (Lancel, 1995a, pp. 409–27). One may make cautious use of the same historian's pages on the 'Spanish War' and 'Hannibal's War'.

## The situation in Carthage in 237 and Hamilcar's departure for Spain

What would we not give for more precise knowledge of the state of mind of those in Carthage when the loss of Sardinia became known! Although we cannot have the picture we would like, the conflicting indications of some of the texts I have just reviewed give some idea of the upheavals that shook the Punic capital at that time. In the centre of the storm, we again find Hamilcar Barca. With the return of peace and security, but also the bitterness of a fresh amputation of Carthage's overseas empire, the time had come to settle old scores. According to Appian (*Iber.*, 4), Hamilcar found himself blamed for having made ill-considered promises to his mercenaries during his command in Sicily, notably to the Celtic contingents fighting under his orders, thus fuelling the rebellion. Threatened with being brought to trial – probably before the Tribunal of the Hundred or Hundred and Four, but Appian is not specific – he seems to have escaped legal proceedings thanks to his connections with influential people in Carthage who were also in public favour. In the forefront – and this is his first historical appearance – was the Hasdrubal who, it seems, had just married Hamilcar's second daughter. While on the subject of this marriage, I must mention a rumour – for it is doubtless significant of the malice of Roman annals regarding the Punic leader, referred to by Cornelius Nepos (*Hamilcar*, III, 2), with a swift echo in Livy (XXI, 2, 4) – according to which a special friendship linked Hamilcar to the handsome Hasdrubal. Apparently it was to avoid seeing this friendship frustrated that Hamilcar gave his daughter's hand to the young man, for, says Cornelius Nepos, Carthaginian family customs forbade a father-in-law to be separated from his son-in-law. The Roman historian may pretend to distance himself by adding that scandalmongers could not fail to attack so great a man – *maledici tanto viro deesse non poterant* – but himself was unable to refrain from reporting the slander! Polybius makes no mention of either the proceedings instituted against Hamilcar, or the allusion to his homosexual leanings, and modern historians agree in viewing this belated alteration to the image of a man whom Cato the Elder held in the highest esteem (Plutarch, *Cato Maior*, 8, 14) as influenced by later Roman historiography (Huss, 1985, p. 286), and perhaps more precisely by Coelius Antipater (Hans-Günther, 1991, p. 116). We may also attribute to the anti-Barcid tradition the statements of Diodorus of Sicily (XXV, 8), according to whom, after the end of the Mercenaries' War, in the period we are examining – the end of 238 to mid-237 – Hamilcar teamed up with Carthage's least desirable elements, using a fortune amassed by dubious means, war booty among others, to ingratiate himself with the people and thus obtain military command over the whole of Libya for an indeterminate period.

To put it bluntly – the word *demokopia* appears in his text – Diodorus is speaking of demagogy in a questionable polemical tone. However, he seems sure that in Carthage during these years state government was developing in a democratic direction. Polybius (VI, 51) places 'in the period when Hannibal's war began' – in other words, some twenty years later – what he considers a deterioration in the Carthaginian constitution, about which, at least in his original outlook, he shared Aristotle's good opinion (Lancel, 1995a, pp. 115–17). In Carthage, he says, 'the voice of the people had become preponderant in deliberations, whereas in Rome the Senate enjoyed the fullness of its authority. Among the Carthaginians the opinion of the greatest number prevailed, among the Romans that of the elite of the citizens.' Let it be said in passing that, with this comparison, we again find the Greek historian's concern to inquire into causes and his oft-remarked tendency to see in the just balance of an aristocratic government in Rome the recipe for its historical success. The distortion in the conduct of public affairs denounced by Polybius might have begun slightly earlier than he says, owing to the great upheaval caused by the Mercenaries' War and even before the blow of losing Sardinia. We saw earlier (above, p. 19) that at a crucial moment in the rebellion led by Spendios and Matho it was the people's assembly, even then, which had imposed Hanno's dismissal from his military command and the appointment of an assistant for Hamilcar. Two or three years later, the same scenario may well have been repeated, ensuring for Hamilcar, besides possible judicial immunity, pre-eminence at the expense of Hanno, who was once again set aside, but among the Elders of Carthage preserved his status of leader of the opposition to the Barcids. To speak of a 'democratic revolution' in regard to the crisis of 238–237 would probably be exaggerated, and it would be risky to connect this episode, as some have done (Picard and Picard, 1970, p. 307), with the formal institution of the annual collegial suffetate in Carthage.

A similar veil of uncertainty, woven by the discrepancies in our sources, surrounds the political circumstances of Hamilcar's departure for Spain. An annalistic tradition, perhaps going back to Fabius Pictor and echoed by Appian (*Hann.*, 2; *Iber.*, 5: cf. also Zonaras, VIII, 17), would have it that the Punic leader left for Spain on his own initiative, without the backing of Carthage's senate. Polybius merely remarks soberly (II, 1, 5) that, once their affairs had been settled in Africa, the Carthaginians dispatched Hamilcar to Spain with an expeditionary force. We shall probably never know anything more, but we can at least advance the hypothesis that Hamilcar would have had little difficulty, before Carthage's senate, in triumphing over the opposition of Hanno, whose desire, as is proved by his entire conduct before and after this time, was that Carthage should concentrate most on consolidating and expanding its African empire. From the very outset of the enterprise, was the ambitious plan to outflank Rome from the far west, or at least limit its expansion on that side, at the forefront of the aims of Hamilcar and his supporters? We shall return later to this fundamental problem; but it must be emphasized that the mines of Andalusia in themselves were a sufficiently attractive target. Let us not forget that Carthage, ruined by the

Mercenaries' War, as well as losing Sardinia had seen Rome impose a heavy additional war indemnity.

Hamilcar probably set out for Spain in the spring or summer of 237, with troops whose composition and numbers are unknown to us. He left Africa, which he was never to see again, at the Pillars of Hercules. In other words, he made his way by land before crossing the Straits of Gibraltar, according to Polybius (II, 1, 6), who is to be preferred to Diodorus (XXV, 10, 1), who suggests that he sailed along the north shores of the Maghreb before crossing the straits. He took with him his son-in-law, Hasdrubal, and also the young Hannibal, then aged nine.

It is on the occasion of this departure by father and son that we see for the first time the indissoluble mingling of history and the Barcid legend. Polybius, again, recounts the legendary episode of Hannibal's oath; he is not the only one to do so, but it was he who gave the account its greatest symbolic power. On the point of leaving Carthage, Hamilcar offered a sacrifice, in order to obtain favourable omens. When the ceremony was over, he summoned the young Hannibal and asked if he would like to come with him on his expedition. When the child enthusiastically agreed, Hamilcar led him before the altar and made him swear that he would never be a friend to the Romans. According to Polybius (III, 11), it was in the evening of his life, in 193, that Hannibal himself revealed his childhood oath in conversation with Antiochus III, with whom he had taken refuge at that time, in order to break down the Seleucid's mistrust of him. Although it appears, with slight variations, in other sources representative of Roman annalistic tradition (for example, Livy, XXI, 1, 4 and XXXV, 19, 3–4), the authenticity of this anecdote has been the subject of impassioned argument by modern critics. Many (for instance, Brisson, 1973, p. 132) reject it, arguing that it did not take shape until the first half of the second century, when Rome was trying to find moral justification for its aggressive policy towards Carthage. But it could hardly take shape earlier, since it was necessary to wait until Hannibal told Antiochus about it in 193!

It is understandable that argument about the reality of this scene goes beyond the level of anecdote. The young Hannibal at his father's side vowing eternal hatred for the Romans is a 'touching scene', a powerful symbol. In the text quoted (III, 11), Polybius uses it as such, as a 'moral proof' of his line of argument, according to which the prime cause of the second Punic War was Hamilcar's implacable animosity towards Rome, an animosity that he strove to pass on to his descendants, like a mission to be accomplished even beyond his own lifetime. Here we find again the spirit of the little story related by Valerius Maximus (above, p. 9), about Hamilcar's sons compared by their father to lion cubs raised to destroy Rome.

The Ancients firmly believed in the effective strength of great characters, and they were not wrong. Livy means nothing different from Polybius by his famous and oft-quoted phrase: '*Angebant ingentis spiritus virum Sicilia Sardiniaque amissae*' (XXI, 1, 5). And a little later he continues, very clearly accusing Hamilcar on the basis of his supposed intent: 'If he had lived longer', he says, 'the Carthaginians, under Hamilcar's command, would have carried into Italy the struggle that they brought under the leadership of Hannibal' (XXI, 2, 2). In the well-chosen words of one of Polybius' best commentators, according to the Greek historian 'Hamilcar throws a bridge between the two Punic Wars' (Pédech, 1964, p. 182). Livy, shortly afterwards, would think no differently from Polybius.

Let us recall that our two main authors, the Latin and the Greek, both believed in Hamilcar's powerful desire for revenge. Even if what little we know tends to lend his actions a personal motive, nevertheless in 237 the Punic general was merely carrying out a policy decided in Carthage because it had prevailed over another. To rebuild itself, and first of all to free itself from a heavy war indemnity, the Punic metropolis was once more taking to the high seas, *en route* for the far West where, according to early tradition, at the end of the second millennium, or at the latest on the brink of the first millennium, Phoenician navigators had established their most distant bridgeheads and put down the first bases for the exploitation of a fabulous Eldorado.

## The Iberian world in the Hellenistic period

In the *oikumene* of the father of ancient geography, Eratosthenes of Cyrene – and at least such as we may try to imagine it (Nicolet, 1988, pp. 74–7) – the Iberian peninsula seemed like a 'subcontinent', as marginalized by its position at the western tip of the known world as India might be at the east. Even in the middle of the third century BC, its massiveness, relief, and the harshness of its climate, very often like that of its inhabitants, had saved it from extensive penetration by outside elements. A traveller like Polybius, who had visited at least its eastern marches – his account is unfortunately lost and survives only in snatches in Pliny the Elder and Posidonius of Apamea – could not fail to be struck by its great diversity and the remarkable coexistence of very varied cultures and levels of culture.

The pre-Celtic and Celtic world of the North-West (the Cantabrian Mountains, Asturia, Galicia, present-day northern Portugal), as well as the plateaux of the Meseta, in the centre of the Peninsula, north of the Tagus, had remained on the fringes of the history being formed since the start of the first millennium BC along the coasts of the Mediterranean basin. On the southern and eastern borders of that 'barbarian' world, in this period, from the Alentejo in the south to Aragon in the north-east, passing through Castilla la Nueva and La Mancha, dwelt peoples known as 'Celtiberian', who would make life difficult for the Barcids in their efforts to expand their Spanish domain. Taking into account a certain unity of civilization, despite their fragmentation into different groups, the name 'Iberian' was commonly given to those peoples who were spread out from southern Portugal and the lower valley of the Guadalquivir as far as Languedoc, by way of Andalusia, the Levant and the maritime side of Catalonia.

What a wealth of differing destinies lay within this Iberian world itself! The earliest entry in history was of the land of Tartessus, that is, the lower valley of the

Baetis (our Guadalquivir). Here agricultural and, more importantly, mineral wealth (the copper and silver-bearing lead of the south slopes of the Sierra Morena) – which was worked in very early times by the Phoenicians settled at Gades (Cádiz) – had favoured the development of a brilliant 'orientalizing' culture (Aubet, 1982, pp. 309–32). In the same period – beginning in the eighth century – on the other side of the Straits of Gibraltar, the Phoenicians had taken advantage of the demographic weakness and cultural paucity of the local populations (the Bastuli) to establish on Andalusia's Mediterranean coast trading-posts and agencies that were very prosperous in early times, chiefly owing to the similar mining resources of the Baetic cordillera. Excavations that have been actively carried out over a quarter of a century on this coast, between Guadarranque and Almeria (Lancel, 1995a, pp. 9–14), have revealed the density of Phoenician establishments in the archaic era, and have also shown that, unlike the Tartessian land of the lower Guadalquivir, they had hardly any cultural heritage.

In contrast, turning northwards and coming to the Spanish Levant, one finds the finest traces of an obviously composite 'Iberian' culture, but which derives some highly original features from this very 'interbreeding'. Its most representative, and certainly most celebrated, jewel is the limestone female bust unearthed at the end of last century at Alcudia de Elche, on the site of the ancient Illici – perhaps the Hellike that we shall see besieged by Hamilcar shortly before his accidental death. This 'Lady of Elche' is commonly dated to the fourth century BC, with perhaps the suspicion that she may belong to the second half of the fifth (Nicolini, 1973, p. 86). In striking and rather unusual fashion – doubt has sometimes been cast on its authenticity – this bust illustrates the successful outcome of a long process of acculturation, which, as it ripened, married Phoenician expressiveness with Greek discipline to bring out the creative capabilities of the Iberian people, whose baroque genius expressed itself more especially in three-dimensional works. This masterpiece of 'high Iberian', as it has been proposed to call the floruit of this culture, from 450 to 200, must not be allowed to conceal other successes. The collection of figured bronzes from Iberian sanctuaries (Nicolini, 1969) is sufficient on its own to proclaim the powerful originality of this art, which asserted itself as early as the sixth century BC, when Graeco-oriental and, above all, Ionian influences travelled from the trading-posts of the Levant into the hinterland, which witnessed the blossoming of schools of workers in bronze who had assimilated to perfection the techniques of lost-wax and full casting. These techniques devoured metal, but copper and lead mines were close at hand, and from earliest antiquity this region had been the first and probably the principal staging-point on the 'tin road' from Britain and the 'Cassiterides islands' (Gras, 1989, p. 102), perhaps the islands situated at the entrance to the deep 'rias' of the south of Galicia. In various religious sites – but chiefly at Despeñaperros (near Santa Elena, Jaén) in the sixth century, and Cerro de los Santos near Albacete in the fourth and third centuries – there would be a growing pile of votive offerings which number among the masterpieces produced by the 'peripheral' cultures of the classical world. And the interest of Iberian output sculpted in stone by no means yields to that of the bronzes. I have already mentioned the 'Lady of Elche'. In the range of 'ladies' represented enthroned in majesty, hieratic in their heavy jewellery and sumptuous garments, which to them weigh nothing, the 'Lady of Baza', discovered a mere twenty or so years ago near Granada, has no less a presence than the bust from Elche. A divine force emanates from her, too.

As we have just seen, this south-east quarter of Spain where Carthage was making ready to return in force had been open to other influences than those of the Semitic world since the dawn of the first millennium BC, when the Phoenicians had established their bridgeheads on Andalusian shores and, by their contribution, had strengthened the orientalizing development of Tartessian culture. The texts relating to the incursion into Andalusia of a Greek adventurer, the Samian Kolaios, in the first half of the seventh century, and those which instance the 'philhellenism' in a barely later period of a mythical Tartessian king, Arganthonios (Herodotus, I, 163; Pliny the Elder, VII, 154–6), are not empty words. A very recent synthesis, assembling the results obtained by Spanish archaeology which has been very active over the past thirty years or so, clearly reveals how Greek trading had blazed a trail in the Peninsula, especially from the arrival of the Phocaeans (Rouillard, 1991). In this regard, the year 600 BC is a key date. The founding of Massilia (Marseille) by Phocaea, that Greek town in Asia Minor cramped into its shoreline with no hinterland, was shortly followed by that of Emporion (Ampurias) on the north coast of Catalonia, around 590–580. There is still much controversy about earlier Greek colonization in Andalusian territory. However, at Mainake, in the very heart of the string of the oldest Phoenician establishments, as subsequently about that of Akra Leuke (the future foundation of Hamilcar, in fact) – the Greeks had, nevertheless, been able to give substance to their existence and influence on the Levant coast by means of *Emporia* ('markets'), that were politically unobtrusive and commercially efficient (Rouillard, 1991, pp. 281–311). There are impressive maps showing the distribution of thousands of Greek vases, particularly fourth-century Attic pottery, brought to light in the Peninsula, and even as far afield as the areas of Portugal north of the Douro (Rouillard, 1991, pp. 120–1, 124–5).

The reader who is familiar with the proverbial commercial expertise of the Phoenicians and Carthaginians may perhaps wonder at the surprising success of Greek competition in Spain, notably during the fifth and sixth centuries BC. That would be to underestimate the exceptional technical quality of the articles in question, in this instance the black-glazed Attic pottery which no Phoenico-Punic products could yet rival until, a little later, Carthage perfected a black-glazed pottery from very hard clay, which was just as sturdy and also lighter (Lancel, 1995a, p. 408). Being commercial realists, the Phoenico-Carthaginians were not slow to act as redistributive traders, dealing in articles that had proved their worth. That these articles were not their own does not mean that they themselves were absent from the vast market provided by the 'exploitable' Spain of that period. Furthermore, they were very much present in an essential field in which their genius had previously imposed itself on the Greek world –

writing. The distribution map of ancient inscriptions in the Iberian peninsula (especially those from the seventh to the fourth centuries BC) shows four main varieties of script corresponding to non-Indo-European dialectal specializations occupying vast geographical sectors; but these variations all go back to a common creation originating from Tartessus, at the latest in the seventh century and, in the final analysis, to the Phoenician alphabet, with a few adaptations. Although Phoenician inscriptions proper appear to be limited to Andalusia's southern coastal fringe, Greek inscriptions are still rarer; they are tightly confined to the Phocaean colony of Emporion (Ampurias), in Catalonia (De Hoz, 1991, pp. 669–78). And a notation of Iberian dialects in Greek characters is attested only in a small part of the Spanish Levant, the region of Alicante and Murcia (Rouillard, 1991, pp. 334–5). This is not surprising: it is also the region of Elche, of the famous bust, where in the whole of Iberian art the imitation of classical Greek art appears most clearly.

## Hamilcar in Spain

All the same, a long-standing cultural influence, and no less ancient and sound trading positions, do not take the place of a political and administrative infrastructure, even less of what we would term military logistics. We lack the necessary information to judge the assessment Hamilcar was able to make when he arrived in Gades (Cádiz) in 237.

The old Phoenician city, keeping watch on the Atlantic, almost an island facing the estuary of the Guadalete, was still welcoming and safe. But beyond? Of the trading posts that had formerly spread at fairly close intervals along the Andalusian coast, on the other side of the 'Pillars of Hercules', some were already long gone: for instance, Chorreras and Toscanos; but it is true that these sites had been abandoned only to the benefit of neighbouring establishments: Morro and Mezquitilla for the first, Cerro del Mar for the other. And the old Phoenician presence had been maintained, it would seem, at Málaga where, even in the era of Augustus, Strabo (III, 4, 2) could still perceive the imprint left by Phoenician town-planning. The Phoenico-Carthaginians were similarly present in Almuñecar, on the site of the ancient Sexi, at Adra, where Abdera had remained unchanged throughout the pre-Roman period. It is thus almost certain that, for Hamilcar and his soldiers, the whole of the coastal strip of lower Andalusia was a friendly area, widely usable as a rearguard base. Incidentally, the native population of this zone, specially around Málaga, called Blasto-Phoenicians by the Greeks and Bastulo-Poeni by the Latins, was the only one to have adopted the Semitic tongue.

Offshore from the Spanish Levant, Carthage had for centuries exercised full and entire sovereignty over Ibiza, thereby controlling all the Balearic archipelago. We shall have occasion to see how vital to it this Mediterranean relay-point was at that time. But in the Peninsula itself, it does not appear that the Carthaginians' strong cultural and commercial presence was matched by a political protectorate. In particular, there is no reason to give other than purely commercial significance to one of the precise geographical locations in the second treaty agreed between Carthage and Rome in 348. The text of this treaty, passed on by Polybius (III, 24), set as the western limit of piracy, trade and possible colonizing undertakings by the Romans a town named Mastia Tarseion, which in all likelihood was a city on the east coast of Spain, if not exactly Cartagena, as is sometimes suggested. This clause in the treaty is without doubt significant of the clear-sightedness of the Carthaginian senate faced with the potential dangers of the Italic city-state's increasing powerfulness. Already confronted with the fierce commercial and cultural competition of the Greeks, Carthage was not anxious to see Rome enter the field as a third party in the Iberian peninsula. From that it is a mere step to interpreting this diplomatic device as an indication of Carthage's hold at that time, by means of military raids, on the entire south-east quarter of Spain as far as its tip at Cape de la Nao; a step which has sometimes been taken (for instance, Picard and Picard, 1970, p. 334) on the basis of the archaeological evidence of destruction suffered by sites in the region in the mid-fourth century. It is commonly agreed nowadays that there is nothing here to give firm evidence of a Carthaginian military presence in this part of the Peninsula in that period (Barcelo, 1988, p. 132) and one is tempted to conclude, with another expert on the terrain, that the difficulties Hamilcar had to face in his venture bear sufficient witness that, before the Barcid reconquest, Carthage was no more than a privileged commercial and cultural partner in the region (Rouillard, 1991, p. 235).

## From Cádiz to Alicante

Reconquest: Polybius' words suggest that this was more or less what it was all about: 're-establishing the Carthaginians' affairs in Iberia', as he defined Hamilcar's mission (II, 1, 6), stretching over nine years, which the Greek historian sums up in a few lines, thus condemning us to follow less reliable guides.

Quite naturally, Hamilcar had in mind the gold and silver mines of the Sierra Morena, direct or indirect control of which formed his prime objective. To achieve this, negotiations were probably easy with 'Tartessian' peoples – such as the Bastetani – whose acculturation was of long standing, although Diodorus includes them among those whom the Carthaginian general had to fight. In contrast, in the foothills of the mountains north of Seville and Córdoba, he had to face the resistance of the Turdetani or Turduli, backed by more northerly Celtiberian tribes commanded by two brothers, one of whom, says Diodorus, was named Istolatios. Hamilcar easily overcame them, and incorporated the 3,000 or so survivors into his own army. Shortly afterwards, a second war episode pitted the Carthaginians against an army raised by another Celtiberian chieftain, named Indortes, who managed to assemble 50,000 men – this figure, which seems exaggerated, is unconfirmed – but was put to flight even before joining battle. If we are to believe Diodorus (XXV, 10, 2), on this occasion Hamilcar resorted to a strategy of terror. After seizing Indortes, whom he had besieged, the Punic leader put out his eyes, tortured and finally crucified him. But he was magnanimous towards enemy soldiers taken prisoner, sending more than 10,000 of them back to their homes. As the Sicilian historian remarks, diplomacy thus alternated with the use of force!

Hamilcar had apparently wasted no time in accomplishing the first part of his mission. The renewal of the silver coinage of Gades, recorded at that time, bears witness to the reorganization of mine-working in the Sierra Morena (Alfaro-Asins, 1988, pp. 75, 126). Although we have no material proof, it is highly probable that the Barcid arranged the transport to Carthage of the precious metals whose scarcity had not long before imperilled the republic at the time of the Mercenaries' War, and which it now so desperately needed in order to pay off its annual war debt to Rome. Some sources report that a few years later, in 231, a Roman embassy came to enquire of Hamilcar the reasons for his presence and activities in Spain. He is said to have replied that he was working to pay the indemnity owed to Rome (Cassius Dio, fragment 46). Though it is probably apocryphal, the anecdote is significant of the ends pursued by the Punic general and, through him, by the Carthaginian senate.

Hamilcar had realized that he could not confine himself to controlling Gades and the river routes of the Guadalquivir and Guadalete, as well as the coastline of lower Andalusia. To make sure of that control, he had to extend his hold eastwards, at least as far as Cape de la Nao, the tip of the Peninsula towards Ibiza; on a clear day, from the promontory one can make out the island where the Carthaginians had for centuries maintained a political and military presence. During several campaigns, which occupied him from 235 to 231, Hamilcar turned towards these Iberian peoples – the Bastetani or Mastians around Murcia, the Contestani around Elche – who, as we saw (above, p. 32), thanks to their contacts with the Greeks, had reached as early as the fourth century a high level not only of artistic flowering but also of material and technical civilization. The weapons produced in the region were renowned in Antiquity, in particular the famous curved sabre, the *falcata*, a fine example of which is preserved in the Madrid Museum.

It was to safeguard his rear in this new phase of Carthaginian control of the Peninsula that Hamilcar, according to Diodorus (XXV, 10, 3: the Sicilian historian is the only one to mention this founding), founded what he intended to be an important city (*megiste*) in the place named in Greek Akra Leuke, the 'White Headland'. People have sometimes tried to see in this city one of the three colonies settled, according to Strabo (III, 4, 6), by Greeks from Marseille south of the Sucro (present-day Jucar). But the term used by Diodorus (*ktizein*) implies without any doubt an act of founding, and it is more plausible that the historian should have naturally transcribed into the Greek form Akra Leuke one of those names beginning *Rus*-which abound in the Punic toponymy of the Mediterranean coastline, especially that of north Africa. It is nevertheless regrettable that not a single archaeological trace enables the site of this foundation to be pinpointed, though it is ordinarily assumed to be at or near Alicante. Even the date remains in doubt: was it 231, as is sometimes stated, or shortly after 235, at the beginning of the series of operations intended to pacify the region? The slightly earlier date seems more likely.

Whatever the truth, with this *ktisma* to crown a splendid career as military leader and politician, Hamilcar's adventurous life was drawing to its close. The end came, so it seems, during the winter of 229–228: eight years, says Cornelius Nepos (*Hamilcar*, 4, 2), after his arrival in Spain; in 227, about nine years after his arrival, according to Polybius (II, 1, 7), and ten years (III, 10, 7) before the start of the second Punic War. At the time Hamilcar had left the bulk of his troops and war elephants in his winter quarters at Akra Leuke and, while his son-in-law Hasdrubal was campaigning elsewhere, he went to lay siege to a town called Helike, often and probably wrongly identified with the Roman Illici, the Elche made famous by the celebrated 'Lady'. For Elche is too close to Alicante, on the outskirts of which the rear base of the Punic leader must have been situated, and if one places Helike there one cannot see in which large river Hamilcar can have drowned while crossing it in retreat. For, if we are to believe Diodorus, that is how he met his death. The king of the Oretani – from the plateaux of La Mancha – came to the assistance of the place under siege. Hamilcar, in a difficult position, accepted the feigned negotiation that was proposed to him and, attacked while retreating, made a point of protecting his two sons who were accompanying him – Hannibal and Hasdrubal the Younger – by diverting the pursuers' attention on to himself. He is supposed to have drowned while crossing on horseback the river that separated him from the main body of his troops – perhaps the Jucar. At least, that is Diodorus' version (XXV, 10, 3–4). In actual fact, the circumstances of Hamilcar's death remain quite vague. Ill informed, or in a hurry to recount what was happening at the same time in Illyria, Polybius (II, 1, 8) renders him honours in three lines, having him fall, weapon in hand, on an anonymous battlefield; while Cornelius Nepos (*Hamilcar*, 4, 2) states precisely that he died in an engagement against the Vettoni, a fairly distant tribe, west of Toledo, in the upper valley of the Tagus. We shall take no notice of the fantastic tale handed down by Appian (*Iber.*, 5), followed by the Byzantine Zonaras (VIII, 19), according to which the Punic leader fell victim to a battle ruse: wood-laden carts which the Spaniards had hitched up to oxen are supposed to have closed in on the Carthaginian soldiers who, taken in by the stratagem, at first laughed but were then thrown into panic when the carts were set on fire, and their leader was killed in the midst of the chaos.

## Hasdrubal the Fair

Hannibal had not quite reached his twentieth year. Despite his early experience and engagements at his father's side, he was too young to succeed him. It was Hamilcar's son-in-law, Hasdrubal, who was chosen by the army, and even if we lack definite testimony, there is no doubt that this choice was ratified by the people in Carthage. There in person, Hasdrubal could pride himself on having been the dead leader's lieutenant for several years. As admiral, he had commanded his navy, but had also been his second-in-command in land battles. In the Punic metropolis, he had certainly maintained useful friendships and support from the time when he had played a far from negligible political role (above, p. 28). Support which – if we are to believe one of our sources, Cornelius Nepos (*Hamilcar*, 3, 3) – he seems to have continued to win for himself by buying it; according to the historian, he was the first man seriously to change public mores in Carthage by his corrupt manoeuvring. But as we shall see, in attempting to draw up a political assessment of his action in Spain, in the case of Hasdrubal and later of Hannibal, the Roman historiographer may have been influenced by the aristocratic opposition to the Barcids in the very heart of the Carthaginian senate. This influence is also perceptible in Livy (XXI, 2, 4), when the Paduan historian thought fit to note that Hasdrubal's appointment to head the Spanish army was made in Carthage with the assent of the people, but against the wish of the men in high places.

Scarcely had he taken office when Hasdrubal assembled his forces, which were joined by reinforcements sent from Africa (Appian, *Iber.*, 6); in all he had 50,000 footsoldiers, 6,000 horsemen and 200 elephants. He returned to the attack on the king of the Oretani, conquered him and avenged Hamilcar by massacring all those whose treachery had brought about his defeat and death. Diodorus says (XXV, 12)) that he seized the 'twelve towns' of the Oretani and 'all the towns in Iberia'. It is very hard to define with a little more precision the geographical reality of Hasdrubal's conquests, and thereby the farthest boundaries of the regions won by him for Carthage's rule. But henceforth a large part of the south-east quarter of the Peninsula became subject to Punic domination. Their submission was obtained also by clever diplomacy (celebrated by Livy, XXI, 2, 5 and 7) in dealing with the Iberian petty kings. Either because he had been left a widower by his first wife – Hamilcar Barca's second daughter – or because in his eyes reasons of state justified bigamy, Hasdrubal married the daughter of one of them. Having thereby become 'one of the family', he had himself acknowledged as supreme chief of the Iberians; *strategos autokrator*, says Diodorus, using the Greek title, the very one conferred by the League of Corinth on the young Alexander in 335.

The name does not occur by mere chance at this point. Of course, there was some distance between Hasdrubal the Fair and the demi-god educated by Aristotle, but it was not vast. To put it another way, less than a century after the hero's death, Alexander's exploits had become the point of reference. The collapse of the *polis* and its transition to a state, in the modern sense of the word, the winning of new territories to the classical culture and the creation of new focal points from which its influence could extend, made concrete by the founding of new mother-cities; the exercise of a policy of fusion-cum-assimilation towards indigenous populations; everything that Alexander's genius had invented for the renewal of the Ancient World was henceforth on the agenda of every great entrepreneur. As Alexander had married an Iranian princess, Roxanne, Hasdrubal married an Iberian princess, and we shall later see Hannibal also follow this example. And as the city of Akra Leuke founded by his father-in-law was not sufficiently emblematic, on the same coast but farther south, at the junction of the Levant and the Andalusian littoral, on a site admirably suited to the development of a large port, the son-in-law founded a new capital. The Romans were to call this Carthago Nova (present-day Cartagena), but its founder named it Qart Hadasht (following the example of the Punic mother-city, which was thus hypostatically duplicated on Iberian soil), or 'new town', as Polybius' Greek transcriptions prove, *kaine polis* beside Karkhedon. What a strange destiny for this Semitic place-name which the successors of Christopher Columbus in the early sixteenth century would give to the great Caribbean port of what would soon be Colombia – the final extension of Carthage across the oceans and centuries, and a consolation prize for those adventurers into ancient history who still sometimes pursue the fantasy of an impossible discovery of America by contemporaries of Hannibal!

Will the excavations being actively carried out at Cartagena (Ramallo *et al.*, 1992) discover one day, beneath the Roman levels, a few vestiges of the palace built by Hasdrubal and seen by Polybius in 133, nearly a century after its construction? The Greek historian speaks of its sumptuousness, adding that it might be indicative of an aspiration to monarchy (X, 10, 5). The exact description that he gives of the site, as a prelude to his account of the siege of the town by Scipio in 210, enables us to visualize fairly clearly the location of the major monuments in the new capital so desired by Hasdrubal; dominating the bay, on an eminence, the temple of Eschmoun-Asclepius to the east, with the 'royal' palace in symmetry with it to the west, on the other side of an artificial canal which linked the well-protected anchorage with the shallow waters of the lagoon. But we do not know the whereabouts of the naval yards and arsenals that strengthened the dynamic potential of this place, which was a real stronghold where were stockpiled the riches amassed by the Barcids, especially the output of the rich silver mines lying in the immediate vicinity of the town. Polybius (XXXIV, 9, 8–11) states that, almost a century later, 40,000 workers – or rather, slaves – were working there to the benefit of the Roman people, bringing in a revenue of 25,000 drachmas per day.

Not long before, the reorganization of the mine-workings of the Sierra Morena had improved the worth of coins minted at Gades shortly before Hamilcar's arrival. These mines, which seem to have been brought into service prior to the Barcid foundation, must also have kept up a supply of good alloy to the mint at Cartagena, the existence of which can only be probable, since there is no attested monetary inscription as there is for Gades, Sexi (Almuñecar) and Ibiza. Anyway, this coinage of the Barcid era poses a particular and important problem beyond purely numismatic perspectives, because we refer to it as a criterion that, among other things, allows us to decide whether the government established in Spain by Hamilcar may legitimately be considered as a monarchy of Hellenistic type, like those founded by Alexander's successors. On the face of one of the coins in this issue, a double shekel with an elephant, the effigy represented as the great Gaditan deity, Herakles-Melqart, with his club, is not necessarily that of Hamilcar, as is sometimes claimed (Picard and Picard, 1970, p. 213; but cf. Acquaro, 1983–4, pp. 83–6). But another effigy of the coinage from the same years is more disturbing; there is nothing to enable us specifically to recognize Hasdrubal, of whom no portrait remains, but the manner of representation is very similar to that seen on the face of coins of the head of the Ptolemaic dynasty, Ptolemy Soter. The Ptolemaic features are more pronounced and the expression more lively, but in both instances there is the same diademmed profile, the same convention of monarchic representation. And although there is controversy over identifying this effigy as a portrait of Hasdrubal, and if, notably, the finest Spanish specialist on this coinage still sees it rather as a beardless image of Herakles-Melqart (Villaronga, 1973, pp. 143–5; 1979, p. 105), the type of coinage remains on the ever-open file of the 'Barcid kingdom'.

Indeed, nothing is more difficult than gauging the political status of this Punic Spain and the nature of its links with the Carthaginian mother-city. External signs with symbolic value, the Cartagena 'palace', types of coinage are, as we have seen, vague or arguable. Moreover, archaeology is no help at all. We are driven to seek answers in the written sources – chiefly Polybius and Diodorus – which themselves depend to a large extent on contemporary Roman annals of the events. The latter are presented in tendentious fashion by writers like Fabius Pictor, himself a Roman senator, whose viewpoint embraced the argument of those who, in the heart of the curia, supported maintaining the status quo *vis-à-vis* Carthage. It was necessary at all costs to dissociate the Punic metropolis from the deeds of Hamilcar, and above all of his successors, Hasdrubal and Hannibal, to demonstrate that Carthage's responsibility was not compromised in Spain by adventurers who were engaged in a strictly personal game and were ruling on their own account. Highly significant of this tendency is the picture painted by Fabius Pictor, and related by Polybius (III, 8), of Hasdrubal's seizing power in Spain. According to the Roman historian, after Hamilcar's death and the appointment of his son-in-law as head of the army, Hasdrubal went to Carthage and tried to abolish the constitution then in force in order to replace it with a form of monarchic rule. Thwarted by the oligarchy in the Council of Elders, he left again for Spain, which from then on he governed without any regard for the Carthaginian senate. Polybius adds that he lends no credence to this version, and clearly taxes Fabius Pictor with incoherence. But his scepticism in this regard is directed mainly against the implication that the Barcids, from Hamilcar to Hannibal, never followed any but their own desires and dragged Carthage willy-nilly into the venture of the second Punic War. Speaking in particular of Hasdrubal, though he does not believe that Hamilcar's son-in-law severed all ties with the motherland, he cannot help suspecting, as we have seen in regard to the palace at Cartagena, that he may have had monarchic aspirations.

The Roman Senate as a whole must have had an overall perception of Hasdrubal as a Hellenistic *basileus*. Nevertheless, it was directly to him, and not to the Carthaginian senate, that the *patres Romani* addressed themselves in a diplomatic approach that was to have heavy consequences, since the treaty in which it concluded imposed on the Carthaginians in the Iberian peninsula a boundary whose crossing, as we shall see, was at the root of the second war against Rome.

We may remember that in 231 an embassy had been sent to Hamilcar, apparently with the sole aim of obtaining information, and had returned to Rome satisfied with the Barcid's reply: his concern was to enable Carthage to acquit itself of its war debts. During the summer or in the autumn of 226, the Roman Senate sent a second embassy to Spain, this time to meet Hasdrubal, armed with a mandate of quite different scope. The meeting probably took place in Cartagena. In Polybius (II, 13, 7), our sole source, a few words suffice to define the agreement then reached, in the terms of which the Carthaginians were forbidden to 'cross the Iber bearing arms'. It would probably be wrong to take this unilateral declaration too literally, suggesting as it does a veritable diktat imposed on Hasdrubal, without anything in return; it is likely that a complementary clause similarly restricted the Romans. However that may be, it is understood that Hasdrubal could be satisfied by an agreement which, in his eyes, was the equivalent of official recognition of all that Carthage had done for more than ten years, and was still doing, to affirm its hegemony in Spain south of the Ebro – at least, if Polybius' Iber is really what we call the Ebro. The conditions that caused Hannibal to unleash the hostilities of the second Punic War will bring us back to this problem of place-names.

Quite naturally, there has been speculation about the reasons which might have pushed Rome to make this approach to Hasdrubal, all the more so because Polybius himself lets us into his opinion on this matter. In the Greek historian's view, it was the Gaulish peril that committed the Roman Senate to cutting its losses in the Iberian peninsula; calm was needed among the Carthaginians in Spain before the Celtic menace in the Po Valley could be confronted (Polybius, II, 22, 9–11). It is sometimes held (Picard, 1967, p. 94) that the great Gaulish campaigns postdated the agreement of 226 by a year, but that is not enough cause to reject this motive. Celtic pressure on the Cisalpine region and northern marches of Etruria was very noticeable at that time. Latent when the treaty of 226 was agreed with Hasdrubal, this pressure materialized brutally some months later when, in the spring of 225, the Gauls of the Po Valley – the Boii around Bologna, the Insubres of the Milanese area, the Taurini of Piedmont – joined by bands of Transalpine Celts (the Gaisates) flooded through the Apennine passes (Polybius, II, 23). Fifty thousand footsoldiers and 20,000 horsemen or soldiers in wagons fell on Etruria. They had already reached Clusium (Chiusi), three long days' march from Rome, when the Roman forces encountered them. After a few setbacks, the troops assembled by the consuls L. Aemilius Papus and C. Atilius Regulus got the better of the Gaulish hordes level with Cape Telamon, on the Etruscan coast slightly north of Cosa. C. Atilius Regulus paid for the success with his life (Polybius, II, 28–31). Rome did not content itself with this sharp setback; two years later, in 223, its armies crossed the Po and invaded the territory of the Insubres. Shortly afterwards, a decisive victory carried off at Clastidium by the consul M. Claudius Marcellus – whose name reappears throughout the second

Punic War – gained Milan for Rome, and the founding of the first Cisalpine Roman colonies, at Piacenza and Cremona, followed immediately. Lastly, in 220, the construction of the Via Flaminia – named after its promoter, the censor Gaius Flaminius – opened from Rome to Rimini a rapid access route to the Po Valley, on the very eve of the second Punic War. Polybius, who narrated this 'Gaulish War' in detail, made no mistake about its importance. He knew that for Hannibal Celtic support was the strategic condition *sine qua non* of his whole venture.

In contrast, the Greek historian breathes not a word of what appears to modern historians to have been the other motive, coupled with full awareness of the imminent danger from the Gauls, for the Romans' approach to Hasdrubal in 226. Earlier (p. 33) I gave a glimpse of the activity of the Greeks in the Iberian peninsula from the seventh century onwards. Its permanent results were the settlements due to Phocaean colonization at the dawn of the sixth century: the founding of Emporion (Ampurias) had swiftly followed that of Massilia (Marseille) around 600 BC. If Rome had no direct interests in Spain to protect at that time – except perhaps for Saguntum, but we shall see later that this raises a thorny question of date – it was a different matter for the Massaliots, who were anxious to preserve their commercial potential in the Spanish Levant and as far as Andalusia. Around 300, the periplus of Pytheas made this Marseillais presence on the shores of the Iberian Sea even more solid. But their principal interests lay in Catalonia, where they kept a watchful eye on their long-established settlements, not only Ampurias but also Rhode (Rosas). And setting the farthest limit to Carthaginian expansion in Spain very much to the north of the Peninsula, at the Ebro, may well have been dictated by consideration for these Marseillais demands. But did the Marseillais also have interests at Saguntum, situated slightly north of Valencia and thus in a very southerly position in relation to the mouth of the Ebro? It is easy to agree that this Iberian port, well placed at the outlet of the Rio Palancia, could have been a major landfall for Phocaean trade. But the inexactness and even silence of our sources have unfortunately encouraged the extrapolations of modern historians. There is nothing to tell us, as has sometimes been suggested (Picard, 1967, p. 95), that Saguntum refused to acknowledge Punic hegemony on Hasdrubal's accession. Also, the fact that in Antiquity (Livy, XXI, 7, 2; Strabo, III, 159) it was regarded as a Greek colony founded by the Ionian city of Zakynthos (Zante) appears to be a fable born of the resemblance of the two place-names. All we know is that in these same years the Saguntines placed themselves under Rome's protection. Polybius (III, 30, 1) dates this alliance to several years before Hannibal assumed command (in 221). Fixing a more precise date divides historians into those who have no hesitation in going back as early as 231 – at the time of the first embassy sent by Rome to Hamilcar, and thus earlier than the treaty of 226 with Hasdrubal – and those who consider that the placing of Saguntum under Roman protection came after this last agreement. In both cases, and even more so if the alliance with Saguntum came after the accord of 226, one runs up against an automatic incompatibility with a treaty that left Carthage with an area of influence covering all the territories south of the Ebro. This is all supposing that Polybius'

Iber is realy the Ebro and not the Jucar, as proposed in an elegant but specious solution advanced by Jérôme Carcopino (1961a, pp. 19–67), to which we shall return.

The course of events leading inexorably to a resumption of the great confrontation with Rome was gathering speed. It appears that, during the last years of his Spanish 'proconsulate', successfully pursuing his skilful policy of assimilation, Hasdrubal had rallied the Iberian tribes near Saguntum, especially the Turboletes. But he perished, the victim of revenge, probably at the beginning of 221. And just as in the case of Hamilcar's demise, our sources diverge on the details of his death. For Polybius (II, 36, 1), who was hardly interested and rids himself in two lines of someone he obviously did not like, Hasdrubal paid with his life for wrongs of a personal nature. In another tradition, of which Livy is the leader (XXI, 2, 6), he was assassinated in his palace at Cartagena by a servant who thus avenged the death of his master, an Iberian prince who had been killed on Hasdrubal's orders. And in the *Punica* (I, 169–81) of Silius Italicus we read of the execution reserved for this dauntless hero under the most refined tortures: a fine example of that baroque build-up which characterizes the quest for pathos in the Latin poetry of the Flavian era.

## Hannibal

On Hasdrubal's death, Hannibal was elected by acclamation to the head of the army in Spain, and the people's assembly in Carthage ratified this appointment. Hamilcar's eldest son was then twenty-six.

In a famous text from which I will quote rather extensively, Livy (XXI, 4) is drawn to the reflection of Hannibal's image in the eyes of the veterans of the army of Spain:

> The old soldiers felt as if the young Hamilcar had been restored to them; in this young man they saw the same vigorous expression, the same fire in his eyes, the same air, the same features. Very soon Hannibal's own qualities, rather than his father's memory, claimed their love and obedience. Never had one nature more perfectly combined the most opposite forms of behaviour, power to command and willingness to obey. So it would be difficult to say whether he was dearer to his commander or to his men: Hasdrubal preferred him above all other officers for courage and vigour in action, and there was no leader with whom the soldiers showed more confidence or boldness. No one was more daring in confronting dangers, or had more sangfroid in the midst of those dangers themselves. He was indefatigable in both body and spirit; he could endure extremes of heat and cold with equanimity; he ate and drank according to his needs, not his pleasure; waking and sleeping, he made no distinction between day and night; what time his duties left him he gave to sleep, nor did he seek it on a soft bed or in silence: he was often to be seen, wrapped in an army cloak, asleep on the ground amid common soldiers on sentry or picket duties. His clothing in no way distinguished him from other young men of his age; but his accoutrements

> and horses were conspicuous. On horseback or on foot he far outshone all other fighting men; he was the first to go into battle, and once it was engaged he was the last to leave the field. These great virtues were matched by his vices: inhuman cruelty, a more than Punic perfidy, no heed for the truth, a total disregard for honour, no fear of the gods, no respect for the sanctity of an oath, no religious scruples. Such was the complex character, compounded of these virtues and vices, of the man who served three years under Hasdrubal's command, overlooking nothing that he needed to do or see in order to become a great leader one day.

I had to quote this entire page because it is such a fine example, not only for its literary quality, which translation does not totally conceal, but also, and perhaps more importantly, because it brings us close to the problems raised regarding Hannibal by Roman historiography, of which Livy is the most prestigious spokesman. He depicts an idealized portrait of the young captain, which may be seen as a stereotype. But the fact cannot be ruled out that certain precise features – 'things seen' – may have been gleaned from eye-witnesses, like Sosylos or Silenos, either directly – we shall see that Livy sometimes refers to the last-named – or indirectly, through Coelius Antipater. But of course it is the moral picture of the young Hannibal which most clearly reveals the bias of the Paduan historian, if only because he straightaway ascribes 'vices' to the young man which he had scarcely had the time to develop. The famous phrase: *Cum hac indole virtutum atque vitiorum triennio sub Hasdrubale meruit* (XXI, 4, 10) is in fact an anticipation, or if one prefers, the conclusion of a 'programme-portrait': on the brink of the third decade in which Hannibal's war is, so to speak, the sole topic, the historian is warning his reader that Rome will have to fight a war leader of genius, but also an adversary fearing neither god nor man. The *inhumana crudelitas*, the *perfidia plus quam Punica*, are therefore slogans whose validity we must test as we go, principally by comparisons with Polybius.

No less emblematic and very useful in this drama is the insistence, from the very first line, on the son's perfect resemblance to his father. It is the physical side of an identification which, on the moral plane, had been forever sanctioned by the famous 'oath' sworn by the child. But it is not out of the question to suppose that this statement rested on a genuine resemblance, which our ignorance of his father's features cannot even enable us to imagine. We must not let slip this occasion to pose the question of the portrait of Hannibal in his youth. In the opening pages of this book, I regretted the absence of a real iconography compared with a very rich imagery. Some people have not so easily resigned themselves to this lack.

Our museums and their storerooms are bulging with marble or bronze effigies whose anonymity ingenious specialists have attempted to penetrate by making learned comparisons. One attribution may well supersede another previously acquired. This is what happened to a fine bronze discovered over half a century ago at Volubilis, in Morocco, and now preserved in the Rabat Museum. It had been successively recognized as Hieron II of Syracuse, then Cleomenes III, then Attalus, before comparisons were made with marbles kept in Copenhagen and

Madrid, and presumed to be effigies of Juba II. It was then identified with the philhellenic and erudite minor Mauretanian king, protégé of Augustus and married by him to another princess in his guardianship, the daughter of Antony and Cleopatra – who had one of his royal residences at Volubilis. But when one compares these images with other busts identified with certainty as portraits of the Mauretanian king – marbles from Cherchel, in Algeria, the ancient Caesarea, his other residence, a marble in the Louvre – one cannot prevent a doubt forming. From that doubt was born another hypothesis, brilliantly upheld, according to which the bronze of Volubilis – and the effigies so like it in Copenhagen and Madrid – are in fact portraits of the young Hannibal (Picard, 1965, pp. 31–4; 1967, pp. 104–8). This is an alluring idea to which it is very tempting to subscribe, so great is the desire to associate the name of the young Punic leader with such a beautifully 'Alexandrian' image. However, this hypothesis is rendered fragile because, in its turn, it is anchored to the recognition, not long ago, by a British numismatist, Edward S. G. Robinson (1956), of this same Hannibal on the face of a finely made silver shekel of the Barcid coinage. Alas! As we saw earlier (pp. 39–40), concerning Hasdrubal, specialists are nowadays inclined to view the effigies on these types of coins as deities. Moreover, it must be admitted that in any case the diademmed profile on this coin bears only a very distant resemblance to the handsome young man of Volubilis. Our consolation for these uncertainties is that at least they allow our imagination full play.

## Hannibal's campaigns in Spain

Did Hannibal have it in mind, from the very day when he took command, to carry the war against Rome into Italy? Livy (XXI, 5, 1) thinks so, and states that, if he did not at once attack Saguntum, it was in order not to provoke a *casus belli* with the Romans straightaway, and more precisely to give the appearance, by intervening elsewhere, of having been dragged into the war by the dynamic of his campaigns against the Celtiberians (XXI, 5, 3). All in all, it was one of the first applications of the 'domino theory'. More positively, Polybius (III, 14, 10) maintains that, although the young general at first avoided any clash with the Saguntines that was likely to mobilize the Romans, this was less for tactical reasons than from concern to broaden and strengthen his authority over the rest of Spain. The Greek historian adds that this doctrine had been bequeathed to him by his father, Hamilcar. If, as we may imagine, Hannibal was well aware of the imminence of the head-on clash with Rome – above all since its legions had eliminated the Gaulish threat in the Po Valley – the need to have at his disposal bigger and safer rear bases in Spain was forced upon him. We shall see later that even before the decisive Roman check on the Metaurus, in Italy itself, the war had begun to be lost for the Carthaginians on Iberian soil when Scipio seized Cartagena in 210.

Hannibal spent just under two years (221–220) in expanding the Carthaginian domain towards the north-west of the Peninsula. His first campaign brought him against the people that our two historians call the Olcadi, whose capital – Althaia in Polybius, Cartala in Livy – he took by storm, which earned him the submission of an entire region that cannot be situated with precision: probably present-day La Mancha, between the upper Guadalquivir and the middle course of the Jucar. Then he brought his booty-laden army back to his winter quarters at Cartagena. In the spring of 220, he engaged battle farther afield against the Vaccaei, notably capturing Hermandica, which is ordinarily identified with Salamanca, in Castile. But Hannibal had ventured far from his bases, into the heart of Celtiberian country. Remnants of the conquered army, joined by exiles from the Olcadi, who had been defeated the preceding year, urged revolt among the Carpetani, on to whose territory Hannibal had retreated: probably the high plateaux of Castilla la Nueva, in the region of Toledo. In an awkward position, the Punic general was wise enough to break off contact and cross the Tagus at a ford. Then he set up camp on the left bank, taking care to leave enough space between his entrenchment and the banks of the Tagus to incite his pursuers to cross the river. When they had committed themselves to this course of action, Hannibal's cavalry overwhelmed them in midstream; those that were able to gain a foothold on the bank were crushed by some forty elephants which charged parallel to the edge. Hannibal put the finishing touch to their rout by recrossing the river with his army and scattering the survivors far and wide. After this defeat and the submission of the population of Castilla la Nueva, no people remained south of the Ebro who could still resist the Carthaginians, chorus Polybius (III, 14, 9) and Livy (XXI, 5, 17) in somewhat summary and geographically inexact fashion, for present-day Aragon remained outside the Punic sphere of influence, not to mention the north-west extremities of the Peninsula.

## Saguntum

Most importantly, the pro-Roman enclave formed by Saguntum, south of what the Spaniards call the Ebro, remained out of reach of the Carthaginians: a thorn in the flesh of Punic Spain, but also a very thorny question for modern historians! In the course of the last half-century, dozens of books and articles in learned publications have tackled the problem of the origins and causes of the second Punic War, and especially the role played in unleashing it by the siege of Saguntum (Christ, 1974, pp. 74–191). The blame lies principally with both an unfortunate summary of some words by Polybius and the distorted – not to mention chronologically inaccurate – presentation of events in the Roman annalistic tradition, chiefly represented for us by Livy, with its concern to show the Senate's diplomacy in the most favourable light.

It is easy to produce a defence of Polybius. His error, if there is one, consists of a merging, when he writes that by attacking Saguntum the Carthaginians 'were infringing both the treaty concluded with Lutatius, which stipulated that each of the two parties would refrain from attacking the other's allies, and the agreement signed with Hasdrubal, by which they had committed themselves not to bear arms beyond the Iber' (III, 30, 3). Reading this sentence rather quickly – as quickly as it had been written – it is possible to realize that Polybius had made a topographical error, somewhat surprising for a man who knew the country and was passionately keen on geography, by placing Saguntum north of the Ebro. An error that was, in any case, committed by certain later sources, like Appian (*Hisp.*, 7, 1), who situates Saguntum between the Ebro and the Pyrenees. In the middle of the present century it was thought possible to resolve this difficulty by imagining that the Iber mentioned in the treaty of 226 was not the Ebro, but the Jucar, which in fact flows into the Mediterranean slightly south of Saguntum (Carcopino, 1961a, pp. 19–67). We have only to look again at Polybius in another place (III, 6, 1–2) to find the right answer, which he expressly indicates when, reporting the opinion of contemporaries on the immediate reasons for the war, he states precisely that, according to them, 'the prime cause was the Carthaginians' siege of Saguntum, and the second the crossing by these same Carthaginians of the river that the natives of the country call the Iber'. And even though, faithful to his constant doctrine of the distinction to be made between 'causes' (*aitiai*) and 'the commencement of events' (*archai*), he saw only the latter, and not true causes – we know that in his view these were to be sought in the Barcids' implacable enmity for the Romans – it is quite clear that the Greek historian distinguished two periods in the unleashing of the war. The capture of Saguntum, which had become the Roman people's ally and was thus protected as such against the Punic enterprise by the already long-established clauses of the treaty of Lutatius (241), was the first *casus belli*, to which Hannibal would soon add another, if necessary, by crossing the Iber (Ebro).

As for Livy, he does not lay himself open to any suspicion of geographical error. He clearly places Saguntum 'beyond the Ebro', from the Roman viewpoint, in other words, south of the river (XXI, 5, 17). But the Roman historian is not free from all incoherence, to the extent that it has been said of his account, 'it is so chaotic that it is completely unusable by historians' (Errington, 1970, p. 51), a statement that is exaggerated, or pessimistic. Thank heaven historians of Antiquity know how to decode their sources, rectify errors, make up for gaps and correct omissions – in fact, these may be said to be their chief pastimes. But it is true that Livy is not the best of guides in this matter; for instance, when he states that conflicts between Saguntines and their neighbours, 'especially the Turdetani' (XXI, 6, 1), were at the root of Hannibal's siege of Saguntum. Actually, hundreds of kilometres separated Saguntum from 'Turdetania', the ancient kingdom of Tartessus, in the middle and lower valley of the Guadalquivir. The land of the Turdetani features in Livy's text only because, in the view of Romans in the Augustan era, this region was symbolic of Carthaginian Spain (Pelletier, 1986). The neighbours with whom the Saguntines had a bone to pick were rather, according to Appian (*Iber.*, 10), the Turboleti (above, p. 43).

A more serious error is that, by situating the preliminaries of the war under the consulship of P. Cornelius Scipio – the father of Africanus – and Ti. Sempronius

Longus, that is, at the earliest after 15 March 218, the legal date of the year's consuls' assuming office, Livy compresses into a few weeks (up to the end of April 218, the approximate date of the movement of Hannibal's troop columns towards Catalonia) a whole series of events which we shall see unfold, in fact, over eighteen months. Livy is fully aware of this absurdity since, at the end of his account of what happened, he feels the need to review the whole of this chronology, implicitly acknowledging that a more spaced-out chronology, such as that of Polybius (III, 17, 9), which makes the siege of Saguntum last eight months, is more probably accurate (XXI, 15, 3–5). If he does not modify his own account, however, there are good reasons. Livy is dependent on his sources, whether Fabius Pictor or Coelius Antipater, in other words Roman annalists, who were behind the shortening of the duration of Hannibal's campaigns in Spain. This contraction was probably 'a political operation of "disinformation", aimed at persuading the reader that because of the swiftness of events Rome had not had the time to come to its ally's assistance; its apparent passivity was thus justified' (Jal, 1988, p. XLIV). In Livy's successors, the time-lag appears even shorter, to demonstrate the Senate's desire to react as quickly as possible; so, for Silius Italicus (II, 391), the Roman embassy declares war on Carthage even before the fall of Saguntum.

Duly illuminated by modern criticism, the comparison of our various sources enables us to restore the succession of events to a likely chronological sequence. Hasdrubal was doubtless still alive when, dissension having broken out at Saguntum, the Saguntines had recourse to the good offices of Rome (Polybius, III, 30, 2), which restored order in the city, very probably by eliminating Carthage's supporters. It has been suggested that this episode belongs to the summer or autumn of 223 (Sumner, 1972, p. 476). Two years later, after Hasdrubal's death, Hannibal, the new commander-in-chief, led his victorious campaigns into the interior of the Pensinsula, at least until the beginning of the winter of 220–219. Worried by the Carthaginians' territorial advance, and perhaps exposed to the intrigues of their neighbours secretly orchestrated by Hannibal, the Saguntines then sent an embassy to Rome (Livy, XXI, 6, 2), even several, according to Polybius (III, 15, 1). Dispatched by the Roman Senate, the ambassadors met Hannibal at Cartagena during the winter of 220–219.

They enjoined the Punic leader to refrain from any action against Saguntum, which had placed itself under their protection. Hannibal reacted indignantly, reminding the ambassadors that not long before Rome had not hesitated to intervene violently in the internal affairs of that city, having notable Saguntines put to death and exiling others. Ironically, the young Punic leader turned against the Romans one of their own favourite arguments in foreign policy: 'The Carthaginians', he said to them, 'could not close their eyes to such an attack, for it was one of their traditional rules of conduct never to leave the oppressed without help' (Polybius, III, 15, 7). As the Greek historian is our sole informant on this exchange and the atmosphere in which it took place, it is worthwhile to pause a little over the fairly surprising commentary it makes on Hannibal's attitude. We shall have occasion to see later that Polybius' opinion of the Punic leader is favourable overall, that he most frequently exonerates him of many of the accusations laid against him by Roman historiography – notably cruelty and barbarity – and even that he cannot praise him enough for the specifically military qualities of an army leader. But in this instance, Polybius' judgement is harsh; Hannibal's demeanour appears to him to be dictated by his impetuous youth, warlike zeal, the encouragement afforded by his recent successes and chiefly his inveterate hatred – despite his youth – for the Romans: 'Prey to a violent anger, totally unreasonable, instead of giving the true causes of his conduct, he took refuge in pretexts without foundation' (III, 15, 9). Would it not have been better, adds Polybius, to demand from the Romans the restitution of Sardinia and the payment which, abusing the situation, they had unjustifiably demanded not so long before? The Greek historian's rationalism here may appear to border on the ingenuous, in the view of those who have been taught by a long series of international conflicts up to a recent date that it is fairly rare to see aggressors display their true aims. Of course, there have been attempts to explain Polybius' opinion. The Greek historian's most recent French editor saw it as an echo of Roman propaganda (de Foucault, 1971, p. 48), which is unlikely, owing to Polybius' frequently noted independence with regard to the bias of the annalists. For his part, the great British commentator interpreted it as the result of the historian's regret and embarrassment on finding that in this instance one of his heroes did not conform to his outline of the causes (*aitiai*) of the war (Walbank, 1983, p. 63). More precisely, by applying here, in relation to a decisive act by Hannibal, an 'interpretation grid' which he would re-use later regarding Philip V, when Demetrius had so little difficulty in persuading the king of Macedonia to engage in what proved to be a short-lived policy of confrontation with Rome, Polybius is giving his readers a sign to show that a war decided on the nod of a head – or a fit of temper – could only lead to failure, however brilliant the strategist (Eckstein, 1989, pp. 1–15). The grapes of wrath, thought Polybius, had no chance of ripening. But it is true that he knew what was going to happen.

Dismissed by Hannibal, according to Polybius (III, 15, 12), the Roman ambassadors embarked for Carthage. But the Greek historian omits to tell us what became of them and, for his part, Livy (XXI, 6, 4) mentions only that, though the principle of such an embassy was decided in the Senate, the ambassadors did not have time to leave Rome, Hannibal in the meantime having attacked Saguntum. The time was the end of the winter of 220–219. Hannibal knew for sure that, having recently and with difficulty contained the Celtic danger in the north of Italy, Rome was now worried about the situation in Illyria, on the shores of the Adriatic, where the intrigues of its former vassal Demetrius of Pharos, who had made an alliance with the regent of Macedonia, Antigonus III (Doson), then with the young king Philip V after his accession in 221, would force its intervention in the Balkans, precisely in the spring of 219. There was every likelihood, therefore, that the Punic leader would have plenty of elbow-room at Saguntum.

The siege lasted some months – eight, specifies Polybius (III, 17, 10), taking hardly any interest in the operational details, although he himself was an expert on siegecraft. But he is careful to say that Hannibal was much involved personally. Livy, perhaps taking his information from Coelius Antipater, reveals that at the start of the siege the general was wounded in the thigh by a javelin when he rashly went near the defence wall (XXI, 7, 10). The place was strong and solidly defended. The citadel rose on the west corner, on an eminence where the 'Bateria dos de Mayo' is now, recalling the capture of the town by Napoleon's armies in 1811. The Saguntines fought well, making use of a terrible weapon, the *falarica*, a kind of javelin, often outsized, whose shaft, bound round with tow smeared with pitch and sulphur, was set alight before being hurled; it was a veritable 'missile', as fearsome for the fire it carried as for its three-foot-long iron tip (Livy, XXI, 8, 11). In his *Punica* (I, 350–64), Silius Italicus described with his usual baroque emphasis the terrifying effects of this weapon which, when it was large, could be launched only by catapult.

Meanwhile, diplomatic tactics were continuing. During the summer of 219, if we follow Livy (XXI, 6, 8), a Roman embassy landed a short distance from the town besieged by Hannibal. Polybius makes no mention of it, as he was concerned with the embassy that the Punic chief had received in his winter quarters at Cartagena some months previously (above, p. 48). In a debate that is still open and widely argued, the question is asked whether this second Roman embassy referred to by Livy – for him, in fact, the first, since the one whose mission had been halted, before the siege of Saguntum, had not in his view had the time to embark – should be identified with the one at Cartagena, when Hannibal had behaved with the high-handedness and passion that we saw condemned by Polybius. Whatever the final solution, we are indebted to Livy for the content, from the Roman and chiefly Carthaginian viewpoint, of the exchanges that occurred at the time of this embassy. We are also indebted to him for enabling us to put a face to this Roman embassy – that of its mission leader, a patrician, P. Valerius Flaccus, former consul for the year 227, who in that role must have prepared the agreement settled the following year with Hasdrubal and who was thus well acquainted with the state of affairs in Spain. Informed of the landing of Rome's envoys, Hannibal seems to have excused himself from receiving them on the pretext of his duties as commander-in-chief. Also, realizing that they would go from there straight to Carthage, he anticipated them by a message addressed to the leaders of what Livy calls the *factio Barcina*, in other words, the clan who, in the heart of the Council of Elders, for over twenty years had faithfully upheld the position of the Barcid family.

At the time of the audience granted to Valerius Flaccus and the other Roman envoys to Carthage, an old acquaintance made himself the spokesman for the Punic aristocracy, in opposition to this clan: Hanno, Hamilcar's rival, whose hostility was to accompany Hannibal throughout the whole of the second Punic War. The speech ascribed to him by Livy (XXI, 10, 2–13) is the first in a series that the Paduan historian delighted in putting in the old Carthaginian senator's mouth, with a belligerent crescendo that would culminate in the harangue delivered after the victory of Cannae in 216; a Pyrrhic victory, Hanno would near enough say (below, p. 112). In the present circumstances, Hanno was brief but to the point. In his view, Hannibal was a dangerous warmonger who must be stopped before it was too late, and the brand he had lit at Saguntum threatened the very walls of Carthage. He therefore proposed to put an immediate end to the operations against Saguntum and to hand Hannibal over to the Romans. The composition of the Council of Elders, with a majority in favour of the Barcid, gave Hanno no chance of being heard, and the Council threw the blame for the conflict on the Saguntines. Meanwhile, at Saguntum, the siege continued. Hannibal had to absent himself for a few weeks to quell a revolt of the Oretani and Carpetani, in La Mancha and Castilla la Nueva: in reaction against the excessive harshness of levies of men, they had attacked the Punic recruiters. But the besieged barely had any respite. In his absence Hannibal entrusted command of operations to Maharbal, son of Himilco, who would be his master of cavalry at Cannae, at least according to Livy's version, and thereby, as we shall see, the originator of a famous saying. According to a legend magnificently illustrated by Silius Italicus (*Punica*, II, 395–456), from his lightning raid into the heart of the Peninsula the Punic leader brought back a marvellous historiated shield, said by the poet to be the work of Galician workers in bronze. Carthage's whole history was inscribed on it in a prodigious miniature, and in a dynamic that projected Hannibal himself beyond the Ebro. Saguntum, whose misfortunes were also depicted on the shield, fell at the end of autumn 219. The town's final days were terrible, the inhabitants driven by starvation to devour the corpses of their nearest and dearest, until the survivors lit an immense pyre and threw themselves upon it, together with their families (Augustine, *City of God*, III, 20). The vast spoils were divided into three kinds: booty in terms of prisoners was left to the soldiers, and precious objects or the proceeds of their sale were sent to Carthage; as for gold and silver, Hannibal put them aside to cover the needs of his future campaigns.

## War is declared

When the fall of Saguntum was announced, feelings ran all the higher in Rome because there was an awareness that very little had been done to aid a friendly city that was under its protection. However, regardless of what Polybius has to say about it, and on this occasion he vigorously attacks two of his Greek sources – ('vulgar tittle-tattle,' he says, 'such as is spouted in barber-shops' (III, 10, 5); what we might call saloon-bar gossip) Sosylos of Lacedaemon and one Chaireas, of whom we know nothing – there was animated debate in the senate for, despite the affront received, the decision to declare war on Carthage was not unanimous.

In the senate, the faction of the Fabii, traditionally reluctant to engage in an active Mediterranean policy, and more especially to intervene in Spain, was still powerful at the end of 219. But for some years the Aemilii had been their rivals in holding the principal magistracies; and, since the victory achieved over the Gauls at Cape Telamon in 225, the Aemilii had been backed by the democratic party, in the person of C. Flaminius, elected consul in 223, in their efforts to weaken the conservative aristocracy's preponderance in the Senate. After 222, the predominance of the Aemilii, together with that of another great patrician family, the Cornelii Scipiones, is increasingly marked in senatorial debates and at the head of the Roman executive. In 219, it was L. Aemilius Paullus – the one we call Aemilius Paullus, at least the first of the two we thus designate – who shared the consulship with the plebeian M. Livius Salinator, but we have seen that they were required by the demands of the war in Illyria against Demetrius of Pharos. And for the year 218, the appointed consuls were P. Cornelius Scipio – father of Africanus – in association with Sempronius Longus, and he, too, was a determined adversary of Carthage.

Although there is disagreement about the date of this debate in the Senate – Silius (I, 675–94), like Livy (XXI, 6, 5–6), placing it after the news of the attack on Saguntum, whereas Zonaras (8, 22), abridging Cassius Dio, puts it after the fall of the town and the dispatch of the second embassy, which seems more likely – our sources, apart from Polybius, agree on the names of the two protagonists who clashed there. On one side a representative of the Cornelii, and by no means the least, L. Cornelius Lentulus Caudinus, 'princeps senatus' or 'leader of the Senate' in 220, high priest in charge since 221, proposed an immediate declaration of war. On the other, Q. Fabius Maximus Verrucosus, twice consul, censor in 230, who was soon to gain fame against Hannibal for his famous tactic of 'playing for time', but who was already one of the most substantial figures of his era, asked only that an embassy be sent to Carthage. This solution prevailed, and as it was decided that it should be led by one of the Fabii clan, probably the old M. Fabius Buteo, one might believe that the party of conciliatory diplomacy had won the day. But among the four other members of the delegation were the two consuls of 219, L. Aemilius Paullus and M. Livius Salinator, which singularly reduced the chances of reaching some arrangement.

The embassy's mandate was simple. It was a matter of asking Carthage whether Hannibal had acted on his own account when he attacked Saguntum, or whether he had followed instructions from the Council of Elders. In the first case, there would be a demand for Hannibal to be handed over, as there had been at the time of the embassy led by Valerius Flaccus but with no decision sanctioning the refusal of the Carthaginian senators at that time. In the second, if Carthage supported Hannibal and officially endorsed his actions, it was committing itself to war.

This time, Hanno did not rise to speak. The reply was given by a senator who remains anonymous, presented by Polybius (III, 20, 10) as the most qualified among his colleagues. His response to the question posed was a subtle reasoned argument. In the first place, a foreign power had no right to demand a reckoning from a Carthaginian general who owed justification of his conduct to his government alone. The only point to be discussed was whether, by attacking Saguntum, this general had or had not contravened a treaty involving Carthage. Now, the only treaty which bound the Punic city was the treaty of Lutatius, concluded in

241 at the end of the first war with Rome, and this treaty could not concern Saguntum, which at that date was not yet allied with the Roman people. As for the agreement signed with Hasdrubal in 226, even supposing that the Saguntines had featured as the subject of a special clause, Carthage did not recognize itself as committed to a pact concluded unbeknown to it by its representative in Spain, and which the Carthaginian senate had not ratified. After all, by behaving in this manner Carthage was doing no more than Rome itself, which had not accepted the treaty concluded in 241 between Lutatius and Hamilcar as it stood, and had worsened the conditions for the Carthaginians after consulting the people (above, p. 3). The Carthaginian orator ended by putting the Roman ambassadors' backs to the wall, using a robust and bold piece of imagery that is typical of Livy's style: 'Let your minds at last be delivered of the plan they have been so long gestating!' (XXI, 18, 12: *quod diu parturit animus vester aliquando pariat.*) The astuteness of the reply and the force of the formal demand were disconcerting to the Roman delegation. Its leader responded with no more than a gesture; pinching the fabric between two fingers, he formed a fold in his toga and added, 'We bring you here peace or war: choose which you please.' Faithful to their line of conduct, the Carthaginians at once replied that it was for him to choose. Then Fabius, smoothing out the fold, declared that it would be war.

Great moments in history sometimes need a setting, and imagery that powerfully conveys the special nature of the event. It matters little whether Fabius' theatrical gesture was real or apocryphal; it was truly symbolic of the deep ambiguity of that moment. A war that could decide the fate of the world had been accepted by Carthage, against its real wish, except in the case of one clan who ardently desired it. There were a number of the Council of Elders who considered that 219 was not the best time to confront the arch-rival, as the conquest of Spain was not over and its complete submission was far from being achieved, whereas Rome, whose eastern flank was calmer since the campaign in Illyria and which was less anxious about the Celts, had perceptibly strengthened itself. However, all the Carthaginian senators (except perhaps Hanno!) were agreed that if the Roman challenge regarding Saguntum was not taken up it would not only do irreparable damage to Punic prestige among the Spaniards but also, at a stroke, ruin the task so patiently undertaken in the Iberian peninsula for more than twenty years, and so necessary for Carthage's renewal after the loss of Sicily and Sardinia. They had therefore been led to assume formal responsibility for the conflict. In Rome, once the matter of Macedonia had been settled, supporters of military intervention against Carthage had not found it too difficult to slip the brakes applied by the prudence of the Fabii. For the Aemilii, the Cornelii Scipiones and their allies, it was no longer merely a matter of going to avenge and reinstate the rights of a small Spanish town which had placed itself under Rome's protection and had been allowed to be crushed. It was a matter of striking Carthage where it would hurt most, in Spain and Africa: this became clear in the spring of 218, when the new consuls were each given two distinct 'provinces'. It fell to P. Cornelius Scipio to lead an army into Spain, while at Lilybaeum, on the western tip of Sicily, T.

Sempronius Longus was to assemble the troops necessary for an expedition to Africa itself. The genius of Hannibal would counter this strategy with another, that was unsuspected in Rome.

## Hannibal's final arrangements in Spain

Hannibal was obviously the least surprised by the turn of events. As there was little chance that Rome would fail to react, even belatedly, to the attack on Saguntum and its subsequent fall, and knowing himself supported in Carthage by the Barcid clan, he had begun to make his arrangements for the realization of a plan of vast scope that had certainly been maturing for a long time. Even though we have no proof, it is probable that in 219, perhaps earlier, he had sounded out the Volcae of Roussillon, then the Salyes and Allobroges, making contact by means of couriers with populations occupying the territories lying along a route which was already forming in his mind. But we do know, as we shall see later, that just before launching his enterprise he received emissaries from the Gauls at Cartagena. The length of journeys at that time, and the slowness of approaches, necessarily required much forward planning before the decision was taken. In the middle of the fifteenth century, according to the findings of a Florentine, the journey from Barcelona to Montpellier took an average of ten days or so; probably rather more in Hannibal's time, with roads that were rougher and less safe, and secure stopping-places uncertain. These delays in communications were consistent, as is illustrated by the story – celebrated in Antiquity – of the Miletan general Histiaeus, who had sent a message by having it written on the freshly-shaven hairy hide of one of his couriers; his hair had had time to grow during the journey, concealing the text!

After the capture of Saguntum, Hannibal had taken up his winter quarters at Cartagena. There he had received the news of the outcome of the Roman embassy to Carthage, thus this would be the beginning of the winter of 219–218. The plan of the coming campaign was perfectly fixed in his mind because, to have rested troops at his disposal later, he sent his Iberian soldiers to their homes for the winter. He himself used the winter of 219–218 to take a whole range of measures, both offensive and defensive. To make sure that Africa was protected, he reinforced its garrisons, sending over Iberian contingents: 13,850 footsoldiers armed with the *cetra* – a little round shield – 1,200 horsemen and 870 Balearic slingers. These figures given by Livy (XXI, 21, 12) are also to be found in Polybius (III, 33), who provides us with the key to such surprising accuracy when he mentions that he himself had read the figures, carved by Hannibal's order on the bronze tablet at Cape Lacinium in southern Italy (below, p. 156). These reinforcements must have been assigned on one hand to the defence of Carthage, and on the other divided between various cities of Punic Africa: in the 'metagonite' (Mauretanian) cities, says Polybius precisely (III, 33, 12–13), in other words, in Massaesylian Numidia, the present-day Constantine in Algeria (Desanges, 1980, p. 188), where

Hannibal levied 4,000 young men, chosen from among the best families, both to reinforce the garrison of the Punic mother-city and to serve as hostages. At the same time, in the other direction, he dispatched large contingents of troops from various corps from Africa to Spain.

There was all the more need for him not to neglect his Spanish defences because he was perfectly well aware that, returning from Carthage, the Roman ambassadors had gone via the north of the Peninsula in an attempt to win over the various populations to Rome's cause (Livy, XXI, 19, 6–8). In particular these were the Bargusii, a people of Catalonia, and the Volciani, who were probably settled close by; perhaps they should be identified with the Volcae, who, as we shall see later, held the Roussillon area. Although the spokesman for the Volciani gave a less than encouraging reply to the Roman envoys – its substance being that the ruins of Saguntum were there to deter anyone else from an alliance with Rome – it was clear that nothing should be left undone to transform the greater part of Spain into the safest possible 'sanctuary'. Hannibal therefore provided his brother Hasdrubal, to whom he entrusted the task of holding the Peninsula, with an infantry reinforced by 11,850 Africans, with the addition of 300 Ligurians and 500 Balearic slingers. Twenty-one elephants were also included as back-up. The cavalry given to Hasdrubal was similarly essentially African: 450 'Libyphoenicians' – half-breed soldiers from the Tunisian Sahel – and, chiefly, 1,800 Numidians and Moors.

These exchanges were just so many cross-links by means of which the Punic leader meant to weave solidarity between Spain and Africa in the testing times ahead. In doing so he acted as both politician and soldier, as he had also done in another area shortly before, probably in 220. It may be remembered that his predecessor, Hasdrubal the Fair, had taken a Spanish woman as his second wife, soon after succeeding Hamilcar. In the same way, we learn from Livy (XXIV, 41, 7) that Hannibal married an Iberian woman from Castulo, one of the most important cities at that time in upper Andalusia, near Linares. Very early on the town had aroused the interest of the Phoenicians of Gades because of its mineral resources, and its ancient wealth had found expression in some of the most beautiful works of orientalizing art. Silius Italicus tells us a little more about the bride. She was called Imilce, not from a Greek name as the Latin poet thinks (*Punica*, III, 97–105), but from a well and truly Punic name: it is quite legitimate to recognize in it the barely modified Semitic root *mlk*, the 'chief', the 'king' (Picard, 1967, p. 119). In contrast, it appears harder to follow Silius any further in his romantic elaborations. Supposedly from this union a son was born, before the very walls of besieged Saguntum. Before leaving for Italy, Hannibal took the mother and still young child to Gades, where he put them on a vessel bound for Carthage, to protect them from the vicissitudes of war. And the poet shows us this Imilce, fixing her gaze on the shores of Spain until the ship's progress hides them from her sight.

In fact, before the great departure, Hannibal really had made a pilgrimage to Gades, says Livy (XXI, 21, 9), in order to fulfil his vows to Hercules and 'to bind himself by new vows' – a piece of information that the dogmatic Polybius, supposing that he knew about it, did not bother to pass on to us. Hercules, or really Melqart, the 'King of the Town' in Phoenician, the tutelary god of Tyre but also the god of Phoenician expansion, who for centuries had had his great temple on the edge of the vast ocean, encouraged all kinds of ventures. We shall see that he had pride of place in the Barcid pantheon, and recall the unanswerable statement which put the final touch to Livy's portrait of Hamilcar's son: *nulla religio*. Does a subtle exegesis give rise to the thought that the Roman historian, who as we shall see refers quite often to the Carthaginian's devoutness, had in this instance echoed a grievance which originated in Punic circles, among those hostile to Hannibal, and which he picked up without really understanding it because he was insufficiently acquainted with the theological disputes peculiar to the Phoenico-Punic world (Picard, 1967, p. 114)? It is an interesting hypothesis, but I think it is more likely that here Livy is closely indebted to his main source, Roman annals, whose spirit of denigration he has adopted with regard to Hannibal's atheism (Huss, 1986, pp. 223–8) or, rather, impiety – a serious accusation in Antiquity, especially in a Roman context. We are once again warned, therefore, of the need for corrections to be applied to the views of the Paduan historian in the history that follows.

# 3

# From Cartagena to the Po Valley

The generally assumed date for the departure from Cartagena is not, at best, before the end of April, and more probably May, 218; a fairly long period which Hannibal used to finalize his plan of action. For the effective realization of the military measures taken by the Punic leader occupied quite a time, with all the to-ings and fro-ings of the African contingents to Spain and Iberian troops to the Mauretanian cities and Carthage. Certainly a period of months, whatever methods of travel were used: completely by land apart from the Straits of Gibraltar, or at least partly by sea, the chief port of embarkation from Spain being Cartagena rather than Cádiz. All the same, it is probable that the sea route was principally used for these journeys. We shall see that the Punic fleet of Africa was still considerable and that hundreds of vessels plied between Carthage and Sicily at the time of the siege of Syracuse in 213–212. But the squadrons based in Spain at the start of 218 were not large: fifty quinqueremes, two quadriremes and five triremes, according to Livy (XXI, 22, 4); but only thirty-two quinqueremes and the five triremes were fit to put to sea. By comparison, for the Spanish theatre of operations alone, where naval means were not called upon to play a determining role, Cornelius Scipio had at his disposal a fleet of sixty quinqueremes, and Sempronius Longus also had sixty in his Sicilian bases. These figures alone are enough to show that Hannibal could not dream of attacking Italy if transporting his troops by sea. And a simple glance at the map adds the finishing touch. Unless it followed the coastline north – but then, reaching the Provençal and Ligurian coasts, it would be confronted by the combined attacks of Marseillais and Roman naval forces – when it left the shores of the Spanish Levant the Punic fleet had an easy crossing only as far as the Balearics, where it could take a break in complete safety. Beyond, towards the east, as well as the possibility of meeting the bad weather which often blows down from the Golfe du Lion and is still feared by sailors, the Punic ships had no island relay points other than Corsica and Sardinia, which had been hostile territory since 238.

## Hannibal's plan and the opposing forces

Hannibal was probably unaware of the exact numbers of naval forces available to the two Roman consuls. But he had all the other data in mind to decide on the details of the plan of action which he perfected during the first months of 218. It will also be accepted that, broadly speaking, he was fully informed of the opposing land forces and available potential. As regards his own camp, it goes without saying; but it is more than likely that his spies ensured he had almost as much knowledge as we do, mainly thanks to Polybius, about Rome's strengths and weaknesses.

Probably on the basis of information that he himself had gleaned from Fabius Pictor, the Greek historian (II, 24) drew up a table of the numbers Rome had been able to assemble a few years earlier, in 225, at the time of the Gaulish invasion (above, p. 41). The spearhead of the Roman army was formed by the two legions of Roman citizens entrusted to each of the two consuls, each comprising 5,200 footsoldiers and 300 horsemen. In all, therefore, a corps of experienced, seasoned troops, of sterling quality; 22,000 men. In addition there were the two legions stationed at Tarentum and in Sicily, each comprising 4,200 infantry and 200 cavalry. The allied troops serving with each of the two consuls and thus fighting alongside the four legions mentioned above totalled 30,000 footsoldiers and 2,000 horsemen. Stationed in reserve at Rome were troops ready to intervene, depending on the course operations might take: of Roman citizens, 20,000 infantry and 1,500 cavalry, reinforced by allied contingents, that is, 30,000 infantry and 2,000 cavalry. To these already considerable numbers must be added a second reserve, which could assemble over 200,000 men, Roman or Campanian citizens, and also the militias of the allied Italic peoples: to the north, the Veneti, Cenomani, Umbri, Sarsinates and Etruscans; in the centre, towards the east flanking Roman territory properly speaking, the Vestini, Marsi, Marrucini, Peligni and Samnites; lastly, to the south, the Iapygians and Messapians in Apulia, and the Lucanians. Adding all these forces together, Polybius arrives at a total of 700,000 footsoldiers and 70,000 horsemen. But of this total the Italic militias, more mediocre in quality and of suspect loyalty, accounted for about half, and when speaking of citizens it is more than likely that the Greek historian included both the *juniores*, of an age to bear arms (from eighteen to forty-six years), and the *seniores*, who formed a reserve.

Figures are one thing, logistic realities another. Though they could be mobilized in theory, in practice it was often difficult to get these human masses to theatres of operations, and they were not easy to train and arm effectively for combat conditions. And Hannibal knew it; but he also knew – and for him this was a fundamental, strategic fact – that Rome could delve into its reserves in Italy to compensate for its losses in men, whereas to make up his own losses he could only hope for massive desertions to his side, or the problematic arrival of external reinforcements.

The heterogeneous nature of the forces that Rome was able to line up for battle also reveals real political complexity, which must be mentioned, since Hannibal could play on the coexistence of a multiplicity of kinds of status in Italy, and did not hesitate to do so.

At the time we are dealing with, Roman territory proper occupied the greater part of central Italy, with a fairly narrow face to the Adriatic, from Pisaurum

(Pesaro) in the north to Hadria in the south; this front was broader on the Tyrrhenian Sea, from Cape Telamon to Cumae. The central Apennines were enveloped in this whole area – around 30,000 sq km – which nevertheless was not completely homogeneous, for several reasons. First, alongside Roman citizens with full rights (*optimo jure*), there were citizens without the right to vote (*sine suffragio*), and thus also without the possibility of candidacy for honours in Rome; they were, however, subject to the military and financial charges of citizens with full rights. Cities without voting rights were for the most part on the northern, eastern and southern fringes of the *ager Romanus*: for example, Caere, on the southern boundary of Etruria, Sena Gallica, in the ancient Gaulish territory on the Adriatic and, in the south, Capua in Campania. Capua had its own institutions, magistrates, senate and people's assemblies, and we shall see that, after Cannae, Hannibal was able to make wily use of this political situation and also of the Campanian elites' desire to regain a status in the Confederation on a level with their former prestige.

Again, a glance at the political map of the period shows that Roman territory was, so to speak, peppered with enclaves formed by colonies with Latin rights: autonomous cities which also had their own particular institutions and magistrates and whose citizens were governed by their own legal system and local laws, but who had the opportunity of residing in Rome, marrying into the Roman citizenry and acquiring Roman citizenship. In return, the Latins were liable to Rome for taxes and participation in the war effort, in the form of sending contingents that were strictly laid down by the *formula togatorum* (Toynbee, 1965, I, pp. 424–37). In the summary which Polybius made of the numbers of men able to be mobilized in 225, the historian enumerates (II, 24, 10) 80,000 footsoldiers and 5,000 horsemen provided by the Latins. All in all, it was a very privileged status – for example, Spoletium (Spoleto) in the north, and Beneventum (Benevento) in the south – and it is understandable that the peoples of *nomen Latinum* showed impeccable loyalty to Rome during the war waged by Hannibal. There remained the territories occupied by the allies, those whose names are mentioned above (p. 58), which, to both north and south, provided the *ager Romanus* and Latin cities with vast protective areas. It was among the allied territories in the south, Apulia, Lucania and Bruttium, that the Punic leader provoked the most serious defections and rallied the most peoples to his side.

## The Punic army's departure from Cartagena

Hannibal was well aware that his army's numbers would dwindle all the way along the route leading him from Cartagena to the Po Valley. He therefore had to swell their ranks to the fullest extent at the time of departure; Polybius (III, 35, 1) estimates that they then numbered around 90,000 footsoldiers and 12,000 horsemen – probably exaggerated figures. We shall see that, before crossing the Pyrenees, Hannibal left to one of his lieutenants – one of the numerous Hannos who appear in this story – 10,000 footsoldiers and 1,000 horsemen, and sent just as many home. He crossed the Pyrenees with the rest of his army, which then comprised, according to Polybius (III, 35, 7), 50,000 footsoldiers and 9,000 horsemen. This means that during the fighting north of the Ebro he must have lost 21,000 men, which seems excessive. Still according to Polybius (III, 60, 5), after crossing the Rhône, the Punic army had no more than 38,000 footsoldiers and slightly more than 8,000 horsemen, or 46,000 men in all: Hannibal would therefore seem to have lost nearly another 13,000 soldiers since his entry into Gaul, although he does not appear to have had to face any serious engagements in that part of the campaign. When he finally reached Italy, only 20,000 infantry and 6,000 cavalry remained to him: this indication is the only sure one, since it figured among the numerical data of the famous inscription of Cape Lacinium (Polybius, III, 56, 4). It would seem, therefore, that 20,000 men disappeared between the Rhône crossing and the arrival in the Po Valley; an enormous figure, however testing and heavy in losses crossing the Alps might have been. In short, from 102,000 men at the departure to 26,000 upon arrival, the losses appear excessive, and since we must hold on to the last figure we must review the first one downwards. It is generally accepted that the numbers on departure must not have exceeded between 60,000 and 70,000 men at the most.

From the purely numerical viewpoint, it was a very large force. They were also courageous troops, probably the best army of the period. Of course, it was not an army of citizens, in which it differed profoundly from the Roman army, which also included auxiliaries, incorporated allied contingents, but whose spearhead was supplied by conscription; the Carthaginian citizens, on the other hand, were incorporated only into territorial units which saw no action outside the defence of Carthage. But the military instrument which Gisco and Hamilcar had used in Sicily had greatly improved since then. The long-held preponderance of mercenaries had noticeably diminished in favour of contingents of soldiers who were also almost 'professional', but more stable; units levied from among the populations subject to Carthage. These still included the 'Libyans', subjects of Carthage in Africa; they had formed the majority of the troops repatriated from Sicily at the end of the first Punic War, and still represented the main mass (12,000 men out of 20,000) of what remained of Hannibal's infantry at the time of his descent of the Italian side of the Alps (Polybius, III, 56, 4). The sobriety and resistance of these men to fatigue and privation were legendary. Those of them who served in the infantry had the bare minimum of weapons: a few javelins, a dagger and a small round shield, the *cetra*. Those whom Hannibal put into the lines at Cannae were equipped with weapons taken from the enemy at Trasimene (Polybius, III, 87, 3; Livy, XXII, 46, 4). The novelty in comparison with the first Punic War was that henceforth fighting alongside them in the infantry units were Iberian footsoldiers, recruited like themselves but from Spanish populations subject to Carthage; there were 8,000 of them among the 20,000 infantrymen who survived the crossing of the Alps. They fought beside other Spaniards who were recruited as mercenaries from peoples who had remained independent, like the Celtiberi of Castile. In battle they used a short double-edged sword, equally useful for cut and thrust, and also a curved sabre, the *falcata* (above, p. 00). They too protected themselves by means of the *cetra*, but those who served in the line, for example at Cannae in 216 (Polybius, III, 114, 2), adopted the long oval shield of the Gauls. Strictly mercenary contingents reinforced this infantry. Men from the Balearics, who were not conscripted by force although their islands were under the Punic protectorate, used javelins, as at the Trebia (Livy, XXI, 55, 6 and 9), but most of all the sling, their speciality: three slings, the length of their straps differing according to the distance of the target to be reached, two being wound round their body and their head (Diodorus, V, 18, 3). It was a formidable weapon, and a missile from one wounded the consul Aemilius Paullus at the battle of Cannae, at the start of the engagement. Ligurians also served as mercenaries, and Hasdrubal received 300 of them in the troop set up for him by his brother to hold Punic Spain (Polybius, III, 33, 16). We know very little of their conditions of service; they were used mainly in the light infantry, as scouts; but at Zama, and even in the battle of the Metaurus, they were to be found fighting in the lines.

I shall speak of the Gauls later. Although they had a very important role in the Punic army – for Hannibal they were a most useful, and frequently sacrificed, rank and file – they did not really come on to the scene until after the arrival in the Po Valley, where Hannibal had planned to incorporate them in order to fill the gaps caused in his army by the Alpine crossing. But as we have seen, the Carthaginian general brought a large cavalry with him, of which 6,000 men survived that ordeal. Auxiliary contingents of Numidians constituted the majority, their commitment to fighting alongside the Carthaginians often harking back to old alliances; we may recall the assistance brought by Naravas to Hamilcar Barca during the Mercenaries' War (above, p. 17). In the rest of this history there will be occasion to assess the services they rendered to Hannibal, from the Trebia to Cannae, and at the time of the raids in Bruttium; but at Zama, owing to the alliance that Scipio had obtained from Massinissa, there were more of them fighting in the Roman ranks, and this was perhaps the principal cause of the Punic defeat. Like the African footsoldiers in the light infantry, they had very basic weapons, consisting of a small round shield, a few javelins and a dagger. The latter was terrifyingly effective in the hands of these virtuosi horsemen, formidable in pursuing units that had been put to flight. Livy (XXII, 29, 5) remarked on their skill, which he said was similar to that of circus riders – the *desultores* – having two horses at once, so that they could leap on to the other when their mount was tired, sometimes even in the midst of battle. It could be said of them that they were to the Carthaginians what the Cossacks were to the Russian armies in the eighteenth and nineteenth centuries.

One of the facets of Hannibal's genius was knowing how to turn this heterogeneous army – incidentally, we must add the Italiots (Samnites, Lucanians, men from the Bruttium and Apulia) who were temporarily incorporated after Cannae – into a whole that is impressive for its cohesiveness throughout fifteen years (218–203). The fact that these men from a diversity of backgrounds had embarked on a venture that kept them all similarly far from their homes and thereby gave them a solidarity may partly explain that cohesiveness. But going even further, it has even been boldly suggested that Hannibal conferred on his army a genuinely 'supranational' dimension (Brizzi, 1984a, p. 138). This is perhaps rather exaggerated, in that it evokes, or suggests, an amalgam of various nationalities in this army's tactical units, small or large. That was not the case; as we shall see, the battle order at Cannae or Zama clearly shows that the soldiers remained grouped by nationality. But the army corps brought together troops of diverse nationalities, and the label of supranationality may be admitted in so far as the conception and quality of command of this heterogeneous army enabled it to be raised to a very high level of strategic homogeneity. The junior officers in command of the base units – the equivalent of the Roman 'turma' for the cavalry, and the 'maniple' for the infantry – had the same origin as their men, with whom they stayed in close contact. At a higher level, in the Numidian cavalry, for example, the leaders might be nationals but also 'Punicized' African superior officers, or even of Carthaginian stock. In the Punic army fighting in Sicily between 212 and 210, command of the Numidians, at first entrusted to a 'Libyphoenician' from Bizerta, Muttines (Livy, XXV, 40, 5, who thus 'Latinizes' the Semitic name 'Mattan'), was subsequently withdrawn from him by the general commanding the expeditionary corps, Hanno, who gave it to his own son (Livy, XXVI, 40, 6). As for the higher command, that of the army corps, it was exercised solely by generals who were all of Carthaginian origin – and probably aristocratic – and who acted as loyal lieutenants to their commander-in-chief. First and foremost, the Barcids: Hasdrubal, the younger brother, left in 218 at the head of the Punic army of Spain this side of the Ebro, who would be killed in 207 at the Metaurus while bringing help to Hannibal; Mago, the last-born, one of the architects of the success on the Trebia, who would be at the centre of command at Cannae alongside his brother, would be sent to carry on the war in Liguria towards the end of the Italian campaign and would die at sea, in 203, on the homeward journey. And then the leaders who distinguished themselves at Trasimene and Cannae, notably: Hasdrubal, who commanded the left wing at Cannae, while Hanno had the right wing; Maharbal, who worked so hard with his cavalry, and Mago the Samnite, Hannibal's chief lieutenant in Bruttium. Between these captains, who were certainly young but precociously seasoned in war by several years of long and difficult campaigns, one may imagine a brotherhood of arms similar to the one which would exist between the future marshals of the Empire in the Napoleonic epic.

## Hannibal's elephants

Almost everything has just been said about Hannibal's army, except for what was probably its most remarkable feature: the part played by elephants. The Carthaginians had not been the first to make military use of them. It was Alexander who originally discovered the use of these beasts for fighting, at the time of the battle of

Arbeles, in 331, then in the Indus valley. But it was Pyrrhus, king of Epirus, who made them known in the West. He had used them in his army at Heraclea, in 280, and their introduction in southern Italy, and then Sicily, certainly created a sensation. They were pachyderms of the Asian species, *Elephas indicus*, carrying a pavilion – the Indian howdah – on their back, usually containing two soldiers, archers, as can be seen notably on a dish from Capena dating from slightly after the exploits of Pyrrhus.

The Carthaginians soon adopted this new military device, whose efficiency they had discovered to their cost in their battles against Pyrrhus. They, too, used them in Sicily, and lined them up in Africa itself against Regulus at the time of the first Punic War. We may recall the terrible use that Hamilcar made of them against the mercenaries trapped in the Gorge of the Saw (above, p. 21) and the contribution they made to Hannibal's first great success in the battle waged on the Tagus in 220. Their frequent portrayal on the reverse of Spain's Punic coinage almost makes the elephant the Barcid totemic animal. And it is these representations, among others, which enable us to classify them, not in the category of Asian elephants, whose shoulder height often reaches 3 metres, nor of the African bush elephants, which exceed that size, but in the variety known as *Loxodonta africana cyclotis* (or *Loxodonta atlantica*): in other words, the forest elephant, which is smaller – from 2.40 to 2.50 metres high at the shoulder – with very obvious physical characteristics: ears with enormous flaps and rounded lobes, a marked concavity in the middle of the back, the head carried high, a ringed trunk instead of smooth as in the Asiatic type, and long tusks.

In his 'Libyan accounts', Herodotus (IV, 191) mentions elephants as early as the fifth century BC on the borders of present-day Tunisia, while the *Periplus of Hanno* (§ 4) places them in the coastal regions of Morocco. In the late fourth century Aristotle, and later Pliny the Elder, would agree in acknowledging their habitat in the foothills of the Moroccan Atlas and in the Rif, not far from the 'Pillars of Hercules'. In these various regions of the ancient Maghreb, more extensively forested then than now, they survived until the first centuries of the Christian era, and their extinction seems due less to climatic variations than to the fact that they were systematically hunted, especially to maintain supplies for the amphitheatres of imperial Rome, a vast consumer of wild animals for its games.

In the spring of 218, Hannibal took with his army a troop of twenty-seven elephants, probably all of the small African variety, with perhaps the exception of one which Pliny the Elder, using a note borrowed from Cato, (*Natural History* VIII, 5, 11) names Surus – for Syrus, 'the Syrian' – that enjoyed the reputation of being the bravest elephant in the Punic army. The elephants' relatively small size prevented them from carrying a combat howdah; they were ridden only by their drivers (mahouts), whom Polybius (III, 46, 7) calls 'Indians' (*Indoi*), not because they were necessarily from India, but because it was a name hallowed by custom. When the drivers were on the point of losing control of their mounts, maddened by the wounds they had received or the din of battle, it was their duty to kill the animal on the spot by driving a blade into the nape of its neck with a mallet. This was what happened notably at the battle of the Metaurus in 207, says Livy (XXVII, 49, 1), where more elephants were killed in this way by their drivers than by the enemy. The historian adds that this procedure had been originated by Hasdrubal, Hannibal's brother, himself the unfortunate hero of the battle of the Metaurus. At Zama, Scipio would have the idea of deeply intersecting his battle-lines by a series of corridors into which the elephants would plunge futilely. Thus, as familiarity with the animals increased, ways of parrying their thrusts were found. Also, no longer did their shrill trumpeting and their ears spread out like sails, which added to their already monstrous bulk, inspire the same terror; not even their trunk, that enormous 'serpent-shaped hand' – as Lucretius (III, 537) described it – which they extended forward in their charge, between their formidable tusks.

## The other side of the Ebro

Just before he left Cartagena, Hannibal received envoys from the Gauls bearing encouraging messages: on either side of the Alps, and especially in the Po Valley, he was awaited with feelings of goodwill (Polybius, III, 34). For his part, the Punic leader sent on ahead emissaries charged with reconnoitring the terrain, chiefly the passes over the Alps, and winning over the Celtic chiefs by offering them presents on his behalf (Livy, XXI, 23, 1). This long first stage, from Cartagena to the Ebro, in June 218, posed no problem; nor did the river-crossing. Better still, when Hannibal, having reached Onussa, was about to cross that boundary beyond which he would be, *de facto*, irrevocably committed to war, he is said to have received divine encouragement in a dream. In his sleep he saw a young man of godlike appearance who introduced himself as the guide appointed by Jupiter to lead Hannibal into Italy: all he had to do was march after him without turning back. Hannibal, seized with awe, at first obeyed; then, moved by an all-too-human curiosity, he could not refrain from looking back, whereupon he saw a snake of extraordinary size moving in the midst of deafening crashes of thunder, and an immense wreckage of trees and smashed houses. And when he asked his young divine guide what this prodigy might be, the answer was the 'Devastation of Italy': Hannibal must go ahead and leave hidden that which was to come. Such is the version given to us by Livy (XXI, 22, 6–9). Polybius (III, 47, 8) who, a little later, in connection with the crossing of the Alps, would deride those historians who quote the intervention of 'gods or the sons of gods', takes good care not to relate this epiphany, which nevertheless featured in his sources. For, in his *Treatise on divination* (I, 49), Cicero echoes it, with slight variations – the serpent, or dragon, becomes a sort of many-headed hydra – as does all later tradition, from Valerius Maximus to Zonaras, by way of Silius Italicus. And all these versions have this basic feature in common: the god's imperative orders, or prohibition, against the central character turning round and looking behind him. Orpheus will not be able to stop himself from turning round to see if Eurydice is really following him, and will lose her. In another divine context, Lot and his family must quit Sodom without turning round, but Lot's wife looks back and is changed into a pillar of salt: both victims of all-too-human curiosity in the face of a manifestation of the sacred. Hannibal, however, is in no way punished for having flouted the ban. And it is here that the episode, as reported by Livy and Cicero, appears as a feature – which has come down to us by way of Coelius Antipater, the source quoted by Cicero – of a propaganda probably orchestrated by Silenos, the Greek historiographer, who accompanied the Punic general throughout his campaigns and was starting to build the legend even before the history was written. Hannibal had received from the gods the mission to carry the war into Italy, and the revelation that he had, against their will, discovered the consequences – the devastation of Italy – in no way brought down their anger upon him.

However, once past the Ebro, the first difficulties arose. On the soil of present-day Catalonia, Hannibal had to confront peoples who had not been subjugated: the Ilergetes, in the region of Lérida; the Bergusii, in the valley of the Segra; and the Ausetani, between Vich and Gerona, as well as 'Lacetania', which Livy situates at the foot of the Pyrenees, perhaps near Ripoll. Polybius mentions the Arenosians in the Val d'Aran and the Andenosians in Andorra (III, 35, 2), and remarks that these first engagements incurred fairly heavy losses in the Punic army. Moreover, Hannibal left in place – therefore in the Catalan hinterland – one of his lieutenants, Hanno, with 10,000 footsoldiers and 1,000 horsemen to hold the countryside, contain the passes and in particular keep a watch on the Bergusii, whose sympathies lay with the Romans. As a precautionary measure, therefore, the Punic leader jettisoned around 10,000 men: according to Livy (XXI, 23, 4–6), 3,000 footsoldiers of the Carpetani, a people recently subdued (above, p. 46), did a U-turn when the army began the mountain crossing; Hannibal did not retain them by force and sent home another 7,000 men whose loyalty seemed in doubt. With his army thus diminished, he crossed the Pyrenees not, it seems, at the col du Perthus but, to avoid the Marseillais colonies of the Catalan coast (Ampurias and Rosas), going via Cerdana, then the col de la Perche and the Têt valley (Bosch-Gimpera, 1965, pp. 135–41). Then, striking out obliquely eastwards, he set up his first camp at Illiberis, on the site of the small present-day town of Elne, slightly south of Perpignan.

The populations of present-day Roussillon were at that time under the leadership of a federation, that of the Volcae Arecomici, Celts who had arrived fairly recently, in the late third century, in a culturally Iberian world. According to Livy (XXI, 24, 2), some of these peoples, fearing that they would fall into the grip of a Punic domination comparable with the one they had heard spoken of on the other side of the Pyrenees, took up arms, and their leaders met at Ruscino, present-day Castel-Roussillon, a short distance from Perpignan. The end of July was already approaching. Hannibal's plan could brook no delay; on confrontation, the Punic leader preferred a conciliatory approach and, says Livy, by means of handing out gifts, managed to get his army past Ruscino unharmed.

Polybius (III, 39) estimates a figure of roughly 1,600 stadia, or some 280 kilometres, for the distance travelled by Hannibal's troops between Emporion

(Ampurias), which in fact they left on the right, and the point where they crossed the Rhône, upstream from the confluence of the Durance – in spite of some doubt, as we shall see, about the exact spot. This presupposes the shortest possible journey from the halt at Illiberis (Elne). It is agreed that, at least as far as Nîmes, Hannibal followed the itinerary chosen exactly a century later by Domitius Ahenobarbus for the road that would bear his name, the 'Via Domitiana', which roughly matches the present-day 'Languedoc motorway'. In other words, the route closest to the shoreline, leaving between him and the sea only the vast stretches of stagnant water that punctuate this flat and lagoon-filled coast. So the Punic troops passed under the shadow of those *oppida* (Pech-Maho, near Sigean; Pech-Redon, near Narbonne; Ensérune, near Béziers; the Pioch du Télégraphe, at Aumes; Ambrussum, north of Lunel; and Nages, near Nîmes) which had been established as look-out posts on the heights dominating the principal line of passage. It has been supposed that Hannibal posted garrisons in these *oppida*, notably at Ensérune (Picard, 1967, pp. 163–5). One thing in favour of this hypothesis is that it ingeniously takes into account the 'falling-off' of 13,000 men which, as we saw above (p. 60), Polybius reveals between the crossing of the Pyrenees and that of the Rhône: they would have disappeared into the *oppida* of the Languedoc. However, the proof of a permanent Punic occupation – at least a dozen years – of these strongholds is still lacking. Certainly, objects of clearly Carthaginian manufacture have been found there, especially amphorae that are totally typical of that style. But the increasingly formally recognized presence of Punic, or at least 'Punicizing', material in these Roussillon and Languedoc sites (Morel, 1986, p. 43) argues more in favour of great activity in these places of Punic *guggas*, those traders who could on occasion also act as intelligence officers. And if it is reasoned that Hannibal needed to maintain permanently the security of a land communications corridor between Spain and Italy, such an argument would apply equally to the rest of his Gaulish itinerary: but he would never have had enough men to dot his entire route with garrisons! There is more reason to think that the Carthaginians, in these areas of Roussillon and Languedoc, did not feel the need to fortify staging-points and that their passage through the region was swift and peaceable. Certainly, it was found that the *oppidum* of Pech-Maho was destroyed and abandoned at the end of the third century, and other destructions in Languedoc have been connected with the Punic advance (Barruol, 1976, p. 683), but there is no proof.

Hannibal reached the vicinity of the Rhône around the end of August 218, rather than the end of September (see Proctor, 1971, p. 58). At very nearly the same moment, P. Cornelius Scipio arrived with his fleet in sight of Marseille, having sailed along the coasts of Etruria and Liguria, and established his camp near the great arm of the Rhône. It may be recalled that, according to the initially conceived plan, he was to make his way, with his two legions, towards Spain. But everything had conspired against him, first to delay his march and then to upset his arrangements.

The delay was due to the Celts of the Po Valley. Concerned about the foundation of two Roman colonies at Piacenza and Cremona some months earlier, in the spring of 218, the Boii (who occupied present-day Emilia around Bologna) had staged an uprising, stimulated by the news, through Hannibal's emissaries, of nearby assistance from that quarter. With the help of the Insubres of the Milanese region, they drove out the Roman colonists and forced them back into Mutina (Modena), to which they laid siege (Polybius, III, 40; Livy, XXI, 25). An initial troop sent against them and led by the praetor L. Manlius Vulso fell into an ambush. It was necessary for the urban praetor C. Atilius Serranus to take the exceptional step of going to his assistance with one of the two legions earlier entrusted to Scipio to be taken to Spain. Scipio had therefore to recruit a fresh legion to replace it, and thus reached Marseille two or three months late, only to learn that Hannibal, foiling all Rome's strategic plans, was already half-way to Italy.

## Crossing the Rhône

Theoretically it could be reckoned that the Punic army would cross the river downstream from the confluence of the Durance, in other words, probably at Beaucaire, where the Rhône flowed more slowly and had a slacker current, therefore being kinder to antique vessels. And in fact, for anyone coming from the Languedoc and wishing to go to Italy, it was at that point, or very near it, where they would have to cross the river, regarding this as the coastal route – in the Roman imperial era it would be the Via Julia Augusta – or take the route which, ascending the valley of the Durance on the left bank, ended up at the Mont-Genèvre pass. The first itinerary, via the coast, was completely ruled out for many reasons, for instance, it would have forced Hannibal to pass through the territory of Marseille, then through its trading-posts Tauroeis (Le Brusc), Olbia (Hyères), Antipolis (Antibes) and Nikaia (Nice). Then, once through this fiercely hostile zone, and also through a number of natural barriers – including the Var – he would have had to face the ambushes of Ligurian brigands in the narrow and twisting Riviera dei Fiori; it took the Romans nearly a century (after the victory of Sextius over the Salyes, or Salluvii) to establish a traffic corridor free of all banditry (Strabo, IV, 6, 3). And first and foremost, passing Beaucaire, or any other point between Arles and Avignon, would have made an encounter between the Punic army and the consular army inevitable, as the latter was already massed in the Crau plain.

In other words, the presence of Scipio's two legions also prevented Hannibal from taking the better road, through the Durance valley, known in Antiquity as the 'Heraclean Way', because it was supposed to have been opened by Heracles–Hercules, the eponymous hero of all the great routes in the ancient world. The concomitant presence, in mid-August 218, of Scipio in the Crau and Hannibal on the approaches of the right bank of the Rhône, somewhere between Nîmes and Villeneuve-lès-Avignon, is a fundamental strategic datum not taken into account by historians and commentators. They generally place the Punic army's crossing of the river downstream of the confluence of the Durance – at Fourques for De

Beer (1969, pp. 122–3); at Beaucaire for Lazenby (1978, p. 36) – on the strength of an indication by Polybius (III, 42, 1), according to which Hannibal crossed the river at a point situated at 'about four days' march from the sea'. And this crossing-point is calculated on the basis of a daily marching distance of between twelve and fifteen kilometres, starting from les Saintes-Maries de la Mer . . . . One forgets that a river like the Rhône builds up its delta powerfully with alluvial deposits, that the Camargue advances on the sea each year by several tens of metres: from les Saintes-Maries to Arles today it is slightly under forty kilometres; in the fourth century AD Ammianus Marcellinus (XV, 11, 16–18) reckoned only eighteen miles – twenty-six kilometres – from Arles to the sea. The distance was even less in Hannibal's time and, allowing his army a march of around fifteen kilometres a day, one arrives at a crossing-point upstream of the confluence of the Durance.

To pinpoint the spot remains a delicate undertaking. We can only keep to the texts which agree, that is, of Polybius (III, 42) and Livy (XXI, 26–7). Both – the Latin in more detail – tell us that on the brink of crossing the Rhône the Punic general ran up against unexpected resistance by some of the Volcae: 'Not being sure', says Livy, 'that they would be able to keep Hannibal away from the western bank, and wanting to use the river as a defence, they had nearly all their men taken across the Rhône and occupied the opposite bank under arms.' The Punic leader could not afford to add to the technical difficulties of the crossing the risk of a confrontation with the Volcae under the worst conditions. He therefore ordered his best lieutenant, Hanno, son of his elder sister and the suffete Bomilcar, to lead a strong detachment of Spaniards to take the Celtic barbarians from the rear. Hanno ascended twenty-five miles of the right bank of the Rhône, as far as a place where his Gaulish guides showed him that the river divided into two arms, embracing a small island, this configuration rendering a crossing easier. The detachment crossed the river, took a day's rest, came down again along the left bank and, after occupying a hill at the rear of the Volcae camp, let Hannibal know by means of smoke signals that he should make ready for a coordinated action.

On the right bank, where the bulk of the Punic army lay, everything was prepared for the river crossing. When Hannibal began to send his army over – the men on masses of small boats and rafts, the horses swimming, pulled across on long reins, except for those which were transported on boats, fully saddled and bridled so that they could be mounted the moment they reached the other bank – the Volcae left their camp and massed on the riverside in great disorder. Then, when Hanno and his men attacked them from the rear, they scattered. All that remained to be done was to finish the river-crossing. The elephants proved to be a headache for their drivers. Our two authors, Polybius and Livy, kindly explained, with a wealth of detail derived from their common source – very probably Coelius Antipater, himself supplied by Silenos – the stratagem employed to get these animals across, 'as they always obeyed their drivers, except when they found themselves faced with a water course' (Polybius, III, 46, 7). Someone had the bright idea of building immense rafts covered with a thick layer of earth, so that the elephants allowed themselves to be led on to them, docilely following two females which acted as guides! Polybius, like the Ancients in general, believed elephants to be incapable of swimming, and portrays those which, maddened with fright, jumped into the river, as walking underwater on the bed of the Rhône but holding their trunks above the water like snorkels (O'Bryhim, 1991, pp. 121–5).

It was here, just after this more picturesque than dramatic crossing, that the first engagement between the Carthaginians and the Romans occurred, limited in scale and the only one before the major confrontations in Italy. Shortly after landing his troops in the Crau, Scipio had sent 300 horsemen as scouts to sound out Hannibal's intentions. They ran into a strong party of Numidians to whom, for his part, the Punic leader had given a similar mission, while the Rhône crossing was completed. There was a brutal cavalry clash, with fairly heavy losses among the Numidians. According to Polybius (III, 45, 4), Scipio immediately set out with his troops to engage battle. If we are to believe Livy (XXI, 29, 6), while Hannibal hesitated between pursuing his planned march towards Italy and accepting combat, his hesitation was ended by the arrival of emissaries from the Cisalpine Boii, who offered to act as guides and assured him of their alliance. But he scarcely needed these last-minute spurs. He ordered his columns to move off at once up the left bank of the Rhône. As for P. Cornelius Scipio, he did not rush off in pursuit of the enemy. As soon as Hannibal had broken off contact, he hastened back to Italy in order to defend the Po Valley. But he did not take his army, which he left with his brother Gnaeus, entrusting him with the mission of invading Spain and taking the offensive against the Punic army which was there under Hasdrubal's command. With a wide-ranging strategic vision, which went beyond immediate concerns, he thus took a decision that was to affect the subsequent war to the advantage of the Romans, since for a number of years Hasdrubal would find himself prevented from sending reinforcements to his brother in Italy.

The reader will have gathered that, in the account of these tumultuous episodes, one topographical detail at least might guide the search for the site of the river-crossing: the 'island' of which Hanno and his men took advantage, going twenty-five miles upriver when they carried out their turning movement. Unfortunately, the bed of a river alters over a period of twenty-two centuries, and this particular feature of the Rhône's course can no longer be pinpointed today with any certainty; one might consider the 'île de la Piboulette', slightly upstream of Saint-Geniès-de-Comolas, or the 'île Vieille', downstream from Pont-Saint-Esprit. But did they exist *then*? Thus historians are divided – and will always be so, failing an improbable archaeological discovery – between several sites, from Villeneuve-lès-Avignon, in the south, just above the confluence of the Durance, to Pont-Saint-Esprit, in the north, the farthest possible upstream limit for the crossing, for Hannibal had to avoid the necessity of crossing the Ardèche beforehand (Figure 3).

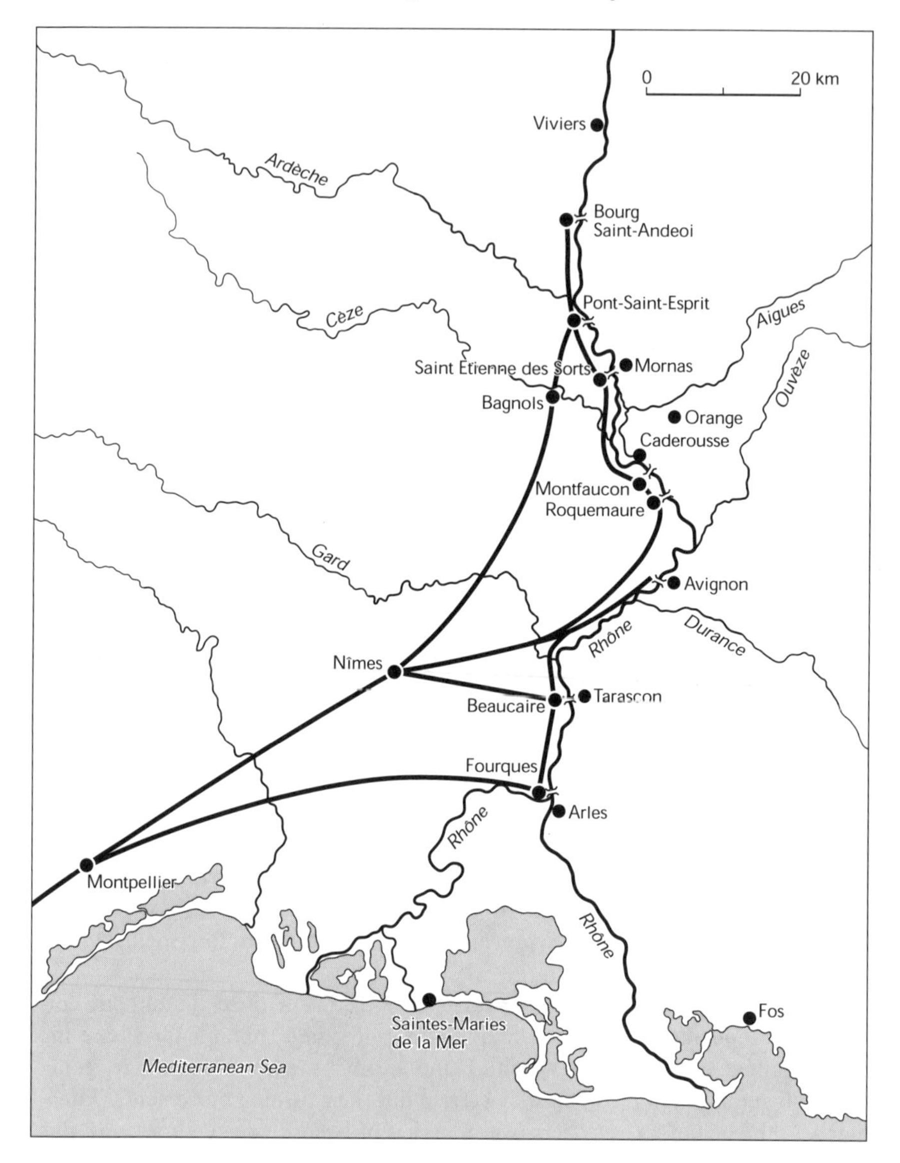


**Figure 3** Crossing the Rhône: various hypotheses; the most probable extend from Roquemaure to Pont-Saint-Esprit (from Seibert, 1988)

## Crossing the Alps

Of all Antiquity's outstanding deeds, probably no other has caused so much ink to flow as Hannibal's crossing of the Alps: immediately after the event, or nearly, pens started to scribble. Livy (XXI, 38, 6) indicates the variants that he finds in his sources; half a century later, Seneca (*Naturales Quaestiones*, III, 6) alludes to these differing versions. And from the early sixteenth century, learned literature has continued to feed on the topic, until it has been blown up out of all proportion. At the end of the nineteenth century, a specialist from Grenoble put the number of books and articles devoted to the question at over three hundred (Chappuis, 1897, p. 355). On the eve of the First World War, an erudite German historian, humorously excusing himself for not having exhaustive information, declared that, because he was not yet a hundred years old, he had not yet covered the whole bibliography relating to the subject! (Kahrstedt, 1913, p. 181). Nowadays he would need a second lifetime to read all that has appeared since.

I will not inflict on the reader a list of all the Alpine passes which the ingenuity of commentators, backed by knowledge of the texts and experience of the mountains, has thought it possible for Hannibal's elephants to cross (Seibert, 1988). The handful of references in the account that follows will suffice to give some idea of the multitude of solutions that have been advanced. And among those solutions I will offer the one which, with one or two variants, seems likely to give the best combination, among many strong probabilities, of the various data available. But first, a word or two to explain the reasons for what may seem to be an obsessive perseverance in this quest.

In the first place, there is the interest of the subject itself which, as we have seen, aroused enormous curiosity even in Antiquity. Of course, on a number of occasions, and especially around 400 BC when they had eventually surged down as far as Rome, reaching the lower slopes of the Capitol, Celtic bands had managed to cross the Alps. Polybius (III, 48) recalls those precedents and, as a man who himself had made the journey, has a tendency to rather rob it of its excitement. But for an entire, organized army, including several tens of thousands of men, with its cavalry, supply corps, and elephants, it was a 'first'. The venture equalled, even eclipsed, those of Alexander, and was elevated to the mythical level of Herculean prowess. From the time of the Renaissance, it was rediscovered in Livy's account and people began to read about it with passionate enthusiasm, at the opening of that famous 'third decade', which for centuries became bedside literature for the well-read and 'scholarly'. And we shall see that Livy, in a different but just as effective way as the baroque résumé by Silius Italicus (III, 465–56), knew how to extract dramatic effects from this mountain epic to hold readers spellbound, enabling them to share the anguish of Hannibal's companions, their intense emotions and, ultimately, the immense joy of having scaled one of the world's greatest natural ramparts. This is the whole import of the short speech addressed by the Punic leader – when the summit of the pass had been reached – to his troops, massed on a vantage point from whose height they could see the entire Po Valley stretched out below them until it disappeared into the distance (Livy, XXI, 35, 8–9). Enchanted by these literary qualities, many a reader, however little bitten by the research 'bug', has been tempted to follow the trail of the Punic soldiers on those mountain paths. However, at the same time, as we shall also see, Livy wildly muddled the tracks, 'contaminating' at least two sources from which he borrows two sections of the route which in fact belong to different itineraries. And trying to recognize on the terrain the topographical features he describes is a temptation to which it is better not to succumb. As has been said, everywhere in this mountainous terrain there are deep ravines and steep slopes, and landslides that lay bare the rock in gigantic scars; also, above the 2,000-metre level, there is plenty of snow in the north-facing hollows. Crossing the Alps with Livy and Polybius in one's hand is an even more fanciful enterprise than trying to find the true site of the battle of Alesia by matching Caesar's text with an Ordnance Survey map.

## Ascending the Rhône Valley and the road through the Alpine foothills

We must therefore take the texts as our starting-point and compare the realities of the terrain only in the case of absolute impossibility. This historico-philological inquiry starts quite naturally at the place where we left Hannibal after his Rhône crossing, on the left bank of the river, somewhere on a level with Orange or Mornas (Figure 4).

Polybius (III, 49, 5) and Livy (XXI, 31, 4) agree in saying that from his crossing-point Hannibal ascended the valley for four days before modifying his route. Everything urged him to hasten his march. He needed to put as much space between his troops and Scipio's army as quickly as possible, since the first unfortunate engagement had dissuaded him from waging on Gaulish soil a battle that did not fit in with his plans. Moreover, it was already the end of August, and any delay carried the risk of adding the problems of bad weather to the natural difficulties of the mountain crossing. It is easy to accept that these four days' rapid march – crossing the Drôme in that season presenting no serious obstacle – brought the Punic army level with Valence, or a little beyond. But what do the texts say? Both Greek and Latin, with one accord, state that Hannibal then reached the 'Island' – *Nesos, Insula* – in other words, a place so called because it was hemmed in among the confluence of two rivers. On one hand, the Rhône; on the other – and here is the first difficulty – a watercourse that can be identified with the Isère only at the price of a double amendment applied, one to Polybius' text by Scaliger, one of the most marvellous scholars of the second half of the sixteenth century, the other to Livy's text by Cluver, a no less estimable Dutch scholar of the early seventeenth century, who read *ibi Isara* where Livy's *Mediceus* (XXI, 31, 4) has *ibi Sarar*. This is what philologists call a 'palmary' emendation – worthy of carrying off the palm! – a perfectly well-founded operation in the view of an editor of ancient texts, who simultaneously recognizes and puts right a known hydronym – it is Strabo's Isar (IV, 1, 11), the Isara of Florus (I, 37, 6) – distorted by a common-or-garden 'haplography', the two adjoining 'i's in the original text having become one because of the copyist's misreading.

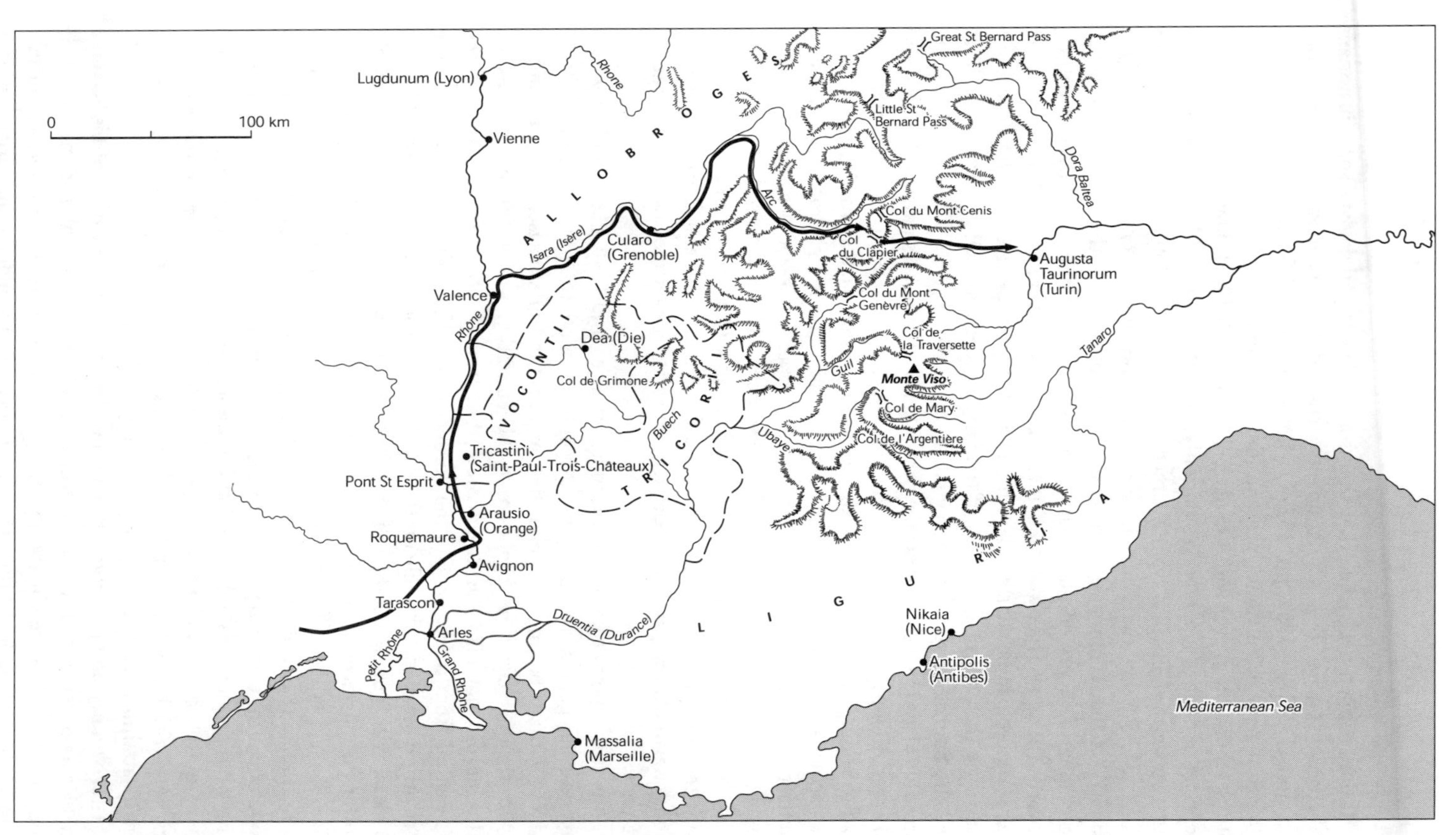


**Figure 4** From the Rhône Valley to the Po Valley (plan by S. Lancel from De Beer, 1969, pp. 144–5, who proposes a different itinerary)

It does happen that, when they themselves are not philologists, some historians rebel against what they see as an unwarranted manipulation of the texts (for example, De Beer, 1969, pp. 132–5, who wants to read Skaras – and not Isaras, after Scaliger – in Polybius' text, and interprets it as the Aygues, a small tributary of the Rhône on a level with Orange). That Hannibal had, however, reached the confluence of the Isère emerges not only from the four days' march indicated by our two sources, but also from the mention, implicit in Polybius, explicit in Livy (XXI, 31, 5), that the Punic leader then found himself on the borders of the country of the Allobroges. Now, it is known, at least for the classical era, when epigraphic data provide landmarks, that the limit of the Allobroges' territory, towards the south, followed the Isère, from Royans as far as the Rhône; but there were Allobrogian pockets south of the Isère, between the river and the Belledonne massif (in the present-day valley of the Grésivaudan), as well as between the Isère and the Bourne, in the Vercors region (Rémy, 1970, p. 207). These overspills had probably already taken place at the time when Hannibal was passing through, and to enter Allobrogian country the Punic leader did not need to cross the river. He had to anticipate the outcome – and we shall see that such a crossing, apart from its particular difficulties, would not have put him on the right road. Having made contact with the Allobroges, Hannibal very opportunely had occasion to exercise his diplomacy, using his good offices to settle a difference between two brothers who were in dispute over which should govern: giving judgement, in compliance with the law, in favour of the elder, the Carthaginian obtained from him provisions, warm clothing and footwear, as well as a strong armed escort as rearguard defence.

It is at this point that our two authors diverge. And Livy, like a rambler whose compass has gone haywire, begins to wander. I quote the passage (XXI, 31, 9) in which, without batting an eyelid, he sums up the route he ascribes to Hannibal: 'Once the quarrels of the Allobroges had been settled, now setting off towards the Alps he did not take the direct route, but veered left to the territory of the Tricastini; from there, passing the borders of the Vocontii, he proceeded to the Tricorii, meeting no obstacle on the way until he reached the Durance.' The text is clear, with not the slightest hint of alteration, but disconcerting. For, to say nothing of the incomprehensible 'veered left' (*ad laevam*), which would have made Hannibal either go west, in relation to the line of the Rhône, or at best northwards, in relation to that of the Isère, the route described by Livy makes the Carthaginian go back south, even if he merely brushed the northern boundaries of the Tricastini, whose region, around Saint-Paul-Trois-Châteaux, still bears their name, and then, quite perceptibly reascending, cross the southern zone of the Vocontii territory (the lower Diois) and, pushing eastwards, reach the Gapençais before finally attaining the Durance in the direction of Embrun.

Livy will say no more about it, and nothing in the continuation of his account enables us to establish precisely at which pass he thinks the Punic army emerged; but after making it rejoin the upper valley of the Durance, by such a curious detour, there is no doubt that in his mind Hannibal's soldiers must have gone up that valley to come out at the Mont-Genèvre pass. In fact, the 'Herculean Way', via the Durance and Mont-Genèvre, was probably the route that the Punic general had originally considered the best solution, but as we have seen (above, p. 67), the presence of Scipio's legions near Marseille at the time when he himself was nearing the Rhône had dissuaded him. The alternative solution, which he had certainly foreseen, lay in passing farther north. Livy had caught wind of it, as can be seen when he blames one of his sources (XXI, 38, 6), Coelius Antipater – although he had followed him in the first section of this northern route, as far as the confluence of the Isère! – for having made Hannibal pass via the Pennine Alps (i.e., the Valaisan Alps), and more exactly via the *Cremonis jugum*, which is not the Grimone pass (an easy mistake!) but, near the 'Tête de Crammont', the present-day Little St Bernard pass. The Latin historian refutes this for the reason that the passage by the Pennine Alps, so he says, would have brought Hannibal out among the Salassi, in the valley of the Dora Baltea, or the Val d'Aosta. Now, adds Livy, it is known for a fact that he came down among the Taurini, in the valley of the Dora Riparia, which slopes more gently down to Turin. Yes, but two passes gave equal access to the territory of the Taurini. Like all Romans of his time, Livy was well acquainted with the Mont-Genèvre pass, which had quite recently come into the limelight because of the journey made in the opposite direction by Caesar, speedily making his way into Gaul in 58 BC, via Briançon, Embrun, Gap, Die, the Rhône valley and Lyon (Caesar, *De bello Gallico*, I, 10, 3–5). But he was unaware of the second pass: we shall soon see which one.

As was suspected by de Saint-Denis (1974, p. 137), it was probably the still-famous passage of Caesar's legions via the Diois on their way to quell the Gauls that inspired Livy to have the Punic army take the same route. Even in our own day the idea still holds ground, as it has been proposed to christen the modern roads (D.93, D.94 and N.94) the 'Hannibal route', crossing the region from Crest to Embrun, by way of Die, Veynes and Gap, where this 'Hannibal route' joins the 'Napoleon route'! A fine trip, to be sure, through the pleasant landscapes of the Drôme and Hautes-Alpes, very 'touristic' and nowadays made so easy by the road plans of French engineers. But Hannibal was no tourist, and why should he have amused himself, in company with around 40,000 men and some twenty elephants, by leap frogging the mountain tracks of the Diois and lower Dévoluy, with passes at over 1,000 metres, like the col de Cabre or, farther north, the col de Grimone which, as we have seen, is not the *Cremonis jugum?*

Nevertheless, some reputedly serious historians have chosen to follow Livy here. Among them is Sir Gavin De Beer, whose initial refusal to accept the Skaras–Isaras correction in Polybius made it easier for him, it is true, to adopt this solution. For him the Skaras was the Aygues and the 'Island' the confluence of this minor watercourse with the Rhône, so he had the Carthaginian ascend across the Tricastin to the Drôme, then go along its left bank as far as Die; next, directly eastwards, by the col de Grimone and Gap, Hannibal rejoined the Durance, which he followed as far as the vicinity of Guillestre. But then, having reached this point, a more specious than accurate discussion over the indications about the passes left by Strabo (IV, 6, 12, quoting Polybius, XXXIV, 10, 18) and Varro suggested to the British scholar that he should make Hannibal deviate from the Durance route, emerging at Mont-Genèvre, and commit him to the Queyras, with a last hestitation over the pass chosen: was it the col de Mary, south of the massif, or rather the col de la Traversette, not far from the Viso, at the very end of the upper valley of the Guil (De Beer, 1969, pp. 160–82)? As wise an expert on these mountains as General Guillaume, who is moreover a careful reader of the texts and experienced in the difficulties of all the documentation, considered that the Traversette remained a good candidate for the title, at least in the eyes of those who continued to trust Livy (Guillaume, 1967, p. 93). At an altitude of almost 3,000 metres – 2,947 to be precise – this pass has in its favour that in summer it retains a thick cloak of snow on the Italian side, perhaps the glacier-snow that we shall see causing Hannibal such difficulties at the start of his downward trek towards the Po Valley. But the altitude in itself was a handicap and anyway, as its name fairly indicates, the 'Traversette' is, rather than a pass, a narrow breach, a 'window' opened in the crest, with very steep access from either side, so difficult to get through in bad weather that at the end of Louis XI's reign the Piedmontese Marquis de Saluces had a tunnel made there, which has since collapsed. And, sharing a smile with Samivel, one may imagine Hannibal's army – but what about the elephants in such a spot? – filing past two by two, if not in single file, for days at a time (Samivel and Norande, 1983, p. 77)!

## Storming the Great Alps

It is sometimes painful to be reasonable; but it is better to be so with Polybius and return with him to the banks of the Isère, on its lower course.

The Greek historian says (III, 50, 1) that for about ten days before undertaking the 'climb' properly speaking (*anabole*), Hannibal travelled 800 stadia, or 148 kilometres, along the river. Polybius is usually accurate enough in the figures he gives for distances for us to trust this one which, calculated from the departure-point of Pont-de-l'Isère, leads roughly to the level of Pontcharra, at the northern tip of the present-day Grésivaudan. And as he adds – followed in this by Livy (XXI, 32, 6) – that, duly escorted by the Allobroges, the Punic army had a peaceful march over this still-flat terrain, there is no cause to invent imaginary difficulties (as in Lazenby, 1978, p. 42), for example having Hannibal do battle with the mountain-dwellers of the Vercors in the gorges of the Bourne; his Gaulish guides would have served their client very ill if they had led him into this dangerous corner! The only hesitation, on this part of the journey, concerns which bank of the Isère: staying on the left bank had the advantage of avoiding crossing the river, whose bed is broad and flow abundant in all seasons near to its confluence with the Rhône; and we saw earlier that there was no need for Hannibal to cross to the right bank to communicate with the Allobroges. The only snags to this itinerary along the left bank are the narrow crossing of the 'bec de l'Échaillon', just when the last foothills of the Vercors have been overcome and the transverse valley of Voreppe has been entered, and then the need to cross the Drac, probably on a level with Comboire; but, before it was channelled quite recently, the Drace, a mountain stream that was nearly dry at the end of summer, divided into several arms and was therefore not a serious obstacle. If Hannibal had gone along the right bank, he would have met much graver difficulties in entering by this first gateway to the Great Alps. Hannibal arrived near Cularo, the site on which Grenoble is based – where probably nothing yet existed, let alone a bridge – more than one and a half centuries before the first mention of the village in a letter from Munatius Plancus addressed to Cicero in 43 BC (*Ad Fam.*, X, 23, 7). Here, in the vicinity of the present-day 'Porte de France', he would have had to take the very narrow passage – even narrower than that of the 'bec de l'Échaillon' – left by the river flowing closest to the last excarpments of the Chartreuse massif, those limestone cliffs of the 'Bastille' which the quarrymen had not yet begun to hack.

Hannibal knew that he could not continue to ascend the upper course of the Isère, which led him into the dead end of the Tarentaise, from which there was no practicable pass. This piece of information, supplied by his Gaulish guides, was one more reason for him to remain on the left bank of the river. He therefore crossed the Grésivaudan by going along the foothills of the Belledonne massif. Having come level with Pontcharra, he lost the benefit of the Allobroges' escort; at the same time he had to choose between two possible routes. Between Pontcharra and Montmélian, the Isère valley widens out to form a bowl several kilometres wide, its floor until quite recently still rendered damp, if not marshy, by the converging waters of the Bréda and Gélon. This feature accounts for the long-observed preference of travellers for a route that leaves the Isère valley at Pontcharra to ascend the small enclosed valley of the Bréda and then, after La Rochette, of the Gélon, to rejoin the left bank of the Arc at Montgilbert (Dion, 1960, pp. 55–6). Early in this century, it was even suggested that, in order to save one or two days' march, on leaving La Rochette Hannibal had cut across the small massif of Les Hurtières and crossed the pass of the Grand-Cucheron to reach the valley of the Arc plainly upstream of Aiguebelle (Azan, 1902, p. 107). This is forgetting that in the mountains a straight line, or simply a short cut, is very rarely the shortest path. It is very probable that Hannibal continued along the Isère as far as its confluence with the Arc, preferring, in order to avoid the bogs of the valley floor, to keep to the terraces formed by the lower slopes on either side (de Saint-Denis, 1974, p. 140). It was probably here, at the foot of the bec d'Aiton for some (Jullian, 1920, p. 480), or rather level with the constriction of Aiguebelle for others (de Saint-Denis, 1974, p. 141), that the first war episode of the Great Alps crossing took place, mentioned by Polybius (III, 50, 3, and relayed by Livy, XXI, 32, 8), when the Allobroges escorting the Punic army left it in order to return home. From then on, Hannibal's only guides were the Boian Gauls who, it may be recalled, had joined him at the Rhône crossing (above, p. 69).

Reaching the Maurienne region, Hannibal was now making his way along ever narrower passes as he ascended the valley of the Arc. The long column of the

Punic army, stretching farther and farther back, became more vulnerable to attack. There the Carthaginians, Livy notes maliciously (XXI, 34, 1), were in danger of becoming victims of their own weapons, cunning and ambush. This is what happened about midway along the valley. Without the precautions taken by its leader, who had placed the horsemen in the front, followed by the wagons and elephants, with the heavy infantry bringing up the rear, the army would have suffered a disaster. Even so, the losses were heavy, and Polybius even specifies (III, 53, 5) that Hannibal spent a whole night with his rearguard troops, cut off from his horsemen and wagons, protected by an enormous isolated rock; one may imagine the torments that the vain search for this rock has cost the seekers.

Finally, on the ninth day after the start of the climb (Polybius, III, 53, 9; Livy, XXI, 35, 4), Hannibal reached the top of the pass. The season, says Polybius, was nearing the 'setting of the Pleiades'. For the Ancients, who read the skies as we read our calendars, this event in the first days of November marked the arrival of winter, at least from Hesiod's time. It was therefore at the very end of October, when the first snows had already whitened the summits. Hannibal set up his camp and waited two days for those lagging behind – both men and beasts – to catch up with him. And to give fresh heart to the exhausted troops, from a kind of balcony with a vast panoramic view, he showed them the Italy which henceforth was theirs for the taking.

But his troubles were not yet over. Livy rightly remarks that, although the Italian side of the Alps presents a shorter journey, it is also steeper. It was here, at the start of the descent, that an event took place which is recounted with astonishing similarity by our two authors (Polybius, III, 54, 5–55; Livy, XXI, 36–7). Behind the descriptive accuracy, the almost tangible portrayal of gestures and attitudes, one senses the hand of Silenos, Hannibal's historiographer, who wrote a day-to-day account of the campaign. But unlike Polybius, less detailed but more coherent, the Latin saw the scenes described through the distorting mirror of Coelius Antipater, from whom he perhaps borrowed the episode of the vinegar (De Sanctis, 1917, pp. 77–8). Hannibal's soldiers had reached a place where the narrowness of the track prevented not only the elephants but even the mules from getting past. It is clear in Polybius, less so in Livy, that a landslide which had turned a naturally steep slope into a real precipice obliged the column to take a path that was impracticable even for the horsemen. It was therefore necessary to abandon that route and set off on a north-facing slope where difficulties of a different, but no less insurmountable, kind awaited the Punic soldiers. There, in fact, a thin layer of fresh snow masked the dangers of steep glacier-snow on which men slid as if on toboggans, while the pack animals, sinking through the crust with their hooves, found themselves caught as if in a trap. Hannibal ordered a return to the rocky wall of the south-facing slope and had the men clear by brute force the path which the landslip had obliterated. In addition to human effort, says Livy, vinegar (or sour wine) was used to dissolve the rock, and there has been much comment on this. Though Polybius breathes not a word of it, the story, in the Roman tradition, was current right up to Ammianus Marcellinus. In fact, what causes the problem is not so much the vinegar, as it is known that in Antiquity every army carried large supplies of it both for the troops' drinking purposes and the maintenance of weapons, but the enormous quantities of wood that would be needed to keep the fires going for the operation. Where on these mountain crests would Hannibal's men have found the 'gigantic trees' (XXI, 37, 2: *arbores immanes*) of which Livy speaks? However, the ordeal was nearly over. The foothills were close; the army rested a while before descending to the plains.

All that remains is to locate this pass which Hannibal had just introduced into history. Professional historians, amateurs and erudite locals have spent a great deal of effort on identifying the place; it is the key part of the immense 'literature' that has grown up on the crossing of the Alps. At the point we have reached, after a process of elimination, sending Hannibal on the route of the upper Maurienne, the number of possibilities has shrunk considerably. At the end of this road, having passed Modane and the village of Bramans, one arrives at the region of Mont-Cenis; there, commentators are divided over three passes. A humanist and mountaineer doctor Marc de Lavis-Traffort, stands out especially; in the middle of this century, after devoting years of his life to it, he probably arrived at the most satisfactory solution to the problem. To his way of thinking, the pass must combine a certain number of distinctive characteristics that are contained in the whole body of the textual data. This boiled down to travelling over the peaks, texts in hand. But this method, which was likely to prove disappointing if applied indiscriminately, might be productive once a cautious historico-philological approach had defined the Alpine sector which it suggested by and large as Hannibal's crossing-point.

Two passes in particular were favoured by scholars: the Petit Mont-Cenis and, chiefly, the col du Clapier (Dion, 1962, p. 538; Huss, 1985, p. 305 Meyer, 1958, p. 241). But after a meticulous examination of the terrain, de Lavis-Traffort gave his preference to a depression which was a twin to that of the Clapier and was very close to it in height (2,482 metres) – that of Savine-Coche. This last pass matched all the discriminant criteria, whereas those that follow fall short of the Clapier: just at the start of the descent towards Italy, there were those deep screes, and also the thick glacier-snow in the shadows, which had given Hannibal so much trouble, but equally, shortly after this tricky area, lay the sunny alpine pasture where the Punic leader was able to give both animals and men a breather. So it was possible to reconstruct the penultimate phase of that testing orderal of crossing the Alps. Still guided by the Boii, leaving the valley of the Arc around Bramans, Hannibal had turned right into the small valley of Ambin, at the entrance to which the fine Roman chapel of Saint-Pierre d'Extravache still marks the route that the Carthaginian initially made famous; then he had gone through the little valley of Savine and set up his camp, the last before the descent, around the small lake. Between the twin depressions, Clapier and Savine-Coche, a promontory on the Italian side dominates the ravine of the Clarée, which enters the Dora Riparia a little upstream from Susa; in the distance is Piedmont, glimpsed through the indentations of the lower valleys.

In 1961 the demonstration by the learned Mauriennais received exceptional recognition, when the title 'pas de Lavis-Traffort' was officially given to the col de Savine-Coche, in homage to the researcher. But the finest acknowledgement of the value of his work seems to me to be the support given shortly afterwards by an eminent scholar from Zurich, who sided with his opinion and abandoned the Clapier for Savine-Coche (Meyer, 1964, pp. 90–101).

# 4

# 'Blitzkrieg' – from the Trebia to Cannae

During the first phase of his great venture, Hannibal's strategical genius had lain in sowing confusion, then catching the enemy unawares. It may be remembered that when, after a brief cavalry engagement, P. Cornelius Scipio had seen Hannibal taking to the Rhône Valley to seek farther north the passage across the Alps that was not accessible to him at Mont-Genèvre, he had given up the idea of pursuit. Leaving the bulk of his troops with his brother Gnaeus, whose mission was, as planned, to take them to Spain, he had re-embarked with all speed and returned to Pisa, after calling in at Genoa (Polybius, III, 56, 5; Livy, XXI, 32, 5; 39, 3). While the Punic leader and his army plunged deeper into the Alpine valleys, Scipio crossed Etruria and, taking command of the unseasoned troops of the praetors L. Manlius Vulso and C. Atilius Serranus, who were still reeling from the blow of their recent failure against the Boii (above, p. 67), he set off for the Po Valley. He made camp at Placentia (Piacenza), beside the river.

A simple glance at the map shows that with this line of march Scipio was clearly expecting the Punic army to sweep down farther north, coming along the Dora Baltea from Aosta. As in his time the only known pass leading from the Celtic region to the Taurini was that of Mont-Genèvre, he had good reason to think that Hannibal would come through the Pennine Alps at the Little St Bernard pass. Probably informed by the Boii that the Romans were unaware of the pass in the Mont-Cenis region, Hannibal had created the element of surprise. The military history of the Great Alps has a wealth of these games of hide-and-seek. In the early sixteenth century, a similar manoeuvre, but in the opposite direction, enabled François I to carry off the victory of Marignan (Melegnano) in 1515; warned that a Swiss army was resolutely awaiting him at the descent from Mont-Genèvre, he had gone through the col de Larche. For his part, Hannibal owed it to his unexpected route that he had been able, once he had reached Piedmont, to take time to rest his troops. Polybius (III, 60, 6) and Livy (XXI, 39, 1–2) both tell of the condition of the half of his army that remained to him – remember the figures from the stele at Cape Lacinium: 20,000 footsoldiers and 6,000 horsemen; men who had endured privations and suffering that had turned them into little short of savages. Soon afterwards, following a three-day siege, the Punic general seized the capital of the Taurini, probably the future Augusta Taurinorum (Turin), and as an example had the throats cut of all those who had resisted. Such terrorism was not gratuitous. Polybius makes it quite clear that the Gauls of the Po Valley were holding back; in theory they were won over to the Punic side, but the approach of the Roman legions called for caution. Hannibal felt that if he was to forge ahead without delay, he had to create a spur that would rally them as quickly as possible.

The news of his arrival in Italy, and then of his capture of the capital of the Taurini, had been greeted with a kind of astonishment in Rome. The second consul, Ti. Sempronius Longus, who had been sent to Sicily to make ready an expedition to Africa, was immediately recalled from Lilybaeum. In the space of only a few months, however, he had done good work, profiting from the alliance of king Hieron of Syracuse, to place not only Sicily but also the Aeolian Islands in a state of defence against the activities of the Punic fleet, seizing Malta, where the garrison surrendered without a fight. But there was no longer any question of attacking Carthage when the enemy was on their own doorstep! About mid-November, leaving the praetor M. Aemilius to guard Sicily, and his lieutenant Sex. Pomponius, with twenty-five warships, to keep a watch on the coasts of Italy, Sempronius arrived with his troops at Ariminum (Rimini) on the Adriatic.

## The first encounter near the Ticinus (late November 218)

Sempronius had not yet been able to join forces with his colleague when the first engagement between the two armies took place. Scipio had crossed the Po, and had then gone westwards to meet Hannibal. He had crossed the Ticinus (Ticino) by means of a temporary bridge, protected by a small fort and under the guard of a detachment. Hannibal was marching in the opposite direction along the bank of the Padus (Po), the Romans, as Polybius says (III, 65, 1), having the river on their left, the Carthaginians on their right. On the eve of this emotionally highly charged first confrontation, the two generals made a point of galvanizing energies. It was the Carthaginian who had most at stake; a kind of 'double or quits'. Should there be a heavy defeat, it would mean the end of a venture that had scarcely begun; if he were to win, he could be sure that the Gauls still standing on the sidelines would rally to his banner and afford him the means to carry on. In this psychological preparation for combat, Polybius and Livy tell us, Hannibal overlooked nothing. Before addressing his men, he put them in the right frame of mind by laying on a kind of dramatic performance. He brought before his troops a group of young mountain-dwelling Gauls who had been taken prisoner during the crossing of the Alps, and provided them with the weapons of their nation and fully equipped horses. By drawing lots, a few pairs were selected to face each other in single combat, the survivor committing himself to serve in the Punic army for the rest of the campaign.

At the outcome of these duels, among the captives who remained spectators, there was less pity for those who had been killed, says Polybius, than for their victors; for the former had been delivered from all their woes, whereas for the latter the worst was yet to come. But – and here was Hannibal's true purpose – what had started as a mere spectacle for his troops turned into a psychodrama for, in the Carthaginian ranks, the soldiers began to feel compassion for their fate, and they too felt that those who had been killed were the lucky ones.

This performance provided the Punic leader with the main theme of a speech which, summarized by Polybius and much elaborated by Livy, but both similar in content, has fortunately been passed down to us in authentic fashion, at least in broad outline, just as it was transcribed by Hannibal's historiographers. The spectacle he had just shown his soldiers, he told them, was the true picture of the fate awaiting them. They had their backs to the wall, in other words, the Alps they had just crossed so painfully. Now they had to conquer or die, or fall into the hands of the enemy. And as the last eventuality could not even be contemplated, they would find in contempt for death the best encouragement to win ever given to men by the immortal gods (Livy, XXI, 44, 9).

Foreseeing that his African cavalry would play a determining role in the fray, at the last moment Hannibal recalled Maharbal and the 500 Numidians he had sent to ravage the lands of Rome's allies, with the advice to spare the Gauls as much as possible. He addressed himself specially to them, so that they should be aware of the rewards to be gained by their valour in combat: each would receive a plot of land, wherever he liked, in Italy, Spain or Africa, with immunity from taxation that would extend to his descendants; any allies who so wished could become citizens of Carthage; as for the slaves who had followed their masters and worked as servants in the army, they would be freed, their masters receiving two slaves in place of one by way of compensation. And, as a pledge of his promises, seizing a lamb in his left hand and a stone in his right, says Livy (XXI, 45, 8), he prayed 'Jupiter and the other gods' – perhaps the pantheon invoked later in his famous oath (below, p. 117) – to strike him dead if he should break his word, like the lamb whose head he shattered with the stone. It is a fine thing that this episode – Polybius, for whom these were unimportant religious trifles, does not say a word about it – should be recounted to us by the one who, in definitive terms, had denounced the Carthaginian's atheism and even impiety (above, pp. 44 and 56).

The inaccurately named battle of the Ticinus in fact took place some distance to the north of the left bank of the Po, in the fairly deep loop described by the river between the Sesia and the Ticino, and roughly equidistant between these two tributaries. What was mainly a preliminary cavalry engagement is generally thought to have taken place around Lomello. The two armies had set up their camps fairly close to each other. As Scipio left with his horsemen and *jaculatores* (lightly armed javelin-throwers) to reconnoitre the enemy forces, he came up against Hannibal, who was also arriving with his cavalry to explore the surroundings. At the first clash, the *jaculatores*, surprised by the speed of the opposing charge, retreated along corridors prepared between the 'turmae' (squadrons) of the Roman cavalry. Hannibal had placed his heavy cavalry in the centre, flanked on the wings by the Numidians, whose task it was to envelop the enemy. And that was what happened. Outflanking the Roman lines, the Numidians cut across their rear and crushed the javelin-throwers. As for the Roman horsemen, after holding out against the African cavalry, in the centre, and inflicting heavy losses on it, they turned tail when they found themselves attacked from the rear by squadrons of Numidians, and fled in small groups.

Some, however, rallied round their leader. Scipio certainly needed this defence. Badly wounded, and in danger of being enveloped by the Numidians and taken prisoner, he was rescued, says Livy, by the intervention of his son, the future Africanus, taking part in his first campaign at the age of just eighteen. Livy adds in all honesty (XXI, 46, 10) that, according to Coelius Antipater, the honour of saving the consul should be credited to a Ligurian slave. This episode was probably presented thus by Silenos, Hannibal's historiographer, and perhaps truthfully. Polybius, who is curiously silent on the subject in his account of the battle, returns to it much later in his laudatory portrait of his hero leaving to conquer Punic Spain in 210 (X, 3). He says he learned from Laelius – the Elder, not the homonymous son, Scipio Aemilianus' inseparable friend, whose name often crops up in Cicero's dialogues – how the young man had singlehandedly saved his father, who was hemmed in by the enemy, while his companions hesitated in the face of danger. This narrative smacks of the hagiography that very soon developed around the figure of Africanus, doubtless with the complicity of the interested party, as we shall see.

Hannibal lost no time in reaping the dividends of this initial success, although Scipio's prompt retreat thwarted a more important gain. The Roman consul hastily distanced himself from the Ticinus, then recrossed the Po and set up a first camp not far from Placentia, west of the Trebia. His flight was so fast that Hannibal, in hot pursuit, arrived too late to cross by the raft bridge that had been thrown across the Ticinus, as this was already destroyed; but he took prisoner several hundred soldiers, engineers in the Roman army who had remained on the west bank of the river. Then he marched for two days back along the north bank of the Po before finding a suitable spot to make a bridge of boats. Leaving his lieutenant, Hasdrubal, to get the bulk of the army across, he himself went immediately over to the south bank to receive emissaries from the Gauls. Having sat on the fence for a long while, they now flew to support the winning side, and came to offer provisions and reinforcements. So everything went as planned. Moreover, when the Carthaginians began to run short of provisions and were preparing to attack the township of Clastidium – the present-day Casteggio, some ten kilometres south of the Po – where they knew the Romans had stored large quantities of grain, the place was handed over to them by its commander, one Dasius, originally from Brundisium (Brindisi), and the Messapians of Calabria. That the traitor was from the south of Italy may not be entirely due to chance, nor his betrayal a matter of luck. It might be seen as the result of the long-term undermining work carried out by Carthage in those regions where Hannibal would soon achieve his finest political successes (Picard and Picard, 1970, p. 239; Brisson, 1973, p. 172). For Rome the surrender of Clastidium was an affront made all the more bitter because its capture four years earlier, in 222, had been one of Marcellus' most significant successes against the Cisalpine Gauls. The Punic leader welcomed the renegades with great consideration, and incorporated the defaulting garrison into his own army. Two days after crossing the Po, he had set up his camp a few kilometres from Scipio's, west of the Trebia.

## The Battle of the Trebia (late December 218)

Scipio, who was not making a good recovery from his wounds, went from one setback to another. In his camp, taking advantage of the slackened vigilance of the small hours, the Gaulish auxiliaries took up their weapons and massacred the Roman soldiers camped beside them. After decapitating the dead – a macabre detail mentioned by Polybius (III, 67, 3), borne out to some extent by the 'severed heads' of Roquepertuse – they went over to the Carthaginians, 2,000 footsoldiers and 200 horsemen in all. Hannibal made use of them as ambassadors, despatched to their respective towns to exhort their compatriots to form an alliance with him. The worst disgrace for the Romans was that the Punic general saw the arrival in his camp of Boii from the Bologna region, who had come to hand over the commissioners sent by Rome to proceed with the division of their lands. Hannibal eagerly welcomed their overtures, but left them their three prisoners so that they could use them as bargaining power to obtain the return of hostages.

According to Polybius (III, 67, 8), Scipio felt these betrayals bitterly. He feared that the contagion of these demonstrations of support would spread throughout the whole Cisalpine region, and felt very insecure where he was, in direct contact with Hannibal. The night after the desertion of the Gaulish auxiliaries, he struck camp, crossed the Trebia and installed himself on the hills overlooking the east bank of the river. This position, which was better protected, also made it easier for him to link up with his colleague Sempronius, whose reinforcements he was awaiting from Ariminum (Rimini). Since the already old, but decisive, work of Kromayer (1912, p. 48), this second camp of Scipio has been taken to be situated at Pieve-Dugliara, very near Rivergaro, where today the road from Piacenza to Genoa, via Bobbio, joins the valley of the Trebia.

Ti. Sempronius Longus arrived there with his troops around mid-December. He was impatient to do battle; if he was to end his consulate with some dazzling action, his weeks, if not his days, were numbered. Hannibal provided him with the opportunity for some preliminary skirmishes. The Carthaginian had noticed that certain Gaulish tribes occupying this region between the Po and the Trebia, with whom he had concluded treaties of friendship, still had dealings with the Romans. Unwilling to tolerate their playing on both sides, he resorted to military persecution, sending strong detachments to ravage their lands. The victims presented themselves at the Roman camp to ask for help, and Sempronius leapt at the chance. He immediately dispatched his cavalry across the Trebia, flanked by a strong body of *jaculatores*. During the limited engagements that followed, the fortunes of war remained uncertain, but the Roman consul received the impression that he had gained the advantage over his adversary – wrongly, as it turned out, for Hannibal, whose plan of action was not yet ready, had preferred to recall his troops (Polybius, III, 69, 13).

Scipio, very wisely, was of the opinion that nothing should be done precipitately; the coming winter would provide the time to train the new recruits in his and his colleague's legions. Furthermore, this same period would act in the Romans' favour; seeing the Carthaginians inactive, it would not be long before the Gauls, with their well-known fickleness, turned against them. Sempronius, however, did not see things in the same way. He had no desire to leave the glory of a victory to the two consuls who would soon be appointed for the year 217, and Scipio's physical incapacity gave him a free hand. As for Hannibal, like Scipio, he reckoned that time would not be in his favour. The keenness of the Gauls would not last for ever; it would be better to profit without delay from the inexperience of the Roman troops, and also from the unavailability of Scipio, a more formidable foe than Sempronius, who was hot-tempered by nature and too self-confident. Lastly, he was well aware that the only salvation for an invading army in a foreign country, logistically insecure, lay in keeping on the move. He therefore actively made his plans, in the fair hope that Sempronius would fall into the trap he was laying for him.

In the area separating the two armies, Hannibal had noticed a spot which, although flat and treeless, was none the less suitable for an ambush because of a steep-sided stream whose banks were sufficiently well provided with undergrowth and plants to afford concealment even for horsemen. The site of this ambush is very probably to be sought in the bed of one of the streams that here flow parallel to the fairly meandering course of the Trebia, which is broken into many small branches: the rio Colomba or the rio Gerosa. In the evening of one of the last days of December – according to Livy (XXI, 54, 7), the eve of the winter solstice – Hannibal summoned his chiefs of staff, in the presence of his young brother Mago, and revealed his plan. Then, taking Mago to one side, he entrusted to him a commando group of 200 men, 100 infantry and 100 cavalry, whom he had personally selected during the day. Each of these men having chosen nine companions-at-arms respectively from their maniple (company of footsoldiers) or *turma* (cavalry division), the final total was a detachment of 1,000 footsoldiers and 1,000 horsemen who set up an ambush under Mago's command. At dawn, Hannibal assembled his Numidian cavalry and sent them across the Trebia, with the instruction to go and prance about before the Roman camp, hurling javelins at the guard posts. Then, retreating, they were to entice the enemy to cross the river.

This act of provocation succeeded beyond all expectations. Sempronius immediately ordered out his cavalry and light infantry – the *jaculatores*: 6,000 men – then put his entire army on the march. That day a bitter sleet was falling, the cold penetrating the bones of the men, who had emerged from their tents on empty stomachs. When, in their pursuit of the Numidians, the footsoldiers plunged into the stream, they found themselves up to their armpits in icy water, and they emerged frozen to the marrow and almost incapable of holding their weapons. In contrast, Hannibal's men had calmly eaten; they had made their limbs supple by the application of oil and grease, which had been doled out to them by their officers, and had armed themselves in front of fires lit around the tents. The battle conditions which, merely on the strength of the forces present might have been considered equally balanced, were therefore tipped in favour of the Carthaginians.

Sempronius could call on two consular armies, or four legions, to which were added the allied contingents, in other words a little over 40,000 men in all. For his part, to the 26,000 men left to him after crossing the Alps, Hannibal had added Gaulish contingents who brought his total force to nearly 40,000 men. But this numerical quasi-equality was deceptive. At the time of the engagement on the Ticinus, Scipio had already discovered to his cost that Hannibal possessed a considerable tactical advantage – his cavalry was over 10,000 strong, if the Gaulish reinforcements were included (Polybius, III, 72, 9) – as against 4,000 Roman cavalry.

Hannibal had sent ahead the Balearic slingers and the light infantry armed with pikes, some 8,000 men, and had then come out himself with the rest of his troops. After proceeding about one and a half kilometres from his camp, he had deployed his heavily armed footsoldiers along a single line: around 20,000 men, Iberians, Gauls and Africans. The 10,000 horsemen were divided into two bodies, placed on the wings, like the elephants, in a forward position. The width of the front thus created may be reckoned at about three kilometres. Opposite, after recalling his horsemen who were fruitlessly tiring themselves out in pursuit of the Numidians, Sempronius had adopted the customary battle order: infantry in the centre, the heavily armed footsoldiers covering the front-line, and the cavalry squadrons on the wings. While in the centre the two heavy infantries fought hand to hand for a long time without any decisive result, the wings of Sempronius' front yielded fairly quickly to the pressure of the Punic horsemen, who were more numerous and more powerful, and to the charging thrusts of the elephants. As the Roman cavalry buckled, it left the infantry's flanks vulnerable, and they were immediately attacked by the pikemen and the Baleares armed with javelins. At that point the men lying in ambush under Mago's command emerged from their hiding-place and attacked the rear of the Roman infantry in the centre, adding still further to the chaos. Let us remember that the Romans were fighting with their backs to the river, and the memory of that crossing, in the freezing early light, did not encourage them to repeat the experience. The only escape was to flee forwards. A few units of legionary infantry, in the centre, managed to pierce the Carthaginian line, inflicting heavy losses on the Africans and, above all, the Gauls, who were facing them. Numbering about 10,000, these survivors were able to regroup and reach Placentia in good order. Of the footsoldiers fighting on the wings, who were massacred in their hundreds near the Trebia by the horsemen and elephants, only a small number were able to escape, like the bulk of the cavalry, and rejoin the other troop at Placentia.

It was an undeniable disaster, and Sempronius convinced no one in Rome – where he went at the end of December to preside over the comitia for the election of the new consuls – that the bad weather could be blamed to minimize his responsibility in the affair. But that bad weather had also limited the size of the Punic victory, by preventing Hannibal from pursuing the routed enemy as far as he would have wished. And, in addition to the losses sustained, the persistent rain and penetrating cold had also ravaged his camp; his men, but chiefly his horses, beasts of burden and the elephants, had been the chief victims of the dreadful weather, although our sources do not agree on the total number. Polybius (III, 74, 11, followed by Zonaras, VIII, 24) says that only one elephant remained; but Livy (XXI, 58, 11) holds that the Punic army still had a small troop of them, since according to him seven of those that had survived the Trebia were to perish a little later in the unfortunate attempt to cross the Apennines. But it would seem that this crossing of the Apennines in the middle of winter – highly improbable on the part of a wise strategist like Hannibal – is an invention of the Paduan historian.

## Overwintering in the Cisalpine region (January–April 217) and the first formulations of an Italian policy

In Rome, the page had just been turned on the calamitous year 218 with the election of the consuls who would come into office in March 217. As always, since this allocation was still statutory, the urns of the *comitia centuriata* had produced the name of one patrician, Cn. Servilius Geminus, scion of a very old family originating from Alba Longa, and one plebeian, but not a mere nobody, C. Flaminius Nepos.

The latter was by no means a newcomer to the head of the Roman state – far from it. As tribune of the plebs in 232, he had been the instigator of the allocation, to the advantage of the Roman popular class, of the *ager Picenus et Gallicus*, the territory on the Adriatic coast occupied before their expulsion by the Gaulish Senones. Since then, the début of his public life, he had been the bête noire of those aristocrats in the Senate who were accustomed to deriving vast profits from exploiting confiscated lands, and who were not at all pleased that members of the plebs should share them amongst themselves. Polybius, who espoused the point of view of the nobles, cannot find words harsh enough to denounce what he considers to be not only a demagogic but politically decadent attitude (II, 21, 8). Flaminius' career, however, had continued brilliantly. In 227, in the capacity of praetor, he was the first governor of the province of Sicily which had been newly added to Rome's possessions at the end of the first Punic War. His election to a first consulship in 223 had been the occasion of a scandal; the nobles had wanted to annul the election because Flaminius, like his colleague P. Furius Philus, had been elected contrary to the auspices. Then these same nobles had wanted to deny them the honours of a triumph against the Insubres, after the victory of the Adda, for not having taken notice of a letter sent to them by the Senate to stop them from engaging battle, as the auspices were unfavourable. The consuls had first won the fight, and read the letter afterwards – a memory that had not left the consul of 217! Shortly before Trasimene, his furious reply to one of his officers who informed him that, on striking camp, it had been impossible to pull a standard from the ground – a very bad omen – was: 'Don't you have a letter from the Senate to give me as well, forbidding me to do battle?' (Livy XXII, 3, 13.) That was enough to give him a reputation for bullheadedness. In 220, while still young, this 'new man' – the epithet applied in Rome to a leader with no family tree – had attained the position of censor; and it was a particularly outstanding censorship if, as Mommsen held, the censor of 220 (and his colleague L. Aemilius Papus) must be credited with the reform which, at that time, in the votes of the comitia, afforded a little more influence to the second-class citizens, thus diminishing the electoral weight of the 'rich'. At all events, the name of Flaminius would remain connected with two achievements of unequal importance but equal brilliance – the famous 'circus', dedicated to the plebs who held their assemblies there, in the southern part of the Campus Martius on the edge of the Tiber; and the Via Flaminia, the great strategic road laid out across the Apennines which, from Rome to Rimini, gave easy access to the north Adriatic. This was the eminent and controversial figure that Hannibal was to encounter along the way.

Unless there were exceptional circumstances, or one was pressed for time – and such had been the case for the Punic leader until the end of December 218 – it was customary in Antiquity for armies not to spend the winter campaigning. Apart from bad weather, the brief hours of daylight and the difficulty of keeping the men provisioned and the animals supplied with fodder discouraged operations. However, if we are to believe Livy, it would be hard to keep up with Hannibal, who seems not to have stayed put after his victory on the Trebia. In the Roman historian's account, he carried the battle to Placentia, where he was wounded (XXI, 57, 8), then several days later went to attack the township of Victumulae, some 140 kilometres distant as the crow flies. Nevertheless, after snatching a little rest for both himself and his men – though Livy does not say where – Hannibal is supposed to have wanted to lead his troops on to Etruria. But while trying to cross the Apennines, he was caught by such a terrible storm, of which the historian gives an apocalyptic description (XXI, 58), that he had no other alternative than to make a U-turn and come back to Placentia, there provoking Sempronius – who had returned from Rome – to combat (XXI, 59, 1–9). After this he withdrew to the Ligures (XXI, 59, 10). All this supposes covering considerable distances – some hundreds of kilometres – in the depths of winter and in the space of a few weeks, or three months at most. This is a really senseless fit of dashing about which is totally unlikely, and should not be admitted on the grounds that Cornelius Nepos and Zonaras follow the same absurd version as Livy.

It is far better to adhere to Polybius even if, in this instance, one has to read between the lines to some extent. One thing is certain: after his victory on the Trebia, Hannibal crossed the river with his army and occupied the comfortable and well-protected camp that Scipio had established on the heights of the right bank (III, 75, 2). Then, not long afterwards, he pushed on as far as Bologna, the capital of his allies the Boii, where he was sheltered from surprise attacks. Not all of them, however – and Livy tactfully (XXII, 1, 3), Polybius more smugly (III, 78, 1–4) – echo an anecdote generally rejected by historians because it seems incompatible with the dignity of a commander-in-chief, and above all too clearly inspired by a tradition mainly concerned with highlighting the famous 'Punic perfidy'. In order to foil conspiracies and attempts on his person, Hannibal is said to have resorted to a 'very Phoenician ruse' (the words *phoinikikon stratagèma* are used by Polybius). He had several wigs made, each suitable to the various stages of life, and wore them in turn, choosing appropriate dress each time; even those closest to him, it seems, had difficulty recognizing him. Perhaps it is one of these 'barber-shop stories' which Polybius usually left to others. But in the relations between the Carthaginians and their newly acquired Gaulish allies, it is a good illustration of the climate of mistrust that had followed the initial embraces.

Polybius naturally suggests Gaulish fickleness, another cliché. In fact, the Gauls had two grievances against the Carthaginian. They had noticed at the Trebia that, while concerned for the lives of his Africans, and even his Iberians, Hannibal had paid little attention to theirs, using them, especially the infantry, as pawns to be the first sacrificed to his tactical choices; undeniably, it was they who had paid the heaviest price for victory. Moreover, they were unhappy to see the war operations still taking place on their own territory, thus with no profit to themselves, and were extremely impatient to penetrate the lands of the allies in Etruria and Umbria, then to trample the *ager Romanus* itself and, under Hannibal's leadership, to repeat the exploit of the Allia, in the early fourth century; who knows, perhaps even to seize Rome. Hannibal was well aware of their expectations and knew that he would have to respond quickly. But for the moment he was mainly concerned with getting a message across to Rome's allies that would be clearly understood from afar.

The prisoners taken at the Ticinus and above all at the Trebia formed two quite distinct groups. The one containing Roman citizens did not have an easy time; their rations were calculated to the last ounce. In contrast, those from territories allied to Rome had the right to every sort of consideration, says Polybius (III, 77, 4). In the end Hannibal assembled them and addressed them: he had not come to make war on them, but on Rome, and his actions in Italy had the sole aim of restoring liberty to the peoples Rome had subjected, and handing back the territories Rome had confiscated. Reinforcing his words with deeds, he sent all these prisoners home without ransom. As we have seen, the surrender of Clastidium had been one of the first results of this policy; its success was now guaranteed.

## Between Emilia and Tuscany (spring 217)

Even before the consuls of 217 assumed office a whole range of military decisions had been taken in Rome, reflecting the growing sense of danger. The prodigies recorded that winter not only in Rome and Latium but also in Etruria and Picenum, even though reported by Livy (XXI, 62, 1) with well-bred positivism, impart the flavour of these fears. The war effort accomplished at that time was unprecedented. Eleven legions, totalling over 100,000 men, were brought under arms. However, not all were destined to go immediately to fight Hannibal. Two were despatched to protect Sicily, another to Sardinia, and two legions, known as 'urban', were raised with the mission of defending Rome. To these five legions were added the two that were already in Spain and, of course, the four consular legions that fought against the Punic army in December 218, whose numbers had to be made up after the enormous losses suffered. Such a war effort was very expensive, and on its own accounted for the devaluations that followed in rapid succession during the second Punic War. In 217, the coin known as the as, which had weighed half a pound since 225, no longer weighed more than a third. By reducing the weight of the bronze coinage on which the army's pay was calculated, the state cut down its expenditure. As has been pointed out (Picard, 1967, p. 171), this measure could not have gone down too badly with small landowners, who were always heavily in debt, as its result was to diminish the value of their debts. In essence, it was this peasantry that bore the burden of conscription.

The four legions engaged against Hannibal at the end of 218 had wintered in the Po Valley; two at Placentia, under the command of Ti. Sempronius Longus. Two others, at first placed under Scipio's command, then under the praetor C. Atilius when Scipio had gone to join his brother Gnaeus in Spain, with the title of proconsul, had been quartered at Cremona. This was done, says Livy (XXI, 56, 9), so that one of those colonies recently established in the Cisalpine region should not singlehandedly have to bear the burden of winter quarters for two armies. These were two safe strongholds: the Cenoman Celts, around Brescia, were making no move, and the Veneti of the lower Po Valley, loyal to Rome, ensured the provisioning of the two towns by way of the river. Hannibal, who had learnt his lesson at Saguntum, which had held him up for months, was anxious not to waste time on a siege. In any case, at the end of the winter the legions were set in motion. At Cremona, C. Atilius received orders to move out his two legions, going down the river and along the Adriatic coast to Rimini, where Servilius took over command. As for the other two, stationed at Placentia, if we follow Livy (XXI, 59, 10), it appears that Sempronius managed to lead them to Lucca, on the Tuscan coast, and thence to Arezzo, where Flaminius took over. The choice of these two 'stopper' positions would seem judicious; Servilius, at Rimini, barred an easy passage to the north of the Apennines and, at Arezzo, Flaminius was covering access through Etruria.

Hannibal did not risk taking the route of present-day Romagna, the flat land from Bologna towards Rimini, Pesaro, Ancona and the Adriatic shore. He knew that if he ventured there it would be easy for Flaminius, setting out from Arezzo, to join Servilius by the upper valley of the Tiber. The route he chose remains in part conjectural. Polybius (III, 78, 6) says that, after carefully gathering information, he decided to avoid the 'major roads', which were too long, and too easy for the Romans to monitor. But in fact hardly any roads existed at that time in upper Etruria; to suggest that he took the via Aurelia, which did not then go beyond the level of Volterra, or the Cassia, which as yet did not reach very far into Umbria from Rome, would presuppose that he had cleared the trickiest part of the route, the crossing of the Tuscan Apennines, then of Etruria as far as Fiesole, the only certain milestone quoted by our sources in the Carthaginian's progress southwards. According to our authors, Hannibal took the shortest way, across a marshy area flooded by a recent rise in the level of the Arno (Livy, XXII, 2, 2). It is generally believed that the Carthaginian chose the itinerary that, from Bologna, made him cross the Apennines by the col de Collina, a pass of modest altitude (952 metres), emerging at Pistoia. There began the boggy zone of the middle valley of the Arno, as far as the environs of Florence. Polybius and Livy use the same words, one in Greek, the other in Latin, to describe the sufferings endured in these marshes, where the water level allowed no camping. Hannibal's long column, with Mago and the Numidian cavalry bringing up the rear behind the Gauls, who were thus prevented from deserting or halting, filed through it for four days and three nights. The men sometimes snatched a few moments' rest, stretched out on the corpses of the pack animals to keep themselves out of the water. Although perched on the one remaining elephant, the general himself suffered greatly. The brutal variations in temperature during that rainy spring, the dampness of the marshes and the long periods without sleep weakened the resistance of the man of whom Livy had written that 'no fatigue could weaken his body or conquer his spirit' (XXI, 4, 5). Because he was unable to treat the ophthalmia he eventually contracted, he lost the sight of one eye in the Arno's marshlands. The image of the handsome, thoughtful and determined young man, whom Hamilcar's veterans had viewed with some emotion when he succeeded Hasdrubal four years earlier, would henceforth be superseded by another, which has come down through the centuries, of the 'one-eyed leader riding a Gaetulian elephant'. Hannibal had just reached the age of thirty.

## Trasimene (21 June 217)

The Carthaginian had emerged from the Arno's swamps near Fiesole before Flaminius, camped by Arezzo, got wind of his arrival. The Roman consul had thus let slip his one and only chance of acting on his own with some hope of success, which would have been to surprise the enemy on his exit from the mountains, or better still, from the marshes (Diana, 1987). Once the Punic army had recovered from its ordeals, its numerical superiority, notably as regards cavalry, would normally protect it from an attack before the two consuls could join forces. Hannibal knew this, and had also learnt enough about Flaminius to be able to judge the decisions of this arrogant man, who was very sensitive to public opinion. Descending southwards from Fiesole, he pillaged, sacked and set ablaze the whole rich region of Chianti, virtually under the nose of the Roman consul, who could not abide to stand idly by as the smoke of burning barns and harvests billowed into the skies of the Etruscan countryside. It was a sight hard to endure for a ruler who, from the outset of his career, had built his reputation on agrarian policy. Leaving his encampment, Flaminius began to follow Hannibal's army, looking out for a favourable chance to attack him. When Hannibal had turned into the Val di Chiana, looking as though he were heading for Rome, Flaminius went towards Cortona; but all of a sudden the Carthaginian bore eastwards, in the direction of Perugia, leaving the mountains of Cortona on his left. One evening at the end of June, Flaminius saw the enemy army disappearing into the narrow gorge that opened up east of Borghetto between the north shore of Lake Trasimene and the foothills of Monte Gualandro (Figure 5).

Once past the defile of Borghetto, the small coastal plain of Tuoro opens out over about two or three kilometres until it is once more enclosed, to the east just before Passignano, by the heights of Montigeto. Beyond, in Antiquity – for the waters have since receded considerably – the hills overhanging the lake, as at Borghetto, left only a very narrow path along the shore, as far as Torricella, until the road cut south-east towards Perugia. There Hannibal set a real rat-trap, which people have tried to reconstruct, with some variants, on the basis of concordant but rather summary indications in Polybius (III, 83) and Livy (XXII, 4).

Having entered the Borghetto defile, Hannibal had gone through the little coastal plain of Tuoro and set up his camp behind the heights of Montigeto. There he had formed an ambush with his soundest troops, the Africans and Iberians. The light infantry – pikemen and Balearic slingers – covered the slopes of the hills facing the lake, on the Vernazzano side. Lastly, on a level with Tuoro, the Gauls and, just after the exit from the Borghetto defile, the cavalry, all duly concealed, closed this hoop-net into which the Roman consul and his army would blindly hurl themselves. This is the reconstruction proposed by De Sanctis (III, 2, 1917, pp. 109–15), which to me seems to take better account of the data supplied by our sources than that of Kromayer (1912, pp. 150–93, followed by Lazenby, 1978, p. 63), which shifts the entire arrangement east of Montigeto and places the location of this gigantic ambush between this site and that of Torricella. More recently, by considerably restricting the boundaries of the battlefield, attempts have been made to localize it in the small 'Conca di Tuoro', that is, only in the western part of the coastal plain, in which Tuoro occupies almost the centre. But the tens of thousands of men – to say nothing of the cavalry – of the combined Punic and Roman forces could hardly have found elbow room in this narrow space, in a crush that would have prevented any progress; and in any case the analysis of the *ustrina* found on the site and deemed to hold the incinerated remains of the battle's victims leaves some doubt over the matter (Susini, 1960, 1964).

When Flaminius had seen Hannibal swallowed up in the Borghetto pass, he had set up camp late in the evening very close by, on the lake shore. At dawn the next day – according to Ovid (*Fasti*, VI, 767–8), 21 June, the summer solstice, a date to which we will adhere rather than an earlier one in the spring, which was recently

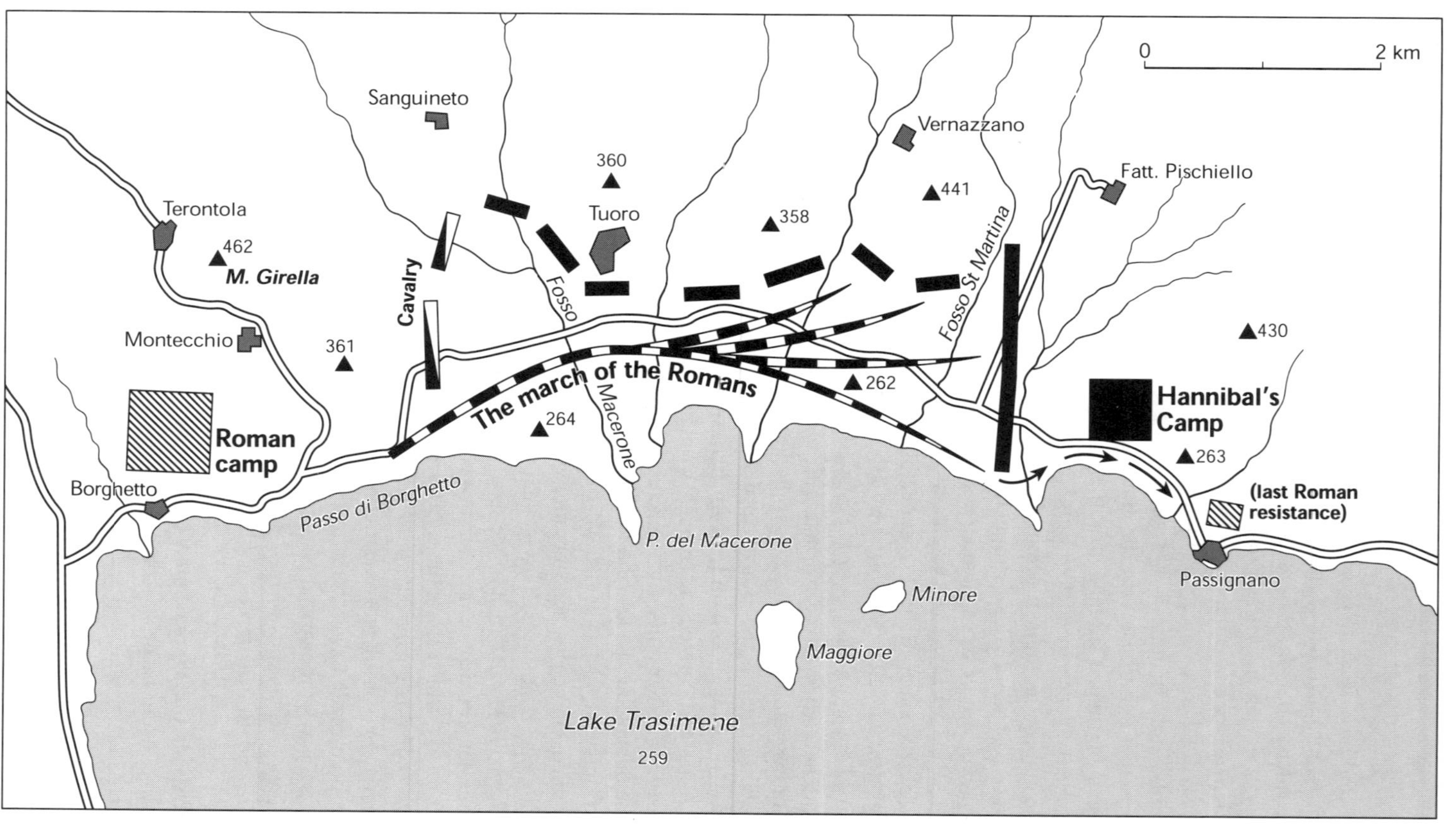


**Figure 5** The battle of Trasimene (from De Sanctis, 1917, summarized by Carcopino, 1961b)

defended in view of the provisioning requirements of the Punic army during the summer of 217 (Desy, 1989) – the consul advanced with his army into the Borghetto pass without sending scouts ahead. In the early morning, a thick mist rising from the lake obscured its shores. When the bulk of the Roman column was committed into the small shoreside plain, at the moment when the advance guard came into contact with his Africans and Iberians, Hannibal gave all his ambush units the signal to attack. The poor visibility, which thwarted all the efforts of the officers – centurions and tribunes – to get the column into battle order quickly, increased the chaos. In the space of three hours, Flaminius witnessed the death of 15,000 men all around him. He himself fell, stricken by a Gaulish lance. Livy (XXII, 6, 3–4) states precisely that it was an Insubrian horseman named Ducarius who, in piercing him with his lance, offered him as an expiatory victim to the shades of his companions-at-arms wiped out by the consul on the banks of the Adda in 223. Probably the worst fate befell the troops of the Roman rearguard, who had just been in time to enter the Borghetto defile without being able to emerge on to the Tuoro plain. Forced back into the lake by the Punic cavalry, the soldiers drowned, weighed down by their armour, or were massacred by the horsemen in the water. Of the entire consular army, only about 6,000 men of the advance guard, who had been able to pierce the wall formed by the Africans and Iberians, managed to escape the net and, once they had reached the heights and the fog had cleared, were able to measure the extent of the disaster. Regrouping, they took refuge close by, near Lake Plestia, where Maharbal, who had been sent in their pursuit with the Iberians and pikemen, took them prisoner shortly afterwards (Alfieri, 1986).

Regarding these prisoners taken by Maharbal, Livy dishonestly attacks Punic 'bad faith' (*Punica religio*: XXII, 6, 12). For, contrary to what he says, Maharbal had not promised them their freedom if they surrendered their arms, but only their lives. And, publicly re-establishing the prerogatives that he held by virtue of his position as supreme commander of the army, Hannibal assembled them with the other prisoners – 15,000 men in all – and explained to them that, in any case, his lieutenant did not have the authority to make them promises. And true to form, he divided the prisoners into two groups. The Romans were entrusted to the guard of various units; as for the allies, before sending them home without ransom, he repeated for their benefit the themes he had already expounded to the captives of the Ticinus and Trebia: he had not come to wage war on the Italians, but rather to restore to them a liberty that had been confiscated by Rome.

Furthermore, Hannibal was careful to render funeral honours not only to his own men – his losses were fairly slight, about 1,500 men, most of whom were Gauls – but also to the chief officers of the Roman army. To this end he had a search made for the body of Flaminius – in vain, says Livy. And it was all the more astonishing because Hannibal carefully collected all the weapons scattered with the corpses over the battlefield; we shall see that he used these chiefly to re-equip his Africans in Roman style. This collection supposes a meticulous search over a fairly limited area. The vain quest for the remains of Flaminius recently suggested an ingenious explanation. As we saw, it was a Gaul who had killed the consul, one of those Gauls whose custom was to keep the heads of their enemies as trophies. And what more precious trophy could there be than the consul's head? Once decapitated, and of course similarly despoiled of its prestigious armour, the body had become anonymous (Brizzi, 1984b, pp. 35–43).

## A summer on the Adriatic

To complete the disaster, Maharbal, dispatched by Hannibal soon afterwards with the cavalry, went ahead to meet the 4,000 horsemen sent as reinforcements by Servilius, as he had not been able to join Flaminius in time. Those who escaped death in an initial engagement came to swell the number of captives.

In Rome consternation reigned. It had fallen to the *praetor peregrinus*, M. Pomponius Matho, from the height of the rostra to admit the defeat to the bewildered throng who had massed in the forum and besieged the curia. Apart from the vastly traumatic effect on a population that had long been unaccustomed to reverses, the political situation was unprecedented. Of the two consuls, one was dead and the other, Servilius, had kept his forces intact, except for his cavalry, but he was blocked at Rimini and cut off from all communication. Such a situation called for exceptional measures, and we shall soon see what they were.

Did Hannibal at that point have the idea of marching on Rome? Livy says nothing about it and Polybius (III, 86, 8) states that he judged that the right moment had not yet arrived, which is most probably the case. The town was protected by Servius' defence wall, originally erected in the middle of the sixth century, but enlarged and notably strengthened after the terrible fear that the Gauls had caused in 390, and the demonstration they had given of the weakness of its defences when they occupied the lower town. Shortly afterwards, in 378, the censors had ordered the reconstruction of the wall with large bonded blocks of tufa from Grotta Oscura in Etruria. In the era we are now discussing, it followed a line eleven kilometres long, punctuated by flanking towers and enclosing over 400 hectares, which made it the biggest defence wall in the whole of the Italian peninsula. At its weakest points, that is, on its eastern flank between the Colline Gate and the Caelimontana Gate, the wall properly speaking was matched both internally and externally by a powerful fortification: on the town side, a broad earthfill, the *agger*, sloped gently up towards the top of the wall and formed a platform on which defenders could circulate and manoeuvre; on the side of open country, a trench was dug to a depth of nearly ten metres. To lay siege to Rome was no easy matter. It required a good deal of mechanical equipment, which first had to be procured, or rather, constructed. Even supposing Hannibal had the desire, the undertaking would have kept the Punic army busy for months, more probably years, turning a war of mobility, in which Hannibal's lively and imaginative strategy had the best chances of success, into a static war that carried the risk of handing back the advantage to the military potential of Rome, which was as yet scarcely tapped. And there was also a strong risk that the ferments of rebellion which had begun to seethe among the people of 'Latin name' might subside.

Hannibal would not have forgotten his dream at Onussa, before leaving Spain, over a year before. The devastating serpent – the long column of the Punic army – had to be allowed to spread its coils over Italian soil, sacking the countryside, provoking in Rome the overwhelming obligation to come to the aid of its allies, and thus providing the Carthaginian with many opportunities for fresh victories; or, if not, compelling Rome to confess its inability to defend them. Moreover, this army needed to become fit again, for its comfortless wintering near Bologna had brought it little rest after so many ordeals. Animals and men suffered from the lack of various necessities, and nearly all were afflicted by, among other things, what Polybius terms the 'itch of hunger' *limopsoros*: III, 87, 2). After Trasimene, the Punic general had passed through Umbria, by way of Perugia and Foligno, where he crossed the Via Flaminia. But there – not at Spoleto, as Livy says (XXII, 9, 1–2), implying that he was going to descend upon Rome – he veered fully eastwards to go down the Chianti Valley and emerge on the rich plains of Picenum. Ten days later, he reached the Adriatic coast, so laden with booty that his troops could hardly transport all that had fallen into his hands (Polybius, III, 86, 9–10).

It was the first time that the Punic army had seen the sea since leaving the shores of the Spanish Levant. Frequently changing the sites of his camp, Hannibal remained on the Adriatic coast, between Picenum and Apulia. It was a land of Cockaigne, where the horses especially benefited. They were bathed in old wine, says Polybius (III, 88, 1), to cure them of their itching skin; an application of oenology that Livy preferred to ignore – was it a scandalous waste, in his eyes? The wounded recovered and all regained their vigour. At the same time as sending a series of messages concerning the most recent events by sea to Carthage, Hannibal re-equipped his Africans Roman-style with the armour and weapons taken from the enemy, doubtless with the *scutum* in particular, the long shield in the form of an ovoid rectangle, which afforded much more protection than the *cetra*. Livy (XXII, 46, 4) would say that at Cannae, with this equipment, it was difficult to distinguish between the African and Roman heavy infantry. With his troops invigorated, the horses sated with fodder, Hannibal resumed his destructive march, ravaging the territory of Hadria, a colony with Latin rights, then that of the Marrucini and the Frentani, forging ahead without opposition as far as Luceria, another Latin colony, and Arpi in Apulia. It was up to Rome to react.

## Q. Fabius Maximus, the general who bided his time

On several occasions during its history, in the hour of danger or simply because the temporary unavailability of the consuls allowed no other solution, Rome had resorted to an exceptional magistracy, limited in time but furnished with full civil and, above all, military powers – the dictatorship. The difficulty in this particular case was that normally the dictator would be appointed by one of the consuls. Now, at the end of June 217, Flaminius was dead and Servilius could not get in touch with the capital. Therefore, an unprecedented event, the matter of electing a dictator had to be left to the *comitia centuriata*, in other words, the people. The choice fell on Q. Fabius Maximus Verrucosus. Twice consul, in 233 and 228, censor in 230, this descendant of an old patrician family – whatever Polybius may think (III, 87, 6), he took from his ancestor Fabius Rullianus the surname Maximus, acquired at the time of the wars against the Samnites – had been a supporter of negotiation with Carthage until the eve of the declaration of war, as we saw earlier (above, p. 52). But the Carthaginians with whom this prudent and wise man would have liked to deal were the Barcids' adversaries; for him Hannibal could be no more than an enemy, and there could be no question of coming to terms with him. The custom was for the dictator himself to choose as adjutant or chief of staff a 'master of cavalry'. But – and here was an equally unprecedented event – it was the people in the *comitia* who appointed, at the same time as the dictator, the master of cavalry in the person of M. Minucius Rufus, a consul in 221, who had distinguished himself in Illyria. As Fabius and Minucius belonged to different, not to say hostile, clans in the Senate, the compromise solution that issued from the voting urns in itself bore the seeds of a future conflict.

The dictator's first concerns were of a religious nature. On taking up office, Fabius convened the Senate, emphasizing that Flaminius' offhandedness with regard to the auspices had probably been more deadly to him than his imprudence. And it was true that in this matter the consul had been something of a recidivist. Prior to Trasimene, he had paid little heed to those signs in which a good Roman could always recognize a divine warning. There had been the well-known affair of the standard that could not be budged from the ground: 'Get it out with a pickaxe', Flaminius had ordered. Shortly before, his horse had suddenly fallen, causing him to hit the ground himself; he had carried on regardless. So a reconciliation with the gods was very necessary. After consulting the Sibylline Books, it was decided to renew with greater solemnity the vow made to the god Mars, and to dedicate a temple to the Erycinian Venus, pledged by the dictator himself. This last gesture was highly significant; Fabius was placing the state under the protection of the goddess of Eryx, whose sanctuary the Roman armies had solidly held during the war in Sicily (above, p. 3). Lastly, the Pontifex Maximus, L. Cornelius Lentulus, submitted to the people the pledge of a 'sacred spring' (*ver sacrum*) of which Livy (XXII, 10 2–6) has preserved the text for us. This was one of the most original features of Roman religion. If the promise, in this instance the safety of Rome and victory over Carthage, was realized in a specific time-span, a pledge was made to sacrifice to the deity the entire production of the following spring. In its fullest form, in Rome's earliest days, the rite had probably included in the sacrifice not only young animals, but also human offspring, and here there is perhaps a curious link with the *molk* sacrifice practised in the tophet at Carthage, that so horrified both Greeks and Romans (Lancel, 1995a, pp. 254–6). It is true that in Rome, during this *ver sacrum*, between the kalends of March and May, sacrifices were confined to the young of sheep, goats, pigs and cows. And very soon the involvement of humans in this ritual had been ingeniously diverted towards colonial expansion. When the animals were slaughtered, a group of young men, sometimes in the company of a totemic animal, left the town to go and set up a new foundation, where Rome would expand with them (Heurgon, 1957).

Next, the conduct of the war demanded all Fabius' attention. With the Senate's agreement, he raised two legions, ordering the conscripts to assemble at Tibur (Tivoli), near Rome. Then, leaving to join Servilius, he made contact with him at Narnia and took command of his two consular legions. Turning south again and picking up the recruits from Tibur *en route*, he regained the Via Latina by way of Praeneste (Palestrina) and, accompanied by his second-in-command, led the other combined legions towards Apulia. At the same time, Fabius had issued an edict, a decision which had been difficult to take and which, even before the operation of his famous delaying tactics, clearly showed that the dictator was not afraid to run the risk of unpopularity. He ordered exposed and defenceless places to be evacuated, says Livy (XXII, 11, 4–5), the evacuated populaces to be resettled and, chiefly, a scorched-earth policy to be strictly applied wherever Hannibal was likely to pass.

Having reached Apulia, Fabius took up a position at Aeclae (Troja), not far from the Punic camp, which was established at Vibinum (Bovino). The dictator refused to accept the offer of combat made to him by Hannibal. The Carthaginian struck camp, followed at a distance by the Roman, who needed all his sangfroid to resist the incessant provocation. It is not always easy to follow the exact itinerary of this 'hare and hounds' pursuit, which took place mainly in Samnite territory, with an incursion into Campania (Alvisi, 1974, pp. 293–313). Hannibal ravaged the region of Benevento, seized Telesia, then by way of Cales entered Campania north of the valley of the Volturnus. He and his troops were now on the soil which produced the already famous Falernian wine, in the heart of one of Italy's richest agricultural regions. There, the dictator needed a strength of mind worthy of ancient standards in order not to depart from the tactics he had adopted, to which he was finding it increasingly difficult to make his master of cavalry, Minucius, adhere: moving in parallel with the enemy, remaining on the high ground, sidestepping an actual engagement but nibbling away little by little at the enemy forces by raids on groups of soldiers who ventured too far from their camp in search of plunder. Was it possible to remain a spectator on the heights of Monte Massico – north of Capua – when all around the smoke was rising from burning farms, when in the autumn at the height of the grape harvest the roots of the vines that made the fortune of the Roman colonists in Campania were systematically cut and destroyed? To make matters worse, Fabius was a victim of the wiliness of the Carthaginian, to whom deserters had pointed out land that belonged to the dictator; Hannibal had the surrounding area razed, ostentatiously avoiding the Roman's property; then he spread the rumour that his selective clemency was a reward for secret dealings (Livy, XXI, 23, 4).

Fabius certainly had no need of this treachery to find himself in difficulties. Not everyone in Rome understood his attitude. In his concern not to jeopardize at one stroke the military potential available to him, some people affected to see in his delaying tactics nothing more than weakness, or even cowardice; they dragged up the nickname *Ovicula*, 'little ewe', that had been given to him in his childhood (Plutarch, *Fabius*, 1, 4–5). He was increasingly challenged from within his army and Livy (XXII, 14) reports that, in sight of the flames that ravaged the territory of the colony of Sinuessa, he was only a hair's-breadth away from a mutiny encouraged by an impassioned address from Minucius. However, one day in autumn 217, Fabius really believed he was going to reap the fruits of his patient observation of the enemy's actions. Through his spies he had learnt that Hannibal was making ready to return to Apulia to spend the season of bad weather, rich with the booty he had amassed throughout the summer. Anticipating him, the dictator had blocked his passage through the Volturnus valley by occupying Casilinum, near Capua. At the same time, he had sent Minucius to guard the narrow crossing of the Via Appia north of Sinuessa. Hannibal's only way out of Campania was through the restricted valley of Callicula, north of Cales. There Fabius went to set up his camp; he posted 4,000 men in the defile, taking up position himself with the bulk of his troops on an eminence that commanded the entry to the pass. But the Punic leader had swiftly assessed the situation and, to foil the trap that had been laid for him, resorted to a ruse which he had perhaps already tried out in the Alps. He had Hasdrubal collect the largest possible quantity of dry wood, which was bound into faggots that were attached to the horns of 2,000 oxen taken from the livestock seized as booty. Very late in the night, these animals were driven towards the high ground dominating the pass, and the faggots were ignited. Deceived by all these lights, the soldiers guarding the defile rushed up the hills. The way was clear for the Punic army, which went through almost without meeting any opposition.

Hannibal returned to Apulia after a slight detour among the Peligni, in the north of Samnite territory. For overwintering, his choice fell on Gereonium, a small town that had been abandoned by its inhabitants in the valley of the Fortorus, which was to be the scene of the last war episodes of 217, at least in Italy. Recalled to Rome for religious ceremonies, Fabius had left Minucius in command, exhorting him to be prudent; it was no small achievement, he told him, to have stopped being beaten by an enemy who had so many times been the victor (Livy, XXII, 18, 10). But Minucius wanted a victory. Failing this, he gained a semi-success at Gereonium – losses more or less balanced out between the two sides – which in Rome the clan hostile to Fabius transformed into a real victory.

A clique had gone into action in favour of granting Minucius the same powers as those of Fabius. Before the people, the tribune of the plebs Marcus Metilius threw down the gauntlet and demanded that a plebiscite should grant the master of cavalry and dictator equal powers. In the Senate, and apparently in accord with Fabius, it was thought that the political game needed cooling down and that the ground should be cut from under this manoeuvring by re-establishing the consuls' normal authority. Servilius was a long way away – we shall see that he was at the time at sea in the Syrtis Minor – but he was still in office. To replace the dead Flaminius, the *comitia centuriata* assembled by Fabius elected M. Atilius Regulus 'suffect consul', one of the sons of the great Regulus, the unlucky hero of the first Punic War. But in the popular camp, opposition was still unrelenting. Largely owing to the commitment of someone whom I shall soon have occasion to mention again, C. Terentius Varro, the plebiscite was adopted. Henceforth there were two dictators, and the problem of sharing the command between them. Back in Apulia, Fabius accepted that the army should be split between the two of them, and Minucius even went to the length of establishing a separate camp.

This was a fine chance for Hannibal to put the boldness of the master of cavalry to the test. Between their two camps, which were quite close, stood a hill that the Punic general decided to make use of in his tactics. Lacking vegetation, the valley of the Fortorus did not lend itself to ambushes, but Hannibal had discovered rocky recesses and even a few caverns in the folds of the terrain. There, in groups of 200 or 300 men, he posted 5,000 footsoldiers and 5,000 horsemen. Then, at first light he had the hill occupied by light troops. It seemed easy to Minucius to conquer this position. He sent in his *velites*, or skirmishers, and next his cavalry and, as Hannibal was sending reinforcements, he advanced with his two legions in battle order. It was then that the soldiers who had been placed in ambush emerged from hiding, catching them from the rear, and placing them in great danger. Fabius in his turn had to come out to restore the fortunes of war. Hannibal stopped the fight.

Even more than Polybius (III, 105, 8–11), Livy (XXII, 30) wanted to bring to a happy conclusion the events of the summer and autumn of 217 which, after causing Rome to tremble, had shattered the cohesiveness of the republic. According to him, Minucius was gracious enough to make honourable amends to the dictator, refusing the very title that he had so desired without deserving it, and burying the bitter memory of the dispute beneath an almost filial homage. One realizes that Livy was an unconditional admirer of Fabius, to the point of having played down, with a certain amount of bias, the real though limited success won by Minucius at the time of the first engagement at Gereonium (Vallet, 1962). All the same, it has to be admitted that the lessons in caution he had given him did not go down well; it was all too dull, and too frustrating to the taste for triumph that the people expected from their generals. The nickname *Cunctator*, which seems to us part and parcel of his name, was never applied in his lifetime to Q. Fabius Maximus, and it could never have been an official title, a *cognomen ex virtute*, as the word itself contained more darkness than light (Rebuffat, 1983). Acknowledging the death of Fabius in 203, shortly before Zama, Livy (XXX, 26, 9) recalls the line of Ennius who, in a succinct phrase, had fixed for all time the rather special place occupied by Fabius in the pantheon of the greatest Romans: *Unus homo nobis cunctando restituit rem* ('One man alone, by his delaying tactics, re-established our situation'). Ennius' *Annals* are dated to 168 or 167; it had taken two generations for a statue to be erected to Q. Fabius Maximus.

## Operations outside Italy

Whether or not Hannibal would lose the war in Italy was a serious question. Looking ahead, one might say that he would lose it in Italy through having lost it in Spain.

Remember (above, p. 69) that, in August 218, giving up the pursuit of Hannibal who had crossed the Rhône and turned northwards, P. Cornelius Scipio had entrusted his two legions to his brother Gnaeus, with the mission of leading them to Spain. He had reached Emporion (Ampurias) and established his rear base there. Making successive landings along the coastline of present-day Catalonia, then advancing deep into the hinterland, he had, by arms but mostly by diplomacy, rapidly won over to the Roman cause a large part of the population of north-eastern Spain, from the Lacetani, at the foot of the Pyrenees, as far as the north bank of the Ebro (Polybius, III, 76; Livy, XXI, 60, 1–4). The troops which Hannibal, before crossing the Pyrenees, had left under Hanno's command took up their position at that time facing the Romans, not far from the fortified town of Kissa, perhaps in the region of Lérida. Scipio easily defeated them and, among other booty, seized the heavy equipment which Hannibal had jettisoned before leaving for Gaul.

Even before he had learnt of the Punic defeat north of the Ebro, Hasdrubal, whom his brother had left to guard Spain south of the river, had crossed it with a relief army. He arrived too late, and had to be content with surprising and massacring the crews of the Roman ships who were off guard. Then, while Cn. Scipio went to make his winter quarters at Tarragona, Hasdrubal, before rejoining his camp at Cartagena, busied himself with strengthening the protection of fortified towns situated south of the Ebro.

During the winter of 218–217, Hasdrubal made serviceable the thirty ships available to him, and fitted out ten others. While his admiral, Himilco, navigated them along the coast, he himself with his army advanced in parallel in the direction of the Ebro. The Carthaginian fleet was moored at the mouth of the river when it was surprised by Scipio's vessels, led by two warships from Marseille acting as pilots (Polybius, III, 95–6; Livy, XXII, 19). This naval battle on the Ebro resulted in severe losses for Carthage. Twenty-five ships had been captured, and henceforth the Roman fleet was in control of the coast, from Catalonia to the Spanish Levant. One squadron even pushed as far as Ibiza, where a delegation of Baleares came to seek Scipio, suing for peace.

In Carthage, where it was well understood that to allow Rome to be the sole naval presence in the Mediterranean would be catastrophic, the response was to arm seventy ships which, having landed at Sardinia, arrived in sight of the Italian coast near Pisa during the summer of 217, with the hope of linking up with Hannibal's army. Near Cosa, on the Etruscan coast, they had already intercepted Roman trading vessels taking supplies to the army in Spain (Livy, XXII, 11, 6). They were immediately pursued by the 120 quinqueremes of which the surviving consul of 217, Cn. Servilius, had taken command after handing over his legions to Q. Fabius Maximus. Better at manoeuvring, they escaped, but had to return to Carthage. Cn. Servilius continued his naval display, making for Africa after a landfall at Lilybaeum in Sicily. He went down as far as the Cercina isles (Kerkenna), from whose inhabitants he exacted a ransom, then, heading back towards Sicily, he seized Kossyra (Pantelleria) in passing. It was clear to Carthage that times had certainly changed; Rome now well and truly dominated the high seas.

It lost no time in taking advantage of the fact. His command having been extended by the granting of a proconsulship, Publius Scipio set sail with a whole armada, landed at Tarragona with 8,000 soldiers and joined his brother Gnaeus. In this summer of 217, Hasdrubal was busy repelling the Celtiberi who had attacked the western marches of Punic Spain. The two Scipios profited from this to cross the Ebro – this was a first for the Roman side – then proceed along the coast of the Spanish Levant. Reaching Saguntum, they did not attack it but came to terms with a notable of the town to have the hostages from various Spanish towns who were held there handed over, making use of the naivety of the fortified town's Punic commander, a man named Bostar (Polybius, III, 98–9; Livy, XXII, 22). Thereupon, as the season of bad weather had arrived, the two brothers retired to their winter quarters north of the Ebro with the feeling that they had prepared the ground well for the reconquest of the South.

## Cannae (2 August 216)

Early in 216, the time had come in Rome for the annual elections to magistracies. In the choice of consuls, the first name to emerge from the urns was that of C. Terentius Varro, elected at the first round. In the preceding autumn, he had supported the proposal to place another dictator, in the person of Minucius, alongside Q. Fabius Maximus. Varro was a 'new man', of modest origins, but Livy, who detested him, has no hesitation in saying that those origins 'were not only humble, but base' (*non humili solum, sed etiam sordido loco ortus*: XXII, 25, 19). His father would appear to have been a butcher, and a retail butcher at that, who employed his son on his stall! Naturally, this was not very likely; but when one knows the contempt of the Roman ruling classes for the small trader – see Cicero, *De officiis*, I, 150–1 – one grasps the import of the remark.

To restore the balance in the face of this plebeian consul, the senatorial nobility put forward the name of Aemilius Paullus, who was somewhat unwilling but in the end easily elected. L. Aemilius Paullus was a descendant of one of Rome's oldest families. Consul in 219, he had won renown in Illyria and had been part of the embassy which declared war on Carthage (above, p. 52). Under the authority of these two consuls were placed the two of 217, Cn. Servilius and M. Atilius Regulus, with the title of proconsuls and therefore with full *imperium* (in other words, full responsibility of command on the field of battle). There was a need for generals to command the army corps that a further war effort had set up; eight legions, although Livy (XXII, 36 1–2) seems to have difficulty in believing this. Moreover, they were legions with greater strength, comprising 5,000 infantry and 300 cavalry, instead of 4,000 and 200 respectively. If allied contingents are added – the same number of footsoldiers and double the number of horsemen – the total of 87,200 men is reached, which is indicated by Livy, and confirmed by Polybius with slightly less precision (the Greek merely says 'eight legions', III, 107, 9). This truly enormous figure – never had so many men been engaged by one side on a field of battle in Antiquity – has sometimes been challenged by modern critics (for example, De Sanctis, 1917, pp. 131–3). Nevertheless, Aemilius Paullus, addressing his troops before they left on campaign, was careful to encourage them by telling them that they would be fighting two to one, and we shall see that Hannibal's forces numbered nearly 50,000 men.

These, then, were the forces that on the Roman side were ready to be deployed on the ground, and these were the generals who would command them. At the highest level was the inharmonious team of the two men who were divided by almost everything. The electoral campaign for the consular elections had been violent, and throughout there had been an undercurrent of bitter hostility by the popular party against the nobles, whom its spokesmen openly accused of deliberately dragging on the war against Hannibal, and even of having brought him into Italy (Livy, XXII, 34, 4). And once he was elected consul, before taking up his command of the armies, Varro had publicly resumed the same grievances (XXII, 38, 6). These exacerbated struggles for a power that had to be shared could only accentuate the split that had already been apparent earlier in those unevenly matched pairs responsible for the previous engagements: P. Cornelius Scipio and Ti. Sempronius Longus in 218, then Cn. Servilius Geminus and C. Flaminius Nepos until June 217, followed by Fabius and Minucius. Now there was a further aggravating factor since, the two consuls having joined forces, the question of the alternate possession of the fasces – the twelve fasces that were the formidable symbol of the *imperium* of each man – conferred supreme authority, now on one, now on the other, over this immense army. In peacetime, the alternation was monthly, but on campaign, it became daily! In these conditions, and above all if the two commanders-in-chief held divergent views on how the war should be conducted, consular collegiality became an empty term. On the day of the battle of Cannae, it was Varro's turn to exercise command. He therefore bore the responsibility for the disaster. But what would Aemilius Paullus have done in his place? By his very presence the other consul was involved in the strategy – if it can be called that – which had been employed.

In a little exhortatory speech to Aemilius Paullus which he ascribes to Q. Fabius Maximus, and by which he establishes a kind of spiritual kinship between the old dictator and the consul, Livy (XXII, 39) reveals another strategic choice, supposed to be that of Fabius and probably also of at least part of the senatorial nobility. It should be enough to encircle Hannibal with the formidable barrier of those tens of thousands of soldiers, reduce him to the state of siege victim within the walls of

Gereonium, and condemn him to starve to death in that little corner of Apulia: in short, to be content to do what Atilius Regulus and Servilius Geminus had done, when left facing Hannibal during the winter of 217–216 and acting in concert, achieving a success that was certain, even if modest (Livy, XXII, 32, 1–3; Polybius, III, 106, 8–11). All very well, but with hindsight it was easier to have a better perception of the situation.

Early in the summer Hannibal, short of provisions at Gereonium, decided to go farther south to a region where a warmer climate hastened the ripening of harvests. His choice fell on the small fortified town of Cannae, on the banks of the Aufidus (present-day Ofanto), where he knew moreover that the Romans stored grain and other farm produce from the countryside around Canusium (Canosa); lands whose richness was proverbial in Antiquity, especially for the quality of its sheep, whose highly renowned wool was at a premium on the market. He set up his camp with his back towards the wind known today in Italy as the *libeccio*, so that the Romans would receive its dust-laden gusts full in the face.

At the end of July, the Roman army came in sight of the enemy troops and set up a first camp some ten kilometres north-west of the position they were occupying, not far from Salapia (Polybius, III, 10, 1). Soon afterwards, Varro made a move to approach the Punic camp and the Roman troops, attacked in marching order, were put in danger from the enemy cavalry. The next day, Aemilius Paullus fortified two camps, one on either side of the Aufidus. Hannibal crossed the river, transferred his camp to the left bank, the side where the larger of the two Roman camps lay, and two days later brought out all his men to offer battle to the Roman army. Aemilius Paullus, who was in command on that day, kept silent, to the great displeasure of his colleague who was, in addition, exasperated by the provocation of the Numidians whose tactics of harassment rendered water-collection duties on the bank of the Aufidus extremely difficult (Polybius, III, 112; Livy, XXII, 45, 1–4).

The next day, 2 August, the handing over of the fasces gave the initiative back to Varro. At sun-up, he in his turn brought out the troops from the big camp and, crossing the river, placed them in battle order on the right bank together with those from the small camp, forming a continuous front facing south (Figure 6). Aemilius Paullus followed for, as Livy says, even if he did not approve he could hardly refuse his help; but he left 10,000 of his troops – one legion and the corresponding allied contingent – to guard the big camp (Polybius, III, 117, 8), which enabled those men who were taken prisoner to avoid the massacre. The development chosen by Varro was as follows: on the right wing, the Roman cavalry – 2,400 men – under the command of Aemilius Paullus, who also commanded an infantry legion and an equal contingent of allied footsoldiers on the same wing. The left wing was under Varro in person who, besides the allied cavalry, commanded two freshly recruited legions, coupled with an equal number – 10,000 men – of allies fighting on foot. The heavy infantry placed in the centre was entrusted to Servilius Geminus and Atilius Regulus.

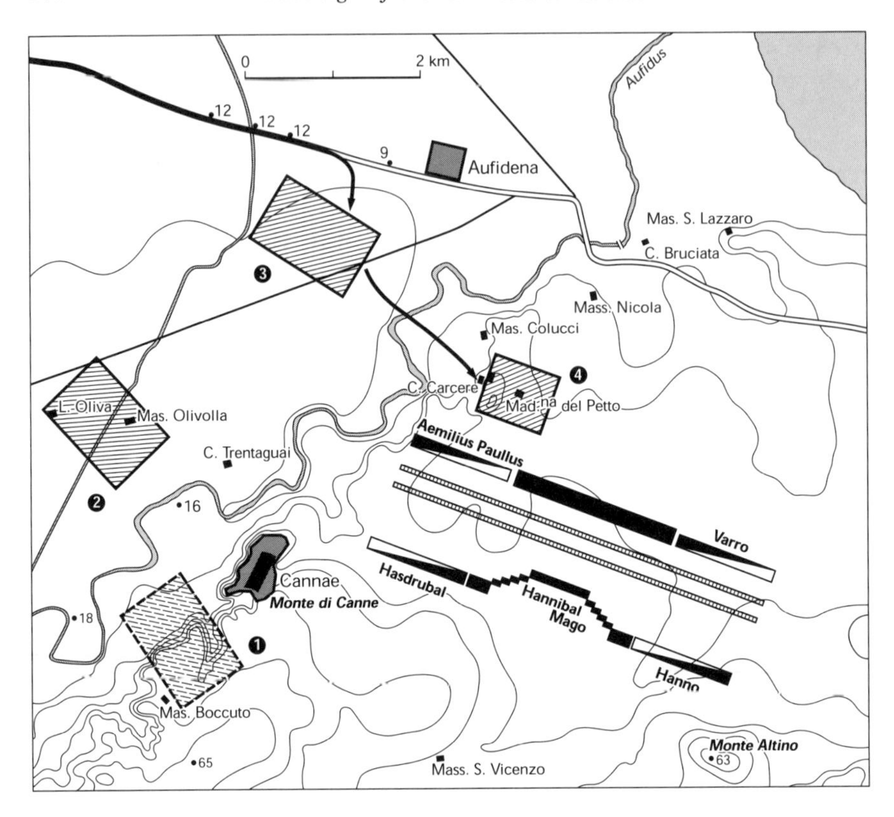


**Figure 6** The Punic and Roman battle order at Cannae: (1) Hannibal's first camp; (2) Hannibal's second camp; (3) main Roman camp; (4) small Roman camp (from Kromayer, 1912)

Polybius (III, 113, 3) noted that, unlike the customary disposition, Varro had lined up the infantry leaving only very narrow gaps between the maniples. Each maniple – the tactical unit of legionary infantry – moreover, presented a narrower than usual front in relation to a depth that is estimated by a great expert on the Roman army of that period to have been about fifty men classically placed in three ranks (Brizzi, 1984a, p. 43). This infantry therefore formed a massive battle corps, a real battering-ram which Hannibal, as we shall see, was able to channel, using its forward thrust to his own advantage. The *velites*, armed with light javelins (the *veruta*), who traditionally engaged in the preliminaries of combat, formed a slim continuous line ahead of the front.

Hannibal first observed how Varro had arranged his troops before ordering his Baleares and light infantry to cross the river; these spread out widely, forming a light protective shield along the front line. Although he had the advantage of a cavalry vastly superior in number – around 10,000 men – he had far fewer footsoldiers, some 40,000 men. He could not, therefore, oppose the Roman infantry with a battle corps of equal strength, and as he had to stretch his front-line to match that of the enemy front, in order to avoid any risk of being surrounded, his line of battle or *acies*, as it was called in Latin, consequently had less depth and less resistance. But his tactical genius realized how to turn this weakness into a strength.

The most solid units of his footsoldiers were those of the African heavy infantry. These he turned into the offensive element of his plan. Divided into two bodies of equal size, these footsoldiers, some 10,000 men, armed Roman-style with the weapons taken from the enemy at Trasimene, were placed on either side of the centre, but slightly to the rear. In the centre, Hannibal put the Gaulish and Spanish footsoldiers, protruding in relation to the line of Africans flanking them to left and right, rather like the *umbo* of a shield, or a crescent with its convex curve facing the enemy. So at the same time a target was offered, and a potential flexibility engineered that could be brought into play when the time was ripe. Gauls and Iberians were ranged in alternating companies, and the sight they presented also alternated, different but equally impressive: naked to the waist behind their shields, the Gauls lined up with the long swords used for cutting; the Iberians could cut and thrust equally well with their *falcata* (above, p. 36), and wore distinctive purple-bordered tunics, whose dazzling whiteness is noted by Livy (XXII, 46, 6). The cavalry was placed on the wings. On the left, along the river, were about 6,000 Iberian and Celtic horsemen, opposite the Roman cavalry and under the command of Hasdrubal. On the right were the African cavalry, especially the Numidians, whom the Aufidus would not hinder in their movements. At their head was Hanno, according to Polybius (III, 114, 7), who is to be preferred to Livy, who suggests Maharbal, the master of cavalry. Taking his brother Mago as second-in-command, Hannibal kept for himself command of the infantry in the centre, where he knew that the most delicate phase of his planned manoeuvre would take place.

In two pages of great clarity, and without seeking dramatic effect, Polybius (III, 115–16) recounts the battle that will be forever famous, not only for the ingenuity of the plan conceived by Hannibal, but also for the precision applied to its execution, the swiftness of its manoeuvres, and the clearsightedness of the choices made by the lieutenants, especially Hasdrubal, when the course of the fight called for their initiative. The elements of the battle are admired to such an extent that in the immense 'literature' spawned by Cannae, often the most pertinent analyses are those inspired by our sources in the tacticians of modern times, from the Renaissance to the nineteenth century (Kussmaul, 1978, pp. 249–57). And as – the only difference being in weaponry – tactical movements on the ground by massed troops have long followed the same patterns, it is not surprising that Hannibal's military masterpiece has influenced the ideas of war theorists, as far as Clausewitz and even beyond (Kertész, 1980, pp. 29–43). On the even of the 1914–18 war, according to Saint-Loup, the Proustian character of the *Côté de Guermantes*, it could be seen inspiring the choices made by the German strategists.

The battle had begun in earnest when the Iberian and Gaulish cavalry of the Carthaginian left wing made contact with the Roman cavalry, who fought valiantly but in the end broke off the action. At that point, as the light troops had fallen back on either side, the infantry engaged combat. As Hannibal had foreseen, Iberians and Gauls yielded under the pressure of the Roman line of infantry, thus doing away with the projecting centre. Pushing back their adversaries, the Romans surged so far ahead that they found themselves between the two corps of African footsoldiers placed on the flanks. All the latter had to do was make a ninety-degree turn, one group to the left, the other to the right, to attack the enemy flanks thus exposed. Simultaneously, Hasdrubal's Iberian and Celtic cavalry, turning behind the Roman lines after routing the Roman right wing, attacked the left wing, which had at first resisted the Numidians opposing them, but scattered when it was thus caught in a pincer movement. All that remained for the Punic cavalry to do was to attack from the rear the Roman infantry who were already trapped in the net that had been formed from the outset of the battle by the tactic of letting the centre yield, itself based on Hannibal's discrimination between strong and weak troops. For, even more than the Iberians, the Gauls, with 4,000 dead, had borne the brunt of a battle that cost the Punic commander fewer than 6,000 men.

On the Roman side, it was absolute disaster. The numbers lost differ between Polybius, who estimates the dead at 70,000, and prisoners at over 10,000, and Livy, who is probably more credible when he acknowledges 'only' 47,000 dead among the infantry, and 2,700 in the cavalry ranks, and estimates the number of prisoners at 19,000. The Roman historian has left a terrifying description of the battlefield, which the Carthaginians scoured the next day to collect the spoils (XXII, 51, 5–9). In those days, when war was fought with blades, except for the wounds caused by missiles from balistas and slings, the injured took a long time to die – especially those whose hamstrings had been slashed by the cutlasses of the Numidian horsemen in their haste to put them *hors de combat* as quickly as possible, and who, the following morning, in the midst of yesterday's dead, still lay bleeding to death. Among the generals, the loss was no less appalling. Most of the Roman military leaders lay on the battlefield, including Cn. Servilius Geminus, consul of the previous year, and M. Minucius, the master of cavalry imposed on Fabius Maximus, as well as twenty-nine tribunes – superior officers – and eighty senators or magistrates with senatorial rank who had voluntarily fought with the troops. Hundreds of Roman knights also lay dead – gold rings, taken from their corpses, filled the baskets that Mago would shortly afterwards take to the Carthaginian senate. Also among the dead was Aemilius Paullus, who had been wounded early in the engagement, and whose death Livy recounts (XXII, 49, 6–11) with the true emotion and dramatic intensity which, here as elsewhere, turn this often mediocre historian into a great writer. When the tribune Cn. Lentulus, seeing him covered in blood at the end of the fight, offered to save him by hoisting him on to his horse, the consul ordered him not to waste the precious time still left to him to escape and warn the senators to put Rome on the defensive; for himself, he preferred to die amid his men and not to have to protect his innocence by blaming his colleague. In fact, Varro, escaping from the massacre with a handful of men, had regrouped the few thousand survivors, a disparate and bewildered bunch, at Canusium.

Was Rome immediately within the victor's reach? On the evening of 2 August 216 Maharbal, the Punic master of cavalry, believed so, and said as much to his leader, whom he visualized dining in the Capitol four days later. Hannibal replied that he needed time to reflect, and it was then that he drew upon himself the rather vexed retort from Maharbal, rendered by Livy in a sentence famous for its conciseness and the vigour of the asyndeton: '*Vincere scis, Hannibal, victoria uti nescis*' (XXII, 51, 2: 'You know how to win a fight, Hannibal, but you do not know how to use your victory'). And Livy, adding that this hesitation doubtless saved the city and the empire (*urbs atque imperium*), sided in advance with those (for example Brisson, 1973, pp. 199–200) who subsequently considered that at that precise moment the fate of the world which we have inherited was poised on a knife-edge. In fact, despite what the victor of El-Alamein may have thought when he deemed Maharbal to be in the right (Montgomery, 1968, p. 98), the objections that held good against a forced march on Rome after Cannae had not changed since Trasimene (above, pp. 96–7). Moreover, Hannibal had other war aims, another plan. After the prisoners had been sorted out, and the Italian allies sent home to their native regions, he addressed the Roman captives, whose ransom he had set at a high price, and his words must be taken seriously. He was not waging a war of extermination, he told them; he was fighting to maintain the status (*dignitas*) of his own country and to ensure its hegemony (*imperium*) (Livy, XXII, 58, 3). Hannibal thus expected Rome to sue for peace; what he wanted was a victory recognized by a treaty that would, to Carthage's advantage, reverse the humiliating situation which had arisen from the treaties of 241 (the loss of Sicily and obligation to pay a heavy indemnity) and 237 (the loss of Sardinia) (Nicolet, 1978, p. 620). And in the following pages we shall see that, to attain this objective, in the wake of Cannae, the Punic commander exerted intense diplomatic activity in the south of Italy, taking advantage of the highly destabilizing effect of his victory which had detached from the Romans part of the Apulians, many Samnites, Lucanians and Bruttians. To march on Rome, to enter Rome, might well be a dream, if not an aim. On several occasions, if we are to believe Livy: in 211, when with his cavalry he would push as far as the town's walls; and in 203, on the point of leaving the Bruttium coast to return to Africa, Hannibal would be plagued with regret at not having tried to force the hand of fate at that time.

# 5

# Declining Fortunes

With the hindsight we enjoy – which was already available to Livy – the formidable thrust which, in the space of two years, had brought Hannibal from Cartagena to Cannae, on three occasions sweeping away powerful armies, appeared to be broken at the end of summer 216. The refusal to march on Rome seems to us to have shattered a dynamic of victory. This evaluation is probably based on an erroneous perception of the personality of Hannibal, whose image is somewhat imprisoned by his breathtaking military successes. In fact, for him as for several others in his wake – statesmen and not only generals – war, according to the famous dictum, was merely the continuation of politics by other means.

Remember (above, p. 84) that Hannibal had only just arrived in the Po Valley in late 218, when, without opposition, he seized Clastidium, which had been handed over to him by the commander of the fort, Dasius, from Brindisi. And it was precisely in the south of Italy that he was counting on the greatest amount of support for a policy which would make Carthage appear as the restorer of former liberties to the old Greek cities of Lucania, Bruttium and Campania, at the same time establishing a *de facto* Carthaginian protectorate over the entire region. Once Rome could be contained in the north of Campania, no longer able to reap the benefits of the valuable relay-points for its fleets – the ports of Pozzuoli and Naples on the Tyrrhenian Sea, Rhegium (Reggio Calabria) in the Straits of Messina, Brindisi and Tarentum on the Adriatic – it would be easier to regain possession of Sicily. Sixty years earlier, Tarentum had appealed to the king of Epirus, Pyrrhus, against the Romans. Obviously, Hannibal knew all about those campaigns, since such knowledge was essential to his own plan. An anecdote concerning a conversation he is supposed to have had with Scipio Africanus at Ephesus, at the time of his exile in 193 – and which is quoted without disguising the fact that it belongs to legend rather than history (below, p. 195) – suggests that he admired Pyrrhus, second only to Alexander (Livy, XXXV, 14, 9; Plutarch, *Flam.*, 21 4). Pyrrhus, stated Hannibal, excelled in the art of siegecraft – in which the Carthaginian was content to be his disciple, and had no ambition to rival him. But above all, he added, he was so well versed in the art of winning over people that the Italiot states and populations would rather be governed by him, a foreign king, than by the Romans, although they had long been the masters of that Italian soil. That was the kind of success that caught the Carthaginian's imagination. It had been a very fleeting success, since after a few years the Epirote had failed in his bid to unite the Greek cities and barbarian natives of Italy under his sceptre. But unlike that brilliant adventurer, Hannibal was not acting for his own personal ends, and could hope to do better than a brave and chivalrous *condottiere*, but very mediocre politician, whatever his most brilliant biographer may say of him (Lévêque, 1957, pp. 660–4).

In 280, after his victory over the legions of P. Valerius Laevinus near Heraclea, Pyrrhus had set out to march on Rome. He went no farther than Praeneste, but sent his friend and confidant Cineas as an ambassador to the Senate to put forward the conditions for peace: in exchange for the return without ransom of the prisoners taken at Heraclea, an alliance would be settled with Rome, and principally, there would be an annulment of all the annexations that had been made for decades at the expense of the Samnites, Lucanians, Daunians and Bruttians, the whole of the south of Italy being formed into a confederation centred on Tarentum. Rome could not accept such a retrograde step, and tradition has it that the censor of 312, the ancient Appius Claudius, blind and paralysed, had himself carried to the Senate to deliver an impassioned speech that swept away the hesitancy of those inclined towards peace.

In the aftermath of Cannae, did Hannibal think of Cineas' embassy? As Ennius would say soon after in a line applicable to both situations: *Qui vincit non est victor nisi victus fatetur* (*Annals*, fr. XXXI, 493: 'The victor is not victorious if the vanquished does not consider himself so'). As Pyrrhus before him, the Carthaginian had a means of sounding out the Romans' intentions. Several thousand prisoners, infantry and cavalry, were crammed into his camp. Ten of them were selected, with the mission of going to Rome to beg for their ransom on the conditions set by Hannibal. The Punic leader sent with them a high-ranking plenipotentiary, Carthalo, whose task was to present the conditions for peace, should he see that any in the Senate were this way inclined (Livy, XXII, 58, 7). But if we are to believe Livy, Carthalo was not received in Rome, and in the Senate it fell to T. Manlius Torquatus to deliver a prosecutor's speech damning those who had yielded to the enemy. Rome did not ransom its prisoners; nor did it grasp the olive branch held out by Hannibal. M. Junius Pera, appointed dictator – he was the last to be so with military powers – and Ti. Sempronius Gracchus, appointed master of cavalry, ordered the mobilization of all young men from the age of seventeen, and as there were not enough free men, 8,000 slaves were specially recruited, paid for and armed by the Roman state at its own expense. An army of four legions and 1,000 horsemen was thus formed, reinforced by contingents of allies and Latins. The war continued.

For the first time, Hannibal divided his army into two bodies. One he entrusted to his brother Mago, with the mission of going southwards, to obtain the active support of the Oscans, Lucanians and inhabitants of Bruttium against Rome, and chiefly the submission of the Greek cities along the coast. From there he was to cross to Carthage to present a complete report on the campaign to the Elders and obtain their backing for what was to follow.

## In the Carthaginian senate

Accompanied notably by Carthalo, the plenipotentiary sent packing by the Roman Senate in the aftermath of Cannae, Mago reached Carthage probably in the late summer of 216. This was the first direct contact that the Barcid family had had with their mother country for many long years and, at the very least, since the departure from Cartagena in the spring of 218. And although during those two years the Council of Elders had had occasion to hold sessions over the conduct of the war, this was the first time that Hannibal was giving an almost personal report, through the medium of his brother. Livy accords suitable importance to the episode and, from his account, one remembers chiefly the singular prominence he gives, in this instance, to the figure of Hanno, the Barcids' principal opponent. Ancient historiography is often at its finest when, using speeches and word portraits in a reconstructed dialogue featuring sometimes bitingly ironic, sometimes vivid and impassioned exchanges, the historian presents the reader with a drama that is truer to historical reality than an objective account.

After emphasizing the scale of the defeats inflicted on the Roman armies, which was rendered more evident by the heap of gold rings deposited at the entrance to the Carthaginian curia (those that had been torn from the knights' fingers on the battlefield of Cannae), Mago ended by asking for reinforcements, as well as supplies and money to pay the soldiers. In the midst of the general rejoicing, and anticipating the almost unanimous agreement that he sensed, a supporter of the Barcids, Himilco, thought he could provoke Hanno. 'Let us listen', he said, 'to a Roman senator here in the senate-house of Carthage!' (Livy, XXIII, 12, 7.) The old strategist refused to give way. He waxed ironic over these costly and far from decisive victories, challenging Mago to say which peoples 'of Latin name' (above, p. 59) had defected from Rome, and how many Roman citizens, even among the extra-urban 'tribes', had rallied to Hannibal. Mago had to admit that not one had done so. But in the heart of the Council the chips were down, and by a vast majority the Carthaginian senators decided to send reinforcements to Italy of 4,000 Numidian cavalry, forty elephants, money and provisions. This was scheduled for summer 215, and did in fact arrive in that period, in the charge of the admiral Bomilcar, at Locri, on the Bruttium coast, where Appius Claudius Pulcher, then praetor in Sicily, vainly tried to intercept him (Livy, XXIII, 41, 10–12). Let me take this opportunity to underline the war effort made by Carthage in 216–215; it is almost unbelievable if one thinks of the relative demographic frailty of its 'African empire'. To the first reinforcement decided upon at that memorable session of the senate, would be added in the spring of 215 a second, more substantial one: the 12,000 footsoldiers, 1,500 horsemen, plus twenty elephants and sixty warships, which Mago would have directed to Italy had the setbacks suffered in Spain not changed their destination (XXIII, 32, 5–6). And we shall see that, at the same time, contingents of roughly equal size would be sent to Sardinia in the hope of winning it back (XXIII, 32, 12). The scope of this effort clearly shows that at that time a large majority in Carthage believed in the possibility of a military victory over Rome, and also that Hannibal, far from being regarded as a *condottiere*, continued to be the general who was legally appointed and loyally supported by his government.

## Capua

After Cannae, Hannibal had marched towards Campania, with the intention of attacking Naples, so that he could have a good port at his disposal. But he was reluctant to embark on a siege, and the sight of the town's defence ramparts deterred him. He changed his route to go farther north, to Capua.

It was not a random choice. Founded about the late sixth century by the Etruscans slightly south of the Volturnus, on the site of present-day Santa Maria Capua Vetere, then a century later subdued by the Samnites, who turned it into the capital of a Campanian state, Capua had come into Rome's orbit soon after the middle of the fourth century, during the upheavals of the 'Latin War'. In the second half of the fourth century, did the city become for a time the 'southern' head of a bicephalous, Romano-Campanian state? The case is still argued, generally to cast doubt upon it (Heurgon, 1969, p. 325). Thus the sovereign right to mint coinage was exercised by Rome alone before the rebellion of 216–211. But it is true that since 334 every Capuan inhabitant had enjoyed Roman citizenship, which he could turn to his personal advantage in Rome, and at the same time exercise his right to contract a marriage, with the possibility of making his fortune there. Also, as well as its official language, Oscan, the city had preserved its municipal magistracies, which were also souvenirs of the ancient Osco-Umbrian culture, with the *meddix tuticus* and the college of the *meddices*. Even if, on the right bank of the Volturnus, it had lost the *ager Falernus* and its vineyards, annexed by Rome, the town was wealthy; like Corinth in Greece, Capua in Italy and the western world was the capital of abundance, and of a luxury symbolized by a market in perfumes that was celebrated throughout the Ancient World, the *Seplasia*. The scented component, in short, of that famous bouquet of the 'delights of Capua', which will be mentioned later.

Hannibal was aware of all this. He also knew that in Capua many felt a nostalgia for their lost independence, based on a national pride nurtured by the Campanians' consciousness of the eminent role they had played, as Rome's instrument, in the policy of Mediterranean expansion that had been carried on for several decades. In Capua the plebeians had been in a state of unrest, at least since the defeat at Trasimene in 217. But the ruling classes were hesitant; they were very much linked with Rome through intermarriage, and moreover, 300 sons from the noblest families served alongside the Romans in Sicily, where they were more or less hostages (Livy, XXIII, 4, 8).

This situation was resolved by the political genius of a local ruler, Pacuvius Calavius, whose name pointed to his Samnite origins, and who was the perfect illustration of the frequently close links of the Campanian aristocracy with the Roman nobility; for he was the son-in-law of Ap. Claudius Pulcher and the father-in-law of M. Livius Salinator, consul for the year 219. According to Livy, whose chronology there is no reason to doubt in this instance, Calavius was *meddix tuticus*, chief magistrate of Capua at the time of Trasimene. To forestall the subversion that was looming, he found an ingenious method of calming down the people's impatience at the same time as placing the local senate under his influence. Livy (XXIII, 3) recounts how he persuaded the people's assembly, which he had convened, that when the new elections were held they could not choose better than these representatives whom they appreciated so little. He thus set the seal of his authority on the forcible reconciliation of both sides. The outcome could then be awaited; in other words, the probable confirmation of Hannibal's ascendancy on the south of Italy and the prospects which such an ascendancy could open up. In the wake of Cannae, the temptation to defect was stronger. However, under pressure from the families who were the most pledged to Rome, a delegation was sent to the surviving consul shortly after the disaster. Livy, who disliked him – above, p. 103 – ascribes to Varro a speech that bears the stamp of bitter lucidity, and is chiefly defeatist in tone, just right to throw the Capuans into Hannibal's arms (XXIII, 5, 4–14). The consul told them quite bluntly that, with the Roman armies in their present state, they could no longer rely on any other than their own forces if they were to avoid falling into the hands of the Numidian and Moorish barbarians, who were rendered still more ferocious by the orders of an inhuman commander. Had they not been ordered to cross rivers on bridges made from mounds of corpses? The accusation will recur later in Florus (I, 22; II, 6). Had they not been taught to feed on human flesh? (In fact, when Hannibal was reviewing supply problems with his lieutenants just before leaving Spain, this suggestion was said to have been made to him by one of his captains, Monomachus, speaking of instances of dire necessity: Polybius, IX, 24, 7.) Here we see pinpointed the trait of *inhumana crudelitas*, sketched by Livy (above, p. 44) as one of the chief components in his moral portrait of Hannibal. But it is probably not without significance that the historian left the matter of enlarging on this trait to someone whom he considered despicable.

All that the Capuans remembered of Varro's speech was his admission of Rome's powerlessness. The same delegates sought out Hannibal and established the bases of an agreement with him: Capua was to keep its laws and magistrates, and no military obligation would be imposed by Carthage on its citizens; moreover, 300 Roman prisoners, left to the choice of the Campanians, would be exchanged for the Capuan horsemen engaged in Sicily. To seal this agreement, Hannibal sent a garrison to occupy and protect Capua, and made his entry into the town, where few were opposed to the defection from Rome. History has preserved the names of Decius Magius, who paid for his pride by being deported to Carthage, and of the son of Calavius, the author of this betrayal, who wanted to kill the Carthaginian under the family roof, and whom his father managed to disarm following a dramatic dialogue which Livy (XXIII, 8–9) delighted in relating, and which may be read also in the superb orchestration by Silius Italicus (XI, 303–68). Before Capua's senate, Hannibal promised that the city would soon be 'the capital of all Italy'. The subject was deliberately flattering and its aim doubtless excessive; but the plan was clearly apparent: it was a matter of containing Rome north of Campania, at the same time establishing a *de facto* protectorate over the south of Italy (and Sicily, whose recapture was part of the programme).

Following two years of a war of movement in which the Roman armies panted after Hannibal, positions were tending to stabilize. Beginning in the autumn of 216, the actual military operations show that the Roman defence line was fixed on a level with the Volturnus, which separated the *ager Falernus* from Capua's territory proper. Astride both banks of the river, the 'stopper' was the town of Casilinum, now covered by modern Capua. There the praetor M. Claudius Marcellus – the consul who conquered the Insubres in 222 (above, p. 41) – who was then in command of the fleet moored at Ostia and had received from the Senate the mission of taking in hand the remnants of Varro's army, set up his headquarters staff and camp. Meanwhile, the dictator M. Junius Pera left Rome for Campania, at the head of 25,000 men, after swelling his army – an unprecedented event – by enrolling several thousand common-law criminals (Livy, XXIII, 14, 3).

In a strong position through Capua's defection, leaving a garrison there, Hannibal first captured Nuceria (Nocera), south of Campania, then set up his camp at Nola. But Marcellus had come to the aid of the town, and his victorious sortie drove the Carthaginian out of it. Taking Acerrae (Acerra) in passing, pillaging and burning it, Hannibal went back towards Casilinum, where he wanted to forestall the expected arrival of M. Junius Pera and his army. Foiled at first before the walls of that part of the town situated on the right bank of the Volturnus, which was held by a modest but resolute garrison of Praenestians, he eventually captured it at the end of the winter and left a garrison to hold it.

In the meantime, Hannibal's soldiers had taken up their winter quarters at Capua. For the first time in three years they slept in a bed, and tradition adds that they were not unaccompanied. A famous page of Livy (XXIII, 18, 10–15) largely gave substance to the idea that the Punic army lost its soul and, above all, its body in those celebrated 'delights'. According to the Paduan historian, a few weeks spent among baths, wine and women – those three highlights in classical Antiquity's life of pleasure – were enough to destroy the fine war instrument forged by Hannibal. In an aphorism that he would shortly afterwards attribute to Marcellus, and which would be repeated after him (Livy, XXIII, 45, 4; Florus, I, 22, 21), 'Capua was Hannibal's Cannae'. But if so, how can it be explained that he was able for over ten years to hold out in southern Italy against Roman armies that were substantially greater in number than the troops he had available? In fact, the adage attributed to Marcellus had more to do with 'psychological action': the Roman soldier had to be convinced that the dynamic of victory no longer existed in the army which had tasted the comforts of human weakness in Capua.

## The great hopes of 215

Italy was not the only scene of confrontation. As we know, Spain had been an important stake in the game since the start of the whole enterprise, with Publius and Gnaeus Scipio waging operations against Hasdrubal that were for a long time indecisive – we shall return to them later – until the arrival of the future Africanus, in 210, radically changed the course of events. But in 215 everything caught fire at once, and all over the place. Sardinia and Sicily in turn, and with varying fortunes, entered the field of battle. And to cap it all, the alliance concluded by Hannibal with king Philip V of Macedonia in the spring of 215 provided an extra touch to the spread of the conflict. Rich in promise for the Carthaginians, but also marked by setbacks – both in Spain and Sardinia – 215 opened a period of uncertainty in which everything still seemed possible for Hannibal, but in which time would henceforth be against him.

At the end of 216, the consuls elected for the year 215 were Ti. Sempronius Gracchus and the patrician L. Postumius Albinus. However, the latter was never able to take up his post as he was massacred, together with his army, by the Boii near Modena at the end of the winter. Hannibal's Gaulish allies took advantage of the pressure exerted by the Punic army in southern Italy. The colonies recently installed at Piacenza and Cremona had to be temporarily abandoned, and a 'suffect consul' to replace Postumius Albinus had to be elected. All eyes turned towards Claudius Marcellus, wreathed in the glory of the success he had achieved a few months earlier at Nola. He was unanimously elected, but his election was quashed for an irregularity – a thunderclap is said to have sounded as he took up his duties. In fact, the senators had taken a poor view of the election of two equally plebeian consuls. He had to stand down in favour of the old Q. Fabius Maximus, appointed consul for the third time, but his service record earned him a proconsulship. While Fabius took over the army which had been led by the dictator M. Junius Pera, and which had its quarters at Teanum (Teano), Marcellus took command of the troops stationed above Suessula, for the protection of Nola. Campania thus remained solidly blocked to the north and east.

Hannibal, who was encamped on Mount Tifata (present-day Monte Vergine, north of Avellino), from where he could monitor Capua and the surrounding area, then sent one of his lieutenants, Himilco, to complete the occupation of Bruttium – present-day Calabria – where he needed plenty of elbow room, both to establish the shortest possible sea links with Carthage and to facilitate connection with Sicily. It took Himilco several months to subdue Petelia (Petilia), but he subsequently obtained the rapid surrender of Consentia (Cosenza). Besieged by the Bruttians who were allies of the Carthaginians, the Greek town of Crotona fell in its turn, as did the port of Locri. Only Rhegium (Reggio Calabria), says Livy

(XXIII, 30, 9), was to remain loyal to Rome to the end. For the Carthaginians, the opportuneness of having at their disposal secure landing-points along these coasts would soon become evident.

In this late third century, Rome's interest in the eastern flank of an increasingly Roman Italy was fairly recent. Beginning in 229, Rome began to intervene against the Illyrians and to set up a kind of protectorate over a whole coastal band of the Adriatic, on the eastern side, of the islands of Issa and Corcyra, on the Dalmatian coast, at Epidamnos and Apollonia, in Epirus (present-day Albania). In 219, one of these princes under the protectorate, Demetrios of Pharos, had tried to shake off the yoke, and Rome had sent against him the two consuls for the year, Aemilius Paullus and M. Livius Salinator (above, p. 52). Demetrios had fled to Macedonia to the young king Philip V. The two men were together at Nemea, in the Argolid, when during the summer of 217 news reached them of the defeat at Trasimene (Polybius, V, 101, 6–7). Soon afterwards, relieved by the peace of Naupactus from the war he was waging against the Aetolians, Philip judged that the time had come to set off in the footsteps of Pyrrhus, or at least to profit from Rome's weak state to seize Illyria. The Cannae disaster persuaded him to make an alliance with Hannibal. In the spring or early summer of 215, an embassy led by Xenophanes disembarked on the shores of Carthaginian-controlled Bruttium, abreast of Cape Lacinium. Not without incident, they reached Campania, and were even intercepted during their return journey. But the agreement had been concluded.

Polybius (VII, 9), who was more curious about treaties and diplomatic means than Livy, has passed on to us the text, which must have been in the archives of the Roman Senate, as it had been seized by the praetor M. Valerius Flaccus, who was in command of the fleet patrolling off the Calabrian coast. This document has for a long time been closely scrutinized and, besides turns of phrase that jar with Polybius' customary Greek, specialists have recognized in it expressions that have more to do with Phoenician diplomacy than with that of the classical world. There is therefore every likelihood that this page transcribes the Punic section of the genuine text of the agreement. It is of considerable interest and justifies the amount of attention it has aroused (Bickerman, 1944, 1952; Chroust, 1974). In his capacity of commanding general, Hannibal pronounces the oath sanctioning the treaty, but he seems to be surrounded by Carthaginian senators (the 'gerontes' of the text) and chiefly flanked by three people designated by name – a Mago, a Myrkan, a Barkomar – who it has been suggested should be regarded as members of the Council of the Hundred and Four (Chroust, 1974, p. 284); but perhaps they could equally well be members of one of those 'commissions', those 'limited councils' that we know were invested, in Carthage, with executive powers (Sznycer, 1978, pp. 579–80; Fantar, 1993, I, pp. 242–6). This raises a slight problem: was the governmental 'entourage' permanently with Hannibal, or had it joined him specially on the occasion of the negotiations with Philip's envoys? But the information is important, and adds to all the other elements that spoil the legend of a Hannibal carrying on a completely personal venture for his own pleasure. Similarly, the deities invoked by him to support the oath he pronounces

(Polybius, VII, 9, 2–3) do not belong to his personal pantheon, but are those of Carthage's official pantheon (Lancel, 1995a, pp. 208–9). Contrary to what Livy says (XXIII, 33, 11), in a not very credible résumé, the text handed down by Polybius reveals that Hannibal's war aims, although remaining fairly fluid in regard to the benefits Carthage hoped to reap from a victory, implied the continuity – and therefore ruled out its destruction – of a Rome which could be negotiated with as with a sovereign state. And the only territorial detail contained in the document was not concerned with Italy; it assured Philip that when the final settlement was agreed Rome would lose, to his own advantage, the Illyrian coastal strip that he and Demetrios of Pharos wished to recover (Polybius, VII, 9, 13–14). This clause also signified Carthage's desire to keep the king of Macedonia away from Italy. Whatever Livy may say, rather summarily (XXIII, 33, 10 and 12), the details of mutual military aid remained vague. At the time of the final ordeal, at Zama in 202, would Philip help Carthage? Livy, as we shall see, says so (XXX, 26, 3); Polybius makes no mention of it, and in general his silence is preferred.

In Sicily, too, fate smiled on Hannibal (Figure 7). Gelon, the eldest son of king Hieron, impressed by the disaster the Romans had suffered at Cannae, was on the brink of denouncing the alliance which his father had loyally upheld for nearly fifty years when he disappeared in rather suspect fashion. But shortly afterwards the ninety-year-old king also died, leaving his grandson Hieronymus, an adolescent of about fifteen years old, as head of the kingdom of Syracuse. This lad, influenced by his entourage, sent an embassy to Hannibal who gave them a warm welcome and, unofficially and personally, saw that they were accompanied on their return to Sicily by a young officer of his headquarters staff named Hannibal, like himself, and two Carthaginians of Syracusan origin, Hippokrates and Epikydes; a draft alliance was worked out. Hieronymus dispatched a delegation to Carthage to conclude a treaty in due and proper form. At first, in the event of success against Rome, he was content to ask for the eastern half of the island as far as the river Himeras (present-day Salso) whose source lies in the central massif of the island, on the high plateau of Henna that Cicero would call 'Sicily's navel' (*umbilicus Siciliae*). Then, succumbing to the flattery of his courtiers, who stressed his illustrious ancestry – he was, on his mother's side, the grandson of Pyrrhus – he went on to demand the whole of the island (Livy, XXIV, 6, 7; Polybius, VII, 4, 1–2). The Carthaginians gave him his head, the main point being that Hieronymus should keep away from Rome. Thereupon, as a first step in waging war on the Romans, the foolish youngster went off to Leontinoi (Lentini), where he was killed in a conspiracy. In the confusion, Syracuse was ready to swing over to the Punic alliance (Marchetti, 1972, pp. 6–11).

In contrast, Carthaginian hopes in Sardinia came to a sudden end. In the spring of 215 Carthage had received a clandestine embassy from a Sardinian leader of Punic origin, Hampsicoras, an approach that was equally encouraged by Hanno, a Carthaginian senator settled on the island (Livy, XXIII, 32, 10; 41, 1–2). According to them, the Sardinians, crushed by taxes and contributions in kind, were ready to rebel against a Roman domination they had impatiently endured since

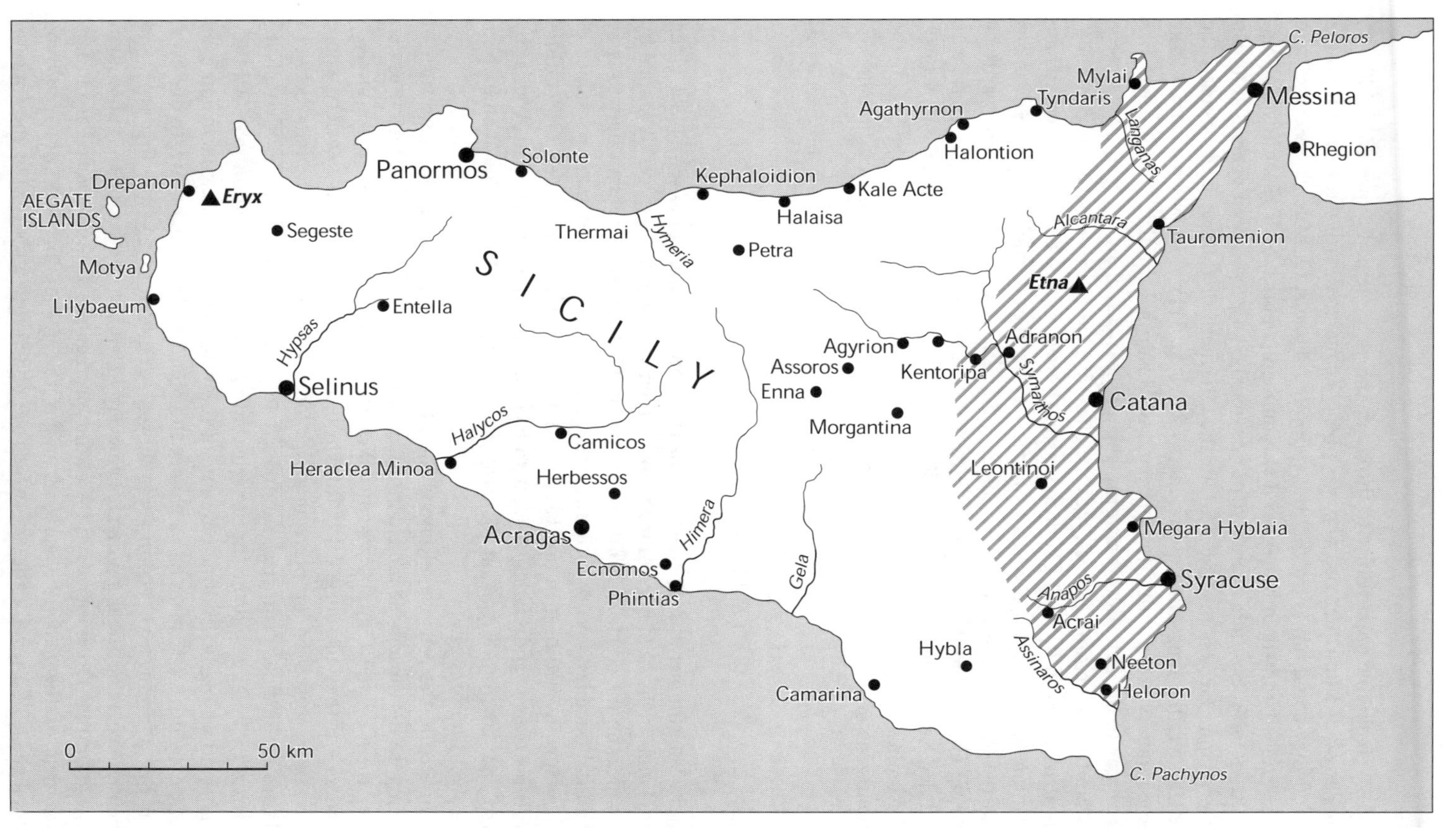


**Figure 7** The Syracusan principality on the east flank of Sicily (from Polybius, *Histoire*, 1970)

238. A favourable opportunity to throw off the yoke seemed to present itself with the arrival of a new praetor, who was poorly acquainted with the area. But on the island they could not know that the appointed praetor, Q. Mucius Scaevola, who was seriously ill, would be replaced at a moment's notice by T. Manlius Torquatus, a victor in Sardinia twenty years previously, an experienced general and man of principle. He was the one who, in the aftermath of Cannae, had opposed the Senate over the ransoming of prisoners (above, p. 111). Carthage had sent a large expeditionary force under the command of Hasdrubal the Bald, but his fleet was driven on to the Balearics by a storm, and a first engagement, unwisely undertaken without these reinforcements, was a defeat for the Sardinians. Finally landing, Hasdrubal linked up with Hampsicoras in the region of Carales (Cagliari), where Manlius had set up his camp. The battle was a real catastrophe for the Sardinians and the Carthaginians, and Manlius completed his success shortly afterwards by seizing Cornus (Santa Caterina di Pittinuri), on the west coast, where those who had fled were sheltering. To cap it all, Hasdrubal and Hanno were taken prisoner. T. Manlius Torquatus was able to return to Rome and announce to the Senate the submission of the Sardinia which he had already subdued for the first time in 235.

## Between Capua and Tarentum (autumn 215–autumn 214)

In the late summer of 215, Hannibal made yet another attempt to seize Nola, aided by Hanno at the head of reinforcements – men and elephants – recently landed by Bomilcar on the coasts of Bruttium (above, p. 112). But after trying vainly to sway the local notables' loyalty to Rome, and clashing with the energetic resistance of Marcellus, he had to give up (Livy, XXIII, 43–6). Hanno returned to Bruttium with his troops, and Hannibal went to take up his winter quarters in Apulia, by Arpi, not far from Foggia, at the base of the Gargano, a land he loved and where we shall find him again.

In Rome, the consular elections for 214 were marked by a dramatic turn of events. In his capacity as the elder outgoing consul, Q. Fabius Maximus presided over them on the Campus Martius. Following a custom that surprises modern readers – if they also forget that Roman institutions belonged to a society whose votes were based on property qualifications, founded on distinctions between classes – the first 'centuries' summoned to vote were those of the 'first class', formed by knights and the 'upper crust' of citizens who served on foot. All they had to do was agree, and the outcome of the vote was a foregone conclusion even before the other centuries had a chance to vote. An additional oddity, to our eyes, was that a 'prerogative' century was chosen at random to have the first vote, and their choice, regarded as a portent, had every likelihood of swaying the subsequent votes. On that December day in 215, the 'prerogative' century picked at random was that of the *juniores* – citizens under the age of forty-six who could be mobilized – of a rural 'tribe' (by which we understand a district) of the Anio, in the countryside east of Rome (Livy, XXIV, 7, 12). The names of the consuls chosen by this vote were T. Otacilius Crassus and M. Aemilius Regillus.

In a completely unaccustomed manner, Fabius spoke out to have the vote quashed. He could easily reject Aemilius Regillus who, as a flamen (priest) of Quirinus, was unable for religious reasons to go away from Rome. As for Titus Otacilius, although he was his nephew by marriage, Fabius showed him no consideration. The burden was too heavy, he said, for the shoulders of a man who, while praetor in 217, at the head of the fleet, had not been capable of ensuring the safety of Italy's coasts. Above all, and here lies the main interest of a harangue which could be suspected of expressing Livy's own feelings about the methods of exercising command at that time, Fabius openly criticized a system that confronted one enemy – Hannibal – who was secure in the length of time he had available to put his strategy into operation, with generals elected for a year who had to step down when they had scarcely completed their campaign preparations. It was clear to all that, in saying this, Q. Fabius Maximus was for the fourth time – not counting his dictatorship of 217 – offering his person to the republic. Summoned to vote afresh, the *juniores* of the Anio saw to it that his name emerged from the urn, associated with that of M. Claudius Marcellus, for whom it was his third consulship.

## THE FIRST POLITICAL AND ECONOMIC CHANGES IN ROME

There must be no mistake about the underlying direction of this vote. The Senate was clearly behind the 'prerogative century' of the Anio. Or, more precisely, this second rectified vote had been inspired by the clan which at that time was in the majority in the Senate, the 'conservative agrarians', of whom the Fabii were the leaders (the 'Delayer's' own son was one of the two consuls for the following year, 213). They also included in their ranks some eminent plebeians, excellent generals, like M. Claudius Marcellus himself, and Q. Fulvius Flaccus, who was elected praetor by the same comitia for 214, and would be consul in 212. The predominance of a clan which, by means of prorogations, could guarantee the continuity of command to be seen from 215 to 208 (the year of Marcellus' death in Apulia), did not rule out the sharing of responsibilities, even though at the cost of lasting exile in a 'province' for the representatives from another faction. Thus P. Cornelius Scipio would be proconsul in Spain for six consecutive years until his death in 211, ensuring, together with his brother Gnaeus, the continuity during that period of a strategy which was to create the conditions for the decisive success of his son, the future Africanus, at Cartagena in 210. In this way the *comitia centuriata* of 214 had brought into play choices that constituted a real turning-point in the concept traditionally held in Rome of the exercise of executive power and the conduct of war.

The year 214, in many respects a pivotal year in the history of the second Punic War, also witnessed if not the final outcome, at least the rapid setting-up of a monetary reform which by itself is symbolic of the adaptations, this time in the economic field, to which Rome had to agree under the formidable pressure of events. As we know, currency is the very sensitive barometer of not only economic difficulties but also political weaknesses. Thus in the autumn of 217, after Trasimene and the disastrous impression it made on central Italy, the unprecedented – and short-lived – issue of gold coins (staters), far from being considered as a healthy sign, was the obvious result of Rome's loss of reliability *vis-à-vis* its Latin allies and the strength of money in the very heart of the republic, and a rather desperate attempt to restore confidence. But above all, in the same period, a succession of devaluations of the basic monetary unit, the as, a bronze coin, and the accelerated reform of the entire system, clearly reveal the distress of the Roman public treasury faced simultaneously with needs that had become enormous and difficulties in obtaining fresh supplies of mintable metal.

It was probably in the same year, 217, that the bronze as, which originally weighed one pound (in Rome slightly over 300 grammes), was devalued to half of this weight, passing soon afterwards to one-third; in 214 the as was worth only one-sixth of a pound; this is the numismatists' *sextans*. Such a rapid tumble called for a vigorous reorganization of the whole system. That was the aim of the creation of a new silver coin – to replace the existing quadrigatus, itself devalued and poorly incorporated into the overall scheme. Some forty years ago, during the American excavations at Morgantina (Sierra Orlando, in the centre of Sicily), the discovery of a cache of money including denarii enabled the date to be pinpointed, as the site of the find, the sanctuary of Demeter and Kore, had been destroyed by Marcellus' soldiers between 214 and 211. So it is possible to date to these years the first issue of the silver denarius which originally bore the helmeted head of Roma on its face, and which for over four centuries would symbolize the permanence and solidity of Roman money. There were, however, two devaluations, the first soon after its creation, probably in 209, when the as itself again lost half its remaining value – this was the 'uncial as' – and the denarius was no longer exchanged against ten, but sixteen, pieces of this basic coinage, which it would partly accompany in its new fall. In these crucial years, such precipitate monetary manipulations say a great deal about the anxieties of the Roman treasury and the economies that became necessary – especially to pay the army's wages – when it had to make massive issues of cash. It must, however, be added that these devaluations and reforms need to be set in a Mediterranean perspective; it has been shown that the devaluation to one-sixth of the as, at which point the denarius was created, was not something confined to Rome alone, but went hand in hand with equivalent measures in Egypt, Etruria and perhaps also in Syracuse during the same period (Nicolet, 1963, pp. 432–6). We may therefore assume *de facto* the existence of an international exchange rate for precious metals, as well as relations between silver and bronze, of which Roman currency would have had to take account.

Aside from these monetary manoeuvres, the Roman state in this period of crisis also resorted to exceptional financial expedients. For, in order to face the expenses of war, the customary *tributum*, which affected only those citizens who were not mobilized in the legions, was inadequate; early in 215 the Senate decided to double the rate of tax (Livy, XXIII, 13, 1). It was still not enough. In the preceding year, 216, after Cannae and shortly before the disappearance of the old king Hieron of Syracuse, Rome had asked him for a loan in silver and grain, which was received by Titus Otacilius, who was then in command of the fleet in Sicily with the rank of propraetor (XXIII, 21, 5). At the same time, to remedy the *penuria argenti*, says Livy (XXIII, 21, 6), in other words, the short supply of cash currency, a kind of state bank was created in Rome, with the appointment of triumvirs from among the highest personages, notably one Aemilius and one Atilius. At the end of the campaign waged in Spain during the summer of 215, which was successful but very costly, Publius and Gnaeus Scipio asked the Senate for fresh subsidies which the public treasury was hard put to it to find. Companies of *publicani* (tax farmers) agreed to provide them, granting long-term credit, through the concession of an additional 'risk premium' (Livy, XXIII, 48–9). In 214, the squadron entrusted to Titus Otacilius, restored to his duties as admiral of the fleet despite Fabius' criticism, was cruelly short of sailors. The Senate passed a law, and the consuls were enabled to order by edict that the crews should be made up to strength by progressive taxes imposed on the wealthiest citizens, the senators providing up to eight sailors with a year's pay. For the first time, wrote Livy (XXIV, 11, 9), the Roman navy – rather on the lines of the Athenian naval 'liturgies' – was fitted out at the expense of private individuals. Like the *tributum*, these enforced taxes had their limits. We shall see this four years later when one of the two consuls for 210, M. Valerius Laevinus, wanted to repeat the operation. Faced with a revolt of the taxpayers, an appeal was made for voluntary contributions from the upper classes – the senators setting an example, swiftly followed by the knights and more comfortably-off plebeians – in the form of their gold and precious objects, then their silver and liquid assets in bronze coins, to be given to the triumvirs in charge of the state bank, against receipts redeemable over several maturity dates (Livy, XXVI, 36). The history of our modern nations is not without such patriotic donations made in the hour of danger, against 'assignats' (in the French Revolution) or treasury bills, often of dubious validity. To the donors in 210, the third portion of reimbursement would not be paid off until 200, and then only by the granting of lands taken from the public domain (Livy, XXXI, 13, 9).

Let us return to 214. The sacrifices and exceptional measures just mentioned give some idea of the colossal war effort made by Rome. The Senate decided to carry on operations with eighteen legions, or more than 100,000 men, not including the allied contingents serving alongside these legions. Moreover, the fleet numbers amounted to 150 vessels. It must be added that these figures, which we read in Livy (XXIV, 11, 2–5), do not include the forces engaged on both land and sea in Spain. When Africanus left to go there, after the death of his father and uncle, he received, says Polybius (X, 19, 1), a sum of 400 talents, or 1,800,000 denarii, equalling two years' pay for his troops: an average of 250,000 denarii has been proposed as the cost of a legion's annual upkeep (Marchetti, 1971). It was an exceedingly heavy financial burden, easier to assess if we recall that when it was created in 214 the denarius was worth ten asses, and if we know that this sum was the equivalent, in that period, of the daily wage of several manual workers.

Hannibal, who was wintering in Arpi, Apulia, was alerted by the Capuans to this extraordinary mobilization, and returned in the spring of 214 to his Mount Tifata camp, above Capua. Then he descended to the Campanian coast, ravaging the territory of Cumae, next unsuccessfully testing the defences of Pozzuoli and Naples. At Lake Avernus, where he had stopped to make a sacrifice, he met a delegation of young Tarentine nobles. Grateful to the Punic leader for having liberated them, some after Trasimene, others after Cannae, they had made themselves the champions of the Carthaginian cause among their compatriots. The prospect of gaining a hold on Tarentum by virtue of having contacts in the place appealed to Hannibal all the more because he was held in check in Campania. After a fresh attempt he had to abandon the hope of taking Nola, which was well defended by Marcellus. On the Volturnus, Casilinum (present-day Capua), a key position, was recaptured by the two consuls' troops.

Hannibal went to Tarentum, sparing its territory the devastation of war. Having reached its walls, he must have decided that the time was not yet ripe; no one came forward to meet him, and M. Valerius Laevinus, commanding the Roman fleet at Brindisi, had caused the town to be placed on the defensive. Autumn had already arrived. As in the preceding year, Hannibal went off to winter in Apulia, which was decidedly his favourite area. This time his choice fell on Salapia, near the coast, half-way between Arpi and Cannae; the terrible memory of 216 dissuaded the Romans from going there to cross swords with him. Here a later tradition, reported by Pliny the Elder (*N.H.*, III, 103), credits him with a liaison with a local prostitute, a story which apparently still filled the little Apulian town with pride three centuries afterwards. They probably showed visitors the house in which this winter love affair had taken place! But the truly astonishing thing would be that Salapia alone should bask in such renown, if we were not indebted to Justin (XXXII, 4, 11) for the knowledge that Hannibal was not a womanizer and, notably, that he respected his female prisoners, to the point where it might be doubted that he was born in Africa, a land given to the pleasures of Venus, as everyone knows. Imilce, the wife to whom he had bidden farewell on the shores of Gades, was very far away, but the history of the Carthaginian's exploits was by no means cluttered with female figures.

## The siege of Syracuse: Archimedes versus Marcellus (214–212)

In Syracuse, after the death of Hieronymus, the situation had remained confused for a long time until Hannibal's envoys, Hippokrates and Epikydes, managed to obtain the top magisterial posts, at an election that was somewhat stormy (Livy, XXIV, 27, 3). In the spring of 214, the praetor Appius Claudius Pulcher was in office at Lilybaeum, on the western horn of Sicily, where he had under his command troops and 100 large vessels ('penteres') which had to confront the switch in Syracuse's alliance. Livy tends to play down his role to the advantage of Marcellus, and in rather imprecise manner has the latter intervening on the island in the early months of 214 (XXIV, 21, 1), while showing him to us protecting Nola against Hannibal, helping Fabius to besiege and capture Casilinum and being subsequently detained for some time at Nola by illness. Marcellus could not have landed in Sicily until the beginning of autumn (Marchetti, 1972, p. 19). But for the Paduan historian the brilliance of his person eclipses the other protagonists, and we have to go back to the little that remains of Polybius' account (VIII, 3–7) in order to give everyone his due.

The two Roman generals shared the task at hand: Appius Claudius, on the landward side, attacked the vast defence wall that girdled 'greater Syracuse', with the huge suburban expanses of the Epipolae; Marcellus, with his large ships, attacked from the sea the lower town, Achradina, the central district which, facing the island of Ortygia, had its own fortifications, the defence walls being washed by the waves. The Romans, who had just taken Leontinoi almost without opposition, had no doubt that they would easily achieve their aim. But Syracuse was strongly defended, especially by the genius of its great son, Archimedes. He was not merely one of the greatest geometricians of all time; a friend, perhaps even a relation, of king Hieron, he had not been too proud to become the city's chief engineer, complementing its defences, and perfecting to a technical level that was extremely high for Antiquity the war machines in which Syracuse had specialized since the time of the tyrant Dionysius in the early fourth century.

Marcellus was not slow to realize the sort of welcome awaiting him. Archimedes used his full range of weapons against the Roman consul, who brought his big ships close to the defence wall, side by side in pairs, thus transformed into platforms from which towers could rise to the level of the top of the wall while, from the other vessels, velites hurled javelins at the defenders posted on the curtain walls. Ballistas and catapults of all calibres and differing ranges hindered or endangered the approach of the enemy ships. Among other strokes of inspiration was a giant 'stone-thrower', whose projectiles, weighing some 350 kilograms, smashed the 'sambuca', a sort of tall ladder, protected by facings, that Marcellus had set up from an assemblage of eight ships, and was trying to place against the sea-defence wall (Plutarch, *Marcellus*, 15). To attack the soldiers on the decks, the Syracusan had had loopholes, at a man's height, made in the walls for archers. Polybius, an expert in siegecraft, as we know, was very interested in all this machinery, and has described in detail the most ingenious invention (VIII, 6): a sort of crane which was placed against the internal face of the defence rampart and which, when a Roman vessel reached the foot of the wall, let fall on it an 'iron hand' that seized it by the prow; then a heavy counterweight, assisted by a winch, lifted the ship with its prow in the air. All that remained to be done was to let it forcefully drop back again to capsize or damage it, together with its crew. It appears, at least according to Polybius, that Marcellus himself had enough sense of humour to joke about his own setbacks. As if that were not enough, later tradition also ascribed to Archimedes the installation of batteries of parabolic mirrors on the heights of Syracuse capable of setting fire to the Roman ships by concentrating the sun's rays on them. Legend, perhaps, but one which the genius of the man who discovered spheroids, as well as the cone and Archimedes' spiral, does not render totally improbable.

For his part, Appius Claudius was having no better luck in his efforts to weaken the landward defences, especially in the north, where a powerful fortress, the Hexapylon, commanded the main entrance. It was decided to lay siege to the town, which was blocked on the seaward side by the Roman fleet that a Carthaginian squadron, smaller in number, stationed on Himilco's orders at Cape Pachynum on the southern tip of the island, dared not attack. Up to the end of 213, when he left for Rome to bid for the consulship, Appius Claudius took command of both the fleet and land troops, freeing Marcellus who, with part of the army, seized towns in the region which had gone over to the Carthaginians: Elorus, Herbita and Megara Hyblaea. The Romans realized, to their cost, that this land of Sicily, which they had so recently annexed, had not been won over to their side. In a letter addressed to the senate in Carthage, Hannibal had convinced them that the time had come to reconquer the island. A large expeditionary force – 25,000 footsoldiers, 3,000 cavalry and twelve elephants – had gained a foothold on the south coast, at Heraclea Minoa. Hippokrates, emerging with several thousand men from Syracuse, which was left to be guarded by Epikydes, had joined this army. Agrigentum, not far distant, had fallen. Henna, in the centre of the island, a real holy city in Sicily, with its temple dedicated to Ceres on the very spot where Proserpine was thought to have been carried off by Pluto, had been held by the Romans, but at the price of a massacre that had outraged the Sicilians.

At the end of the summer of 212 however, Marcellus, who had kept his command in Sicily with the title of proconsul, achieved his ends, though not without difficulty. Having learnt from a deserter that, in honour of the feast of Artemis, there would at least be rivers of wine running in the town even if other provisions were lacking, he resolved to take advantage of this to have his men scale the wall protecting the entire plateau of Epipolae, but at the part where it was lowest near the port of Trogilus and the tower known as 'Galeagris'. As the defenders were all drunk, it was child's play for the chosen commando group, with the help of ladders, to gain access to the covered way and, once they had reached the Hexapylon, to come down and open a postern gate through which Marcellus and his troops poured. Soon afterwards, following a betrayal, the surrender of the Euryalus fort, which to the west commanded the major corner of the fortification, gave him control of the entire upper and suburban part of the town. Sheltering behind their own defence wall, there remained the lower town, Achradina, and the island of Ortygia (Nasos), which was connected to Achradina by a narrow isthmus. Of the two promoters of Syracusan alliance with Carthage against Rome, one, Hippokrates, who was fighting outside the town, had already succumbed. When the other, Epikydes, deserted the besieged fortress to flee by sea to Agrigentum, the end was in sight. It was made easier by another act of betrayal, by one of the commanders of the garrison, a Spaniard serving in the Carthaginian army. In the sea-defence wall protecting the island on the side of the big port, he had a gate opened near to the fountain of Arethusa.

At last Marcellus was master of one of the most beautiful towns in the Ancient World, and also one of the most opulent, where royal treasures and works of art had been amassed over the five centuries since its foundation by the Corinthians. All that was most noteworthy was methodically set aside to be sent to Rome. The rest was left to be pillaged. And in that autumn of 212, Syracuse's brilliant defender met his end in the role of absent-minded old professor. Amid the noise and fury created by the sacking of the town, completely engrossed in the figures he was tracing in the sand of his abacus, Archimedes was killed by a soldier who did not recognize the great man (Livy, XXV, 31, 9). Marcellus, adds Livy, was sorry for the death and took care to ensure that this learned man was given a fitting burial. One hundred and thirty-seven years later, Cicero, who was quaestor at Lilybaeum and visiting Syracuse as a tourist, searched for the tomb, which he knew to be surmounted by a small column, itself bearing a sphere and a cylinder. He did, indeed, find it, as he relates in his *Tusculanes* (V, 66), but it was overgrown with brambles and eroded by time and weather. A surprising oversight on the part of the Syracusans; but Archimedes had no need of a monument in order to be immortal.

## From the Capture of Tarentum to the Loss of Capua (212–211)

Sicily was not yet totally and definitively lost to Carthage. It would not be so until two years later, with the fall of Agrigentum, victim of a disagreement between the commander Hanno, Himilco's successor at the head of the Carthaginian expeditionary force, and his master of cavalry Muttines, a brilliant soldier of 'Libyphoenician' origin, who took revenge for the insults of his commander-in-chief by handing over the town to the Romans. But the fall of Syracuse was a cruel blow for Hannibal.

Furthermore, in the same period, the noose around Capua was growing ever tighter. And Apulia was no longer that 'sanctuary' where he liked to build up his forces during the winter; Arpi had been recaptured in the spring of 213 by the new consul, Cunctator's son, who bore the same name as his father, Q. Fabius Maximus. The Punic leader had spent the greater part of summer 213 in the region of Salento, the heel of the Italian 'boot', south of Lecce. From there, in fine weather, one can see on the eastern horizon the mountains of Albania, which might provide a Macedonian reinforcement, though that was highly unlikely. Most importantly, he could keep his eye on Tarentum; after a fruitless first attempt (above, p. 124), he had not lost hope of profiting from secret contacts in the place to lay hands on a good port that would be so useful both for communications with Carthage and the prospect of combined operations with Philip of Macedonia.

Although Livy (XXV, 11, 20) hesitates over this point of chronology, the successful attempt on Tarentum is dated to the early winter of 213–212. And the account left by the Roman historian can be superimposed so exactly on Polybius' text (VIII, 24–34), fortunately preserved, that one might think Livy had purely and simply translated it (De Sanctis, 1917, pp. 365–6; Wuillemier, 1939, p. 150). In Polybius, the clarity of detail, the precision of his rendering of matters of secondary importance to the account, and above all, the fact that everything seems to be observed from the Carthaginian standpoint, leads one to think that in this narration he has closely followed the version written by Silenos, Hannibal's historiographer (Walbank, 1967, II, pp. 100–1). Livy also probably goes back to Silenos, but by way of Coelius Antipater; hence the distortions and dissonances to be found in comparison with Polybius, which rule out mere copying from the Achaean.

As we may read it in both writers, and also in Appian (*Hann.*, 32–3), the history of the capture of Tarentum is a marvellous illustration of Hannibal's ability to use things and people to his own ends, and by other means than great strategy. In this instance he had been helped by Rome's clumsiness; following an escape attempt, Tarentines held hostage had been hurled down from the Tarpeian rock. In Tarentum this massacre had provoked much ill-feeling. One evening, thirteen young men emerged from the town's defence wall and approached the Punic camp. Two of them, Nico and Philemenos, advanced as far as the sentry-posts and had themselves brought before Hannibal, to whom they explained their grievances against Rome and their intention to hand over the town to the Carthaginians. The Punic leader's response may be imagined; he gave them a new rendezvous and let them take a few head of cattle, as supposed booty, to allay suspicions on their return to Tarentum. At a second meeting, the terms for the surrender of the town were set: the Carthaginians would liberate it without imposing the slightest tribute, and would respect its liberties and franchises, compensating themselves only by the pillaging of Roman property.

Philemenos, a renowned hunter, increased these nocturnal sorties, earning by his distribution of game the good graces of the garrison commander – a member of the *gens* Livia, whose name Livy prefers to keep quiet so as not to offend this illustrious family – and of the soldiers posted in the tower which, in the eastern part of the wall, guarded the second gate after the 'Temenide Gate'. In this way he succeeded in getting the postern opened at the slightest sound of a whistle. It was decided to act on the day when the governor of the town would be giving a party at the Mouseion, near the agora and thus at the other extremity of the town. While Nico remained on the spot, Philemenos joined Hannibal. An elite troop was formed, composed of 10,000 men of the light infantry and horsemen, who left the camp early in the morning in order to cover in one stretch the three days' march separating them from Tarentum (Polybius, VIII, 26, 2–5). Some few kilometres ahead, a party of eighty Numidians preceded the column, both to form a screen and to give the impression of a simple pillaging raid. At about twenty kilometres from the town, Hannibal called a halt for the evening meal and to give his officers their instructions. By dusk the next day, the troop had already left to reach the town's walls at dead of night.

Meanwhile, in Tarentum, C. Livius was unconcernedly feasting, putting off serious matters till the morrow, principally the dispatch of his cavalry to deal with the Numidian looters. Nico and his friends joined in the festivities and brought the Roman captain home very late, thus ensuring that all was calm and alarm-free. Then they met in the eastern part of the town which, *intra muros*, was occupied by tombs, in an exception – which Polybius (VIII, 28, 6–7) explains as the result of an oracle – to the rule in the classical world that pushed cemeteries outside defence walls. Massed around the tomb of Pythionikos, they waited to respond to the signal – a fire – that Hannibal was to make to them from the tumulus of Apollo Hyacinthus. When the signal was received, they rushed to the Temenide Gate, killed the guards and let in the bulk of the troops, 2,000 horsemen remaining outside the walls to deal with any eventuality. Meanwhile, a second column of 1,000 Africans arrived before the other gate, the one which Philemenos was in the habit of using when returning from his hunting expeditions. The latter showed himself first, together with three of his comrades carrying an enormous boar on a stretcher. At the sound of the whistle, the officer of the guard unsuspectingly opened the gate and was taken by surprise whilst admiring the beast; some thirty Africans burst through the wicket, slaughtered the guards and opened the main gate. The two columns that had entered by two different means of ingress then converged towards the agora. There Hannibal ordered 2,000 Gauls, divided into three sections, led by Tarentines, to occupy the town but to spare the inhabitants. Running to assemble at the sound of the Roman trumpets, which Philemenos and his companions had seized, the men of the garrison were easy prey for the Punic soldiers posted in the streets and on the agora. At daybreak, Hannibal had only to gather the Tarentines together to reassure them about their fate.

Certainly, the town had been taken, but its particular configuration prevented the Punic leader from achieving his real aim. For, with C. Livius, several thousand of the town's Roman defenders had retreated to the citadel, at the tip of the isthmus separating the bay of Tarentum properly speaking – the present-day Mare Grande – from the vast natural basin – the Mare Piccolo – that sheltered the Tarentine fleet. So the Romans kept control of the sole access channel. Hannibal quickly gave up any idea of taking the fortress by brute force; he lacked the means and knew from experience, as events had just shown him, that the only swift and economical way to take a fortified town was by trickery and treachery. At least, to prevent a return offensive to the town from the garrison shut in the citadel, which was separated by a wall and a trench, he increased the entrenchment by creating another ditch and two stockades. Principally, to get out the boats that were caught in the trap, he had the brilliant idea of transporting them on wagons, or rollers, along the line of one of the town's roads, perhaps the present-day Corso ai Due Mari (Polybius, VIII, 34, 9–11; Livy, XXV, 11, 16).

Even incomplete, this success had a kind of impetus. In the months that followed, Metapontum and Thurioi fell. Nearby Lucania was in a state of ferment. The leader of the confederation of Lucanian tribes which had until then remained loyal to Rome came to an understanding with Mago the Samnite, who was in command in Bruttium, to lay a trap for the proconsul Ti. Sempronius Gracchus who, according to the more probable of the two versions given by Livy (XXV, 16–17), fell at the place known as Campi Veteres. At Herdonea, in Apulia, the praetor Cn. Fulvius Flaccus learned at the expense of his army – he lost 16,000 men – how much it could still cost to attack Hannibal without due consideration. The latter, during the winter of 212–211, kept to Bruttium, divided between his desire to finish off the work begun in Tarentum and a concern to preserve Capua. The second affair won the day.

The symbol less of a strategy than of the Italian policy that Hannibal had been striving to pursue since Cannae, Capua was increasingly under threat. Of the twenty-three legions that Rome could henceforth bring into line, four, reinforced by allied contingents, were besieging the Campanian city, under the command of the two consuls of 212, Q. Fulvius Flaccus and Ap. Claudius Pulcher, who were prorogued the following year with the title of proconsul. From the Senate they had received an order not to leave Capua until they had taken it by storm (Livy, XXVI, 1, 2). In the spring of 211, leaving the bulk of his equipment and most heavily armed troops in Bruttium, Hannibal set off for Campania. In an engagement destined to break through the encirclement, where he himself fought alongside his Campanian allies, the Carthaginian lost several thousand men. He decided to create a diversion, and perhaps fulfil a dream.

## At the walls of Rome

As the old Fabius Maximus had clearly seen, Hannibal was not coming to besiege Rome, but to raise the siege of Capua (Livy, XXVI, 8, 5). When it became known in the Senate that he had managed to get his army across the Volturnus, using a bridge constructed of boats, it was decided to summon to the rescue part of the forces massed around Capua. From Campania to Latium a race began between Hannibal and the proconsul Q. Fulvius Flaccus, who was returning in haste with 15,000 men, footsoldiers and cavalry. Knowing that the Carthaginian army had taken the interior road, the via Latina, the proconsul sent couriers to prepare stopover points along the coastal route, the via Appia. Flaccus was one day behind his enemy, but he had the advantage of being on his own ground. Reaching the Porta Capena, he crossed the town from south to north and set up his camp, in the north-east, outside the walls, between the Esquiline and Colline Gates, more or less on the spot where, much later. Tiberius would place the Rome garrison, those praetorian cohorts formed by his predecessor, Augustus, at the very beginning of the principate. Delayed by the needs of his supply corps, then by bridges that had been cut at Fregellae on the Liris, Hannibal appears to have gone by way of

Frusinum (Frosinone) and Anagni, then veered off slightly to the right on a level with Tusculum, to set up a first camp some dozen kilometres east of Rome. Polybius, on the other hand, has Hannibal crossing Samnite territory in his march on Rome (IX, 5, 8), following a route which he does not state precisely, but which was situated perceptibly farther eastwards and matches the one ascribed to him also by Livy a little later, copying Coelius Antipater (XXVI, 11, 10–13), but on the return journey! Let me add that modern critics (Walbank, 1967, pp. 122–4; Lazenby, 1978, pp. 121–2; Huss, 1985, p. 371) incline towards this mountainous route, despite its difficulties and the surprising length of a detour that brought the Carthaginian army to the level of Reate (Rieti) before having it redescend south-westwards to approach Rome by the right bank of the Anio, not far from its confluence with the Tiber.

As may be imagined, the town was in turmoil. The Senate was in continuous session in the forum and, while the matrons went to implore the gods in their temples, all strategic points, especially the Capitol and the citadel, were reinforced by troops under the responsibility of the urban praetor C. Calpurnius Piso. When Hannibal drew even closer, setting up camp first on the Anio, three miles – fewer than five kilometres – from the walls, there had to be a reaction, all the more so because the Carthaginian, with 2,000 horsemen, came prancing up to the Colline Gate, examining the defence walls and making a reconnaissance of the location. Flaccus sent his cavalry to drive them off, and there was a movement of real panic when a large party of Numidian deserters, who were quartered on the Aventine, received the order to take part in the fight; seeing them descending on the Esquiline at the double, people believed, says Livy (XXVI, 10, 5–6), that the enemy was already within the gates.

Some days later, the two armies really came face to face under Rome's walls and – another major disagreement between Polybius (IX, 6–9) and Livy (XXVI, 11) that must be noted – according to the Greek historian, on the Roman side it was not the army corps taken from Capua that were set against Hannibal, but the young recruits of the second legion, freshly raised by the new consuls who had entered office in the spring of 211, Cn. Fulvius Centimalus and P. Sulpicius Galba. And as luck would have it, these recruits had presented themselves for enrolment on the very day of Hannibal's arrival! The mere sight of these raw recruits, lined up in battle order in front of the ramparts, is supposed to have given him pause for reflection; something one may hesitate to believe. But Livy's account is hardly more gratifying for lovers of 'war games', or even quite simply for historians. Flaccus and the two consuls supposedly did not refuse to fight, but downpours of thick hail, which the gods renewed the next day, prevented the adversaries from doing battle. And, shaken by this omen, the Hannibal whom Livy portrays elsewhere as so heedless of divine will, is said to have decided to retrace his steps, additionally annoyed to learn that at the very moment when he reached Rome's walls so little heed was paid to his arrival that contingents raised as reinforcements were then departing for Spain. As the ultimate blow to his pride, he learned from a prisoner that the land on which he had set up camp on the banks of the Anio had just been sold to Rome! And in reprisal he summoned the town crier to order him to auction the bankers' shops around the forum in Rome.... All these touches say more about Livy than about Hannibal; the historian shows here that he is sensitive to the interplay of passionate feelings, to disconcerting human freedom in the face of all determinism (Ducos, 1987, pp. 132–47). Whereby he becomes a writer, in the strongest sense of the term, and therefore sometimes very inconvenient for us. It is easier to believe Polybius when, to explain Hannibal's departure from the scene, he points out that the Carthaginian had gleaned enough booty from the Roman campaign, and more importantly, had calculated that enough time had elapsed since his leaving Campania for Ap. Claudius Pulcher, the consul who had remained at Capua, to become worried and lift the siege of the town to hasten to Rome's assistance.

But he miscalculated. At Capua, a majority of the local senate, believing themselves to have been deserted by Carthage, and still trusting in the clemency of Rome, opened the town's gates to its army. The suppression was merciless; several dozen notables of the town were beaten with rods and beheaded, and all Campanian citizens, not only in Capua, but also Atella and Calatia, were sold into slavery. The town of Capua itself was not destroyed, in consideration of the richness of the land, but it was politically sterilized. The city that had been Campania's pride was turned into a large agricultural township that was totally deprived of any communal organ, its lands and buildings, public or private, becoming the property of the Roman people. Every year, a prefect would come from Rome to 'lay down the law'.

Could Hannibal have any inkling of the terrible impression this tragic denouement would have on the peoples in all those Italic and Greek cities in which, albeit in fragile fashion, he had sometimes managed to inculcate the idea that the history of the region might take a different course? Probably, but he had already chosen his path. After the Roman venture, he went straight back to join Mago the Samnite in Bruttium. In Apulia, the friendly towns fell one after the other. Following Arpi, Salapia passed to the Romans in 210. Tarentum was lost in 209, and with it the hope of restoring to Carthage mastery of the region's territorial waters. Hannibal, who had dreamed of ruling in southern Italy on behalf of Carthage, imperceptibly became a prisoner in Calabria.

# 6

# Setbacks

Within the still limited confines of the Mediterranean world which, at the end of the third century BC, lived broadly in a state of cultural symbiosis, the second Punic War – or 'Hannibal's War' – was the first world war in the history of humankind. After igniting Spain, crossing the south of Gaul and the north of Italy, it had ravaged central Italy and continued to rage in south Italy. Nor, as we have seen, had it spared Sardinia and Sicily. The conflict had even spilled over beyond the western part of the Mediterranean basin with Philip of Macedon's entry into the war. As early as 215, the stationing of a fleet of fifty vessels at Brindisi, under the command of M. Valerius Laevinus, had prevented the king from following up his treaty of alliance with Hannibal by carrying the offensive on to Italian soil. But he had opened a front in Illyria, then on the north-west flank of continental Greece. To be more exact, it was Laevinus who had decided the second front by concluding an alliance agreement in the autumn of 212 between Rome and the Aetolians, the king of Macedonia's ancient adversaries. And it is in the framework of the operations carried out in Illyria and Greece that we see most clearly one of Carthage's major weaknesses in this war.

Massive intervention by the Punic fleet would have severed Laevinus' communications, probably destroyed his squadron and at the same time made possible the transfer of the Macedonian contingents to the south of Italy. But we saw earlier how Bomilcar, the man in charge of the Carthaginian navy in Sicilian waters, had avoided combat at Syracuse. The same admiral would be content a little later, in 211–210, to block the citadel of Tarentum without managing to achieve its surrender. Even in this period, it becomes clear that the inadequacy of the Punic fleet will weigh very heavily in Carthage's final defeat (de Saint-Denis, 1976, pp. 80–4). In this globalization of the war, by leaving mastery of the sea to Rome, Carthage deprived itself of its strongest trump card in order to avoid a multiplication of fronts and thus the dissipation of its own efforts.

## Operations in Spain up to the death of P. and Cn. Scipio (216–211)

The combined operations of the two Scipios south of the Ebro at the end of 217 (above, p. 103) had made Hasdrubal realize his precarious situation in the Spain that was in his charge. In the spring of 216, an initial batch of reinforcements – 4,000 infantry, 500 horsemen – had enabled him to quell an uprising of the Tartessians, a people who had nevertheless long been within the Punic sphere of influence (Livy, XXIII, 26–7), unless, as has been suggested (Scullard, 1930, p. 47), Livy, who was not conversant with facts about Spain, confused them with the Turdetani (above, p. 35). But shortly afterwards, the swiftly spread news that he had received orders from Carthage to go to Italy with his army had again swayed part of Spain over to Rome's side. Warned by Hasdrubal, Carthage's senate had not altered its choice of strategy: Hannibal's brother must hasten his preparations for departure to Italy; but to take his place in Spain and hold the country they sent a general named Himilco, with an army and a fleet. P. and Cn. Scipio did not make the mistake of underestimating their adversary. They assembled their forces near the Ebro to bar Hasdrubal's route. An important encounter took place in the autumn of 216. If we are to believe Livy (XXIII, 29, 6–13), it appears that the Carthaginian general was the victim chiefly of the lack of enthusiasm of his Spanish footsoldiers, who were placed in the centre of his battle line, because on the whole they would rather be defeated in Spain by yielding than take the chancy road to Italy in the role of victors. Despite the vigorous engagement of his wing troops – Carthaginians on one side and Africans on the other – and himself thwarted by the desertion of his cavalry, Hasdrubal was unable to avoid a defeat, combined with heavy losses, which ruined his hopes of going on to Italy, with an army now very much depleted. At the end of 216, the Scipios were able to report to Rome, where the disaster of Cannae was still being bewailed, that on their side at least the danger was averted. The more so because, as soon as Hasdrubal's defeat was known in Carthage, it was decided to send to Spain – and not as originally planned to Italy as reinforcements for Hannibal – his younger brother Mago, with his fleet and troops (Livy, XXIII, 32, 11).

According to Livy, who is our only source here, despite these reinforcements, between 215 and 212 the Carthaginians went from one setback to another in the Iberian peninsula; but his chronology often appears suspect and his topographical indications uncertain. For example, the Roman historian refers successively, in 215 then in 214, to two Carthaginian attacks against the town of Iliturgi, very probably an urban site in Andalusia, near Jaén; in both instances (XXIII, 49, 5–11 and XXIV, 42, 8–10) these attacks were repulsed by the Romans, with heavy losses on the Carthaginian side. Two parallel narratives have long been suspected in this repetition (De Sanctis, 1917, p. 247, note 76). It was perhaps in 214, as Livy says, that Castulo, in upper Andalusia, near Linares, went over to the Romans, a defection that was felt all the more keenly by the Carthaginians because the town had been a longstanding ally and was the place where the young Hannibal had found his Spanish bride, Imilce (above, p. 55). The Paduan also dates to the same year, 214, Rome's reparation for a humiliation, with the recapture of Saguntum, the siege and capture of which in 219 had been the start of the whole affair. But as he adds (XXIV, 42, 9) that it was the eighth year the town had been in enemy hands, this recapture should rather be dated to 212.

P. Cornelius Scipio was then in his sixth proconsulship, patiently nibbling away at the Carthaginian positions in the peninsula, with the assistance of his brother Gnaeus. They now had three Punic generals to contend with: in addition to Hannibal's two brothers, there was another Hasdrubal, Gisco's son, who was to fight for about ten years in Spain and then Africa; at the end of 212, he had joined camps with Mago, Hannibal's younger brother. The two Scipios decided to divide their army, which they believed to be sufficient in number, with the addition of 20,000 recently recruited Celtiberians. Publius took two-thirds to fight against the combined forces of Mago and Hasdrubal Gisco, Gnaeus having the task of attacking Hasdrubal Barca at the head of the remaining third, which included the Celtiberian reinforcements (Livy, XXV, 32, 1–8).

At the very beginning of 211, Publius Scipio was the first to go on campaign. He seems to have advanced southwards to about the level of Castulo (Appian, *Iber.*, 16), when he was harassed by the Numidian cavalry serving in the Carthaginian ranks, commanded by a young leader destined for a long and fine future, making his first direct intervention in the conflict. Massinissa was not seventeen, as Livy makes out, but about twenty-five; by order of his father Gaia, who reigned over the Massylian Numidians, it seems that he had already had a victorious encounter in Africa itself with the other Numidian king, Syphax, who with an army trained by a Roman instructor, had dared to attack the Carthaginian forces (Livy, XXIV, 48–9). Publius, who found himself encircled by Massinissa's cavalry, learning moreover of the imminent arrival of Indibilis, at the head of 7,500 Suessetani, resolved to break out of the circle by going to meet Indibilis by night. The proconsul fell in this combat, pierced by a lance. At the same time, his brother Gnaeus, abandoned by his Celtiberian allies, decided to beat a retreat northwards. Pursued by the Numidian cavalry, and soon caught by the forces of the three Punic generals, which had joined, Gnaeus hastily took up a position on a bare and stony hill where, for want of an entrenchment, he died under the sheer weight of numbers, barely a month after his brother. Pliny the Elder (*H. N.*, III, 9) placed the site of Cn. Scipio's fall at Ilorci; perhaps the present-day place known as Lorqui, some twenty kilometres north of Murcia (Scullard, 1930, pp. 50–1).

There was something tragic about the fate of the two Scipios, dying in the Spain they had so valiantly defended for seven years, and at the very moment when almost everywhere, and especially in Italy, the fortunes of war were once again smiling on Rome. At least their army's survivors made the Carthaginians pay dearly for the death of the two leaders. Having retreated and dug in this side of the Ebro, the Roman soldiers, assembled in military comitia, proclaimed as general not Publius Scipio's lieutenant, Tiberius Fonteius, who was by no means undeserving, but a Roman knight called Lucius Marcius Septimus, whose personal charisma had made a great impression and who galvanized the army's energies so well that he succeeded in surprising the Carthaginians in their camp and inflicting heavy losses (Livy, XXV, 39). Several weeks later, when the Roman Senate received from Lucius Marcius a report of his exploits, at the head of which the new general gave himself the title 'propraetor', many senators pulled a wry face; it was not customary in Rome – or Carthage – for generals to be proclaimed by their troops (Livy, XXVI, 2, 1–2). But Lucius Marcius was forgiven. He had won enormous booty in the Carthaginian camp, among other trophies a silver shield – which became a gold shield in Pliny the Elder (*H.N.*, XXXV, 14) – bearing on its *umbo* a portrait in relief of Hasdrubal Barca, and weighing 137 pounds. In memory of this victory, the shield, given the name 'Marcius' shield', was to remain hanging in the Capitoline temple in Rome until the fire that destroyed it in 83 BC.

## The young Scipio is appointed to head the army of Spain

Capua's surrender at the end of spring 211 made it unnecessary to keep the troops that had besieged it on the site. On the Senate's orders, the general in command, the praetor C. Claudius Nero, embarked at Pozzuoli with several thousand footsoldiers and about a thousand horsemen, landed at Tarragona and went immediately to the Ebro to add these new contingents to the army he took over from Tiberius Fonteius and Lucius Marcius. Shortly afterwards, he was lucky enough to surprise Hasdrubal Barca, who had inopportunely camped in a defile, the defile of the 'Black Stones' (*Ad Lapides Atros*) among the Ausetani, in other words, rather than south of the Ebro (Lazenby, 1978, p. 132), where it was not likely that he could have ventured, in the Pyrenean foothills of upper Catalonia (Huss, 1985, p. 375). In an awkward position, Hasdrubal is supposed to have promised to quit Spain, together with his army, if the Roman general would let him go; but on the day fixed for the negotiation, he asked for a postponement on the pretext of some religious interdict, and in the end took advantage of a thick fog to make his escape, leaving the unhappy praetor to meditate on the *fraus Punica* (Livy, XXVI, 17).

In Rome where, after the fall of Capua and Hannibal's increasing confinement in the south of Italy, growing attention was being paid to the Iberian front, there was concern to choose for the army of Spain a leader who would measure up to its strategic importance and also to the memory of the two great generals who had died. Whatever Livy may say, and here again his chronology vacillates, Nero was probably allowed to complete his period of command to the end of 211; at all events, there is no mention of his early recall. Nevertheless, the appointment of a new commander for the army of Spain was the subject of an exceptional procedure. The consuls in office, C. Fulvius Centimalus and P. Sulpicius Galba, summoned the *comitia centuriata* – an adequate electoral body – but proceeded in an extraordinary fashion, outside the 'normal course' of general elections, to the nomination of a general who was given a proconsular *imperium*. And the chosen man was no less extraordinary, as he was the young P. Cornelius Scipio (Figure 8).

The reader may recall the first appearance of the future Africanus in this history (above, p. 84). It was at the end of November 218, and the young man

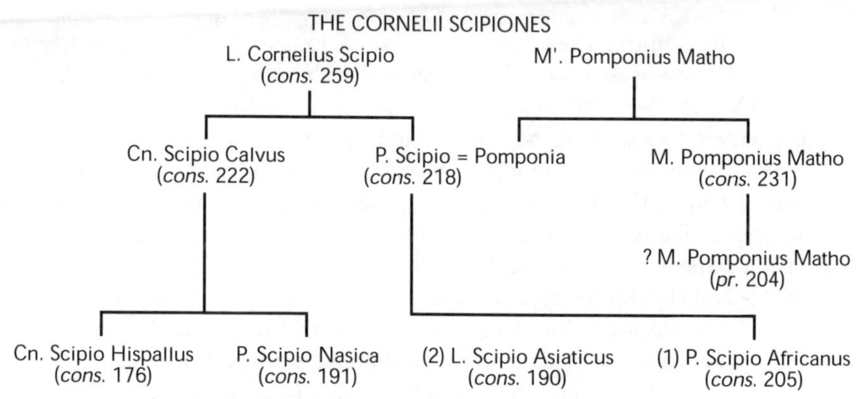


**Figure 8** Three generations of Cornelii Scipiones

had rescued his father, who had been wounded at the battle of the Ticinus and was in grave danger of being taken prisoner. Two years later, barely twenty years old, at this time military tribune and by virtue of this rank a corps commander of one of the legions engaged in the battle, in Livy (XXII, 53) we see him, after the disaster of Cannae, taking command of the small group of young officers who, in the face of defeatist machinations, took an oath never to betray the republic. It was clear, says the historian, that the fates had chosen him to wage this war. Thus, *a posteriori*, the youth of this budding general appears to have been studded with premonitory signs.

Polybius, too, lapses into hagiography, but without being fooled by it, as is shown by the account he gives of his hero's election to the curule aedileship in 213. Scipio was then twenty-two or twenty-three years old, and to attain the aedileship *suo anno*, as the Romans said, he would normally have had to wait ten years or so. But it is true that in those terrible years, with the losses sustained on the battlefields by the senatorial nobility, there was less concern about the legal age. Polybius who, through the intermediary of his patron, Scipio Aemilianus, had access to the family archives, has given a detailed account of the circumstances of the future Africanus' accession to the aedileship (X, 4–5). In fact, he presented himself in order to make certain of the election of his own brother, Lucius, counting on his personal popularity to ensure that their joint candidacies would triumph, with the consent of his mother, Pomponia, from whom he had demanded the indispensable *toga candida*. The authority of paterfamilias had been delegated to this worthy woman, in the absence of her sons' father in Spain, and what convinced her was the account given by her son of a dream in which he saw himself elected, together with his brother, and returning to the house to be embraced by his joyful and proud mother. Polybius adds that he does not believe this story about the dream, but that in the end it was a clever ploy because it allowed the idea that Scipio was in communication with the gods to gain credence in public opinion: the superior man is free to turn the credulity of the common herd to his own profit.

The equally admiring Livy, for his part, did not hesitate to remark that, despite his youth, Scipio was astonishingly preoccupied with his own image. He had, says Livy (XXVI, 19, 3–9), the singular art of giving weight to the slightest of his actions, undertaking nothing, whether in public or private, without taking himself off to the Capitol for long periods. This custom, which perhaps reminded the Romans of Numa, the sorcerer-king, had given rise to the belief that he was of divine origin; like Alexander the Great, he was even said to be the issue of a monstrous serpent which had sometimes been seen in his mother's bed. Scipio let people talk and kept up the mystery. Considering the times in which he lived and the means at his disposal, this highly organized man, of rare precocity, appears in our sources as an unparalleled manipulator of public opinion. With the capture of Cartagena, we shall see how the general was able to achieve such a powerful influence over his soldiers by making use of all these methods.

## The capture of Cartagena (210)

The Senate had thus placed at the head of the army of Spain a young man aged barely twenty-five, and more importantly, one who had not yet held either a consulship or even a praetorship; such a responsible command had therefore been entrusted to a virtual *privatus*, whose cursus was empty of the highest magistracies. It was quite without precedent, and Livy (XXVI, 18, 5–6) rather unconvincingly explains it by the refusal of the republic's greatest public servants to take on a post that was reputedly difficult. It is easier to believe, following Mommsen, that the Senate – and more narrowly, the faction of the Cornelii at its centre – had acted in such a way that Scipio was the sole candidate (cf. Scullard, 1951, p. 66). Whatever the truth of the matter, the new commander left Ostia with thirty ships, which landed 10,000 infantry and 1,000 cavalry at Ampurias. From there, with the ships following him along the coast, Scipio reached Tarragona. During his rounds of the allies and the winter quarters of the various corps of his own army, he conspicuously kept Lucius Marcius, the avenger of his father and uncle, at his side. Such was his aura that the other's prestige could only be of use to him without putting him in the shade.

Early in the spring of 210, the general was joined by the propraetor who had been appointed as his assistant, a perceptibly older senator, M. Junius Silanus, a member of a family who were friends of the Scipios. He left him with several thousand men to guard the regions situated this side of the Ebro, and took the bulk of his forces – 25,000 footsoldiers and 2,500 horsemen – across the river. He had obtained information about the position of the three Carthaginian armies and so had learnt that Hasdrubal, the son of Gisco, was stationed somewhere between Gades and the mouth of the Tagus, on the Atlantic; that Mago held the hinterland of Castulo, in upper Andalusia, and that Hasdrubal Barca was, not at Saguntum, as Livy says (XXVI, 20, 6) with obvious distaste for Iberian geography, but among the Carpetani, in Castilla la Nueva. He had calculated that none of them was fewer than ten days' march from Carthago Nova (Cartagena), the capital of the Barcid 'kingdom' founded some fifteen years before by Hamilcar's son-in-law (above, pp. 38–9), and of paramount strategic importance. Scipio also knew that it was defended by barely a thousand men-at-arms. He resolved to strike a mighty blow and seize Cartagena.

He took into his confidence only C. Laelius, the prefect of his fleet, a 'new man' whose brilliant service achievements we shall see in the campaigns in Spain and Africa, but who was to have nothing more than a modest political career, entirely in the shadow of the great man who was his patron. And it was from Laelius, who outlived his protector and whom he met at the end of his life, around 160 BC, that Polybius gleaned at first hand the exact details that fill out his account of the capture of Cartagena.

With Laelius making his way along the coast and Scipio with his troops coming overland, they are supposed to have reached the town simultaneously in the space of seven days; this figure is to be found in both Polybius and Livy, and must be assumed to be wrong – bearing in mind the distance (over 400 kilometres) separating Cartagena from the mouth of the Ebro – rather than admitting, in company with several critics, that the departure-point cannot have been the Ebro, but the Jucar (above, p. 47 and Walbank, 1967, pp. 204–5). At all events, the Roman fleet dropped anchor opposite the town's sea frontage, at the end of the narrow and deep bay that opens to the south. Scipio set up camp to the east. To the west and north, a lagoon – the present-day Almájar is what remains – connected with the bay by a channel, lapped against the town's fortifications on the landward side; in this way it provided a double entrenchment, and it could be assumed that, in the event of an attack, the ramparts on this side would have fewer defenders. But Scipio had learnt from fishermen who were familiar with the area that the lagoon was fairly shallow, permanently fordable in almost every part and, most importantly, that towards evening, probably owing to a land wind which usually rose about then – in addition to a very slight tide in the Mediterranean – a large amount of its water emptied out, leaving very little depth. The Roman immediately saw how he could make use of this and, in his speech before the battle, did not fail to tell his soldiers that at the right moment Neptune, who had appeared to him in a dream as he slept, would come to their aid.

The attack was in two stages. Scipio's troops first repulsed a sortie from the Carthaginian garrison before going on to attack on the east side, on the narrow strip of land that formed the isthmus between the end of the bay and the lagoon. This first assault failed. But Scipio, without withdrawing any troops from the isthmus, in anticipation of the evening drop in the level of the lagoon, had positioned on its north and west shores 500 men armed with long ladders. At the ebb tide, when the water began to recede and run through the outlet leading to the sea, many saw this as proof of the complicity between the gods and the sorcerer-general. With water barely up to their waists, sometimes only to their knees, they crossed without difficulty. While they gained a foothold on the defence wall, so poorly defended at these points, others attacked the gate, on the east, which soon yielded. Only the citadel remained, close to the sea wall, and this surrendered without a fight.

The booty taken was as vast as expected: an enormous amount of war material, notably what constituted the artillery of that period, catapults and other large missile-projectors; sixty-three transport vessels, many still laden with their cargoes. There was, in addition, all the gold and silver resulting from the looting and confiscations carried out in Spain for nearly thirty years and amassed in Cartagena as if in a giant safe by Hamilcar's son-in-law and his successors. Scipio adopted the attitude towards prisoners that was necessary to serve Rome's cause among the Spanish populations. He immediately freed Cartagena's citizens, whom he looked on less as Carthage's allies than as its hostages. And the hostages properly speaking – men, women and children held at Cartagena – were restored to their nearest and dearest without delay, or handed over to the ambassadors of their respective cities who happened to be there. Polybius (X, 18–19) and Livy (XXVI, 49) similarly pay tribute to the Roman general's concern that the common soldiery should have respect for the captives. But the Latin historian, in addition, delights in recounting the pleasant story of 'Scipio's self-restraint'. As a gift, some of his soldiers had brought him a young Spanish maiden of exceptional beauty. Scipio summoned her parents and betrothed, a young Celtiberian prince, to whom he handed back the young woman, asking him only to be a friend to the Roman people in future. And when the young prince, overwhelmed with gratitude, laid at his feet the gold he had brought to buy back his fiancée, Scipio urged him to keep it, and look on it as a wedding present. In an era when, for an ambitious artist, there could be no greater or more glorious title than to be known as a 'painter of history', we know how much Poussin – with the painting kept in the Pushkin Museum in Moscow – or François Lemoyne 'milked' the scene evoked by Livy (XXVI, 50) when creating their canvases.

## From Scipio's victory at Baecula (Bailén) to Hasdrubal Barca's arrival in Italy (209–early 207)

The capture of Cartagena was the brilliant result of a strategic plan that was a work of genius for both its boldness and rapidity of execution, quite on a par with Hannibal's dazzling advances in Italy in the years 218–216. By seizing their principal base, Scipio had in a few days severed the key communications link of the Carthaginians in Spain with their mother-city. But the three Punic armies that held the country were still intact.

Leaving a garrison at Cartagena, with the approach of winter Scipio had gone back to his quarters at Tarragona. On the return journey, he began to reap the dividends of his victory and his treatment of prisoners and hostages. The first to rally to him was Edeco, probably the chief of the Edetani, on the Levant coast between the Jucar and Ebro. Much more seriously for the Carthaginians, Andobales and Mandonios, two chiefs of the Ilergetes, between Aragon and upper

Catalonia, soon defected, and many minor Iberian princes followed their example (Polybius, X, 35). Hasdrubal Barca watched his allies desert him, one after another, and his forces dwindle as those of the Romans swelled. He resolved to do battle as quickly as possible, with the thought at the back of his mind that, if he did not emerge as the victor, he would gather around him and the remains of his army the largest possible number of Celtiberians to go and join his brother in Italy.

For his part, Scipio was also looking for battle. He left his Tarragona quarters in early spring – of 209 for Livy, who put the capture of Cartagena in 210: see XXVII, 7, 5–6 – strengthened by all those who had rallied to him. The encounter took place at Baecula (Bailén), some forty kilometres north of Jaén, on the right bank of the Guadalquivir, where Hasdrubal had taken up a position to bar the Roman's access to Baetica (present-day Andalusia). The solidity of the position held by the Carthaginian made Scipio hesitate at first. Then, fearing that if he simply marked time it would give Mago and the other Hasdrubal, Gisco's son, the opportunity to come to the rescue, he decided to engage comabt. Here again, his determination served him well; Hasdrubal had not finished bringing his troops out of their entrenchment when he was attacked on the right by Laelius and on the left by Scipio himself. Hannibal's brother preferred to break off the engagement, save his war booty and funds, and leave with his elephants and the residue of his army for the valley of the Tagus, thence to reach Castile and the Pyrenean foothills by way of Navarre. Fearing the arrival of the two other Carthaginian armies, Scipio did not go in pursuit.

The victory at Baecula laid open to Scipio the route of the lower valley of the Guadalquivir, which he would take two years later. For the moment, it completed the rallying process that the seizure of Cartagena had started among the Iberians. And the Spanish leaders who now pressed around the Roman general like vassals around their suzerain made him an act of allegiance as they had formerly done to the Barcids; they saluted him with the title of king. Nothing could place Scipio in greater difficulties *vis-à-vis* the Senate in Rome where, since the end of the sixth century the republic had been based first and foremost on the *odium regni*, a profound loathing for royalty (Martin, 1994, p. 333). When Edeco and then Andobales, on a personal basis, had saluted him thus, he had let it pass – not that he had not noticed, as Polybius says (X, 40, 3), but because he was already sufficiently acquainted with the Spanish mentality and its liking for monarchy. But this public proclamation and enthronement by the masses were unacceptable. Scipio tried to make it be understood that 'the title of king, which is great everywhere else, was intolerable to Rome' (Livy, XXVII, 19, 4). The Spaniards were at liberty to acknowledge that he had the spirit of a king, as long as they did not use the word! It is not certain that the 'barbarians', as the historian has it, fully appreciated the true greatness that such an attitude revealed. One might even suspect that they were a little disappointed. But Scipio consoled them by agreeing to accept the title of *imperator* which, he disclosed on this occasion, his soldiers had already conferred upon him. Was this not the same title (above, p. 38) that

Hamilcar's son-in-law, Hasdrubal the Fair, had accepted from the Iberian minor kings?

If we follow Livy, while the Roman general tarried a little to receive the submission of the peoples of Spain, then returned to his Tarragona quarters and sent detachments to keep watch over the southern foothills of the Pyrenees, the two other Punic generals, Mago and Hasdrubal Gisco, joined Hannibal's brother to confer with him. All three were agreed in thinking that, after the last Roman victories, the only region which still remained absolutely loyal to Carthage was henceforth the lower valley of the Guadalquivir and the Gades area, on the coast. It was decided that Hasdrubal Gisco would take refuge in this sanctuary with his army, enlarged by the addition of Mago's, while Mago himself would go to the Balearic Islands with funds for the enrolment of mercenaries. Massinissa, who for the time being was still serving alongside the Carthaginians, was given the mission of carrying out regular raids, at the head of 3,000 horsemen, mainly to ravage the towns and territory of Rome's new allies.

As for Hannibal's younger brother, applying a strategic plan that had already been decided in the Council of Elders at Carthage – a project known to the Romans as the result of a bold incursion at Utica, where he had taken prisoners, by M. Valerius Messalla, prefect of the fleet of Sicily – he gathered as many Celtiberian soldiers as he could and went off to cross the Pyrenees by a western pass. The choice of such a route – forced upon him by Roman surveillance to the east – perceptibly longer than Hannibal's in 218, necessarily delayed his progress, which was further slowed down by recruiting, as he went, contingents levied from among the Gauls, who were attracted by the enormous quantities of gold that he carried in his wagons (Livy, XXVII, 36, 2). Hasdrubal thus spent the best part of 208 between the Pyrenees and the Alps, and had to wait for the end of winter to cross the latter at a point unknown to us. According to Livy (XXVII, 39, 7) and Appian (*Hann.*, 52), he followed in his brother's footsteps. That would have been pushing the family spirit a little too far, since nothing obliged him to make the detours that had cost Hannibal and his army five months of suffering. It is more likely, as is commonly thought (e.g. de Sanctis, 1917, p. 561), that he took the Durance and Mont-Genèvre route which presented him with no obstacles. In Rome, they could follow his progress without being able to oppose it. Ambassadors from Marseille had first gone to announce the Carthaginian's arrival in Gaul to the Roman Senate, which had dispatched observers with the task of examining the situation, liaising with the Marseillais allies. They therefore knew that the spring of 207 would see Hasdrubal emerging into the Po Valley with his army; it was a serious threat, but would be no surprise.

## The death of Marcellus (summer 208)

Hannibal, too, was certainly aware that his brother was preparing to give him a helping hand at the other extremity of Italy. After such an accumulation of setbacks since the capture of Syracuse – Capua's surrender in 211, the capitulation of Salapia in 210, the fall of Tarentum in 209, not to mention Spain, the linchpin of the whole enterprise, whose collapse he was witnessing – here lay his great hope. Meanwhile, he had to hold firm, and not allow himself to be incarcerated in his Calabrian hideout.

In the early summer of 209, when he had learnt that Tarentum was besieged by Q. Fabius Maximus, who had just taken on his fifth consulship and been glorified – in preference to another great celebrity, T. Manlius Torquatus – with the title of 'princeps senatus', or leader of the Senate, Hannibal had done his best to avert the city's fall. Against him, the principal generals of the Roman army had shared their roles: while Fabius prepared to attack Tarentum, the other consul, Q. Fulvius Flaccus, was to 'pen' Hannibal in Bruttium as much as possible; but it fell to Marcellus, with an extension of his proconsulship, to play an active part in preventing the Carthaginian from coming to the besieged city's aid, and to try to make contact with him. As Hannibal had gone up into Apulia as far as Canusium and was trying to raise the populations against Rome, Marcellus hastened to stage an encounter. On the first occasion Hannibal pulled back, before agreeing to fight. The luck of war had initially favoured him, but shortly afterwards Marcellus took his revenge and forced Hannibal to retreat, although he was unable to go in pursuit as he had suffered such heavy losses in his ranks. He even withdrew for several months to Venusia, so that his army could lick its wounds. Hannibal had then gone to the aid of Tarentum, by a series of forced marches, but it was already too late. The town had fallen, more by treachery than force of arms, and Fabius had seized a booty that was almost on a par with that taken at Syracuse three years earlier. It was a real windfall for Rome's public finances, which were in a parlous state. The Carthaginian had retreated to Metapontum, where he tried in vain to lure Fabius into an ambush; getting the gods on his side, the consul had had the auspices taken and had thus scented the trap (Livy, XXVII, 16, 12–16).

Unlike the Romans, who were gradually extending their hold over the south of Italy and were able to rebuild their forces, whether Hannibal was victorious or evenly matched with his foes he was now losing both ground and men. Early in 208, hopes began to rise in Rome that one mighty blow could be struck that would put an end to the war now entering its eleventh year. For lethargy was spreading; in the preceding year twelve out of thirty colonies, some of them very ancient, such as Ardea, had offered the pretext that they were ruined and refused point blank to provide contingents or subsidies. Now, early in 208, Etruria showed signs of disturbance and threatened an uprising; hostages had to be taken at Arretium (Arezzo), where Varro, the consul who had survived Cannae, had to keep a garrison with a legion he commanded in his role of propraetor.

Despite the criticism that his long period of inaction at Venusia in the preceding year had earned him, Marcellus was elected consul for the fourth time. His colleague, Titus Quinctius Crispinus, had immediately gone to Bruttium, where he replaced Fulvius Flaccus. He first attacked Locri, but Hannibal's approach soon caused him to abandon the siege, and he went off to join Marcellus, who had brought his army out of Venusia. The two consuls' intention was to join forces in order to wage a battle with Hannibal which they wanted to be decisive. He was marching towards Locri, but made an about-turn to confront them. The two armies made contact between Venusia and Bantia (Banzi), on the border of Apulia and Lucania. Between their respective camps, which were very close, lay a wooded hill where Hannibal had immediately stationed a strong detachment of Numidian cavalry, to cover every eventuality and chiefly to surprise enemy patrols. The two consuls had the unfortunate idea of reconnoitring the terrain for themselves. Emerging from their camp with a small escort, they fell into the ambush. Crispinus, badly wounded, managed to get away by the skin of his teeth, but Marcellus fell, pierced by a lance. Hannibal, who had come to have a high regard for this adversary, gave him military honours and had him buried on the spot.

The two consuls, who had desired to avenge Cannae, had actually only succeeded in making 208 even more disastrous than 216, because Crispinus did not survive his injuries and the year was thus marked by the death in combat of two consuls, an unprecedented event, as Livy emphasizes. At the time, Marcellus was over sixty and, with Polybius (X, 32), one may well be surprised that such a seasoned army leader so recklessly exposed himself to danger – temerity of which Hannibal would not have been guilty, adds the Greek historian, forgetting that our hero had been wounded below Saguntum's walls in the autumn of 219 (above, p. 50) because he had incautiously approached them too closely; but it is true that he was then only twenty-seven or twenty-eight. This unhappy end by no means tarnished the general's image. Marcellus lived on in Roman memory as a great captain who, although lacking real strategical genius, had had the necessary drive and tenacity to make an effective defence of Campania in its time of greatest danger, then to capture Syracuse, and finally to combine his efforts with those of Fabius and Flaccus to turn the south of Italy into a shrinking prison where, from one season to the next, Hannibal had less and less space in which to move around. A tradition that seems to go back to Posidonius of Apamea, gleaned by Plutarch (*Fabius*, 19, 4; *Marcellus*, 9, 7), beautifully sums up this picture: Fabius had been Rome's shield, Marcellus its sword. Now another sword had to be found.

## THE BATTLE OF THE METAURUS (SUMMER 207), OR THE END OF THE ILLUSION

Before burying Marcellus, Hannibal had removed his signet-ring. He had it in mind to make use of it to regain possession of Salapia by trickery. Lost to him two years earlier, the town had been one of his favourite wintering-places, of which he had nothing but fond memories (above, p. 124). But Crispinus, knowing that his colleague's seal was in the Carthaginian's hands, had put the neighbouring cities on their guard. When the people of Salapia received a letter bearing Marcellus' seal and announcing his forthcoming arrival they were not taken in by the ruse. When Hannibal arrived one fine night at the gate of the town, a few hundred

Roman deserters who made up his advance guard were allowed to pass under the raised portcullis, but then it fell again behind these renegades, who were slaughtered. Greatly vexed, Hannibal went back to Bruttium, where his lieutenant Mago the Samnite, besieged in Locri, was finding it increasingly difficult to offer resistance. The siege was lifted thanks to Hannibal's arrival, and he spent the winter of 208–207 there.

In Rome, as the consuls in office were both dead, an *ad hoc* dictator, T. Manlius Torquatus, presided over the elections for the year 207, which took place under pressure from Hasdrubal's imminent and expected arrival in the north of Italy, accompanied by a strong army. To confront the threat that the two brothers would join forces, Marcellus' death, and the battle fatigue and age of the two other front-rank Roman generals, Fabius Maximus and Fulvius Flaccus, imposed on the Senate the difficult choice of a general who simultaneously had dynamism, was thoroughly experienced and belonged to one of the dominant clans. There was no question of bringing Scipio back from Spain, where his proconsulship was extended. The name that emerged belonged to a patrician, Gaius Claudius Nero: at the side of Fulvius Flaccus, he had won renown at Suessula and around Capua as praetor, then propraetor, in 212 and 211, and we have seen (above, p. 136) that he was able to take Hannibal by surprise in Upper Catalonia during his period of command in the last months of 211. The way in which Hasdrubal's brother had avoided a confrontation then had left him with a desire for revenge. Elected with him, to temper his hotheadedness, was the old Marcus Livius Salinator, the consul who had defeated the Illyrians in 219, and who needed a little persuading because he had lived some ten years in a sort of internal exile, having been accused – wrongly, in his opinion – of peculation (Livy, XXVII, 34).

With a total strength of twenty-three legions, including the four serving in Spain, Roman forces in that year regained the record numbers of the second Punic War, which had already been reached in 211. To keep Hannibal in Lucania and Bruttium, besides the two legions under his command, Claudius Nero could count on equal numbers of troops, commanded by praetors, at Capua, in the Tarentum region and in Bruttium; in all, seven legions, to which allied contingents were added. The task of checking Hasdrubal in Gaul, in other words, northern Italy, was entrusted to Salinator with his two consular legions, reinforced by the two legions of the praetor L. Porcius Licinus, and those commanded in Etruria by C. Terentius Varro, consul in 216, now with the rank of propraetor.

Hasdrubal arrived in the Po Valley around the end of April or beginning of May. His army, which upon its departure had probably equalled that of his brother ten years earlier, had suffered less from an easier and shorter crossing of the Alps. And while Hannibal, on his descent of the Italian slopes, had had to do battle in the depths of winter, Hasdrubal reached Cisalpine Gaul in fine weather and with a rested army. This doubtless explains why those in Rome did not believe it possible to halt his advance along the line of the Po, which would, moreover, have involved a dangerous incursion by Roman troops into the territory of the Insubres where, apart from Piacenza and Cremona, they had no rear bases and their lines of communication were very uncertain. It had been decided to ensure the defence of central Italy at all costs, level with the north of Etruria and what was still known in Livy's time as the *ager Gallicus*, or the former territory of the Gaulish Senones on the Adriatic, between Ancona and Ravenna.

In Rome people's fears were mounting, materializing in the form of prodigies. To allay the first and ward off the others, a supplication of the gods was decreed (Livy, XXVII, 37, 1), and the pontiffs decided that a choir of three times nine young maidens should go through the town singing a hymn in honour of Juno Regina, composed by Livius Andronicus, one of the leading Latin poets, born in slavery in Tarentum, and taking his family name from his emancipation by the consul Livius Salinator's father.

The time that Hasdrubal had gained in the Alps he lost at Placentia, which he besieged. If he were to succeed, the symbolic weight of the undertaking would in all probability be very potent. Rome's most advanced outpost in Celtic territory, the colony of Placentia dated from the very year, 218, that had witnessed the outbreak of this war and, after his success on the Trebia, Hannibal had judged the place to be too well defended for him to take it on. The capture of Placentia would have provided Hasdrubal with a valuable rearguard bastion and could not have failed to create a considerable stir in the north among the tribes of the Insubres, and in the south among the Boii, whose territory he would have to cross and whose alliance, or at the very least their neutrality, was essential to him. Perhaps, too, Hannibal's brother hoped to entice to the vicinity of Placentia the two legions of the praetor Porcius Licinus, and on mounting his campaign to repeat Hannibal's initial success on the Trebia. But the town's resistance discouraged him. When he reckoned that he had recruited enough Gaulish auxiliaries, and the season was far enough advanced to provision his troops and cavalry with fodder and grain, he lifted the siege and set off southwards. Unlike Hannibal in the spring of 217 (above, p. 91), he did not attempt to cross the Apennines in order to penetrate into Etruria. He chose to leave Italy's great spine on his right and descend through Romagna, along the Adriatic. At the same time, he addressed a letter to Hannibal and entrusted it to a squad of couriers composed of four Gaulish and two Numidian horsemen. We shall see shortly what became of the messengers and their letter.

Even before receiving his brother's couriers and arranging with him the strategy of their joining forces, Hannibal knew that he would have to go a good part of the way north in order to meet him. He was well aware of the advantage to be drawn from a common pooling of their men, and the destabilization that would be wreaked in Rome by a victory won in central Italy, Umbria or among the Pelignians, for instance. He also weighed the risks of the manoeuvre, in the first place the possible loss of Bruttium, if not in its entirety, at least Locri and Crotona, if he left it defenceless for a few months, These were the ports on which he could still rely to receive aid from Carthage, to ensure links with the Macedonians and even, in the last resort, if all were lost, to re-embark for Africa with the residue of his army. That is why he was in no hurry to leave his winter quarters. He took the time to assemble the detachments that were scattered in the various garrisons in Calabria and marched with his army into Lucania, where he set up his camp beside Grumentum, a city that had always remained loyal to him. From Venusia, the consul Claudius Nero came to meet him with his two legions, augmented by the two legions of the proconsul Fulvius Flaccus, drawn from Bruttium: in total, 40,000 footsoldiers and 2,500 cavalry; even if this figure quoted by Livy (XXVII, 40, 14) seems excessive, we are talking of forces that well outnumbered those available to the Carthaginian. A fight in which Hannibal suffered more losses than his adversary did not prevent him from pushing on to Venusia, where his encounter with the enemy went against him once more. His situation was becoming critical. Under cover of night, and by mountain paths so as to avoid any engagement, he reached Metapontum, adding its garrison to his troops, and ordering his lieutenant and nephew, Hanno, who was in command of Metapontum, to go and form another army in Bruttium. With his forces thus increased, Hannibal returned to Venusia by the same roundabout route, then took up a position at Canusium (Canosa) in Apulia.

Meanwhile, the messengers dispatched by Hasdrubal to his brother had ridden flat out almost the length of the peninsula. When they learned that Hannibal had gone from Venusia to Metapontum, they intended to join him there, but mistook the route and went to Tarentum, where they were taken prisoner by soldiers of the propraetor in command, Q. Claudius Flamen. The letter they were carrying fell into the hands of the consul Claudius Nero, who thus learned that Hasdrubal was giving his brother a rendezvous in Umbria. He sent the letter to the Senate, at the same time informing them of the initiative he was immediately going to take, which was all the more daring because it was not customary for a consul to go, on his own initiative, beyond the bounds of the 'province' (to be understood less as a geographical district than as a theatre of operations) which had been assigned to him. He dispatched couriers to prepare bivouacs for him on the route he intended to take, along the coast on the eastern fringe of the Samnites' territory and Picenum. Taking the best sections of his army, 1,000 horsemen and 6,000 infantry, and leaving his lieutenant Quintus Catius to guard his camp, facing Hannibal, to put the latter off the scent he pretended to attack a neighbouring Lucanian town that was held by a Punic garrison, but then, leaving by night, he went in a series of forced marches to Picenum. Had Hannibal got wind of the consul's precipitate manoeuvre? What is certain is that he did not budge. Even if he had wanted to go in pursuit, he probably lacked the means. For, contrary to what is sometimes said (Picard, 1967, p. 197; Brisson, 1973, p. 262), it was not just a 'curtain of troops' that Claudius Nero had left facing him, as a snare to mislead him, but well and truly the bulk of his army, around 30,000 men, and it seems that the proconsul Fulvius Flaccus, one of the best generals Rome could bring to bear, was present at the time in Canusium alongside the legate Quintus Catius (De Sanctis, 1917, III, 2, p. 574). In any case, the extreme rapidity of Nero's march, by night as well as by day, discouraged any thoughts of pursuit. In only a few days, his light troops, unencumbered by baggage, had reached the camp of Livius

Salinator, in the neighbourhood of Sena Gallica (Senigallia), near which the practor L. Porcius Licinius had also set up his own.

Hasdrubal's camp, too, was quite close by, and Nero arrived at night in order not to draw his attention, and to avoid creating a second entrenchment or even enlarging that of his colleague, his officers and men were received in their tents by their counterparts in Livius' legions. But this stratagem did not deceive the experienced eye of the Carthaginian who, from his forward positions, could see greater numbers of troops and horses that were worn from recent heavy riding; nor did it deceive his ears, as he could hear redoubled trumpet signals from the consul's camp, a sign of the presence of both consuls together. Worried, he decided to break away and intended to recross the Metaurus by night with his army. As neither Livy nor Polybius, in the extract devoted to the episode (XI, 1–3), throws any light on the matter, we shall never know what Hannibal's brother could have had in mind in risking this withdrawal. Did he perhaps mean to go far enough up the river on the left bank to be able to join the Via Flaminia and upper valley of the Tiber, and from there to march on Rome? But Claudius Nero had parried this eventuality in advance when he wrote to the senators to send the two urban legions to Narnia, a strategic point between Sabinum and Umbria (Livy, XXVII, 43, 8–9). At all events, this ill-prepared move came to a sudden end. Deprived of its guides, who had fled, the column wandered along the river's meanders, looking for a non-existent ford, without making much progress. Pursued by the Roman army, Hasdrubal was forced to do battle, his back to the Metaurus, in the worst possible conditions. On the Roman left wing, Livius Salinator withstood the blow of the main Punic battle corps, composed chiefly of Spanish soldiers, and personally led by Hasdrubal. Behind his elephants, he had placed in the centre the Ligurian contingents recently recruited as he crossed the Alps. On the Roman right wing, Claudius Nero confronted the Gaulish auxiliaries; but a hill that covered the left of the Carthaginian line-up impeded his action. He made his troops draw back, pass in a column behind the Roman battle front, then extend beyond its left wing; from then on he was in a position to attack Hasdrubal's right flank. This manoeuvre decided the outcome of the fight. When he saw that all was lost, Hasdrubal refused to survive the disaster. He rode his horse at a Roman cohort, and died with his weapons in his hand.

Not long afterwards, while life in Rome resumed its normal course amid general rejoicing, following three days of prayer decreed by the Senate, and as Livy says (XXVII, 51, 10), even business was picking up again to peacetime levels after twelve years of war, the consul Claudius Nero returned to his camp near Canusium. He had Hasdrubal's head flung down in front of the Carthaginian lines. Hannibal could see his African soldiers in chains, and the consul even allowed two of them to cross the lines to bring tidings of the disaster. Did Hannibal then really declare that he saw this as a sign of Carthage's ultimate fate (Livy, XXVII, 51, 12)? As Montesquieu remarked, nothing would have been more 'apt to throw into despair the peoples who had sided with him, and discourage an army that expected such great rewards after the war'. He at least showed that the blow had struck home; gathering all his people together, including the Metapontum garrison, Hannibal went to take refuge in the extreme tip of Bruttium.

## The end of the war in Spain

Hasdrubal Barca's departure had considerably reduced Carthaginian forces in the Iberian peninsula. To fill this void it was decided in Carthage to send additional contingents from Africa, under the command of a general named Hanno, who came to join Mago, Hannibal's last brother, after raising Celtiberian auxiliaries. Silanus, the second-in-command whose term of office had been extended like that of his superior, marched against them with 10,000 infantry and 500 horsemen. Hanno was taken prisoner and the Celtiberians scattered, but Mago, with his cavalry intact and 2,000 of his footsoldiers, withdrew in good order to join Hasdrubal, son of Gisco, in the Gades (Cádiz) region.

Now, late in 207, Scipio would have liked to bring the Spanish front to an end. He went personally to Baetica to attack Hasdrubal, but when he realized that, in order to give his army cover, the Punic general had dispersed the men among the walls of the various strongholds in the lower Guadalquivir valley, he had to give up the undertaking. In his entourage, however, he had his brother Lucius, with whom – as we saw earlier (p. 137) – he had recently been elected to the aedileship. Lucius, who would follow his career in his brother's shadow, would be praetor in 193 and consul in 190, and we do not know exactly in what rank he was serving in Spain at Publius' side. To him fell the honour of capturing a town that Livy calls Orongis (XXVIII, 3, 2), possibly situated in the north-east environs of Granada (Lazenby, 1978, p. 144), and perhaps more precisely at Baza, where, it may be recalled, one of the most beautiful Spanish 'ladies' was discovered (above, p. 33). The capture of this town in upper Andalusia was a minor achievement, but Scipio probably wanted to demonstrate that Hasdrubal Gisco's delaying tactics were not catching him unprepared.

In the spring of 206, the Punic general brought his troops out from the towns where they had taken up their winter quarters. Recruitment drives carried out by Mago had considerably reinforced them. Between the two of them, the Carthaginian generals were able to line up 50,000 footsoldiers – even 60,000 according to Polybius (XI, 20, 2) – and 4,500 cavalry. At Tarragona, where rumours of this massive mobilization had reached him, Scipio had only four legions available; it was imperative that he increased their number, if for no other reason than to match his adversary's strength. With the reinforcements brought by Silanus, levied thanks to the support of Culchas, an Iberian prince, and the contingents that he could add to the troops himself, between Tarragona and Castulo, he managed to arrive at 45,000 footsoldiers and around 3,000 horsemen. But Scipio remembered that the last-minute defection of the Celtiberians had been at the root of his father's and uncle's defeat. The Iberians in the ranks would be there chiefly to make an impression on the opposition. To win a victory, he relied on his legions alone.

The decisive encounter of this war in Spain took place at Ilipa (Silpia for Livy, XXVIII, 12, 14), supposedly situated some fifteen kilometres north of Seville, at Alcalá del Río, on the right bank of the Guadalquivir (Lazenby, 1978, p. 145). While Scipio was busy setting up his camp, he suffered an initial attack by cavalry led by Mago and Massinissa, with his Numidians; but the Roman had foreseen this eventuality and massed a large troop of horsemen behind a nearby hill, and they put the attackers to flight. After a few days of skirmishes, in which the two armies, arranged in combat lines, took stock of each other, battle was engaged and, although the forces drawn up were more or less equal, two tactics effected by Scipio assured him of gaining the upper hand. Over the preceding days, the proconsul had noticed that in the mornings Hasdrubal was slow to bring out his troops, and that he placed his Africans – the hard nucleus of his army – in the centre and his elephants on the two wings; and Scipio himself, on those days, emerging even later from his camp, lined up the Romans in the centre facing the Africans, and placed his Iberians on the wings. The day he decided to do battle, not only did he catch Hasdrubal unawares by leaving his camp at dawn, but above all he deployed his infantry in opposite order to his usual placement, the Iberians in the centre and the Romans on the wings. Rather than in Livy (XXVIII, 14–15), one may read in Polybius (XI, 22–4) the details of the manoeuvres ordered by Scipio, which the Greek historian has retraced with his customary technical precision when dealing with military matters. In the very early morning, the Roman general had sent his cavalry and velites to harass the Carthaginian army, which had not yet completed its deployment. Several hours later, he recalled his cavalry and light infantry and, opening the ranks among the Iberian footsoldiers in the centre, let them through to the rear, in two groups which took up their position behind the two wings, the velites in front of the horsemen. Only then did he advance the entire front. But – and here is the essential tactical arrangement – when he came within a few hundred metres of the enemy line of battle, while the Iberian soldiers in the centre continued to advance slowly, preserving their original alignment, he made his wings, in other words his legionary infantry, now backed by the velites and cavalry, execute a ninety-degree turn, left for the right wing, which he commanded, and the opposite for the left wing, led by M. Junius Silanus and L. Marcius Septimus. Caught in a pincer movement, the Iberian soldiers on the wings of Hasdrubal's army were driven from the field and scattered, whereas the best elements, the Africans and Carthaginian veterans in the centre, made hardly any contact with Scipio's Spanish infantry – who had mainly featured as 'extras' – and took little active part. Towards the end of the day, conquered more by fatigue and heat than by their engagement in the combat, they retreated, at first in good order, then in a rout that only a violent storm prevented from turning into a catastrophe. Thus, with a tactical plan recalling that of Cannae, but more skilfully worked out as regards the manoeuvre of the wings, Scipio had carried off a victory – and this too was a lesson he had learnt from Hannibal – similarly based on discrimination between weak and strong troops.

Hasdrubal Gisco, who had found refuge at Gades, would go from there to Africa, where we shall soon see him again. Shortly afterwards, the old city gave Mago to understand that a reconquest of Spain was no longer appropriate. The Barcid epic came to an end late in 206 where the adventure of the Phoenicians in the West had begun at the close of the second millennium BC. With the rebellions of Mandonios and Indibilis, Roman Spain was born amid the final spasms of Punic Spain. Iliturgi and Castulo still had to be taken by brute force, and Sucro's insurrection quelled but, before he departed for Rome in 205, leaving the Peninsula to his successors, L. Cornelius Lentulus and L. Manlius Acidinus, Scipio had accomplished what posterity might consider to be the founding act of the Romanization of Spain (Grimal, 1975, p. 140). A few kilometres from Ilipa, which had witnessed the ruin of Carthaginian power, on the site that would now be known as Italica (Santiponce, north-west of Seville), he had founded a 'village' (*vicus*) of Roman citizens by settling his veterans there; a century and a half later, Caesar would make it a town where, even later, two emperors would be born whose names by themselves symbolize Rome's mastery of the inhabited world at the apogee of its power, Trajan and his successor, Hadrian.

## Hannibal at Cape Lacinium

As a good Roman, Livy had no liking for Hannibal. Nevertheless, he could not help admiring him. In 206, he says, no action was taken against Hannibal (XXVIII, 12, 1), adding that if he took no warlike initiative, after the cruel blow he had suffered on the Metaurus, the Romans, for their part, left him in peace. They still regarded him as a force to be reckoned with, comments Livy, even though everything was falling about his ears. And the historian particularly emphasizes, as an almost miraculous feat, that during the thirteen years – he should in fact have said fifteen – in which he was making war so far from his homeland, in foreign and most often hostile territory, with a heterogeneous and even ill-assorted army, whose provisions and pay were sometimes very chancy, there was never any revolt. So great was the leader's influence, even more remarkable in reverses than successes, and so strong the bond he had been able to create between all those men, and between the men and himself. How much more astounding, he says, that this army, which was still large despite all the losses, could have survived without an uprising – or survived purely and simply – receiving nothing from Carthage for years, and confined in a small corner of Bruttium. For in 205, Scipio, commanding in Sicily, crossed the Straits of Messina and, with the support of Rhegium which was still loyal, recaptured Locri. And if one attempted to trace on a map the boundaries of the territory in which the Carthaginian and his army would mark time for another three years, one would probably be correct in situating them between Catanzaro, Cosenza and Crotona, sheltered on the west side by the mountains of the Calabrian Apennines, extending their presence to the north at the most as far as the deep hollow formed

**Figure 9** Southern Italy and Sicily: the theatres of operations, 214–203. Shading indicates the last bridgehead held by Hannibal between 205 and 203 in Bruttium (from De Beer, 1969)

at the south of the Gulf of Tarentum; the delights of Crotona and that coast immersed in the old Greek culture, bordered by the wild Sila, where the Carthaginian soldiers and the brigands of Bruttium lived together with the wolves (Figure 9).

Hannibal had had several good reasons, mentioned earlier, for maintaining at all costs the broadest possible bridgehead on these farthest shores of south Italy, and notably in 213 for making an effort – poorly rewarded, and soon a waste of time – to seize Tarentum, the best port in the region. In 206, one of those reasons swiftly became obsolete.

The reader may remember the treaty concluded in 215 between Hannibal, on behalf of Carthage, and king Philip V of Macedon (above, pp. 117–18). Although not stipulated as exactly as Livy claims (XXIII, 33, 11), the treaty did not rule out that Philip could transport and land reinforcements for the Carthaginian army in south Italy. As early as 215, the Roman fleet stationed at Brindisi, with a strength of over fifty vessels, patrolled along the Italian coasts of the Adriatic and in the Gulf of Tarentum to prevent any incursion by the Macedonians. In the four years that followed, from 214 to 210, it was the task of the praetor M. Valerius Laevinus, whose command had been extended several times, to keep surveillance over the Dalmatian and Greek coasts, from Apollonia and Oricum – which he captured in 214 – in the north of Epirus (present-day Albania), to the Gulf of Corinth. Late in 212, on behalf of Rome, Laevinus had signed a treaty of alliance with the Aetolians – the main confederation opposed to the Macedonians, between Dorida to the east and Acarnania to the west – reserving all war booty for Rome, but guaranteeing the Aetolians the profits of territorial conquests (Livy, XXVI, 24). Laevinus, judging that Philip was henceforth too wrapped up in the war with his neighbours to bother about Italy and pursue the treaty agreed with Hannibal, was able to withdraw peacefully to Corcyra (Corfu), which had been under Roman sway since 228.

Let me take this opportunity to remark, parenthetically, on the unhappy case of political conscience presented to Greece for the first time by a Roman intervention provoked by Greeks. Polybius, always so attentive to matters concerning his native country, expressed this case of conscience, in a manner clearly intended to be prophetic, in a speech – which is perhaps apocryphal but nevertheless reveals a state of mind – that he ascribes to Lykiskos, a delegate of the Acarnanians, before the Lacedaemonian assembly. In their desire to defeat Philip and bring down the Macedonians, says Lykiskos, the Aetolians did not realize that they had attracted from the West a cloud which, for the moment, enveloped only the Macedonians, but would soon bring great ills on all the Greeks (Polybius, IX, 37, 10). Indeed, for some years events had borne out the truth of the sombre predictions of Agelaos of Naupactus (Polybius, V, 103, 9), who in 217 had been sufficiently farsighted to see that, whether Carthage or Rome turned out to be the victor, Greece ran a heavy risk of paying the price of the war.

M. Valerius Laevinus, who became consul in 210, had been replaced on the Macedonian front by the proconsul P. Sulpicius Galba, who had pursued the policy of alliance with the Aetolians against Philip, and also with king Attalus of Pergamum, who had become their commander. Although he had twice been victorious against Sulpicius and the Aetolians, in the spring of 208 Philip was prepared to accept a peace plan supported by a whole range of neutral states (Athens, Chios, Rhodes and even Ptolemaic Egypt), and proposed by a mediator, a petty Epirote king who at the time was allied to the Aetolians and the Romans against Philip. What chiefly motivated this convergence of diplomatic efforts to end the war, says Livy (XXVII, 30, 10), was the widespread feeling that no pretext for intervention in Greece should be afforded to the Romans and the king of

Pergamum. But the Aetolians' demands dashed these peace plans. And far from calming down, the conflict tended to become even more 'internationalized'; in the summer of 208 Philip received reinforcements of not only a Carthaginian fleet – to be the sole Punic contribution to his war effort against Rome – but also some vessels from King Prusias of Bithynia (Livy, XXVII, 30, 16).

But clouds were gathering over Philip's head. Even if he had ever considered it, there was now no longer any question of his going to help Hannibal. In 207, to the north of his Macedonian kingdom the Thracians and the Maedi were growing restive. The allies of Attalus, the Romans now attacked Euboea, where they seized Oreos. In 206, Philip deemed it more expedient to impose a separate peace on the Aetolians, at which the Romans, their allies since 211, feigned indignation. In reality, Rome wanted first and foremost to consolidate the positions it had held in Illyria for some fifteen years. As for Philip, some months later he grasped the olive branch extended to him by the Epirotes who had come to propose a general peace and, forgetting the treaty agreed with Hannibal, he made peace with Rome in 205 at Phoinike. He did not do too badly out of it, receiving Atintania, north of Epirus. In return, Rome was guaranteed possession of the land of the Parthinians, in the centre and north of present-day Albania. The future Roman Illyricum, the western slopes of the Balkans, thus began to take shape and, with the prospect of the decisive battles that would soon confront it in Macedonia, Rome had multiplied and consolidated its bases.

What reasons still remained to Hannibal, in 205, to hold on in Bruttium? To put this question would be to forget that he was not waging 'his' war, but was conducting the campaign, even though with great strategical freedom, on the orders of Carthage's government. And in Carthage, at the very time when the Roman Senate was preparing to allow Scipio the strategic initiative of landing an army in Africa, the rulers apparently still believed that the strongest possible pressure must continue to be exerted on Italy. The terrible disappointment born of Hasdrubal's failure had not altered this choice. In the autumn of 206, while he was at Gades, the youngest of the Barcids, Mago, had received orders from Carthage to take his available fleet to the north of Italy, there to recruit as many Gauls and Ligurians as possible and then to try to join Hannibal. Having exacted a ransom from the public coffers and the inhabitants of Gades to augment the funds sent from Carthage, and then vainly attempted a raid on Cartagena, Mago went to Ibiza which, as we know (above, p. 34), had been Carthaginian territory for a very long time. From there he pushed on as far as Majorca, where his welcome was such that he had to retreat to Minorca, which he easily overcame and where he spent the winter.

At the end of the following spring (205), with some thirty warships and a transport fleet carrying 12,000 footsoldiers and 2,000 horsemen, Mago made the journey from Minorca to the Ligurian coast without a break – a real nautical feat in Antiquity, even in the high season. He took Genoa without difficulty, reached an agreement with the Ligurian Ingauni, Carthage's traditional allies since the first Punic War, stored his booty securely in the stronghold of Savona and sent his ships back to Carthage, keeping only a dozen or so to defend the port. During the summer of 205 Mago received reinforcements from Carthage. Meanwhile, the Ligurians overtly – for them the Roman armies seemed safely distant – and the Gauls of the Po Valley more discreetly, swelled his army's numbers. The Roman Senate had been alerted to this new danger by the praetor Spurius Lucretius who, stationed at Ariminum (Rimini), had the duty of keeping all north Italy under surveillance. To bar Mago's route, it was decided to effect large-scale troop movements. M. Livius Salinator, proconsul for Etruria with two legions, received orders to rendezvous with Lucretius near Rimini. At the same time, the urban praetor Cn. Servilius Caepio was given the task of putting the two legions he held in reserve in Rome on the road for Etruria. It was M. Valerius Laevinus, back from his proconsulship in Sicily, who was charged with leading them to Arretium (Arezzo), which had been left stripped of men since the departure for Rimini of Salinator's two legions. Thus, from both sides of the Apennines, possible access to central Italy was blocked. For nearly two years Mago and his army occupied the land of the Insubres. But during the summer of 203, near Milan, he agreed to take on the four Roman legions. Despite the support of the elephants, the battle, which soon went against the Carthaginians, turned to a rout when Mago, who was fighting in the front line, fell from his horse, pierced through the thigh. Hannibal's brother was able to retreat and regain the Ligurian coast where ships awaited him. But several days later, off the coast of Sardinia, he died at sea from the effect of his wounds.

Hannibal had assuredly heard of his brother's successful landing in Liguria; but he could hardly have nursed many illusions about Mago's chances of combining their forces in central Italy. The more so because he himself no longer had the means to make the journey to meet him half-way, his forces diminished, subjected to a tight blockade in Bruttium, and cut off from any help that might come from Carthage. Livy (XXVIII, 46, 14) mentions the capture, in the summer of 205, off the coast of Sardinia, of eighty Carthaginian cargo vessels which, according to Coelius Antipater, were carrying wheat and provisions to Hannibal. For the first time in thirteen years, he had totally lost the initiative. Condemned to enforced inactivity, he was at least lucky that his 'house arrest' was in that ancient city of Crotona, on which nearly four centuries of Greek culture had laid a thick patina of elegance and refinement. In the sixth century, Pythagoras had stayed there; before they were eliminated by their neighbours, the Sybarites had communicated their proverbial *joie de vivre* to the inhabitants of Crotona, whose women were beautiful. If we are to believe Cicero and Pliny the Elder, Zeuxis, in the fourth century, had been spoilt for choice when it came to selecting models for his painting of Helen, which the town had commissioned for the temple of Hera at Cape Lacinium.

There, precisely, Hannibal had spent the summer of 205. On the site described by Livy (XXIV, 3, 3–7), surrounded by a sacred wood where the pasture of all kinds of animals – mostly cattle – constituted the sanctuary's wealth, nothing remains today but a marble Doric column, which gives rise to the present-day name of Capo Colonna. It is a modest sea-mark for local mariners and the sole vestige of a proud peripteral temple, whose colonnade one may imagine reflecting that of a similar great and famous temple also dedicated to Hera, the 'basilica' of Paestum. But in Hannibal's time, this sanctuary which Pyrrhus had spared some decades earlier housed treasures in its *cella*, among others a gold column which Hannibal had been curious enough to probe to see if it was merely gold-plated. And when he found it was truly solid gold, he had been sorely tempted to take possession of it. But Hera (Juno) had appeared to him in a dream, threatening to take away the sight of his one remaining eye if he were to deprive *her* of her column. So Hannibal wisely gave up the idea of theft and even, using the gold 'appropriated' from his drilling of the body of the column, had a little heifer fashioned – emblem of the herd which in the nearby sacred wood brought the temple a good income – and placed on top of the column. Recorded by Cicero (*De divinatione*, I, 24, 48), who had it from Coelius Antipater, himself indebted for the information to Silenos of Kale Akte, Hannibal's personal historiographer, this anecdote typifies those which, having come down to us after reworkings of various sources, call for very delicate 'decoding'. As one of the most subtle interpreters of Hannibal's exploits has recently suggested, this little story may possibly find its richest significance if it is related to the euhemerism which flourished at the time on the Ionian coasts (Brizzi, 1983, pp. 243–51). During those years, in Rome, Ennius published his *Euhemerus* and thus gained a wide audience for that curious utopian novel – the *Historia sacrata, Hiera Anagraphe*, for the most part lost – in which Euhemerus of Messina claimed to have discovered on an island in the Indian Ocean, off the coast of Arabia, a gold column on which was inscribed the most ancient history, a theogony of very human origins, of the greatest Greek gods, Uranus, Kronos and Zeus.

In contrast, neither mythical nor of doubtful reality, for Polybius saw it with his own eyes some decades later, is the long inscription – *ingens titulus*: Livy, XXVIII, 46, 16 – that Hannibal had engraved on an altar – a bronze tablet, according to Polybius (III, 33, 18), which he dedicated in the temple of Juno Lacinia. On it in a bilingual text, Greek and Punic, was the list of his achievements, his *res gestae*, as Livy says, using two Latin words that irresistibly bring to mind other *res gestae* accomplished two centuries later, those of Augustus' political testament, preserved in the bilingual copy, Greek and Latin, of the monument of Ancyra (Ankara, Turkey). Of the text that Hannibal had had carved Polybius retained only the numerical data of the forces brought by the Carthaginian to attack Italy (above, p. 54). That is a great pity for, apart from the purely factual aspect of this document, how valuable it would have been to learn its tone. On the Ancyra monument Augustus speaks in the first person and, although at the beginning of the text he boasts of having restored the republic, his tone is that of a monarch. What would it have been for Hannibal's *res gestae*? We must take care not to seek too much from a text whose content will unfortunately remain forever unknown to us. But the mere fact of its existence gives rise to the suspicion that Hannibal may not have expressed himself simply as a general who had been given a mandate by his Carthaginian republic, but as a Hellenistic *hegemon*, recounting his exploits not only in Punic but also in Greek, perhaps through philhellenism but, more importantly, because only Greek, which was the international language in that period, could guarantee him the widest circulation. The Cape Lacinium inscription was probably the memorial to a huge ambition.

# 7

# Zama

While Carthage, by keeping Hannibal in Bruttium and Mago in the Po Valley, still lived in hopes of swaying and inclining Italy towards peace, weary as it was of nearly fifteen years' war waged on its soil, Rome decided to carry the conflict into Africa. As we shall see, during the summer of 204 the armada led by Scipio would disembark on African shores. This landing occurred at the end of a slow political ripening process within the Roman Senate, and also as the outcome of a lengthy diplomatic preparation. The Romans were well aware that the war could not be waged on Carthage's territory with any likelihood of success unless they could rely on the neutrality, or better still the alliance, of the native princes.

In the late third century BC, with the exception of Carthage's own domain, which in the east may be roughly superimposed on present-day Tunisia, three kingdoms shared North Africa (Figure 10). In the far west, a Moorish realm controlled the north of present-day Morocco: despite its strategic position, opposite the Spanish shore of the Straits, it had remained on the fringe of the conflict, even though its king, Baga, had been led on two occasions into becoming indirectly a party to it by indicating his alliance with Massinissa. From Moulouya – Strabo's Mulucha (XVII, 3, 9) – the vast domain of the Numidians stretched eastwards, itself divided into two kingdoms. The more important of the two, in the years immediately preceding the end of the second Punic War, was the western kingdom of the Massaesylians, which occupied a vast territory, covering over two-thirds of present-day Algeria, besides a fringe of eastern Morocco. This extensive realm was bipolar; its king, Syphax, had his capital at Siga (Takembrit), in Orania and, thanks to recently published archaeological excavations (Rakob, 1979, pp. 149–57), we have lately come to know of the mausoleum he had built on an eminence overlooking the town. At the eastern extremity of his kingdom, Syphax had a second capital, Cirta (Constantine); there is still argument over whether this eastern capital was formerly in the Massaesylian domain (Desanges, 1978b, p. 646), or whether Cirta acquired the status of second capital only after Syphax's annexation, in 205, of the kingdom of the Massylian Numidians (Camps, 1980, pp. 102–3). The latter was much more limited in extent, with a probably very narrow maritime strip, between the peninsula of Collo, in Algeria, and Khroumiria, in the north-west littoral region of Tunisia. The Medracen, north-

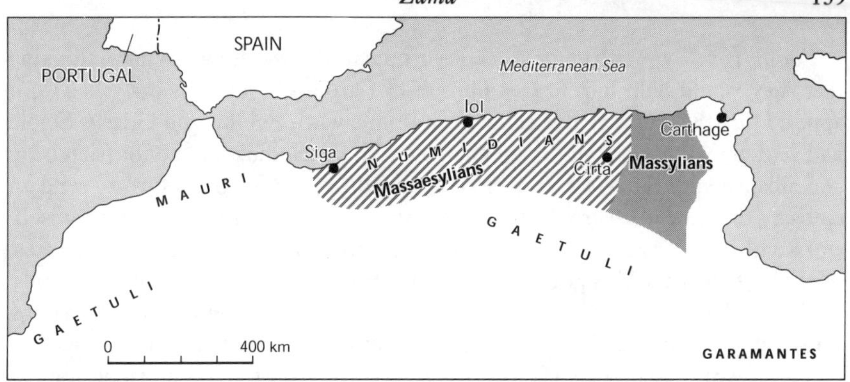


**Figure 10** Syphax's Massaesylian Numidian kingdom (*hatched*) and the Massylian kingdom (*dotted*) inherited by Massinissa at the end of the third century (drawing by S. Lancel based on a map by G. Camps)

east of Batna – a monument that is remarkable for the syncretism it presents between a native architectural style and an Egypto-Greek architectonic setting – is sometimes seen as the dynastic mausoleum of the Massylians (Camps, 1973, p. 516). In the period under discussion, Massinissa, after various vicissitudes, was soon to succeed his father Gaia as head of this Massylian kingdom, for a reign that would last over half a century.

## The view of the Numidian princes

As may be imagined, these indigenous princes had not remained passive spectators of the struggle between Rome and Carthage. They had sided with one or the other, alternating their loyalties. Gaia, the Massylian king, had supplied Carthage with contingents which had been sent to Spain under Massinissa, who had fought alongside the Carthaginians between 212 and 206; remember that in 211 (above, p. 135) the young Massylian chief had played a far from negligible role in the defeat of Publius and Gnaeus Scipio. But afterwards, Massinissa had contributed to the downfall of Carthaginian power; sensing a change in the wind after the crushing defeat suffered by the Punic army at Ilipa, he had sought an interview with the future Africanus, the son and nephew of the victims of 211, and this took place not far from Gades in 206 (Livy, XXVIII, 35). He offered his support to the Roman general if Rome should bring the war to Africa. Scipio, who had been able to assess the value of the Massylian cavalry, accepted. At this juncture, as Gaia, his father, had died, Massinissa had to return in haste to his kingdom, escorted as far as his frontier by 4,000 of king Baga's Moors. He ultimately triumphed over his rivals in 205 but, attacked by Syphax, whom Carthage encouraged to take advantage of the temporary weakness of the Massylian kingdom, he had to go into exile for a time in the region of the *Emporia* (Syrtis Minor), while he waited for the Roman fleet to land in Africa.

For his part, Syphax had for several years inclined towards the Romans, thinking that they would help him to free himself of Carthage's yoke. As early as 213, it appears that the initiative had come from Rome, when Publius and Gnaeus Scipio had sent ambassadors from Spain charged with concluding a treaty of friendship and alliance with the Massaesylian king. In 210, it was Syphax's turn to send an embassy to Rome to assure the senators that they had no trustier ally than himself; and Rome seems to have responded to these advances by appointing three delegates, in return, to take the king gifts of a toga and purple tunic, an ivory curule chair and a golden goblet weighing five pounds (Livy, XXVII, 4, 5–9). But Syphax was of a wait-and-see nature, and in 206 was still committed to a Carthaginian alliance.

This is why Scipio, accompanied by Laelius, had made the crossing that summer from Cartagena to Siga in two quinqueremes, to visit the Massaesylian king. Arriving in sight of the port of Siga, at the mouth of the Tafna, by pure chance they had come upon Hasdrubal Gisco's triremes, as after the defeat at Ilipa he had embarked at Gades to return to Carthage and had made landfall at Siga. It was out of the question for these adversaries to engage in combat on neutral ground, so to speak. Syphax urged both sides to enjoy his hospitality. Hasdrubal emerged from this unexpected encounter even more impressed than Syphax by Scipio. With such a man, he said, 'the Carthaginians should not so much seek to explain how they had lost Spain as how they were going to keep Africa' (Livy, XXVIII, 18, 9). The treaty concluded, Scipio went back to Cartagena believing he had won the Numidian king's alliance. He was wrong. Syphax had been flattered to use his good offices, but was not anxious to have Carthage on his back, as its intact presence in Africa was still something to be feared. Moreover, he had become its immediate neighbour since, profiting from Massinissa's difficulties with regard to the succession, he had annexed the Massylian kingdom on its eastern flank. As for the Carthaginians, given the imminence of war on their soil, it was of the utmost importance for them to preserve the Numidian king's friendship. Around the close of 205, this friendship was sealed by the marriage which united the ageing Massaesylian king, whose children were already grown up, and Hasdrubal's daughter Sophonisba – in reality Sophoniba, as in the best of Livy's manuscripts, transcribing the Punic Çafonbaal, 'she whom Baal has protected'. Young, beautiful, well educated, a musician, endowed with both wit and charm, Sophonisba had everything to attract and hold a man. She enslaved Syphax, who immediately bound himself under oath to a treaty of alliance with Carthage. For good measure, Hasdrubal, who was acquainted with the king's opportunism, made him send a delegation to Scipio, who was then in Sicily, to inform the Roman consul that, if he pursued his plan of landing in Africa and attacking Carthage on its own ground, he would find himself confronting Syphax (Livy, XXIX, 23).

## Scipio's consulship (205)

The victorious Scipio had returned from Spain late in 206. To give an account of all that had happened, he was given an audience by the Senate which, in these circumstances, to welcome a general returning from campaign, assembled outside the town wall, on the Campus Martius, or to be more exact in the temple of Bellona – not far from the vestiges of the 'portico of Octavia' still visible today. There he emphasized his dazzling service record, in the hope of being rewarded with a triumph. But it was not customary for the honours of a triumph to be awarded to an army leader, however glorious, who had not yet held a consulship, or even a praetorship. Scipio did not insist; he made his entry into Rome on foot, and deposited in the public Treasury 14,342 pounds of silver in ingots – the equivalent of almost a million denarii! – and a considerable quantity of silver coins.

The triumph he had not received from the Senate he won in the streets of Rome when the time came soon afterwards for elections for the year 205. At the assembly of the comitia, says Livy (XXVIII, 38, 8), people rushed into the town, not so much to vote as to catch a glimpse of Scipio. His house, situated behind the Veteres Tabernae (the 'old shops') on the edge of the Forum, a site that would later be occupied by the Basilica Sempronia, then by the Basilica Julia in Caesar's time, was in a state of siege. He was surrounded at the Capitol – a temple where, as we know (above, p. 138), he was accustomed to go and meditate – where he sacrificed 100 oxen to Jupiter, a hecatomb he had pledged to the god when he was still in Spain. At the comitia presided over by L. Veturius Philo, the patrician outgoing consul and friend of the Cornelii Scipiones, Scipio was elected consul with P. Licinius Crassus as his colleague; the latter was a plebeian, but an uncommon family inheritance made him the first in his line to bear the nickname Dives (the 'Wealthy'), which was passed on from one generation to the next until the Crassus who, nearing the end of the Republic, would form the first 'triumvirate' with Caesar and Pompey. Licinius Crassus had been Pontifex Maximus since 212, and this office, the most important in Rome in the religious sphere, prevented him from leaving Italian soil. So when the Senate allocated provinces to the new consuls when they took up office in the spring of 205, there was no drawing of lots. Bruttium, where it was essential to continue a tight blockade of Hannibal, fell to Crassus, while Scipio received Sicily.

Why Sicily? There was no longer any combat to pursue, but it was the stepping-stone to Africa. It was a repetition of the situation in 218 – but in far more favourable conditions, after making a clean sweep of the Syracusan principality – when the second consul, Ti. Sempronius Longus, had been sent there to make ready for a possible expedition to Africa (above, p. 82). For this had been the theme of Scipio's electoral campaign, almost given the backing of the entire nation by his election to the consulship. The crossing to Africa, firmly planted in Scipio's mind and desired by the people, was the subject of argument in the Senate. Livy made Fabius Maximus the spokesman for senatorial opposition to this choice of strategy (XXVIII, 40–2). At the time, two years before his death, he was the 'princeps senatus'; by virtue of this rank he presided over the upper assembly and was the first to speak, and indeed it was he who argued for another policy, one that was more sensitive to the sufferings endured for over twelve years by Italian farmers, and the sacrifices already made by the colonies and allies. He was of the opinion that no risks should be taken and that, by combining all the Roman forces, they should bring matters to an end as quickly as possible, on Italian soil, with a Hannibal who was more than ever driven on to the defensive and henceforth hemmed in with the sea at his back. Besides, he was less jealous of Scipio's youthful renown than profoundly disturbed, like the old Roman political class around him, by the young general's ambition. In a confused way, he sensed that with and behind Scipio, a new class of rulers was rising who would be increasingly inclined to seek support from the people. From the army, too; it is very likely that the Senate had got wind of the 'imperatorial' – if not 'imperial' – salutation that the general had recently accepted from his soldiers in Spain (above, p. 141). And Fabius also had a fear of going overseas: neither he nor his clan could be relied on to promote the imperialist policy that would unfailingly result from a military expedition to the south of Sicily (Grimal, 1975, pp. 138–9).

Pleading his cause in favour of his African plan, Scipio astutely stressed all the trump cards at his disposal, which had not been available fifty years earlier to Regulus, whose unfortunate experience Fabius had held up as a frightening example. From now on Carthage was enfeebled, its Numidian allies unreliable and even ready to change sides, like Massinissa, and its mercenaries prompt to rebel, as the recent past had demonstrated. But his speech to the Senate did not go down well, for a rumour was current that if he failed he would take his case to the people. It was another old celebrity, Q. Fulvius Flaccus, who put him with his back to the wall. Would he leave it to the Senate to allocate the provinces and adhere to their decision, or would he go to the comitia? Scipio replied evasively, declaring that he would act in the interests of the state. This left the threat of a resort to the people's vote hanging over the assembly. The senators preferred not to risk losing face, and when Scipio finally said that he would abide by their decision, it was on those conditions that he received Sicily as his province from the Senate, with the authorization to proceed to Africa if he judged such a strategy to be in keeping with the state's interests. Never in its history had Rome issued a blank cheque of such importance to one of its generals.

## The Africa landing

With the exception of the expedition to Locri, mentioned earlier (above, p. 151), Scipio spent the whole of 205 in making preparations. It was no small matter to bring together the forces he needed. Perhaps because the Senate rather resented his having somewhat forced its hand, it had not authorized him to raise a new army at the republic's expense. But he had at his disposal in Sicily the veterans of the two legions who had survived the Cannae disaster by flight and who, after serving for several months in Campania in 216–215, had been exiled for ten years in Sicily as a disciplinary measure (Livy, XXIII, 25, 7). Many had subsequently redeemed themselves and had gained experience that could prove invaluable, notably at Syracuse under Marcellus' command. To these seasoned troops, that he would find on the spot, Scipio added the volunteers, numbering 7,000, whom he had recruited mainly in Umbria, the Sabine region, among the Marsi and Peligni; the whole of central Italy mobilized to support him. To the thirty warships awaiting him at Lilybaeum he was able to add another thirty – twenty quinqueremes, ten quadriremes – hastily put into construction, their over-green wood having to be dried out in the shipyards of Palermo throughout the winter of 205–204. Livy (XXVIII, 45, 14–20) gleefully draws up a list of all the voluntary suppliers of Scipio's future army; among others the Etruscan workyards of Populonia (for the heavy iron equipment), Perusia and Clusium (for timber), Tarquinii and Volterra (for keels and sailcloth). As for the inhabitants of Arezzo, they were outstanding for their generosity in every field of equipment, from hand-mills – for the unground grain supplied to each soldier for his daily bread – to projectiles, including all the requirements of troops on campaign: axes, shovels, sickles, baskets, and so on.

Early in 204 the new consuls took up office: the patrician M. Cornelius Cethegus and P. Sempronius Tuditanus, a plebeian who, as military tribune at Cannae in 216, had conducted himself admirably (Livy, XXII, 50, 6–11). With the title of proconsul, Scipio had had his command extended for a year and the praetor appointed for Sicily, M. Pomponius Matho, was one of his cousins on his mother's side. This was a stroke of luck for Scipio who, while making his preparations to leave for Africa with his army in the spring of 204, had been harshly indicted before the Senate by Q. Fabius Maximus. The latter held him responsible for the disturbances – mutinies and retaliatory ill-treatment between the legate Pleminius and his officers – which had occurred at Locri when the town was recaptured in the preceding year. The proconsul, whom many senators criticized also for his overt philhellenism – a serious accusation in Rome at that time – was rescued from this tight spot by the dictator who had just presided over the elections in the absence of Crassus, kept in Bruttium by illness. Q. Caecilius Metellus, who was to remain one of Scipio's most solid supporters throughout the following years, proposed that M. Pomponius Matho, the praetor appointed for the province of Sicily, should go to Locri to preside over a commission of enquiry. It is easy to suppose that Pomponius threw his whole weight behind the withdrawal of the case against his cousin. At that time Scipio's family, in the narrowest sense of the term, had the wind in their sails. A signal honour was bestowed on the house when, shortly afterwards, in April 204, another of his cousins, Scipio Nasica – the son of Gnaeus who had died in Spain – was chosen by the Senate, as being Rome's 'best citizen', to go to Ostia and amid great pomp receive the 'Idaean Mother', in other words the sacred stone of Pessinus, in Phrygia, which had been handed over by Attalus of Pergamum, then Rome's ally. The Sibylline Books had foretold – and this prediction had just been discovered – that the enemy who was ensconced in Italy could be driven out and defeated if the cult of Cybele, the 'Mother of the Gods', was introduced in Rome. Nasica, then aged about twenty-five, had not even held a quaestorship, and the Senate's choice was somewhat puzzling even to Livy himself (XXIX, 14, 9), who must have had his own ideas on the subject but takes care not to share them with us.

During the summer of 204, Scipio made his quarters at Lilybaeum (Marsala) and decided with Pomponius which contingents should embark for Africa. On the overall strength, between the various figures provided by his sources, Livy hesitates to opt for the largest, 35,000 men, infantry and cavalry combined, but it is the most probable for an expedition of this size. Its core was formed by the veterans of Cannae, who made up the fifth and sixth legions; they were the most seasoned soldiers and also the most highly motivated by the prospect of a victory that would be their redemption. When they left Lilybaeum, the armada carrying these men was probably the most impressive that had ever been seen departing from Sicilian shores: 400 transport vessels, escorted on either side by twenty warships. Scipio himself, with his brother Lucius as second-in-command, was in charge of the fleet on the right; leading the twenty ships on the left flank was the prefect of the fleet, Laelius, and a young plebeian quaestor, a *homo novus* into the bargain, who would soon make a name for himself, M. Porcius Cato, the future censor.

If we are to believe Livy, Scipio, on the eve of departure, gave instructions to the helmsmen to head for the *Emporia*, or Syrtis Minor, or, if preferred, the Gulf of Gabes and southern coasts of present-day Tunisia. But, still according to the Latin historian, on the morning of the third day the fleet was in sight of Cape Bon (the 'promontory of Mercury'). Thereupon, as a fog had descended, hiding the coast, and night had fallen, Scipio chose to drop anchor temporarily. The next day, wind dispersed the fog and revealed the African coast once more. The nearest promontory was no longer Cape Bon, but the one called in the Latin text the *Pulchri promontorium*, or the promontory of Apollo, the 'beautiful god', today the Ras el-Mekki, which ends the Bay of Carthage to the north-west (Desanges, 1980, p. 210).

Apparently, instead of sending the Roman fleet south of Cape Bon, the wind had pushed it to the other side, westwards. So, according to Livy's version, Scipio had originally intended to land near Kelibia, like Agathocles in the past and, more recently, Regulus, or at the farthest, around Hammamet but, driven off course by Aeolus, he accepted the augury that caused him to land on the promontory of Apollo, in the vicinity of Utica. It is difficult to believe, however, that the proconsul left the choice of his destination to the whims of the winds. It is more likely, as Gsell thought (1921, III, p. 213), that although fog delayed him when he was off Cape Bon, he was not diverted from his goal by the wind but had already, upon his departure, settled on the neighbourhood of Utica as his landing-point. As for the *emporia* indicated to the helmsmen as the destination on the eve of departure, if it is not one of Livy's errors, it may well have been a decoy intended for the Carthaginian spies who must have swarmed in and around Lilybaeum; but would this false piece of information, crossing the sea more swiftly than Scipio, really have had the time to 'panic' Carthage? This raises the problem of optical communications, which were certainly in operation between the Punic mother-city and the fortresses of Cape Bon (Lancel, 1995b, p. 402), and were theoretically possible in fine weather but very uncertain between Cape Bon and the belvederes of western Sicily.

## The battle of the Great Plains

The Roman fleet at anchor in the shelter of the Ras el-Mekki had not passed unnoticed in Carthage, where the city's gates were immediately closed, while the defenders took up their positions on the ramparts. Hasdrubal Gisco had been given the task of hastily forming an army, which was not yet ready, and which the Carthaginian general, who was then camped about forty kilometres from Carthage (200 stadia: Appian, *Lib.*, 9), probably in the Medjerda valley, did not want to engage in battle before the arrival of Syphax's Numidians. Meanwhile, directly after Scipio's landing, a group of horsemen had been sent against him, but they had easily been put to flight by the Roman cavalry in a skirmish where their leader, Hanno, had perished. A few days later, the Roman proconsul moved into the immediate environs of Utica, where he set up his camp. Carthage sent a fresh detachment of cavalry against him, commanded by yet another Hanno, the son of Hamilcar, who took the time to recruit horsemen, mainly Numidian, to swell his forces before installing himself in a place known as Salaeca, some twenty-two kilometres from Scipio's camp; perhaps present-day Henchir el-Bey, not far from Mateur. Appian (*Lib.*, 14) locates the engagement more precisely at the site known as 'Agathocles' Tower', a small ruin on the edge of the western foothills of the djebel Menzel Ghoul. In the meantime, Massinissa had joined Scipio with his own cavalry. Their combined action, with the Numidian leader luring the Carthaginian cavalry out of its entrenchments and offering it as easy prey to Scipio's horsemen, who were hidden among the nearby hills, turned this battle into a small disaster for Carthage, which lost 2,000 horsemen, including over 200 Carthaginian nobles and Hanno himself.

In late summer, after seizing Salaeca, Scipio came to besiege Utica, which was blockaded on the seaward side by his fleet. The Roman army, with siege machines sent from Sicily, had taken up position on a hillock overlooking the defence wall, west of the town. But it was well fortified. When Scipio found himself threatened by the combined arrival of the army finally assembled by Hasdrubal, 30,000 footsoldiers and 3,000 horsemen strong, and that of Syphax, with his 10,000 cavalry and several tens of thousands of footsoldiers, he withdrew, after forty days of useless siege. It was now late autumn. In order to spend the winter sheltered from surprise attack, and chiefly to avoid being caught between Utica and these two armies, he set up camp on a promontory that extended fairly far into the sea east of Utica, its tip, which today projects only slightly in the alluvial deposit of the Medjerda delta (above, p. 16), now occupied by the village of Galaat el-Andless. Caesar, who was familiar with it, would say later that it was a particularly suitable place for a camp (*De bello civili*, II, 24). Scipio left his name

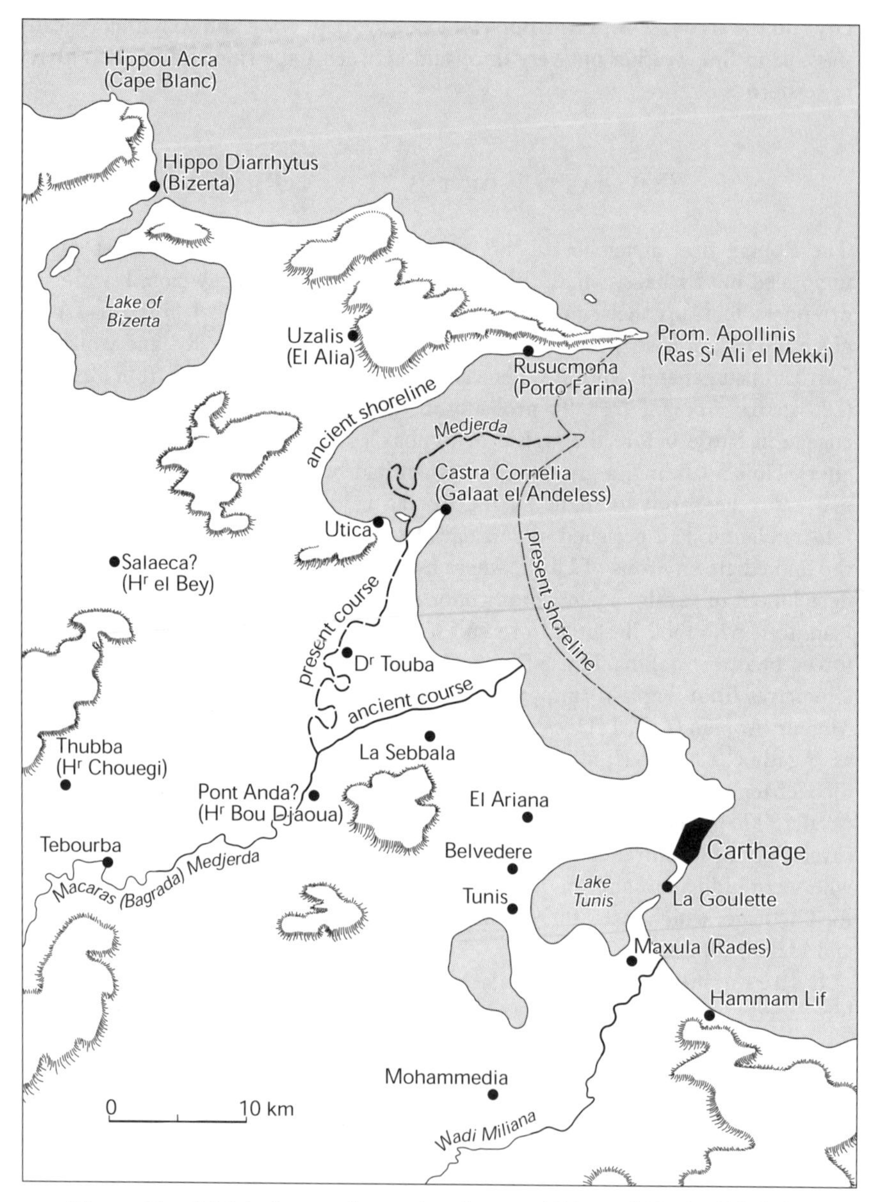


**Figure 11** Scipio's theatre of operations between Utica and Tunis, 203–201 (from Polybius, *Histoire*, 1970)

to the site, which was known as Castra Cornelia (Figure 11) until the end of Antiquity. But there was not much to show for this first campaign, which ended with the coming of winter, and the Roman general, entrenched on his promontory, was besieged in his turn by the two allied armies of Hasdrubal and Syphax, who were quartered about a dozen kilometres away. For his provisions he was dependent on what could reach him by sea, with the heavy risk of its being intercepted by Carthage's fleets, which were very close by. And in theory his term of office would expire in the spring of 203.

Scipio's command was extended in March of that year, but not for an indeterminate period, until the end of the war, as Livy wrongly states (XXX, 1, 10). But he did not waste his time during that winter of 204–203. Did he really hope to win Syphax away from his Carthaginian alliance? So says Polybius (XIV, 1, 3), whom we must follow here, as his preserved text is the basis for all subsequent accounts, including Livy's. Fearing the possibility of engaging combat with an army that was vastly superior in number and on its home ground, Scipio is said to have taken the initiative of holding secret talks with the Massaesylian king. The latter's attitude remained along the lines of the Siga meeting (above, p. 160): his role was that of peacemaker, in no way desirous of breaking with Carthage, whose cause he had espoused when he married Sophonisba. But the Carthaginians would have to quit Italy at the same time as the Romans withdrew from Africa. Presented to the respective senates of the two antagonists, both exhausted by fifteen years of war, the proposal might have had some chance of success, not only in Carthage, where Hannibal's situation in Bruttium no longer left much hope, but also in Rome, to which a peace gained on these terms would have left Spain as the spoils of war. But Scipio did not see things that way; he wanted his victory.

However, Scipio feigned an interest in the talks, with an idea at the back of his mind. His liaison officers had reported to him how the enemy had constructed their camps; cabins made of wood and branches for the Carthaginians, and simple huts of reeds and foliage – the famous *mappalia* – for the Numidians, often constructed outside the entrenchment. He resolved to carry out a surprise attack on the two camps and set fire to them, and had his officers accompanied by observers disguised as slaves to inform him about the access and layout of the sites. In early spring, when he had assembled all the necessary information, he had 2,000 of his footsoldiers stationed on the hill overlooking Utica that he had occupied at the time of his earlier siege attempt, simultaneously relaunching his ships. That was to throw the enemy off the scent, while guarding against any possible sortie from Utica's garrison against his own camp during the operation he planned. He spent an evening in action; leaving enough troops to guard his camp, he set off so as to reach the proximity of the two enemy camps by midnight. He then sent Laelius and Massinissa ahead, with half the legionaries and all the Massylians; their mission was to set Syphax's camp ablaze first; he himself, with the remaining troops, would wait until the fire had done its work on the Numidian camp before attacking Hasdrubal's camp. The operation succeeded beyond all hopes. Both leaders managed to flee, but their two armies were largely destroyed. Polybius (XIV, 5, 15) has no hesitation in saying that, of all the acts of war undertaken by Scipio, this was the finest and most daring. In fact, with almost no losses in his own ranks, he had thus re-established the balance of forces in his favour and created the conditions for a victorious offensive.

Scipio lost no time in exploiting his advantage, the more so because Hasdrubal and Syphax, for their part, had not delayed in partly rebuilding their forces. In the late spring of 203, they were once again able to line up 30,000 men, who were camped in the Great Plains, five days' march from Utica, in the middle valley of the Medjerda in the vicinity of Souk el-Khemis. The Roman general went to meet them there and, after several days of observation and skirmishes, joined battle, placing his cavalry on the right, Massinissa and his Massylians on the left; the latter were faced by the Carthaginian cavalry, while Syphax's Massaesylians were opposite the Italian cavalry; in the centre, Scipio's two legions were confronted by 4,000 Celtiberians recruited in Spain by Hasdrubal. Only these last sustained the clash; Hasdrubal and Syphax took advantage of their resistance to beat a retreat.

In Carthage's senate, the consequences of this defeat were immediately apparent; after Utica it would bring the Punic metropolis into the front-line, and the decision was taken to recall Hannibal from Italy without any further ado.

## Sophonisba

While he himself was exerting direct pressure on Carthage by going to occupy Tunis (Livy, XXX, 9, 10–12), Scipio had sent Laelius and Massinissa in pursuit of Syphax, who had taken refuge in Numidia. He could not be reached, but the greater part of the Massylian domain – the east of the present-day Constantine region and a western fringe of Tunisia – was henceforth liberated from the usurpation of the Massaesylian king. The latter, however, restricted to his former domain, would not accept the situation. He returned to the campaign with a hastily formed army, large in number but of undisciplined novices, and set up his camp near that of the Romans, probably a short distance east of Cirta (Constantine). On 23 June, according to an allusion by Ovid (*Fasti*, VI, 769), there was an engagement between the two cavalries. The Massaesylian horsemen, superior in number, were about to gain the upper hand when the Roman infantry entered the action. While trying to bring his cavalry back into combat – for they were beginning to yield – Syphax was thrown by his badly wounded horse. Taken prisoner, he was handed over to Laelius. Scipio's legate acceded to the earnest plea of Massinissa, who asked if he could go ahead of him with his cavalry to Cirta, where the remains of the vanquished king's army had taken refuge; the sight of Syphax in chains, he said, would break down the last vestiges of resistance.

The site of Constantine is extraordinary, its rocks slashed as if with a sabre by the gorges of the Rummel, and defended towards the west by inaccessible escarpments; one needs to have seen it, at least once, in order to understand the passions that are born in the austere confines of a natural fortress, and let oneself be swayed by the piteous content that flows through the pages Livy devotes to this episode. In Antiquity this stronghold was as it still continued to be in the middle of the nineteenth century, the impregnable quadrilateral of some fifteen hectares, culminating in the north in the Casbah, ever the seat of power in this eagle's eyrie, where one can imagine the palace which witnessed the end of the drama. Like the French of General Damremont, centuries later in 1837, Massinissa presented himself before its walls by passing through the narrow isthmus that separates the citadel from the hillock of the Coudiat Aty, the only possible means of access, to the south-west. But *he* had no need to make a breach in the wall. As he had foreseen, the sight of the dethroned king, in chains, opened the gates to him.

He immediately rushed to the palace. If we are to believe Diodorus (XXVII, 7), before Carthage gave preference to the marriage with Syphax, Sophonisba had been promised to the young Massylian prince, although he had never seen her. The young woman prostrated herself before him, clasping his knees, as suppliants were wont to do then. Nobly acknowledging a defeat that was also, and chiefly, hers since she had largely inspired the attitude of the Massaesylian king, she begged him to let her die rather than allow her to fall into Roman hands. Totally captivated – *amore captivae victor captus*, as Livy prettily expresses it (XXX, 12, 18) – Massinissa gave his promise. But before reaching this extreme, his dawning love for the beautiful Carthaginian suggested that marriage could save her from captivity and keep her alive. The ceremony was performed forthwith, unknown to Laelius, who had not yet arrived; furious at being presented with the *fait accompli*, the legate referred the matter to his superior to be settled.

The scene for the denouement was Scipio's camp. The proconsul had just received Syphax – who would end his life in Italy under 'house arrest' at Tibur (Tivoli) – and the Massaesylian had not hesitated to cast the blame for the madness that had made him take up arms against Rome on the pernicious seduction of the Carthaginian woman. This was enough to worry Scipio, who had learnt of Massinissa's sudden impulse, so to speak. The proconsul reasoned with the young prince, and appealed to his duties as an ally; the Carthaginian woman's life belonged to Rome, and he must hand her over. As he could not save her alive from captivity, Massinissa resolved to free her by death, as she herself had wished. There is no doubt that it was a painful decision for him. But Sophonisba died like a queen, a goblet of poison in her hand, a greater person than the ephemeral husband who had sacrificed her for reasons of state. The supreme tragic character, celebrated by the painters of the European classical age, the heroine of so many operas and tragedies, Sophonisba is indebted to Livy for her prime place in the gallery of exceptional women, from Dido to Kahena, who adorn the ancient history of North Africa (Camps, 1992). The following day, before the assembled soldiers, for the first time Scipio saluted Massinissa with the title of king, and gave him the insignia, including an ivory sceptre: in Latin, *scipio*.

## Hannibal's return to Africa

In Carthage, where too many hopes had been placed on the Numidian king's help, Syphax's defeat and capture were felt bitterly. None of our sources throws any light on the debates that must assuredly have stirred the Council of Elders, but there was a majority decision to send a deputation to Scipio. As was suspected a little later in Rome, the underlying intention, at least of the Barcid clan at the heart of the senate, may have been to play for time, leaving Hannibal enough to get back to Africa and with his army operational once again. At all events, during the summer of 203 thirty Carthaginian senators – probably the same limited council we saw at work during the Mercenaries' War (above, p. 21) – travelled to Tunis, where Scipio had returned after Massinissa's 'enthronement'. They prostrated themselves before him, following the oriental ceremonial of 'proskynesis' which the emperors would later value, but which at that time was offensive to Roman customs. When, after the violation of the truce, Scipio sent three of his officers to protest to Carthage, they did not fail to remind the senators of this act of submission, which to them had seemed surprising (Polybius, XV, 1, 6–7).

The speeches made in Tunis by the Thirty matched this humility; they acknowledged the wrongs done by Carthage, its initiative in the unleashing of hostilities but, at least according to Livy (XXX, 16, 5), they laid responsibility at the door of Hannibal and his clan. They finished by appealing to the generosity of their victor. Scipio laid down his conditions: Carthage was to return its prisoners, the deserters and fugitive slaves; it must withdraw its troops from south Italy and the Po Valley, which Mago, defeated and wounded, was in any case preparing to leave. The Carthaginians must give up all claim to Spain and the islands situated between Italy and Africa, in other words, evacuate the Balearic Islands, and notably Ibiza, where they had maintained a presence since the middle of the seventh century. They must hand over all but twenty of their warships, pay an indemnity of 5,000 talents and, lastly, supply the Roman army with enormous quantities of grain for its subsistence.

Scipio had laid his cards on the table. It was clear that he did not envisage taking Carthage by sheer force. He had been unable to take Utica, and was well aware that Carthage's defence walls, which he could see gleaming at sunset on the other side of Lake Tunis, would present him with a resistance that would be insurmountable within a reasonable time-span. And we, with hindsight, know that between 149 and 146 they would manage to hold off the attacks of the best Roman generals for more than three years (Lancel, 1995a, pp. 415–27). Now, Rome wanted only to have done with this exhausting war. After the deadly perils encountered in Italy a few years earlier, to render Carthage forever harmless, deprive it of its navy and reduce it to its African territory was an outcome that would have been unhoped for not long before.

Scipio had given the envoys three days in which to bring him a reply from their principals. Carthage's senate accepted his terms, though not without reservations – at least among the Barcid clan. Any truce was good if it allowed Hannibal to get back from Italy and, who knows, reverse the situation. Going by way of Pozzuoli and escorted by one of Scipio's lieutenants, Q. Fulvius Gillo, a Carthaginian delegation arrived in Rome in the autumn of 203, with the task of arranging a treaty. They were received *extra muros*, on the Campus Martius, in the temple of Bellona, with a rather chilly welcome. The ambassadors did not disarm the senators' hostility by laying the blame on Hannibal. And as, while clearing Carthage of all responsibility for the conflict, they stated that their mission was purely and simply to ask for a return to the conditions of the peace treaty concluded in 241 with Lutatius (above, p. 3), they were put into a difficult situation by the older *patres* present, who knew this treaty very well because they had had a hand in drawing it up. They pleaded their lack of years as an excuse for their ignorance of certain of the treaty's clauses. The accusation 'Punic trickery' (*fraus Punica*) then burst forth from all sides (Livy, XXX, 22, 6). In fact, the Carthaginian ambassadors were mainly bearing the brunt of the hostility towards Scipio among certain sections of the Roman Senate, in particular the Servilii, an old family from Alba Longa who had managed to get two members to the consulship in 203, Cn. Servilius Caepio and C. Servilius Geminus. At the time, both were absent from Rome, Caepio in Bruttium, where he was keeping a watch on Hannibal, and Geminus in Etruria. By virtue of his title of *princeps senatus* – in place of Q. Fabius Maximus, who was dying, if not already dead – M. Livius Salinator proposed an adjournment of the debate while awaiting the arrival of Geminus, who was nearest to Rome. They could not deliberate on such an important matter, he said, in the absence of the consul. This was virtually setting aside the talks Scipio had engaged in at Tunis. Q. Caecilius Metellus, a loyal supporter of the proconsul, came to the rescue by pointing out that no one was more fitted to assess the Carthaginian negotiators' true intentions than the man who, through his victories, had reduced Carthage to the point of negotiation. According to Livy, the last word lay with M. Valerius Laevinus, consul of the year 210, who suggested having the ambassadors sent back under strong guard and writing to Scipio to tell him to continue the war. Probably more credible is the version of Cassius Dio (fragment 56, 77), according to which the Senate at first rejected any discussion as long as the Carthaginians still had armies on Italian soil; but after the departure of Mago and Hannibal, the conditions set by the proconsul were adopted, though not without long arguments. And we know for certain, thanks to Polybius (XV, 1, 3), whose narrative is again available from early 202, that the Roman Senate and people ratified the treaty on the terms laid down by Scipio, probably during the winter of 203–202.

While peace was being discussed in Rome, Hannibal had resigned himself to leaving Bruttium, not without bitterness and regret, as Livy suggests (XXX, 20), which one can well believe. To complement the transport fleet sent to him from Carthage, he had had ships built (Appian, *Hann.*, 58), and was thus able to transport by sea the elite of his army, probably between 15,000 and 20,000 men, who would constitute the third line of his battle order at Zama. He set foot on the shores of the Tunisian Sahel at Leptis Minus (Lemta), between Thapsus (Ras Dimass) and Ruspina (Monastir). Thus in the autumn of 203 he rediscovered an Africa which he had left while still a child (above, p. 30), and which had become quite alien to him.

He set up camp near the place where he had landed, at Hadrumetum (Sousse). There are many reasons to explain why he chose at first to remain some distance from the Punic mother-city. Hannibal mistrusted the Carthaginian senators, who were too often dominated by the political faction led by his family's old enemy,

Hanno, whom he considered to be the real author of his final failure in Italy because of the man's cowardice, jealousy and defamatory attacks. And perhaps he had also got wind of the way in which Carthage's delegates, first of all with Scipio then in Rome, had tried to exonerate the city of any initiative in the war, laying the blame solely upon him. By taking up his winter quarters at Byzacena he was keeping his distance from Carthage's government, at the same time putting enough space between his forces and Scipio's army to maintain complete freedom to manoeuvre for the time being. He was providing himself with the possibility of obtaining reinforcements and supplies and preparing for a possible encounter, away from enemy surveillance. Moreover, on this coast, the Punic general was on his 'home' ground; he owned properties there, and his personal safety was assured.

## The battle of Zama

The truce granted by Scipio following the first talks in autumn 203 had lasted a few months when it was broken by Carthage in early spring 202.

Two large convoys had departed, one from Sardinia, the other from Sicily, to reprovision the Roman army. The first arrived safe and sound, but the second, after rounding Cape Bon, was caught in a storm. The escort vessels were able to reach Apollo's promontory (the Ras el-Mekki), but the majority of the 200 cargo ships were driven ashore, some on the island of Aegimura (Zembra), the rest on the west coast of Cape Bon at a point which Livy (XXX, 24, 9) calls Aquae Calidae ('Hot Waters'), very probably the old thermal bathing resort of Aquae Carpitanae, still in use at Korbous, opposite Carthage, on the other side of the bay; which is as much as to say that the shipwrecks took place with the whole town as spectators. This was tempting prey for a hungry population; but to seize it would be to break the truce. That, however, was the decision taken: fifty warships commanded by an admiral named Hasdrubal went to take possession of the wrecked transport vessels and towed them into Carthage's port.

Scipio learned of this violation of the truce at the same time that he received news of the ratification in Rome of the treaty prepared under his supervision. He decided, however, to make one last approach before a total break. He sent three of his lieutenants to Carthage to inform the senate of the ratification and demand reparations for the act of piracy. The haughty attitude of the Romans and their ironic allusions to the salvation that the Carthaginians seemed to expect of Hannibal set the senate against them, and few senators were in favour of returning the ships and their cargo. According to some sources (Diodorus, XXVII, 12; Appian, *Libyca*, 34), the crowd would even have offered them rough treatment if two leaders of the anti-Barcid faction, the old Hanno and one Hasdrubal, known as 'the Kid' (Haedus), had not intervened. But other rulers wanted to make the break irretrievable. They laid a trap. To the Roman quinquereme carrying Scipio's three emissaries back to Castra Cornelia (Galaat el-Andless) they supplied an escort of two triremes, with instructions to withdraw as soon as the mouth of the Medjerda was passed; then three triremes lying in ambush were to ram and attack it. The plan only half succeeded; most of the soldiers on board the Roman vessel were killed, but Scipio's three officers escaped safe and sound.

Resumption of hostilities had become inevitable. Before returning to the campaign, Scipio entrusted the guarding of his camp to one of the three emissaries sent back from Carthage, L. Baebius Dives. The latter shortly afterwards saw the arrival at Castra Cornelia of the Carthaginian negotiators returning from Italy with their Roman escorts. Knowing the treatment that had just been inflicted on Scipio's emissaries, the Carthaginian diplomats' hearts were in their boots. But, says Polybius (XV, 4, 5–12), Scipio had no wish to make them pay for the disloyalty of their own people; he had them released and accompanied back to their home.

For his part, Hannibal had probably not waited for the violation of the truce to hasten his own preparations, although the chronology of his actions during the winter of 203–202 is uncertain. He made provisions of wheat, bought horses, made sure of the alliance of several Numidian tribal chiefs, for example, the Areacids, otherwise unknown (Appian, *Libyca*, 33); and a Massylian prince, Mazaetullis, who had recently had a brush with Massinissa, is said to have brought him 1,000 horsemen. In contrast, the help which Vermina, Syphax's son, is supposed to have provided is more questionable, and Diodorus (XXVII, 10) is not to be believed when he affirms that Hannibal massacred 4,000 horsemen who, after serving under Syphax, had betrayed him for Massinissa and now came to offer him their help. The Carthaginian had too great a need of Numidians to alienate them by such a slaughter. But one can accept a piece of information supplied by Polybius (XV, 3, 5), according to which Hannibal, who needed to make up his cavalry, turned to a Numidian relative of Syphax, Tychaios. The latter, fearing that he would bear the brunt of Massinissa's ambition if the Romans got the upper hand, willingly offered to join him with 2,000 cavalry.

After the truce was broken, Scipio had sent messages to Massinissa, inviting him to assemble as large a troop as possible and join him at top speed in the valley of the Medjerda. As for himself, without giving further quarter, one after the other he seized the towns in this region, which at that time was so rich and densely populated (see Lancel, 1995a, pp. 269–72), laid them waste and reduced their inhabitants to slavery. At Hadrumetum Hannibal received a delegation from Carthage's senate, overwhelmed by this devastation, begging him to march on the enemy without delay. He replied haughtily that he knew what he had to do; but a few days later he moved his army and went to camp near Zama.

Of the site of Zama, Polybius (XV, 5, 3, summarized by Livy, XXX, 29, 2) says only that it was situated five days' march from Carthage in a westerly direction. Modern scholars now agree in identifying it, between two homonymous localities, with Zama Regia, a place attested many times subsequently in sources of the Roman period, owing its qualification of 'Regia' to the fact that it was a royal residence of the Numidian princes. But there is still speculation about the exact location of this city: either the present-day Seba Biar, seventeen kilometres north-east of Maktar or, more probably, thirty kilometres north of the last site, in the place known as Jama, where important ruins may be seen and whose toponymy still evokes that famous name (Desanges, 1980, pp. 322–3).

But why Zama? Why this site so far to the south-west of the lower valley of the Medjerda which Scipio was supposed to be ravaging at that time? Neither Polybius nor Livy bothers to pinpoint the position of the Roman who, possibly, had very recently moved farther west, in the river's middle valley, to go and meet Massinissa. Perhaps too, as some have thought (Huss, 1985, p. 416), it was Hannibal's intention, by going straight in the direction of the Massylian kingdom, to fall upon Massinissa before he could link up with Scipio. At all events, once he had arrived at Zama, the Carthaginian sent out scouts to reconnoitre the Roman positions. Arrested by Scipio's patrols, they were taken to the Roman general who ordered a superior officer – a tribune – to show them round all the camp installations at their leisure and escort them back, advising them to report everything faithfully to their leader. By doing this Scipio was probably knowingly imitating the actions of Xerxes – which he could have read about in Herodotus, *Histories*, VII, 146 – who had earlier given a similar welcome to the Greek spies sent to Sardis, where the Persian army was encamped. This audacious self-confidence piqued Hannibal's curiosity, and he let Scipio know that he desired to meet him before resorting to arms. Soon afterwards, he learned of Massinissa's arrival in the Roman camp at the head of 6,000 footsoldiers and 4,000 horsemen. Before a battle which carried the risk of being decisive and in which he had the most to lose, perhaps a final negotiation was possible. But, once he had been joined and reinforced by Massinissa, it was Scipio who was now in a strong position to impose these last-chance talks.

Thereupon the Roman general struck camp and went to set up a new one at a place which Polybius calls Margaron (XV, 5, 14), and which Livy (XXX, 29, 9), although he closely follows Polybius here, calls Naraggara. Hence the confusion of modern philologists, who wonder into which of the two texts the error could have slipped; unless one is forced to admit, with a recent commentator, that here we are faced with two slightly differing transcriptions of the same Punic place-name, and that the locality must have been 'Nahargara' or 'Nahrgara' (Nizza, 1980, pp. 85–8). The presence in Livy's manuscript of the variant 'Narcara' adds some weight to this hypothesis. It remains to find the exact location. A Naraggara was known in the Roman period: it is the present-day area of Sakhiet Sidi Youssef, on the Algerian–Tunisian frontier, which presents us with the major difficulty that it is a long way – about 100 kilometres to the west – from Zama/Jama. But place-names are often duplicated – as we have just seen in the case of Zama – and there is nothing to deny the existence of a homonymous site in the near vicinity of Zama, towards the north, probably between the Wadi Tessa and the Wadi Siliana. Ancient historiography did not ask all these questions. Following Cornelius Nepos, a contemporary of Cicero, it placed the encounter at Zama (*apud Zamam*, says Nepos less precisely, *Hannibal*, VI, 3): a name that cracks like a whip or resounds like a trumpet-call for that famous battle which brought face to face the two greatest generals of the era, and probably of all Antiquity.

There is no serious reason to doubt the historic veracity of their interview prior to the battle. Although seeking dramatic effect was not his forte, Polybius, who mentions it, was in a good position to know the truth of the matter because of his familiarity with the Scipios' circle. Whereas Livy gives it a fuller orchestration, which can be found pictorially represented in the great Gobelins tapestry based on a cartoon by Jules Romain, the Greek recounts it soberly, as it doubtless unfolded, just between the two men, in the presence of only a few escort cavalrymen from either side. There was much at stake for Hannibal; victory would only allow him to liberate Carthage's African territory, whereas defeat would subject the city-state to Rome's terms. But Hannibal was a living legend. According to Polybius, he tried to intimidate his foe, who was some dozen years younger. He proposed that Scipio should obtain his essential demands without risk; Carthage would give up Sicily, Sardinia, Spain and all the islands situated between Africa and Italy. This was a less heavy price than the conditions recently laid down by the proconsul and accepted, it may be recalled, by the Council of Elders before the violation of the truce. Scipio refused; either Carthage placed itself in Rome's hands or the whole matter must be ended by resorting to arms.

Battle commenced the next day, on a fine morning in the summer or autumn of 202. Hannibal was able to line up around 50,000 men, including Baleares, Gauls, Ligures and Mauri, recruited as mercenaries by Mago some years earlier. The solid nucleus of his army was made up of his infantry, strong in Spanish, African and also Italian veterans, brought back from Bruttium, and Carthaginian and Libyan footsoldiers recently enrolled by Hasdrubal Gisco. According to Appian (*Libyca*, 41), on the opposing side Scipio was able to draw up 23,000 footsoldiers, plus 6,000 of Massinissa's infantry. Above all, he had the advantage over the Carthaginian of a better and larger cavalry. On the other hand, Hannibal had eighty elephants which he placed in the forefront of the battle line; behind them he put the mercenaries. His second line was made up of the Libyans and Carthaginians from Hasdrubal's ex-army. The very doubtful presence at their side of a phalanx of Macedonians is mentioned only by Livy (XXX, 26, 3 and 33, 5). He held his third line about a stadium (roughly 200 metres) to the rear; it was composed of his veterans from Italy, in short, the old guard, in the midst of whom he took up his own position. On his left wing, he was flanked by the allied Numidian cavalry; on his right, by the Carthaginian cavalry. Such positioning allows us at least to guess at his tactical intentions. His cavalry was too weak to undertake the enveloping movements that had succeeded so well at Cannae. At the most, he could make use of them to keep the more powerful enemy cavalry away from the action and avert the threat that this could wield over his veterans; he did so but, as we shall see, without the hoped-for result. First and foremost he relied on his infantry, deployed in such a way as to engage in several successive combats. The charge of the elephants was to be the prelude to the attack by the mercenaries, before his second line fell on the enemy infantry. He kept in reserve the best soldiers of his third line, either to complete the work at the end of the action or to prevent or limit any headlong flight should the engagement fail. On the opposite side, Scipio divided his infantry into three lines, following the deployment that was still customary in the Roman army in that period. In the first line were the youngest, the *hastati* (in fact armed with the *pilum* and not the spear, *hasta*), then the *principes* and lastly, in the third line, the *triarii*, veterans, armed with the defensive lance, who could be relied on to retrieve difficult situations. But, instead of placing the maniples in staggered rows, with the companies of *principes* plugging the gaps in the companies of *hastati*, he arranged them one behind the other so that there were deep corridors at right angles to the front line, in order to channel the charging elephants; other corridors parallel to the front were to facilitate the manoeuvres and replacement of his light units, the velites. To the left of the battle line, Laelius was in charge of the Italian cavalry, and on the right Massinissa commanded all the contingents he had brought, cavalry and infantry, part of the latter, lightly armed, being held in reserve behind the Roman lines.

Reading Polybius, it seems that the battle had two very distinct phases. After the skirmishes launched on either side by the horsemen, the elephants' charge did not achieve the success that Hannibal had counted on; some of them went off to the right, others were engulfed in the corridors arranged by Scipio and crossed far into the battlefield without doing much harm to the Roman lines. Similarly, the infantry's fighting did not live up to the plans of the Carthaginian leader, who had hoped that the thrusts of his mercenaries would cause havoc among the Roman front-line. Instead, the mercenaries crumbled before Scipio's *hastati*, and Hannibal's second line went into action amid confusion. As both groups were retreating in disorder into the space that he had left free in front of the third line, Hannibal did not allow them to mingle with his old guard; he ordered the first row of his veterans to present their spears so as to ward them off and force them to retreat to right and left of his front line. That was when the second phase of the battle began. Scipio reassembled his *hastati* and made them form a central position, while the *principes* of the second line and the *triarii* of the third framed them to right and left. The two armies were now both reduced to a single line of the same length. In this new front-to-front battle, Hannibal's old guard might have won the day. But while the outcome was still uncertain, Laelius and Massinissa returned with their horsemen from the pursuit of the Carthaginian cavalry that had been taking place in the distance. Attacked from the rear, Hannibal's veterans were slaughtered where they stood. At the end of the day, the Romans had lost barely 2,000 men, but on the opposing side 20,000 men lay on the ground, and as many were taken prisoner. Hannibal, with a small escort of cavalry, did not stay his flight until he reached Hadrumetum.

## The Peace of 201 and Hannibal's Laughter

There should be no surprise that Hannibal, following his defeat, should have first taken refuge at Hadrumetum. He must certainly have had in mind the fate – often crucifixion – of many Carthaginian generals who had been harshly punished by the Tribunal of the Hundred because the luck of war had not gone their way. To return to the mother-city in a state of emergency, directly after the disaster, virtually alone and without support, would have placed him at the mercy of his enemies. Although our sources are mute on this point, stopping off at Hadrumetum probably allowed him to obtain guarantees and be able to present himself in Carthage with an adequate escort.

In any case, he did not tarry in Byzacena, as we find him shortly afterwards in Carthage. Thirty-six years after his departure for Spain with his father Hamilcar, he once again saw the city he had left when still a child. Before the Council of Elders to whom he reported he made no attempt to disguise the truth; he stated quite simply that he had lost not only the battle but the war, and that Carthage had no other salvation than to seek and obtain peace (Livy, XXX, 35, 11). Scipio, for his part, had lost no time after Zama. He had gone with all speed to Utica, laden with enormous booty after pillaging Hannibal's camp, and immediately set out for Carthage with his fleet. He had already rounded Cape Carthage (Sidi-Bou-Saïd) when he saw coming to meet him a Carthaginian vessel, decked like a suppliant with strips of cloth and olive branches and carrying the heralds' caduceus attached to its prow. On board were ten ambassadors, the top-ranking citizens of the state among whom, says Appian (*Libyca*, 49), were the chief supporters of the peace party, Hanno and Hasdrubal Haedus (the Kid). They implored Scipio's protection, and the Roman ordered them to go to Tunis.

It was there, in the camp he had occupied earlier, that he received thirty Carthaginian ambassadors. Did this delegation comprise the same members as the one he had received in the same place the year before (above, p. 170)? We do not know. The envoys paid the price for their perfidy by the scornful reception they were given. As for the price of the defeat, it was very heavy. Of course, Carthage would continue to exist as a theoretically independent nation, with its laws and according to its customs, and without being subjected to military occupation. But the new conditions imposed by Scipio worsened its status as a nation that was deprived of its arms and even subjugated in its external relations. Its war fleet was henceforth limited to the purely symbolic number of ten triremes, and it must hand over its elephants; it was forbidden to make war on any people outside Africa, and even in Africa itself was not to undertake any action without Rome's authorization. The financial terms were no less heavy; the war indemnity set by Scipio was 10,000 Euboic talents – a Greek monetary unit of international worth, one talent equalling twenty-six kilogrammes of silver – in comparison with the 2,200 talents demanded in 241 at the end of the first Punic War (above, p. 3). This vast sum was payable, in equal amounts, over fifty years; a real millstone round the city's neck, but we shall see that, paradoxically, it did fairly little to slow down the state's economic development. As a guarantee of its commitment to observing all these clauses, Carthage would hand over 100 hostages, to be chosen by the Roman general, and would naturally restore without delay the ships and cargoes seized the year before when the truce was broken.

Of all the terms laid down by Scipio, those which must have weighed most heavily on Carthage's future, together with the ban on its fighting with anyone else on African soil without Rome's consent, were those relating to the limitation of the territory it could now occupy. Polybius (XV, 18, 2) and Livy (XXX, 37, 2) use very nearly the same words: the Carthaginians would keep the towns and territories they had possessed before starting the war against the Romans. Appian (*Libyca*, 54) is more explicit, both chronologically and spatially, when he states precisely that Carthage would keep the regions it controlled within the 'Phoenician trenches' at the time of Scipio's landing in Africa. We know that a system of trenches, probably established shortly after the middle of the third century, gave concrete form to the administrative boundaries of the Punic state and protected its territory (Lancel, 1995a, pp. 261–5). But although the archaeological reality of the fortified frontier creates problems for us today, it appears that this demarcation was sometimes uncertain and thus an object of contention even for its contemporaries themselves. To the north-west and west things were fairly clear, and the trail of these *fossae Punicae* hardly disputable from their beginning on the shore of Thabraca (Tabarka) as far as the vicinity of Maktar. But what about farther south? And were the *Emporia* of Syrtis Minor, for example, encompassed by these trenches? Theoretically no, but when, several decades later, Massinissa laid hands on the region of the *Emporia*, the Carthaginians affirmed, in a list of grievances addressed to Rome, that this region had been included in the boundaries set by Scipio to be under their permanent control (Livy, XXXIV, 62, 9–10). So, besides taking into account the 'Phoenician trenches', Scipio had also taken a hand in defining limits, which of necessity were flawed by all the imprecisions of ancient 'chorography'. This intervention is implicitly acknowledged by Polybius (XV, 18, 5) when, in connection with the domain of the Massylian Numidians which Carthage had to hand back to Massinissa, he situates these restitutions 'within frontiers which will later be demarcated'. A whole series of time-bombs were thus *de facto* put in place, which would irrecoverably undermine Carthage's future until the day, fifty years later, when one last burst, one final desperate act of resistance, would seal its death warrant (Lancela, 1995, pp. 411–12).

Back in Carthage, the ambassadors set out Scipio's terms before the people's assembly, as Livy would have it (XXX, 37, 7), or more probably, as Polybius says (XV, 19, 1), before the Council of Elders. Room for manoeuvre was so tight that a single voice was raised against the proposed treaty; it remains anonymous in Polybius, but according to Livy belonged to a man called Gisco. Hannibal, exasperated by this absurdly hard-line attitude, is said to have got to his feet, seized Gisco and hurled him down from the platform. And when the senators expressed their indignation at his action, he asked them to forgive the roughness of his manners, which were those of a soldier brought up from childhood on the battlefield and not accustomed to parliamentary practices. He continued by urgently advising that they should agree without argument to conditions which, bearing in mind the relative forces involved, could have been worse.

The year 202 was drawing to a close when the ambassadors, duly escorted, arrived in Rome to obtain ratification of the treaty from the Senate. They were already present, it seems, when elections brought Cn. Cornelius Lentulus, in association with P. Aelius Paetus, to the consulship for the year 201. The first-named made vain attempts to have Africa allotted to him as province and thus, to Scipio's detriment, gain an easy victory if the peace talks were to fail, or the honour of being the consul who would give his name to that peace. By allocating Sicily to him, the Senate granted him only command of naval operations if the war were not brought to an end. Scipio kept his proconsulship in Africa with full authority over all land operations. In fact, the war was well and truly over. Received shortly afterwards by the Senate, the Carthaginian envoys, headed by Hasdrubal Haedus, declared their country's agreement to the conditions imposed by Scipio. And on their return to Africa, in the summer of 201, they visited the proconsul who ratified the treaty, surrounded by the fetials, priests who specialized in the rituals of war and peace, who had come from Rome for this occasion.

Four thousand captives then emerged from the Carthaginian gaols, among them a senator, Q. Terentius Culleo. A few months later Scipio re-embarked his army at Utica and landed at Lilybaeum. Before his triumph properly speaking, his journey through Italy was a triumphal parade. Syphax, a prisoner at Tibur, had just died and therefore had no part in the victor's triumphal procession in Rome. But behind Scipio's chariot in a prominent position walked Q. Terentius Culleo, wearing the enfranchised slave's hat (the *pilleus*); the gesture of a man forever the faithful henchman of the one who had restored his liberty. And that was perhaps, as has been suggested (Nicolet, 1977, p. 450), the first and powerful intrusion of a personal clientele into a patron's political game. Was the nickname Africanus added to Scipio's name from the date of that day of glory? And to whom did he owe it? His soldiers, the people, his family? Livy asks these questions without supplying the answer, but notes that his hero was the first Roman general to go down to posterity bearing the name of a conquered people, and he seems rather inclined to believe that the gods themselves placed this crown of immortality on his head.

In Carthage it was a time of mourning. The distress had reached its peak when Scipio ordered the entire Carthaginian fleet, with the exception of ten vessels, to be burnt in the bay facing the town. The whole of Carthage had gathered on the sea front, on the maritime defence wall whose line has been fairly exactly restored by recent excavations (Lancel, 1995a, pp. 152–5), to watch the ships burn with as much desolation as if the city itself had been set on fire, as Livy says (XXX, 43, 12), and he was aware of the outcome. For him it was a premonition of the blazing inferno which the town would become half a century later through the actions of another Scipio. The Carthaginians had no need, to add to their sufferings, to anticipate the misfortunes that lay ahead. Although Carthage had become a land-based power, and its agricultural vocation had asserted itself for at least two centuries in the lands around Cape Bon, the valleys of the Medjerda and the Wadi Miliana, although solid ramparts gave protection on African soil to a state that for nearly half a century had ceased to be the unchallenged master of the high seas, they knew the role that had been played from the very beginning by those 'wooden ramparts', which the Delphic oracle had once predicted would be the salvation of Athens against the Persians in the bay of Salamis. The people of Carthage were only too well aware of that. In the Council of Elders, the members of the oligarchy, wealthy landowners in the rural areas – the very ones who made up the anti-Barcid faction – were less so. There was unrestrained lamentation when the time came to pay the first annual instalment of the war reparations. A legend reported by Livy (XXX, 44, 4–11) would have it that Hannibal burst into bitter laughter amid all the weeping. And when Hasdrubal Haedus rebuked him for it, Hannibal revealed his contempt for these shopkeepers who had remained unmoved as stone when their homeland was placed under Rome's supervision but now wept, incapable of understanding that they were bewailing the least of their misfortunes. What followed would prove him right.

## Hannibal's suffetate

One of Hannibal's recent historiographers was doubtless correct in crediting Scipio with the freedom retained by the Punic leader after Zama and the peace of 201 (De Beer, 1969, p. 290). And perhaps, too, as the British historian suggests, besides the esteem in which he held his adversary, the Roman thought that it might be expedient for Rome, once the decision was taken to allow the Carthaginian state to survive, not to deprive it of the services of the man who seemed most capable, at least for the time being, of allowing it to honour the financial commitments resulting from the treaty.

But the question is, what did Hannibal do during the years immediately following the peace of 201? According to Cornelius Nepos (*Hannibal*, VII, 1–4), who is the only one to supply this information, he remained at the head of the army; indeed, it may well be that this army was kept at a significant level despite the treaty's clause that was so harsh for Carthage by forbidding it to wage even a defensive war without Rome's authorization. But reference to Mago, Hannibal's young brother, at the side of his older sibling, when we know that he had already died of his wounds in 203, renders the testimony of Nepos more than suspect, and in any case we cannot follow him when he adds that the Punic leader continued to make war in Africa – against whom? – until the consulship of P. Sulpicius Galba and C. Aurelius Cotta, consuls for the year 200. Probably echoing this tradition, I must mention a legend reported by a later Latin writer, Aurelius Victor (*De Caesaribus*, 37, 3), according to which Hannibal, fearing the pernicious effects of idleness on his soldiers, employed them to plant a massive expanse of olive trees. Indeed, this he could well have done in the interval of almost a year between his return from Italy in late autumn 203 and his engagement against Scipio in the summer or autumn of 202, while he had his quarters at Hadrumetum. But he could have done this with more continuity in the few years that followed Zama.

We know that this part of old Byzacium – the present-day Tunisian Sahel – Hannibal's favourite place, was a great producer of olive oil in that period (Lancel, 1995a, pp. 276–7). We must admit, however, that these years of Hannibal's career remain obscure. The historian of Antiquity has often to be resigned to admitting ignorance rather than seeking, at any price, to build bridges of guesswork between the too rare and fragile points of certainty.

We are back on firm ground with the year 196, when the joint consuls were M. Claudius Marcellus, son of the great Marcellus of the Fabii clan, and a patrician, L. Furius Purpureo, a supporter of Scipio. In that year Hannibal was elected suffete, in company with a colleague whom he no doubt eclipsed and whose name history has not retained – unless the Barcid clan carried enough weight at that time for him to be elected alone to the suffetate, something which happened for the consulship only once in the entire history of republican Rome, in 52 BC, to Pompey's advantage. In Carthage, since the people's assembly had begun to encroach on the prerogatives of the Council of Elders – and Polybius, in a celebrated text (VI, 51), places this 'democratic' development at the start of the Barcid era (Lancel, 1995a, pp. 118–19) – the power of the suffetes and their influence in the state had been strengthened. Hannibal profited from it to settle a few scores.

When he entered office, he made use of a disagreement, certainly relating to financial matters, with a magistrate whom Livy (XXXIII, 46, 3) describes as a *quaestor*, using the Latin term for the post, in order to attack the powerful 'class of judges' (*ordo judicum*). Hannibal summoned the quaestor to give an account of his actions. The latter, who belonged to the faction opposed to the Barcid and was not afraid of him since, on leaving his office he would enter the rank of the judges, irremovable magistrates, ignored the summons. Hannibal had him arrested and brought before the people's assembly. Seeing that they were very receptive to the indictment he was building up against both the quaestor and the *ordo judicum*, the suffete proposed and immediately called for a vote on a law, by the terms of which the judges would in future be elected annually, none being able to hold the office for two years in succession. If Livy accurately records the facts, it would seem that the Council of Elders was not consulted before the decision was taken by the people's assembly, and also that the control exercised by the assembly could lead directly to the senior magistrates' adopting demagogic attitudes. In this particular context, however, we must take into account Hannibal's personal influence, and not be too hasty to read a truly democratic measure into this constitutional reform, which certainly targeted the oligarchy (Kotula, 1984). It is not surprising that the suffete did everything possible to keep the Elders on the sidelines. There were those among them – probably the same ones who had been opposing Barcid policy for the past forty years – whom he would do his best to force to restore their ill-gotten gains, in order to alleviate, if not abolish, the contributions of ordinary citizens to payment of the war indemnity. As his act of checking the accounts had enabled him to assess how much public finances were losing on the various revenues (basically land and sea taxes), owing to the misappropriation of funds carried on to the profit of a few oligarchs, he declared before the people's assembly that by demanding the repayment of all the sums embezzled the state would be rich enough to acquit itself of its financial obligations to Rome without the need to tax private individuals. And, adds Livy (XXXIII, 47, 2), he kept his word. Many of the Elders must then have remembered the famous 'laughter' of 201; and naturally, in the minds of those who were compelled to make restitution, Hannibal's fate was sealed.

## The paradox of Carthage's prosperity after Zama

In Carthage, after the traumatic spectacle of its fleet in flames, life carried on. Apart from the warships, the town's vital parts had not been affected and, with the exception of the final phase, which had certainly been very destructive around Utica and in the Medjerda valley, this dreadful war of more than twenty years had wreaked its ravages outside Carthage's territory. It had waged the war mainly using Africans, Spaniards, Gauls and Italiots, and comparatively few of its own sons had died in the fighting.

Of course, at the same time as its overseas possessions, Carthage had lost the exploitation of Spanish mines, and very probably control of the tin route, as well. In Africa itself, its horizons, formerly very broad on the maritime side of the present-day Maghreb, had shrunk. But its local economic potential remained intact. The patient work accomplished by Punic agronomy which the name of Mago had brought to a high degree of renown as early as the late fourth century (Lancel, 1995a, pp. 273–9), now yielded its full fruits. Recalling those years of the early second century, Appian (*Libyca*, 67) emphasizes Carthage's recovered power and its demographic increase during the period that followed, when its enforced pacifism enabled it to benefit to the full from its varied productivity, notably in the agricultural domain. Ten years after Zama, Carthage was able to propose to Rome, which refused, that it should pay off in advance the forty annual sums of war indemnity which still remained to be settled (Livy, XXXVI, 4, 7). The two countries had emerged equally depleted from their long conflict. But while Rome, in 200, again confronted Philip of Macedon, then engaged in a war against Antiochus of Syria, Carthage was able to invest in its own development the silver formerly expended to arm warships, recruit mercenaries and maintain armies. Such is the usual revenge of the defeated.

The proof of this rediscovered prosperity is varied. In the first place, textual sources bear witness to it, as we have just seen in Livy's reference to Carthage's proposal in 191 to settle ahead of time the sums still owing from the treaty of 201. But, by recounting the size of the grain supplies agreed to by Carthage for Rome, at its request and in exchange for money, as well as for the subsistence of Roman armies on campaign, the historian also bears witness to Punic agriculture's capacity to hive off large exportable surpluses during the period immediately following the end of the war. In 200, 200,000 bushels of wheat – remember that a bushel, *modius*, represents 8.75 litres – were exported to Rome, and the same amount to Macedonia, for the supply corps of the Roman expeditionary force (Livy, XXXI, 19, 2). Ten years later, in 191, much larger quantities, including 500,000 bushels of barley destined for the Roman army, were requested by the Senate's envoys and supplied by Carthage, which was even pleased enough with itself to offer the provisions gratis, but the Senate refused (Livy, XXXVI, 4, 9). In 171, again, Carthaginian representatives went to Rome to announce that a similar supply of barley, plus a million bushels of wheat, were ready for dispatch; on Rome's orders, they were transported to Macedonia (Livy, XLIII, 6).

These were mass supplies, in a framework of official transactions between one state and another. On the level of ordinary commercial practices, a Latin literary text from the early second century attests that private Carthaginian trade was still active in Italy. The dialogues of the *Poenulus* (The Carthaginian) by Plautus, enacted on Roman stages around 190 BC, clearly show that the Romans of that period had a direct and familiar acquaintance with Punic traders. The one shown in the play, under the passe-partout name of Hanno, appears to be sketched with no underlying hostility, but simply in the bantering tones ordinarily used about foreign bazaar merchants. Hanno is a *gugga* (a generic nickname that is certainly pejorative), with rings in his ears and, like his slaves, wears a beltless tunic. As a good Carthaginian trader, he knows every language while pretending not to (*Poenulus*, v. 112), which in Plautus' comedy gives us some thirty lines of jargon in which, not always easily, people have recognized the language then spoken in Carthage, as perceived by Roman ears, and in a transcription further distorted by the manuscript version of the text (Sznycer, 1967). As Latin was known in Carthage, so Punic was known in Rome, in that period, if for no other reason than contact with the numerous Carthaginian slaves procured in the spoils of war – and since we are speaking of Plautus, the comedy writer of the following generation, Terence, was probably one of them. It would be nice to know what Hanno and his fellow-traders came to Italy to sell. Farm produce, for sure; remember Cato's famous fig which, on the eve of the third Punic War, he would bring to the Senate to impress his colleagues with the claim that it had been picked three days earlier in Carthage! But there would also have been manufactured products – especially that to which texts pay little attention, but which archaeology attests by the score, the only indestructible one of them all – pottery.

In this vast 'common market' for pottery constituted by the western part of the Mediterranean basin, the industrial and commercial presence of the Carthaginians seems to have remained important after the end of the third century. A noticeable re-evaluation of this Carthaginian presence has recently been made, following, first, recent excavations in Carthage – the great hotbed of archaeological investigations on the coast of the Spanish Levant. Second, at the same time, more successful identification has been made of numerous series of black-glazed pottery from the period – successors to the undecorated Attic pottery of the fourth century. Of course, precise datings sometimes remain difficult for the various series. But without too much risk of error it may be suggested that, of the vast amounts of Punic or 'Punicizing' black-glazed pottery found in Spain, but also in Sicily and Italy, as far as Rome, a large proportion arrived there, after Zama, in the baggage of the Carthaginian *guggas* (Morel, 1980, 1982, 1986; Lancel, 1995a, pp. 406–9). In the opposite direction – and here the dates are more reliable – from the first years of the second century, originating from Italy, and more precisely the Naples region, a wave of high-quality pottery products, known as 'Campanian A' pottery, poured into Carthage. This appellation is given to crockery – mainly goblets, plates and bowls – which is remarkable for its clay, of deep ochre, delicately refined and well baked, and above all for its glaze, which is robust, rather a bluish-black, often with metallic glints. The French excavations in recent years on the hill of Byrsa allow us to place the 'peak' of these imports of Campanian pottery in the second quarter of the second century. Its massive presence, which does not exclude that of local products, must not be interpreted as a weakening in Carthage's economic prosperity at that time. In the very active flow of trade between North Africa and central and southern Italy, Italian importers were certainly making no gifts to the Punic metropolis, which compensated for its imports of manufactured products by exporting its own products and agricultural surpluses.

There can be no trading by sea without a commercial fleet. And unless it is agreed, rather absurdly, that everything arriving at and leaving Carthage was transported under the Roman flag, a Carthaginian mercantile fleet must have continued to exist after Zama. This existence poses the problem of ports, and more broadly that of Carthage's urban development, to which the most recent archaeology bears massive witness. Concerning the ports, more precisely, we come to the most striking paradox in the archaeological dossier of Carthage for that period, since it appears from the publication of American and British excavations in the main port area of the city that its definitive state, whose image is still continued in the present-day lagoons, is datable to after Zama (Lancel, 1995a, pp. 172–92). Nothing is more significant of Carthage's regained economic health than the fashioning of the artifical islet of the circular port, and the establishment on this islet and on the perimeter of the harbour basin of installations and fine monumental decor – described by Appian (*Libyca*, 96) – which number among the great achievements of the Hellenistic world. There is therefore nothing more upsetting for the historian who is anxious to check the coherence of his sources, since the completion of this port, which according to Appian could hold 220 warships, is obviously at odds with the clause of the 201 treaty which limited the number to ten. At least one must take note here of the technical prowess, the effort made in town planning, so noticeable too in the German and French excavation sites related to dwelling areas. In the site's central position, the area bordering on the sea developed at that time both in the sense of a search for more habitable space – the monumental sea-gate disappeared and the defence wall was moved farther forward on to the shore – and of a more sumptuous layout for dwellings, which became houses with a peristyle. On the south slope of the hill of Byrsa a whole new quarter appeared, on land hitherto occupied by areas of metal workshops, which were themselves underlain by a much older burial-place. There, well dated by Campanian pottery and the stamps on Rhodian amphorae which, I must add in passing, indicate commercial traffic along an east–west axis, in the earliest years of the second century collective dwellings are to be seen emerging, laid out according to a concerted town-planning scheme, separated by regular roads at right angles, and showing by their overall plans and internal arrangements an evident concern for standardization (Lancel, 1995a, pp. 152–72). The excavations revealed that this zone developed over a quarter of a century, but the rigorousness of its conception, and its originality, combined with the probable date of its commencement, argue in favour of the hypothesis that in the course of his suffetate it was Hannibal who conceived the idea and laid the first stone. Shall we not see that, to fill the last years of his exile, he would become a town planner in Armenia and Bithynia?

In those years of the early second century BC, Carthage thus appears to be an astonishingly prosperous city, though subject to supervision, with no other ambition than to enjoy itself and its riches, and so without a future in the constantly changing Hellenistic world. Slightly more than a century earlier, Alexander had irresistibly set in motion a dynamic of political appropriation of the world to which Roman imperialism would be the true heir. Hannibal was sufficiently well informed and clear-sighted to be aware of it, and also that in the middle term his homeland would bear the cost of an evolution that he could foresee. Could he be satisfied with being the wise administrator of a post-war prosperity? Was he hatching plans to extract Carthage from this gilded mediocrity? If so, his enemies in Rome and Carthage itself did not leave him the time to bring them to fruition. They precipitated him willy-nilly into the eastern mêlée, where he would be a spectator rather than a participant.

# 8

# Exile

Scarcely had the war against Hannibal ended when Rome's attention was drawn to the East. On 22 June 217, in other words, the day after Flaminius' death at Trasimene, Antiochus III of Syria was defeated at Raphia, south of Palestine, not far from Gaza, by the man who then ruled Lagid Egypt, Ptolemy IV Philopator. The event probably passed unnoticed in Rome. Nevertheless, it marked a fleeting era, a time of fragile equilibrium between the three great Hellenistic powers born of the dismemberment of Alexander's empire, Macedonia, Seleucid Asia and Ptolemaic Egypt. Fifteen years later, the Romans could no longer remain unaware of Antiochus. Held in check towards the south, he had immediately started upon what Maurice Holleaux (1957, p. 320) has called his 'anabasis', or military advance up-country; retracing Alexander's steps, he restored the power of the Seleucid dynasty in Armenia, then in Bactriana, returning to Seleucia in 205 with the Achaemenid title of 'Great King', at once rendered by the Greeks, among whom his mighty feats had most reverberated, by the name Antiochus the Great.

Thereupon Ptolemy Philopator died, as did his sister–wife Arsinoe, who was probably murdered. The Ptolemaic kingdom fell into the hands of Ptolemy V Epiphanes, a child aged five – actually those of a guardianship council, led by the old Sosibios and Agathocles, the dead king's favourite, who was highly unpopular in Egypt. There were rumblings of rebellion in the Delta, and already the Theban region had seceded. The time might seem ripe for Antiochus, but also for Philip of Macedon, to profit from the difficulties of the Egyptian empire, which was united from Cyrenaica to Palestine, but splintered and sprawling – hence weak – around the whole perimeter of the Aegean, with its possessions spreading from Thrace to the coasts of Cilicia and Cyprus, by way of Thera, in the Cyclades, and Samos. During the winter of 203–202, the Macedonian and the Seleucid concluded a pact allowing each on his own side to grab pieces of the Ptolemaic kingdom (Polybius, XV, 20). Antiochus at once invaded Palestine. The siege of Gaza kept him a long time, but at the latest in 200–199 he had achieved the conquest of Syria Coele – 'hollow Syria': the Jordan depression – and Palestine. Tyre, the old Phoenician metropolis and mother-city of Carthage, was also subjugated. For his part, Philip had not wasted any time. He hurled himself on Thrace and reached as far as

Chalcedon, on the Bosphorus; on the way back he seized Thasos. The following year, 201, he occupied Samos and laid siege to Chios. Shortly afterwards, south of the Chios canal, he was forced to confront the allied fleets of the Rhodians and Attalus of Pergamum. It was a semi-success. He had captured the royal ship, but Attalus had been able to flee; in the autumn of 201 he and the Rhodians sent ambassadors to Rome to denounce Macedonian acts of aggression on the Hellespont and in the Aegean Sea.

## Rome's entry into war with Philip

In the Senate the envoys from Pergamum and Rhodes were given an attentive hearing. The reply, which was deferred, came at the end of 201 with the election to the consulship of P. Sulpicius Galba, in association with C. Aurelius Cotta. It had not been forgotten that in 210, with the rank of proconsul, Galba had succeeded Laevinus on the Macedonian front (above, p. 153). It is therefore not surprising to learn that soon afterwards Galba obtained, 'by the luck of the draw', as Livy says in all seriousness (XXXI, 6, 1), the province of Macedonia. In the minds of the senators the war appeared to have been settled. The decision needed to be implemented. In the spring of 201, the Senate sent three *legati* – and by no means negligible men: C. Claudius Nero, the victor of the Metaurus, P. Sempronius Tuditanus, author of the treaty of Phoinike in 205, and the young M. Aemilius Lepidus – to deliver an ultimatum to Philip. The king must refrain from any act of war against the Greeks and accept an arbitrated penalty for the damage he had caused Attalus and the Rhodians (Polybius, XVI, 34, 3–4). It was the youngest of these ambassadors who finally met Philip near Abydos, not far from Pergamum, in the late summer of 200. Meanwhile, In Rome, the *comitia centuriata*, duly admonished by the consul Sulpicius Galba (Livy, XXXI, 7), had voted for war after an initial show of reluctance. Aemilius Lepidus notified Philip of the Roman *indictio belli*. In vain did the Macedonian king reply that in his conflict with the Rhodians they were the aggressors, and that he had in no way infringed the clauses of the peace of Phoinike; Rome declared war on him.

In the history of the world in that period probably no initiative bore heavier consequences, and modern historians have racked their brains to find an explanation. Philip was not threatening Rome and had most carefully refrained from provoking it. But his alliance with Hannibal in 215 had not been forgotten and, even if that alliance had remained something of a dead letter, Macedonia was still a kind of bogeyman in Roman public opinion. One may recall the rumour, certainly false, but with an echo in Livy (above, p. 175), of the presence of a Macedonian phalanx at the side of the Carthaginians at Zama. As for the Syrio-Macedonian pact, true, for the moment its target was only Egypt, but should not that menacing coalition be broken, first by attacking the one member who was within striking distance (Holleaux, 1957, p. 341) – and, if possible, without waiting until Philip ended up controlling the whole Aegean. Furthermore, after the fall of Carthage and Scipio's triumph, now that there was no more glory to acquire in the West, there were laurels to be gleaned in the East. There no longer seems any doubt that, when the decision was taken, the ambitions of the 'eastern lobby' weighed pretty heavily (Badian, 1958, p. 66). However that may be, history maintains that this preventive war against Philip of Macedon was the birth certificate of Roman imperialism in the *pars Orientis* of the known world (Veyne, 1975, pp. 838–9).

## Flamininus and the 'Liberty of Greece'

At the end of 200, Sulpicius launched his campaign. While his lieutenant, L. Apustius, ravaged the Macedonian frontier in the north, a Roman squadron was sent to Piraeus to protect the Athenians, the only ones remaining of all the Greeks to show sympathy towards Rome. In the spring of 199, still in office, Galba carried off a success at Ottolobos, on the Erigon, that at least had the result of warming up the Aetolians, who had been Rome's allies since the first Macedonian war but until then had remained sitting on the fence to see what happened. In late 199, realizing that he would have to secure his western frontier, and foreseeing that the Romans would now approach Macedonia via Epirus, in order to get closer to their Aetolian allies, Philip occupied the gorges of the Aous near Antiogneia (in the mountainous region in the south of present-day Albania), simultaneously barring passage to Epirus, in the south, and to Thessaly, on the south-east side. Galba's successor, P. Villius Tappulus, had used a good part of his period of command in pacifying a mutiny that had broken out among his troops. Hardly had he made contact with Philip on the Aous when he was replaced by the consul for 198, to whom the luck of the draw had given Macedonia. T. Quinctius Flamininus landed at Corcyra in early spring with large reinforcements.

Like Scipio in Spain, Flamininus arrived in Greece with a plan and a vision. Also like Scipio, he was a patrician and had reached the consulship at an early age, taking short cuts; he was barely thirty and had not held a praetorship. Again like Scipio, he was philhellenic, an attitude of mind that was suspect in Rome, but a virtue among Greeks. Flamininus had immediately gone to Epirus and from there had reached the Aous. A confrontation with Philip, obtained for him by the Epirotes, gave him the opportunity to present a manifesto: if Philip desired peace, he had to give up all his possessions in Greece, even the hereditary ones, including Thessaly. The Macedonian king indignantly refused and soon afterwards had to beat a retreat as far as Tempe, his defences in the gorge having been won over by the Romans. Meanwhile, Flamininus invaded Thessaly and emerged on the Gulf of Corinth, but an attack launched on the stronghold, which was defended by a Macedonian garrison, failed.

Towards the end of the year negotiations opened in Locris, at Nikaia near Thermopylae, between Philip and the Roman consul, flanked by his allies: Pergamanians, Rhodians, Aetolians and even Achaeans, who had ultimately deserted the Macedonian. Their demands brought the negotiations to an abrupt close, together with parallel negotiations that had begun before the Senate in Rome at Flamininus' suggestion, as he wanted to play for time in the hope that his command would be extended in the form of a proconsulship, which he obtained. The decisive engagement took place a few months later, in June 197, in Thessaly. The two adversaries clashed on the southern slopes of a chain of hills, the Cynoscephalae (*Kynos Kephalai*, 'the dogs' heads'). On this uneven terrain the Roman legions gained the upper hand over the Macedonian phalanxes, who had been reputedly invincible since the time of Alexander. Philip abandoned the struggle.

At Tempe, where the peace talks were being held, Philip declared that he accepted the conditions he had previously rejected. In Rome, where the government was preoccupied with a rebellion of the Gauls in the Cisalpine region and a huge insurrection in Spain, they were just as eager as Flamininus to have done with the Macedonian war. Adopted by the Senate, the decree regulating the peace stipulated that Philip must restore all the towns where he maintained a garrison before the date of the Isthmian Games (Polybius, XVIII, 44, 4).

The latter, which were the most famous in Greece after the Olympic Games, took place in the magnificent setting of Corinth at the beginning of 196. Flamininus knew of the Greeks' concern, fanned by the words of the Aetolians who, furious that the proconsul had denied them the status of allies, went about saying that Greece was simply exchanging masters. He decided on a dramatic stroke, a dazzling manifesto, and it has recently been emphasized that, to make a solemn affirmation of the Greeks' freedom, Flamininus could not have chosen a better spot than Corinth, where since the early fifth century this theme had been linked with the history of the city as pan-Hellenic capital (Ferrary, 1988, pp. 86–8). Before the opening of the Isthmian competitions, a herald, preceded by a trumpet-call, delivered the following proclamation: 'The Senate of Rome and T. Quinctus, general-in-chief, having defeated king Philip, leave in freedom to follow their own laws, without tribute or garrison, the Corinthians, Rhodians, Locrians, Euboeans, Achaeans of Phtiotis, the Magnesians, Thessalians and Perrhaebians' (Polybius, XVIII, 46, 5; Livy, XXXIII, 32, 5). By listing them in this way, Rome guaranteed their liberty to the Greeks who already enjoyed it and granted it to Philip's former subjects. As a temporary measure, however, several strongholds – notably those that Philip himself cynically designated 'the fetters of Greece': Demetrias in Thessaly, Chalcis in Euboea and Acrocorinth – stayed occupied by Roman garrisons. These represented precautions against Antiochus, who had just crossed the Hellespont and passed into Europe.

## Antiochus' exploits and Hannibal's departure into exile

After avenging the humiliation of Raphia and regaining Syria Coele, Antiochus had waited two years before profiting from the Romano-Macedonian war to pursue his advantage in Asia Minor. From 198, Philip's difficulties left the field open for him. In 197 he launched a great expedition by both land and sea. In Lycia, on the south coast of present-day Turkey, he accepted the submission of the cities, such as Xanthos, that were dependent on Ptolemy, then, striking farther to the west and north, he undertook to re-establish his rule over the Greek towns bordering the Aegean, spurred on by the news of Philip's rout at Cynoscephalae. Astute enough to handle the Rhodians tactfully, leaving them control of former Ptolemaic possessions, like Halicarnassus and Samos, and to respect the sovereignty of Eumenes, Attalus' successor, over the principality of Pergamum and its hereditary fiefs, he easily seized the great Ptolemaic city of Ephesus, captured Abydos before the winter of 197 and from there crossed into the Thracian Chersonese in the spring of 196 (Figure 12).

Before crossing the straits, however, Antiochus had run into resistance from two cities that had formerly been allies of Attalus of Pergamum, Smyrna in Ionia and, farther north, Lampsacus in Aeolis. Doubtless advised by Eumenes, Attalus' successor, the two towns – Lampsacus, moreover, by virtue of belonging to the Troad, claiming a mythical and distant kinship with the town founded by Aeneas – turned to Rome and sent ambassadors to ask for its arbitration. After defending the Greeks of Greece properly speaking against Philip, the Romans were now being solicited by the Greeks of Asia. Antiochus in his turn made use of diplomacy, and from Lysimachia, on the Gallipoli peninsula, where he was residing at the time, he dispatched ambassadors to Corinth, in the period of the Isthmian Games, their mission being to congratulate and mollify the Romans, but they received a fairly chilly reception. In return, a Roman embassy, led by L. Cornelius Lentulus, consul for the year 199, who was appointed as mediator between Ptolemy and Antiochus, arrived at Lysimachia in the autumn of 196. He was accompanied by three commissioners whom we shall find resuming the negotiations in the spring of 193. The king was resolute; he denied the Romans the right to interfere in Asia's affairs. As for the Thracian Chersonese, he considered that by occupying it he was doing no more than retrieving possession of something that had belonged to the Seleucids for more than a century. He concluded by throwing a piece of completely unexpected news at the Senate's envoys. He announced that Ptolemaic Egypt, weary of war, was resigned to giving up its fiefs of Syria and Asia Minor and that the reconciliation would soon be sealed by the betrothal of the young Ptolemy V to his daughter Cleopatra. At that point a rumour, which soon proved to be false, of Ptolemy's death interrupted the talks and the king, leaving behind his second son Seleucus, went off to winter at Antioch. The following spring (195) he returned to Thrace with increased forces.

He was still in Thrace, during the summer of 195, when the event occurred that would place his own destiny for a few years on a course with Hannibal's.

As may be recalled (above, p. 181), the Carthaginian had made some firm enemies at Carthage in the year of his suffetate. Livy (XXXIII, 45, 6), who here follows Polybius, whose text is unfortunately missing for the years 196–192, correctly dates the events – unlike Nepos (*Hannibal*, 7) and later Appian

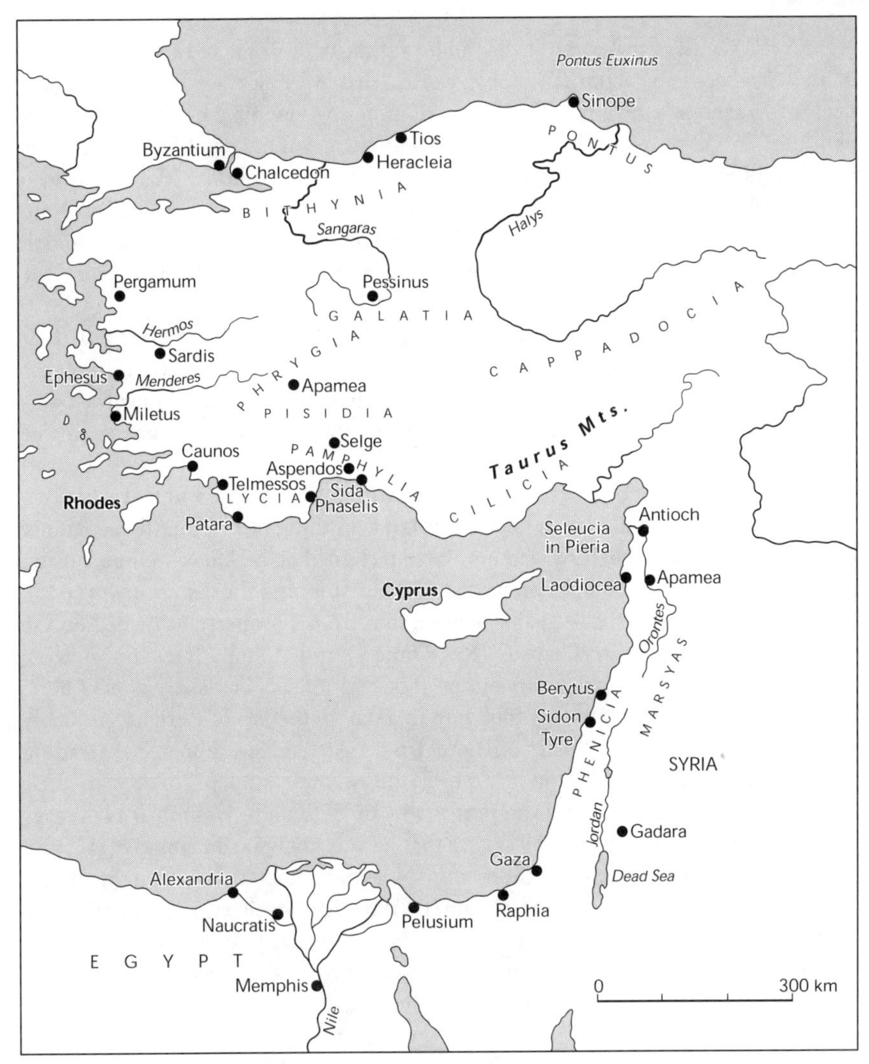


**Figure 12** Asia Minor (present-day Turkey), Syria-Phoenicia and Lower Egypt in the Hellenistic era (from Polybius, *Histoire*, 1970, p. 1498)

(*Syr.*, 4), who place them in 196 – and recounts that members of the faction hostile to Hannibal in the Council of Elders wrote letter upon letter to their correspondents in Rome denouncing the secret contacts which, according to them, Hannibal was having with Antiochus. There was a debate in the Senate, where Scipio – who had been censor in 199 and *princeps senatus* in 198 – brought his full weight to bear against those he saw lending a favourable ear to what he viewed as a baseless accusation. And as Livy remarks (XXXIII, 47, 4), apparently summarizing here a speech delivered by Africanus and reproduced at least in part in Polybius' missing text, 'it was unworthy of the Roman people to subscribe to the hatred of

Hannibal's accusers and commit the public authority of Rome to the machinations of the Carthaginian factions' – noble words, that were not heeded. The Senate decided to send an embassy with the task of indicting Hannibal before the Council of Elders in Carthage for having plotted war with Antiochus. The envoys were Cn. Servilius Caepio, consul for the year 203, and M. Claudius Marcellus, who had completed his consulship in the spring of 195, both from families hostile to the Scipios. Because of his intimate knowledge of Carthage, they were joined by Q. Terentius Culleo, the senator whom Africanus had liberated from the Carthaginian prisons in 202.

In order not to awaken Hannibal's suspicions, those who had arranged their visit suggested spreading the rumour that they were there to settle differences which had arisen between Carthage and Massinissa. But the one concerned was not deceived. For a long time he had foreseen the possibility of having to flee without warning. He was seen in public, as usual, all day; but at nightfall, instead of going home, he went to a gate of the town, without changing, and there met two servants who awaited him with horses but knew nothing of his intentions. Riding throughout the night, hell for leather, over terrain that he knew well and using relays arranged beforehand, he traversed without stopping the distance – over 150 kilometres as the crow flies – that separated him from a property he owned on the edge of the sea, between Thapsus (Ras Dimass) and Acholla (Henchir Botria); perhaps Ras Kaboudia, which juts out on this coast of the Tunisian Sahel. There, ready to cast off, was a ship that took him in a day to the isle of Cercina, probably the biggest of the Kerkennah, offshore from Sfax. A few Phoenician trading vessels had dropped anchor in the port, one of their stopping-places in their dealings between the East and the port towns of Byzacium. Hannibal was recognized, but answered questions by saying that he was going on an embassy to Tyre. Moreover, fearing that one of those ships, leaving under cover of night, might announce at Thapsus or Hadrumetum that he had been seen at Cercina, he thought up a typical stratagem. He had a sacrifice prepared, followed by a banquet to which crews and traders were invited; and to give all these people shelter from the full summer sun, he asked the captains for the loan of their sails, taking care to leave his own vessel fully equipped. And when everyone was happily drunk at a party that went on well into the night, he discreetly weighed anchor. By the time it was known in Carthage that he had left the town, then that he had been spotted at Cercina, he had already reached Tyre. Almost symbolically, Carthage's greatest son found his first refuge in that Phoenician mother-city from which Dido had come over six centuries before.

## Hannibal with Antiochus during the 'cold war' with Rome (195–192)

Hannibal received a warm welcome at Tyre, where he had made contacts whose usefulness we shall see later. From there he went to Antioch, where he thought he would meet the Seleucid king. He saw only the eldest son, with the same name, for Antiochus had left in the spring for Ephesus and Thrace, as we know. It was therefore at Ephesus that Hannibal met him on his return from the Hellespont, in the autumn of 195. By accusing him of making secret pacts with Antiochus, Hannibal's enemies in Carthage and, in Rome, the senators determined on his downfall, had pushed him into the king's arms. Would the latter welcome him with equally open arms?

Antiochus weighed his options. In the 'cold war' (the phrase used by E. Badian (1959)) which set him against Rome and would last until late 192 before becoming open warfare, Hannibal's presence at his side could be a trump card. There was no one in that period who could match his experience in war, the breadth of his strategic vision or his tactical capabilities in all the configurations of land engagements. But in this instance, there was another side to the coin. Since he was the object of such fear for the Romans, the Punic general might equally dissuade them from entering a war with the Seleucid king or incite them to do battle in order to rid themselves of this threat once and for all. Moreover, the guest might prove to be rather a nuisance. How could the greatest general of the era be confined to the office of a military adviser, even of the highest rank, when he had been accustomed for over twenty years to being commander-in-chief, accountable to no one? These doubts that must have filled Antiochus' mind when he greeted Hannibal would be clearly set out by his ally, the *strategos* (commander) of the Aetolians, Thoas, in 192 (Livy, XXXV, 42). And as we shall see, in the engagement that was to begin against Rome, they would lead to the Carthaginian's being deprived of the share he had hoped for in the initiative.

For the time being Hannibal had to champ at the bit. For him 194 was an empty year, as it was for his great adversary Scipio Africanus, who held a rather lacklustre second consulship. Two triumphs were celebrated in Rome during that year, both setting two of his political rivals on a pedestal. The first, in spring, belonged to Cato, for his feats of arms in Spain. He had brought back substantial booty, but chiefly boasted that he had distributed a large part of it to his soldiers in the field, saying that it was better for many Romans to come home with pockets full of silver than for a small number to return with gold. And the image of the upright politician began to take hold with the expression he used in his speech to the Senate on this occasion, when he prided himself on having kept for his own use only 'what he had eaten and drunk' (Kienast, 1973, p. 163, fr. 171). The second, in the autumn, sumptuous in a different way, had been that of Flamininus, and was exceptional for the number and quality of the works of art to be seen in the procession – taken from Philip, states Livy precisely (XXXIV, 52, 4), rather than seized from the Greek cities. As for Antiochus, he had profited from this armed peace to strengthen his presence in Thrace. While restoring Lysimachia (he said that he wanted to make it the princely residence of his second son Seleucus), he had at the same time gained land to the west by annexing Ainos and Maroneia. At the other extremity of his empire, he had consolidated the peace concluded with Egypt in 195 by marrying his daughter Cleopatra, following the conventional betrothal of those times, to Ptolemy V Epiphanes. The wedding had taken place in late autumn 194 at Raphia, in Palestine, on the frontier between the two empires. Was Antiochus counting on his daughter to bring Egypt under Seleucid influence? She was at least the first in a long line of Cleopatras, the last of whom, as we know, was the most famous.

The obstinate resistance of Lampsacus and Smyrna, however, was a thorn in Antiochus' flesh. Remember that they had appealed to Rome, with the support of Eumenes of Pergamum, who rejected the Seleucid's advances and had even refused the offer of marriage to one of Antiochus' daughters. In the winter of 194–193 he dispatched two plenipotentiaries to Rome to propose to the Senate on his behalf a treaty of friendship involving – an essential for him – recognition of his full and entire sovereignty over both Asia Minor and Thrace. The Senate delegated negotiations to Flamininus. Fresh from his triumph, he gloried in his prestige as champion of liberty for the Greeks. However, while protesting the Roman people's vocation to defend Hellenism wherever it might be, therefore in Asia as well as in Greece proper, it did not prevent him from making a rather cynical proposition to the king's ambassadors. As a prior condition to the treaty sought by the king, he must keep out of Europe if he wanted Rome not to interfere in the fate of the Greek cities in Asia (Livy, XXXIV, 58, 2). Antiochus set great store by Thrace, an inheritance from his great-grandfather Seleucus I. His ambassadors replied that they must refer the matter to their sovereign and asked the Senate not to rush matters.

The door had thus been left open for negotiations, which resumed the following spring in Asia Minor. A high-ranking delegation was sent by sea, led by P. Sulpicius Galba, 'repeat consul' for the year 200, who took with him P. Villius Tappulus, the consul for 199, and P. Aelius Paetus, who had held the consulship in 201 and censorship in 199. The three ambassadors were well acquainted with the background, as they had already taken part in the Lysimachia talks with Lentulus in the autumn of 196. The Senate had given them instructions to go first to confer with Eumenes. They therefore disembarked at Elaea, then went up to Pergamum, where Eumenes, who had everything to lose by a strengthening of Seleucid dominance in Asia, exhorted them to show intransigence in their dealings with the king. Thereupon, as Sulpicius Galba had fallen ill, Villius Tappulus, accompanied by Paetus, although our sources here omit his name, went to Ephesus only to find that Antiochus was occupied in waging war against the rebels in Pisidia. So the Roman delegation moved on to Apamea in Pisidia, where the Seleucid king joined them for meetings which had no more success than the negotiations carried on in Rome the preceding winter. There was another contretemps in the form of the death of the king's eldest son and co-regent, Antiochus, whom his father had sent to Syria to guard the southern marches of his kingdom while he himself was busy in Pisidia. In respect for the Seleucid court's mourning, the Romans withdrew for a time to Pergamum. In the autumn of 193, talks at last resumed at Ephesus, and Sulpicius Galba, who had recovered, took part in them, together with the other two legates. But the discussions were all the less likely to have a successful outcome because the introduction into the meetings of delegates from the autonomous Greek cities, duly admonished by Eumenes, caused them to degenerate into a violent altercation (Livy, XXXV, 17, 2: *ex disceptatione altercationem fecerunt*). It was more than Antiochus could endure. After the departure of the Romans, war became the order of the day for his councils.

Though involuntarily, Hannibal had played a role in the Ephesus discussions. It may be recalled that Villius had stayed a few days there before going with Paetus to meet the king at Apamea in Pisidia. Hannibal was also there and, says Livy (XXXV, 14, 2–3), the Roman had a number of meetings with the exile to try to get to know what he had in mind and reassure him about Rome's intentions towards him. In fact, and Polybius (III, 11, 2) recognizes it more clearly than Livy, the former consul deliberately courted Hannibal in order to compromise him in Antiochus' eyes and undermine the already fragile trust evinced by the king; as we shall see, that was indeed what happened. And here the Latin historian, who would later be followed by Appian (*Syr.*, 9–10) and Plutarch (*Flam.*, 21), while taking care to quote his source (Claudius Quadrigarius), could not resist the temptation to let legend break into history and, so to speak, suspend time for a while so that Hannibal and Scipio could have a tête-à-tête at Ephesus. Appian, who lacked the Paduan's critical sense, and feared nothing, goes as far as to show them conversing in the town's gymnasia, the Carthaginian even inviting Scipio to his table at the end of the day. In this conversation Africanus is supposed to have asked Hannibal who, in his opinion, was the greatest general of all time, to which he replied, unsurprisingly, 'Alexander'. Then, when asked who came next, Hannibal said 'Pyrrhus', both for his knowledge of siegecraft and his mastery of the difficult art of diplomacy. As for the third greatest, he answered straight away that it was himself. Scipio laughed and asked him what he would have said if he had defeated him, to which Hannibal replied that in that case he would have placed himself ahead of Alexander, Pyrrhus and all the rest. Scipio was left wondering, both disturbed and enchanted by the flattery wrapped up in Punic wiliness, which in this joust between generals placed him out of the contest.

We are indebted to Maurice Holleaux for having demonstrated, in an earlier dissertation whose elegance equals its precision, that although Scipio may well have journeyed in late 193 in the Aegean, where signs of his presence have been discovered at Delos, he could not have taken part in that delegation and been in Ephesus during the summer (Holleaux, 1957, pp. 184–207). The simple reason is that in the same period he was in Carthage, on a senatorial mission that also included two of his political friends, C. Cornelius Cethegus, who had been made censor the year before, and M. Minucius Rufus. And this mission was itself the indirect outcome of a venture undertaken by Hannibal in his home country, through an intermediary, which at the cost of retracing my steps I must now relate.

If we are to believe Livy (XXXIV, 61, 6), during 193, probably before the Ephesus discussions, the Punic leader had for a time succeeded in persuading

Antiochus to support the principle of a large-scale strategic plan. For Hannibal this would entail setting out for Africa with a hundred or so decked warships carrying 10,000 infantry and 1,000 cavalry, and pushing Carthage, when it saw these forces which would be joined by others on the spot, to resume the war against Rome. Should he fail to persuade his compatriots, Hannibal could at least go on to Italy with the armada obtained from Antiochus and there stir up rebellions, while the king, attacking the Romans from the rear, could go into Greece. Such is the grandiose and, when all is said and done, unrealistic plan ascribed to Hannibal by Livy (XXXIV, 60, 3–6), Justin (XXXI, 3, 7–10) and Appian (*Syr.*, 7), as if the passionate but clear-sighted Carthaginian could for one moment have believed in the success of such a venturesome undertaking, or the Seleucid king, who moreover did not dream of waging a war of extermination against Rome, would have given his consent to a plan that would virtually mobilize his entire war fleet. On the other hand, both men could have considered the viability of sending a lighter expeditionary corps to Africa that would, by means of suitable political preparation, be capable of creating in Carthage the conditions for an uprising against subjection to Rome. Faced with the new eastern ambitions of the Senate, Antiochus too could see the advantage of what, if it succeeded, could turn out to be not only a temporary diversion but also an element in the restoration of a balance in the Mediterranean that had been upset for nearly a decade to the sole benefit of Rome.

To prepare the ground in Carthage, Hannibal had the idea of sending a Tyrian merchant, named Ariston, whose *savoir-faire* he had already been able to assess from earlier missions. With Antiochus' agreement, Ariston, furnished with secret recognition signs, was to make contact with the Barcid's supporters in the Punic metropolis. Were those he spoke to indiscreet or imprudent? The Tyrian and his mission were soon the subject of every conversation, to the point where he was swiftly brought before the Council of Elders to explain the reasons for his presence in Carthage. Ariston had been very careful not to give any kind of written document to anyone at all, but it was argued that, very surprisingly for a businessman, he had contacted only members of the Barcid faction in the town. He was about to be thrown into prison, when some expressed the opinion that it was hardly good commercial policy to arrest a foreign trader, Phoenician to boot, without any serious reason. There might well be reciprocal harsh treatment. The Council retired without taking action. As for the Tyrian, he decided to leave the following night, but before taking to the seas again he played the Carthaginians at their own game (Livy, XXXIV, 61, 14: *Punico ingenio inter Poenos usus*). At nightfall, he put up a poster on the suffetes' court for all to read the next morning, saying that the instructions received by Ariston were in fact addressed to all the Elders, without exception. By compromising everybody, the Tyrian quashed charges against Hannibal's partisans. In Carthage's senate it was nevertheless decided to send an embassy to Rome to report the matter and, adds Livy (XXXIV, 61, 16), who is content to link the two mandates given to the ambassadors in simple coordination, at the same time to complain of Massinissa's recent encroachments. It may be recalled that two years earlier arguments between the Numidian king and the Carthaginians had already been the pretext justifying the Roman deputation, whose real purpose had been to lay hands on Hannibal (above, p. 192). But this time, with the argument concerning the region of the *Emporia*, especially Leptis Magna, at the border of the two Syrtes, there began the real series of Numidian encroachments that would be a true *via crucis* for Carthage.

Massinissa counter-attacked by sending an embassy to the Senate in his turn. To hear him, by virtue of the rights of the original occupants – the indigenous Libyans – Carthage legitimately held only the area of ground covered at Byrsa, when the town was founded, by the famous ox-hide! (See Lancel 1995a, pp. 24–5.) More seriously, the Carthaginians defended their frontiers by a legal argument; they pointed out that the disputed territory was included within the boundaries allocated to them by Scipio when he set the limits in 201. In the period now under consideration, some dozen years later, the Senate was still endeavouring to strike an equal balance between the Numidians and Carthage. Sent to the spot with two colleagues on an arbitration mission, Africanus returned without having settled anything. As has been suggested (Desanges, 1995), Rome probably feared a possible agreement between Carthage and Antiochus. As long as it had no elbow-room in its eastern engagement, which was still full of pitfalls, the Senate would handle Carthage carefully. Hannibal's presence with Antiochus had enabled it, diminished though it was, to remain an international power in spite of everything.

## The torment of Antiochus' failure (192–189)

The Carthaginian's position at the Seleucid king's court had emerged weakened from the meetings at Ephesus. Villius' courtesy towards him had produced its effect. After the failure of the talks, he had been excluded from a council where the king's advisers, led by the Acarnanian Alexander, previously one of Philip of Macedon's counsellors, urged him to enter a war in which the Punic leader would have no other role than to lure the Romans to Africa to create a diversion (Livy, XXXV, 18, 8). At this point Hannibal, appalled that he could be suspected of the slightest accommodating attitude in regard to Rome, when his entire life demonstrated the exact opposite, had the meeting with Antiochus during which he recounted the story of the 'oath' that, while still a child, he had sworn to his father Hamilcar never to be a friend to the Romans (above, p. 30). The king's trust was restored, so it seems, but history was not to provide any striking confirmation.

It is no easy matter to assess Antiochus' frame of mind when faced with the eventuality of war with Rome which loomed on the horizon. Some critics have seen him as 'an indecisive monarch facing a grave decision to be taken, overwhelmed by the death of his son, dominated by his advisers' (Pédech, 1964, p. 232). Concerned first and foremost with maintaining in their entirety the possessions he had inherited from his forefathers, having just retrieved them, the Seleucid was anything but an adventurer. But neither was he at the mercy of events. What he wanted was for Rome to leave him free to do as he wished on the Hellespont side. To put pressure on the Senate and Flamininus, who had been sent on a tour in Greece with three other legates during the winter of 193–192, Antiochus could rely on the Aetolians. At the time of the spring assembly of the Aetolian Confederation, early in 192, Thoas called a vote on a decree by the terms of which – certainly submitted in advance to the king – the Seleucid was invited to deliver Greece and settle the difference between them and the Romans. Antiochus was obviously paying the Romans in their own coin: 'borrowing their tactics, he now practised, like them and against them, a Hellenic policy. To put pressure on him, they upheld the cause of the Hellenes of Asia; to put pressure on them, he championed that of the Hellenes of Europe, and especially the Aetolians' (Holleaux, 1957, p. 394). All the same, he had to take other facts into consideration. During the summer of 192, Nabis, tyrant of Sparta, was wiped out by the armies of the Achaean Confederation, led by Philopoemen, which mustered the Greeks of the Peloponnese who were overtly pro-Roman. Moreover, far from coming to his assistance, Philip of Macedon remained loyal to the Roman alliance to which his defeat at Cynoscephalae had condemned him. Antiochus might well fear then that the balance of forces could alter to his detriment and that he could soon find himself in a worse position in regard to Rome (Will, 1967, p. 171). At that point, the Thessalian stronghold, Demetrias, which had been held by the Romans since 196, defected and fell into the Aetolians' hands. Was that the trigger? In autumn 192, Antiochus resolved to send a modest expeditionary force into Thessaly: 10,000 footsoldiers, 500 horsemen and a few elephants.

Thus without yet being declared, war was engaged *de facto*, but it was not Hannibal's concern. At the council that had preceded the decision, the Carthaginian had even found himself denied command of the small squadron which it had at first been planned to give him to lead a diversionary action in Africa. He owed this snub to Thoas, whom Antiochus preferred to listen to, all the more so because the Aetolian assured him of the only thing he wanted to hear: that his arrival in Greece would be enough to cause a mass rising of the Greeks, ready to join the Aetolians. This showed a poor knowledge of the Greeks, who were divided and, in many instances, had been forced willy-nilly into friendship with Rome since the Isthmian Games of 196; and it was to overlook the true weight of the Achaean Confederation. Above all, Hannibal, who had learnt to understand what motivated Rome, must have thought it showed scant knowledge of the Romans to imagine that, freed from their worries in Spain and less preoccupied in Cisalpine Gaul, they would not react to an affront in Greece under the gaze of Philip of Macedon, a neutral but interested spectator.

Hannibal followed the activities with a critical eye. If the strategy adopted appeared absurd to him, he could have nothing but mistrust for the Seleucid army's principal tactical weapon, the Macedonian phalanx bristling with its spears – the famous 'sarissa', six metres long – like a hedgehog with its spines. It certainly formed a barrier that was difficult to broach, but was static and not very manoeuvrable. It was a war weapon that belonged to the past, since in fifteen years of battles waged in Italy, Spain and Africa, first he and then the Romans, imitating and equalling the master, had put into operation tactics that made use of mobility, enveloping, encircling or dynamically breaking up the enemy forces. An anecdote recorded by Aulus Gellius (*Attic Nights*, V, 5), who was always fond of 'antiquities' – but who unfortunately does not give his source – is a good illustration of the Carthaginan's doubts and how he stood aloof from the king's court. One day Antiochus had complacently shown him his army on exercises, deployed on a field for manoeuvres, all the cavalry's gold and silver trappings gleaming in the sunlight, as were the ornaments on the chariots with their fitted scythes. There were the dromedaries and the Asian elephants, enormous caparisoned beasts each surmounted by a howdah carrying archers, unlike those used by the Punic armies. And when the Seleucid asked him if all that should be enough when confronting the Romans, Hannibal is supposed to have replied, with irreverent irony, that it should certainly provide enough war booty, however greedy they were! One must, of course, allow for the frustration of a man who was seeing all the controls slip out of his grasp. But for all its pomp, this army nevertheless meant business (Bar-Kochva, 1976, pp. 94–103).

The first successes achieved by Antiochus – notably the capture of the fortified town of Chalcis in the autumn of 192 and seizure of the island of Euboea – had not altered the Carthaginian's negative opinion of the strategy being employed. At an important war council held at Demetrias during the winter of 192–191, Hannibal, who until then had been kept out of things, made an intervention, of which Livy (XXXVI, 7) has preserved an echo, and in the absence of Polybius we have no choice but to follow him. The Carthaginian reduced to their real importance, which was minimal, the advantages obtained by the king up to that point. When all was said and done, apart from the Aetolians, he had attracted to his camp only peoples who lacked their own military power – Euboeans and Boeotians – and whom he could foresee turning to Rome as soon as they saw its armies begin to bite. His own plan for the conduct of operations had not changed; he was merely adapting it to the current situation. For the moment, the most important matter was to gain mastery of the seas. He advised Antiochus to strengthen his numbers considerably, as they were far too light even for a modest expeditionary force; also to complement his naval forces as quickly as possible, and station part of them at Corcyra, to block off the Romans' passage from the Adriatic. At the same time, a squadron would skirt the south of Italy and Sicily to launch an attack on Rome from the western side. Lastly, Antiochus would concentrate all his land forces on the right bank of the Aous, in its lower course, to close the principal access to Greece for the Romans, in the north-west, from the Illyrian coastline (Cabanes, 1976, p. 281). It may be recalled that at the end of 199 it was there, or slightly upstream, that Philip of Macedon had intended to bar the way to Vilius Tappulus, then Flamininus. To be put into effect, such a broad-ranging plan involved the mobilization of considerable resources, notably naval, and a necessarily long period of preparation. Now, at the point he had reached, Antiochus had neither the one nor the other at his disposal. That is why one may question whether Hannibal actually advanced these War School proposals, which were brilliant but about as unrealistic as the famous plan of 193 (above, p. 196). For Livy, as for the underlying Roman annalistic tradition, it was important to make it appear, if necessary against all probability, that the Carthaginian was still public enemy number one.

Again according to Livy, in addition Hannibal insistently advocated alliance with Philip, who he said must be led, by diplomacy and, if necessary by force – brandishing the threat of intervention by Seleucus, the king's son, on his eastern frontiers from Thrace – to co-operate against Rome. This could be no more than a pious hope, since Hannibal and Antiochus could not fail to be aware that Philip had already ceased playing his waiting game. In November 192 the praetor M. Baebius Tamphilus had gone to Illyria with a few troops, chiefly to keep an eye on the Macedonian. He was quickly reassured; Philip warned him of Antiochus' entry into Thessaly and promised him his assistance. And if he acted thus it was not merely, as Livy affirms (XXXVI, 8), because he was vexed to see Antiochus, instead of himself, giving honourable burial to the Macedonian soldiers who had fallen at Cynoscephalae four years earlier. Philip had everything to gain and nothing to lose from remaining loyal to the Roman alliance.

To bring Rome into war, a *casus belli* was still wanting. Through imprudence or deliberately, it was one of Antiochus' lieutenants, Menippus, who provided it at the end of autumn 192, when he massacred 300 Romans garrisoned at Delium, a small town in Boeotia near Tanagra. They certainly should not have been there, as in theory Flamininus had repatriated all his men at the end of 196, but the damage was done. Voted in the comitia by the people, ratified by the Senate, war against Antiochus was actively made ready by one of the two consuls elected for 191 who had received Greece as his province. M' Acilius Glabrio was a 'new man', a friend of Scipio and under his protection since 201 when, at the time a tribune of the plebs, and with the backing of another tribune, Q. Minucius Thermus (Scullard, 1951, p. 81), he had helped Africanus to get the better of the machinations of Cornelius Lentulus, who was aiming to deprive him of the benefits of his victory at Zama (above, p. 179). Like his patron and like Flamininus himself, Glabrio was a philhellene, a trend increasingly mistrusted by the Senate. So, to keep an eye on the consul, two 'watchdogs', M. Porcius Cato and L. Valerius Flaccus – who had been joint consuls in 195 and would be co-censors in 184 – enrolled in the army as military tribunes (Grimal, 1975, p. 192).

Rome had set a real steamroller in motion. At the end of February 191, Acilius Glabrio landed at Apollonia with 20,000 footsoldiers and 2,000 horsemen who immediately set off for Thessaly, where Baebius Tamphilus and Philip of Macedon were already in action against Antiochus' Aetolian allies. Within a few weeks Thessaly was occupied. From Chalcis in Euboea the Seleucid king went to meet the Romans in the direction of Lamia, and decided to contain them in the gorge of Thermopylae, ever the gateway to central Greece, and renowned since the sacrifice of Leonidas in 480. It was there that Acilius Glabrio came to encounter him in mid-April. Deployed on the high ground, the king's archers and spear-throwers harassed Acilius' troops on their right flank, and they could not manage to get at the phalanx, which was solidly entrenched in the gorge, when Cato, who had made a night march across the mountains with 2,000 men, fell on the Seleucid's rearguard troops. A disorderly retreat followed. Antiochus was back in Chalcis at the end of April, and at Ephesus a little later, having crossed the sea with what was left of his army. He had lost the match in Greece in a single battle in which Hannibal had not even taken part. But the latter was soon to be seen taking over the role of admiral.

## The War in the Aegean and Asia: Hannibal in Command at Sea

Antiochus relied on his Aetolian allies to hold the Romans in Greece, at least for a while. In fact they proved quite a headache for Acilius Glabrio, who easily subjugated the Boeotians, Phocidians and Chalcidians, but vainly spent the summer outside the walls of Naupactus while Philip of Macedon took advantage of the situation to regain positions in Thessaly, particularly at Demetrias. This greatly displeased Flamininus who, seeing his great diplomatic *oeuvre* of summer 196 unravelling, and being at the time the Senate's delegate with the Achaeans in the Peloponnese, interceded with Acilius to obtain an honourable peace with Rome for the Aetolians (Livy, XXXVI, 34–5).

The end of the war in Greece left the Romans with their hands free to pursue Antiochus in Asia. The king had fortified the Thracian Chersonese, notably the stronghold of Lysimachia, and ordered the commander of his navy, Polyxenidas, a Rhodian exile, to put it on a general state of alert. Hannibal had learnt from his informers, and warned the king, that at the end of the spring a strong Roman squadron had set off from Ostia in fifty decked vessels – troop transport ships with greater capacity than open vessels – which had been joined *en route* by six ships supplied by Carthage and twenty-five other ships provided by the Italian allies. At Piraeus, the twenty-five quinqueremes of Atilius Serranus, the outgoing praetor, further reinforced this fleet, which was placed under the command of C. Livius Salinator, son of one of the two victors on the Metaurus. In opposition, the fleet commanded by Polyxenidas was no less impressive: seventy decked ships and at least an equal number of open vessels. It was in the interest of the Seleucid king's admiral to intercept the Roman fleet and, if possible, defeat it before it could join up with the friendly naval forces of Eumenes of Pergamum and the Rhodians. But, at first anchored at Delos, the Roman ships picked up speed; having reached Phocaea, they acquired the reinforcement of some fifty units of Eumenes' squadron. Now inferior in number, Polyxenidas' fleet had to engage in combat before the arrival of the Rhodians. The fight took place near Cape Korykos, a not easily identifiable promontory on the present-day Turkish coast bordering the arm of sea that separates it from the island of Chios. We may read in Livy (XXXVI, 44–5) the detailed but slightly awkward account – the historian was more at ease when relating land actions – of this naval battle, where the balance was tilted in the Romans' favour chiefly by the superiority of their marine forces in their attacks on the ships.

The end of 191 had come, and with it the time of consular elections in Rome, held early that year. As Livy baldly says (XXXVI, 45, 9), all eyes were on Africanus to end the war against Antiochus. But Scipio had already held a second consulship in 194, and those terrible years between 215 and 207 were over, when under the pressure of events men like Fabius Maximus, Fulvius Flaccus or Claudius Marcellus had been able to hold the supreme office up to four and five times, sometimes without a break. To get over the difficulty, the comitia elected C. Laelius, Africanus' friend and debtor, and his brother Lucius. It remained to be seen who would have the 'province' of Greece, in other words Asia. According to Livy (XXXVII, 1, 7–10), at Laelius' suggestion the choice was referred to the Senate rather than left to the luck of the draw. And Publius put an end to the debate that was starting by declaring that if Greece should be allocated to Lucius, he would go with him as legate. We are indebted to Cicero for another version (*Philippics*, XI, 17) which is more offensive to Lucius: Greece – and therefore Asia – having fallen by lot to him, the Senate annulled the allocation in favour of Laelius; but Africanus protested and announced his intention of serving at his brother's side, and the Senate acquiesced in this solution. Livy's version is probably to be preferred, but in both instances it was the personal weight of Africanus, restoring the balance against the defects in Lucius' image, that carried the decision. Twenty-five years after the fraternal collaboration of the two Scipios in Spain, between 217 and 211, the succeeding generation witnessed the engagement in the same fight of two other brothers from the most celebrated family of the era. And it was possible that Hannibal might once again come face to face with his great adversary of 202, similarly playing second fiddle!

But if the event was to take place, it could not do so at once. In fact, it did not happen. For the time being, in the early months of 190, it was still a matter of who would achieve naval mastery in the Aegean. Antiochus knew that it was useless to fortify the Chersonese if the fleet did not hold the Hellespont. He had to increase his forces at sea, and first by making good his losses. It was then that Hannibal received the mission of going to the ports of Syria-Phoenicia, and probably especially to Tyre, to muster and arm a reinforcement squadron. A little later, the commander of the Seleucid fleet, Polyxenidas, scored a lucky hit against the Rhodian fleet, wiping out a good part of it in the channels of Samos. In April, when the new Roman admiral, the praetor M. Aemilius Regillus, arrived to relieve Livius Salinator, the situation on the Asian coasts of the Aegean was far from favourable to the coalition members. In late spring at Samos, where he had concentrated his forces, Regillus came within inches of responding favourably to the overtures of Antiochus who, worried by the news of the Scipios' arrival in Macedonia, was asking to negotiate. The Rhodians were not against holding talks, but Eumenes of Pergamum was opposed.

Meanwhile it had been learnt at Samos that Hannibal was coming northward with the fleet which had been assembled in Phoenicia. It was the Rhodians, with thirty-six vessels, who went to meet him. The two fleets made contact in the height of summer – Livy, XXXVII, 23, 2: probably in August – off the coast of Pamphylia, more precisely, not far from the peninsula of Side (Figure 12). The fleet armed by Hannibal was clearly superior in number; the Carthaginian commanded its left wing, on the side of the open sea, the right one being under the orders of a Seleucid dignitary, Apollonios. Thanks to his numerical superiority, Hannibal had the first advantage against the opposing admiral, Eudamos. But soon the Rhodians' experience at sea, which was unequalled in the Mediterranean at that time, their skill at manoeuvring, the quality and agility of their quadriremes, allowed them to regain the upper hand. At the end of the day, Hannibal, whose losses were heavier, retreated to Coracaesium (present-day Alanya), a little east of Side. He was then nearly sixty, and one can imagine what a physical ordeal this naval battle must have been for him, in the unhealthy humidity of the Pamphylian coast in the height of summer. Apparently he stayed where he was, blockaded by the Rhodian fleet, the larger part of which patrolled along the east coasts of Lycia to keep him under surveillance.

Hannibal was out of the game, but so were the majority of the Rhodians, while Eumenes was stationed farther north to defend his kingdom and prepare passage for the Scipios. Antiochus thought it a good opportunity to take his revenge for Korykos. The decisive engagement between the Selucid fleet and the Roman one, reinforced by a small Rhodian squadron, took place not far from the site of the first battle, in the vicinity of Myonnesos. Polyxenidas had left the port of Ephesus with a fleet slightly outnumbering that of Regillus. But once again, the handling qualities of the Rhodian ships and the skills of their helmsmen, under the command of Eudamos, tipped the victory to their side. Livy (XXXVII, 30, 3–4) notes the destructive use of fire-ships, in which the Rhodian vessels carried containers filled with a mixture of flaming pitch and sulphur at their prow, on the end of long poles that could be lowered by a system of cables to set fire to the enemy ship. The Seleucid fleet returned to port after losing forty-two ships, no longer in any position to control the Aegean.

Antiochus had evacuated the stronghold of Lysimachia, which was difficult to defend without any naval backing. When the Scipios and their army reached it in the autumn of 190, they halted there and reprovisioned before crossing the Hellespont, while Regillus recaptured Phocaea. From Sardis, in Lydia, where he had withdrawn after the defeat of his fleet, Antiochus sent a plenipotentiary, Heraclides of Byzantium, to the Roman consul. The king declared himself prepared to pay the Romans an indemnity of half their war costs and, as well as his possessions in Europe, to give up the three towns whose resistance had been at the origin of the conflict, Lampsacus, Smyrna and Alexandria Troas. On his brother's advice, Lucius replied that the king must settle the entire expenses of a war which he had provoked, and withdraw from all land situated on this side of the Taurus mountains; in other words, abandon the whole of Asia Minor (Polybius, XXI, 14, 7–8; Livy, XXXVII, 35, 8–10). The king's envoy knew that such demands were not acceptable to his master, but he had secret instructions which he was to reveal to

Publius alone; the king would, without ransom, restore Africanus' son, who had fallen into his hands at the start of the conflict – under circumstances that have remained obscure (Livy, XXXVII, 34, 5–6). In addition, if Publius helped him to obtain peace on the conditions he was proposing, the king offered him a sum of money to be set by himself, and also a share in the revenues from his states (Polybius (XXI, 15, 3–4) and Livy (XXXVII, 36, 2) even speak of Scipio's participation in the running of the Seleucid empire). In this offer, which was of course rejected, one recognizes the impossibility of contact between two mental attitudes that were radically opposed because of their respective pasts. Africanus did not put on an air of offended virtue; he replied soberly that he would gratefully accept the return of his son and in exchange for this courteous behaviour he advised Antiochus to agree to the conditions put to him by the Romans if he wanted to avoid war.

Several weeks later, probably in January 189, the two armies met not far from Magnesia on the Sipylus, at the confluence of the Phrygius and the Hermus. There is an impressive description in Livy (XXXVII, 40; the corresponding text in Polybius is missing) of the royal forces, which were numerous and powerful, but whose disparate nature and lack of cohesion are revealed by their sheer variety. In the absence of Publius, whom illness had kept at Elaea, and because of the scant confidence accorded to Lucius in military matters, effective command of the legions had been entrusted to the consul for 192, Cn. Domitius Ahenobarbus, while Eumenes of Pergamum commanded the right wing, where his own contingents of infantry and cavalry were concentrated. They were both the architects of a victory which cost Antiochus 50,000 men. Not long afterwards the king drew his own conclusions, sending to the Scipios at Sardis plenipotentiaries who obtained peace on the terms already fixed, which would be ratified in 188 by the treaty of Apamea. Antiochus was obliged to pay an enormous sum as war indemnity, 15,000 Euboic talents, as compared with the 10,000 talents imposed on Carthage twelve years before (above, p. 177). Furthermore, the king had to hand over to the Romans those men they considered to be their most implacable enemies, the Aetolian Thoas and, above all, Hannibal. When he had resumed the fight against Rome, the exile had become a 'rebel' in the Latin sense of the word, and Publius could no longer do anything for him. Returning to Italy in the autumn of 189, Lucius Cornelius Scipio was given a triumph, which he celebrated in Rome in November, in a more spectacular fashion, says Livy (XXXVII, 59, 2), than had his brother in 201. But the nickname Asiaticus that he bore from then on did not have the same brilliance as Africanus.

## Between history and legend: Hannibal's last years

Antiochus had not handed over Hannibal. Would he have done so even if he could? Our sources are silent on the part played by the exile in the fighting at

Magnesia on the Sipylus, where his presence could hardly have gone unnoticed, unless it is rather absurdly supposed that he was as passive and discreet as Fabrice del Dongo on the battlefield at Waterloo.

From the heat haze of the gulf of Antalya where he had dug himself in during the height of summer 190 after the naval battle of Side, Hannibal emerged for a series of wanderings that would end in Bithynia a few short years later, but the route and chronology are equally uncertain. Reading Cornelius Nepos (*Hann.*, 9) and Justin (XXXII, 4, 3), who are unfortunately not the most reliable guides – but there are no others – it would seem that from the coast of Pamphylia Hannibal headed for Crete. The nearest large island, Cyprus, had remained a Ptolemaic possession, thus allied to Rome, and therefore forbidden to the exile. As for Phoenicia, which was in theory an asylum for the Carthaginian but was Seleucid territory, could it still take him in when its master was compelled by treaty to extradite the fugitive? At first Crete, which had remained aloof from all the fighting, offered him a temporary refuge, while waiting for something better (and this is what Nepos says, *Hann.*, 9, 1). Was it Hannibal's intention to use it as a springboard for a return to Africa and resumption of the struggle? Can it be affirmed that from there he went to Cyrene (Picard, 1967, p. 227)? That is perhaps to base too much on an obvious error by Nepos (*Hann.*, 8, 1–2) who, speaking of 193, confused the mission entrusted to Ariston (above, p. 196) with a pseudo-incursion by Hannibal himself into Cyrenaica at the head of a small fleet; and it is not enough to modify the date given by Nepos to restore some veracity to this account. In any case, it is hardly likely that the Carthaginian was able to stay long at Gortyna, where he had landed. Crete at that time was a den of pirates, and many Roman and Italian prisoners were stagnating there. During the summer of 189, the praetor Q. Fabius Labeo, taking over from Regillus at the head of the Roman fleet, had left Ephesus for Crete and, once on the island, dispatched detachments all over the place to free captives, in particular at Gortyna, where 4,000 of them regained their liberty, says Livy (XXXVII, 60, 6), though not breathing a word about Hannibal's presence. Could he have escaped this police operation if he was still in the area, or had just arrived there? The chronology of his stay remains vague, and all we know of it, still through Nepos and Justin, is the exile's wily riposte to the cupidity of the Cretans, which was proverbial (Polybius, VI, 46–7). He had arrived among them with his entire fortune, in gold and silver coin, and to keep it safe he had the idea of hiding the greater part of it inside a few bronze statues, casually left in full view in his garden; and placed in their temple to Artemis, to be guarded by the Cretans, he left some terracotta jars filled with lead but covered with a thin layer of gold and silver. This story must of course be taken for what it is worth. In these obscure years when Hannibal was on the fringes of history, 'hagiographers' who are not always well inspired take over from historians.

What is true is that Antiochus' discomfiture and his retreat from Asia Minor to the greater profit of Eumenes of Pergamum – the 'oriental Massinissa' (Holleaux, 1957, p. 425) – pushed Hannibal to the periphery of the Hellenistic East. Between the Black and Caspian seas, Armenia, which only under Trajan would be part of the last series of provinces acquired for the Empire, was among the places he visited. Our sources (Strabo, XI, 14, 6; Plutarch, *Lucullus*, 31, 4–5) both mention the presence of the exile at the court of 'king' Artaxias, and this may have been the second stage in his wanderings after Crete. Attracted by the site of the upper valley of the Araxes where, dominated by the mass of Ararat, it still marks the boundary between Turkey and Armenia, he is said to have outlined plans for a new capital and shown them to Artaxias, who asked him personally to oversee the building of the town that took the name Artaxata. Modern historians are divided over how much credence should be given to this story. It has been pointed out, notably by G. Brizzi (1984a, p. 84), that although the satrap of Armenia had been able to take advantage of Antiochus' misfortunes to shake off his supervision, he had then come under Rome's eye. Yes, but Armenia was a long way away, and that Roman rule very theoretical. And what we shall soon see of Hannibal's very real town-planning activities with Prusias of Bithynia rather argues in favour of the historical reality of his first attempts in the shadow of the mountains of Atropatene.

In 190, before going to confront Antiochus at Magnesia on the Sipylus, the Scipios had been able, by the use of clever messages, to detach Prusias from the Seleucid alliance and persuade him to become, according to the diplomatic term then employed in Rome, the 'friend of the Roman people' (Polybius, XXI, 11). Prusias thus found himself in the same camp as his powerful and rival neighbour in the south, Eumenes of Pergamum. But the situation had subsequently developed. Mysia (or Phrygia 'Epicteta') had become an apple of discord for the two kingdoms. Formerly given by Antiochus to Attalus, Eumenes' predecessor, then seized by Prusias around 196, in conformity with the redistributions decided on at Apamea in 188, the region should have been restored to Eumenes (Polybius, XXI, 46, 10). Rome's delay in intervening – it would do so only in 183 – had allowed the disagreement to escalate until it became open war in 186.

Was it perhaps at this time or a little earlier – I have already mentioned the difficulty of establishing a precise chronology – that Hannibal was welcomed by Prusias? Like Antiochus in the recent past, the Bithynian might derive some advantage from the exile's advice, even if it meant repudiating and betraying him should the need arise. Before handing him over, he had the opportunity to make use of his talents, both civilian and military. He confronted Eumenes on both land and sea. In the account of Hannibal's prowess in the role of admiral, left to us by the Nepos–Justin duo, the stratagem of pots full of poisonous snakes echoes the idea of the hollow statues of Gortyna. During a naval battle on the Sea of Marmara, the Carthaginian is supposed to have thought up the means of both seizing Eumenes' flagship and victoriously resisting an enemy fleet that was superior in number. Before the engagement he sent the king a herald holding a caduceus, the bearer of a message to be put into his own hands. The letter was fanciful, but its acceptance by the one to whom it was addressed clearly picked him out as a target for the Bithynian ships. Eumenes narrowly missed being taken prisoner. And when his more numerous vessels closely hemmed in the Bithynian ships, catapults showered them with jars filled with snakes, which scattered among the banks of oarsmen, creating panic. As so often happens in this literature, one grasps the merging of a trick of war that was probably real, the messenger sent to identify the royal vessel – though in general that would have been recognizable on its own – and a 'stratagem' obligingly elaborated for its picturesqueness. Jérôme Carcopino (1961b, p. 173) is almost alone in giving Cornelius Nepos the amused blessing of a great historian. Sir Gavin De Beer goes one better (1969, p. 299), calling it the first example of 'biological warfare'. Please yourself.

Prusias had his capital at Nicomedia, today Izmit, at the end of a narrow bay where the Sea of Marmara plunges eastward, turning the Bithynian peninsula beyond the Bosphorus into a hyphen between Europe and Asia. His territorial claims on the Phrygian side explain why he desired to have a second, more southerly, capital. Was it he or Hannibal who chose for the new town the site on the north-west foothills of the 'Olympus of Bithynia', present-day Ulu Dag? This would be Prusa, now Bursa, one of the most pleasant cities in modern Anatolia, for a long time the Ottoman capital, and Pliny the Elder (*N.H.*, V, 148) did not entertain the slightest doubt that its architect was Hannibal. After Artaxata, this was a second *ktisma*, a founding act that admitted the one who accomplished it into the closed circle of Hellenistic sovereigns, even if he did not pass on his name to it. And probably the undertaking reminded Hannibal, now in his sixties, of what he had seen as a child, when his father Hamilcar Barca founded Akra Leuke, and later as a young man watching the building of Cartagena from the plans of his brother-in-law Hasdrubal.

It is in these Bithynian years that we must place the writings traditionally ascribed to the exile, one probably genuine, the other incontestably apocryphal. The first, among other writings in Greek by Hannibal, is mentioned by Cornelius Nepos (*Hann.*, 13, 2), unfortunately without the slightest analysis. It is a speech addressed to the Rhodians on the subject of the acts committed in Asia by Cn. Manlius Vulso. And this text, which is obviously anti-Roman propaganda, cannot be much later than the campaign waged by the consul for 189. After receiving from L. Scipio command of the Roman expeditionary corps at Ephesus in the spring of 189, Vulso had used the pretext of the presence of a Galatian contingent in Antiochus' army to launch a vast punitive expedition against the Gallogreeks, apparently without the formal order of the Senate. This raid lasting several months had taken him across Caria, then Phrygia, to the heart of Anatolia where, around Ancyra (Ankara), the Tectosagi had settled, the principal Galatian confederation that had emerged from the great Celtic invasion of the early third century. The consul was brutal and greedy, and the rabble serving under him were tarred with the same brush. In a rather remarkably antimilitarist page, Livy (XXXVIII, 24, following Polybius, XXI, 38) makes a meal of the violence and extortionate demands committed by one of his centurions, who was soon smiling on the other side of his face. His victim, a Galatian princess named Chiomara – whose sensitive virtue was also hymned by Plutarch, Valerius Maximus and

Florus – had avenged her outraged dignity by having one of her slaves decapitate him. True, the Greeks of the maritime provinces of Asia Minor took a rather favourable view of the punishment meted out to the Gallogreeks, whom they feared, but the main beneficiary of the operation was Eumenes of Pergamum, of whom the Rhodians were jealous. It was fairly easy to stir them up by emphasizing the overt brutality of the Roman consul and his troops, presenting a very disagreeable image of Roman imperialism. What a pity that Hannibal's argument has not come down to us.

On the other hand, in the edition of R. Merkelbach (1954, pp. 51–73) we may read the texts contained in the papyrus fragments preserved at Hamburg (*P. Hamb.* 129). Among the letters falsely attributed to Alexander the Great and his father Philip, is a letter, no less false, addressed by Hannibal to the Athenians. The 'king of the Carthaginians' – as he was described – announced the crushing defeat suffered by the Romans at Cannae, and in a style at once prophetic and obscure let it be understood that an uprising by the Greeks could bring about the end of Roman domination in the East and the ruin of Rome itself. There is now agreement (Candiloro, 1965, pp. 171–7; Brizzi, 1984b, pp. 87–102) in dating this anti-Roman attack to 190–185. It probably gains its full meaning if compared, as Arnaldo Momigliano was first to do (1979, pp. 53–4), with a very curious text by Antisthenes of Rhodes, a contemporary of Polybius. A long fragment of his history of the years 190–188 has come down to us thanks to Phlego of Tralles, a freedman and secretary to the emperor Hadrian. There we find an account according to which, around 189, the Roman general Publius, smitten with madness when he was in the panhellenic sanctuary of Naupactus, in Aetolian country, started to make wild prophecies in Greek about the end of Roman domination: a king would come from Asia to avenge the evil that the Romans had done to the Greeks. There is scarcely any doubt that, in this text, 'Publius' represents Scipio Africanus who was at the time, as we have seen, second-in-command to his brother Lucius in Asia Minor. But who was the 'king from Asia'? One thinks first of Antiochus. But it is not impossible that Hannibal is meant, likened to a Hellenistic sovereign. It is probable that in the years immediately following the defeat of Philip of Macedon in 197, then of Antiochus in 190–189, many in Greece, and perhaps especially in Aetolia, looked towards Hannibal as a possible saviour. And since we are reduced to hypothesis in this area, we may listen to the very alluring suggestion of G. Brizzi (1984b, p. 101), for whom 'Hannibal's letter to the Athenians' may have been circulated in pamphlet form just after the exile's death in 183, in order to exploit the emotion that his passing could have aroused in the Greek world.

## *Donec Bithynio libeat vigilare tyranno* (Juvenal, X, 162)

This same year, 183, witnessed the disappearance, within months of one another – all the ancient historians of the time, Polybius (XXIII, 12–14) in the forefront, underlined this chronological coincidence – of the three most outstanding generals, war leaders and statesmen of their generation: a Greek, Philopoemen, a Roman, Scipio, and the Carthaginian, Hannibal. *Strategos* (commander) to the Achaeans for the eighth time in twenty-five years, Philopoemen had fallen into an ambush in Messenia and, thrown into a dungeon, had been forced to take the poison that was offered to him. Polybius, who was related to him, wrote the biography of the man whom Plutarch (*Philop*., I, 7) would call 'the last of the Greeks', and who was honoured on his death by the institution of a real heroic cult.

For Scipio, there were neither cult nor statues, apart from those erected to him in the hearts of Romans – the finest and most enduring, as Tacitus somewhere ascribes to Tiberius, who certainly did not merit any. Two years after the brothers' return from their campaign in Asia against Antiochus (on the chronology, which is a delicate matter, see Adam, 1982, pp. LVII–LXXIII), Lucius, the consul in office for 190, was indicted at Cato's instigation. He was accused of not having accounted for part of the sum paid to him by Antiochus before the signing of the treaty of Apamea in 188, by way of an advance on the war indemnity. The dispute was about 500 talents, as compared with the 15,000 that the Scipios' victory over the Seleucid king had brought into the Roman coffers. Publius was at the time 'princeps senatus'. Taking up his brother's defence and by his action denying *ipso facto* the assembly's right to inspect the generals' administration, he tore up the accounts books which, according to tradition, would have proved Lucius' innocence, adding with disdain that the accuser could always go and search the debris to find what he was looking for (Polybius, XXIII, 14, 6–8). Africanus' extraordinary *auctoritas* caused the accusation to be dropped. But Cato was tenacious. Three years later, in 184, he was elected censor at the same time as his patron, the patrician L. Valerius Flaccus. And at that time he gave a tribune of the plebs named M. Naevius the task of putting Scipio on the carpet, dragging up again the approaches made by Antiochus to Publius in the autumn of 190, when the king had restored his son to him without ransom and unsuccessfully made the proposals mentioned above (p. 204). In Cato's circle, all they wanted to recall of those contacts was how much evidence they showed of Africanus' proclivity to treat another king, enemy of the Roman people, on equal terms. Scipio answered his accuser with scorn and, from the height of the rostra, invited the crowd to accompany him to the Capitol to pray the gods to do Rome the kindness of always granting it rulers in his image in years to come (Livy, XXXVIII, 51, 8–14)! It seems that all the people followed him to the Capitol and made a tour of the city's temples with him. But, says the historian, this day of glory, which repeated that of his triumph, was the last one for Scipio. Taking advantage of the deferment of the legal proceedings, and leaving his brother Lucius to plead his case, he retired to an estate he had at Liternum, on the Campanian coast near Cumae, where he died prematurely the following year. In the imperial era, two and a half centuries later, people went there as tourists or pilgrims. Seneca (*Letters to Lucilius*, 86, 1–5) admired the defences of this small fortified castle, was moved by the modesty of the old-fashioned baths, and wondered whether the funerary altar before which he had just invoked the spirit of the great man was really his tomb. Probably, since his epitaph, attributed to Ennius and which must be quoted exactly as Valerius Maximus (5, 3, 2b) has passed it down to us, made him say, 'Ungrateful fatherland, thou hast not even my bones!'

During the months when Scipio was coming to the end of his life at Liternum, the Senate had received from Eumenes of Pergamum an embassy led by his brother Athenaios, which had come to complain that Prusias, in his war operations, had had the benefit of reinforcements sent by Philip of Macedon, who was related to him by marriage. The Senate dispatched Flamininus to Prusias. Had this specialist in Greek affairs the sole mission of settling a difference between two neighbours? Could it really be true that Rome was unaware of Hannibal's presence at the king of Bithynia's court? However unlikely such unawareness may seem, our sources (Plutarch, *Flam.*, 20, 5; Appian, *Syr.*, 43; Livy, XXXIX, 51, 1–2) sometimes suggest none the less that Flamininus was surprised when he arrived at Prusias' court, and reproached the king there and then. Cornelius Nepos (*Hann.*, 12, 2) is the only one to state clearly that the former consul had already received the information in Rome at the time of the Bithynian ambassadors' arrival, and had informed the Senate. Flamininus would then have been given instructions to make sure that Hannibal was there in person. And here is the second uncertainty: was it Flamininus, as our texts generally say – Nepos in particular – who asked Prusias for Hannibal's head, or was it a deliberate betrayal by the Bithynian in order to get himself into Rome's good graces? Hardly likely to have any fond feelings for Prusias – and the picture of spinelessness given by Corneille in his *Nicomède* is a fairly exact expression – our historical memory has tended to retain the second hypothesis, which ancient tradition does not favour so clearly.

At all events, Hannibal was on his guard. He realized that the Romans were implacably determined to destroy him (Hans-Günther, 1989, pp. 241–50) and harboured no illusions about Prusias, whose feebleness he knew. He had a refuge at Libyssa on the south coast of the Bithynian peninsula, slightly west of Nicomedia; a real fox's lair, according to Plutarch (*Flam.*, 20, 7), with many entrances and exits, and seven underground tunnels leading from the house to the outside. When Hannibal was warned that Prusias' soldiers were already in the hall, he sent servants to explore the other ways out. They too were already guarded by the king's henchmen. He then resorted to the poison that he always carried on him, ready for such an eventuality. Before having him empty the goblet, Livy (XXXIX, 51, 9–11) puts into his mouth the obviously fictitious last words which are nevertheless interesting for the reflection they give of the emotions that must have been aroused in certain circles, in Rome and elsewhere, by the inglorious demise of the old man – Hannibal was then sixty-three. A poor bird stripped of its feathers by age, says Plutarch (*Flam.*, 21, 1), that it would have been better to leave alive. Calling the gods as his witness to the discourtesy of the Romans and the treachery of Prusias, in the end Hannibal turned against Rome the accusation, which had been launched against himself innumerable times, of *fides Punica*.

# 9

# Heritage, Legend and Image

*Les Enfants d'Alexandre* (Alexander's Children) is a nice title for a recent book by J. Sirinelli (1994) on the conqueror's immediate and later heritage. Sirinelli goes beyond the *diadochi* and the successors, the library of Alexandria, the autumn roses of late Hellenism, Greece post-Greece. Hannibal, in contrast, is someone without descendants, even metaphorical ones. In comparison with all those 'illustrious men' – assembled in the great tome in which dear old Chrysale in Molière's *Les Femmes Savantes* kept his neckbands pressed – he is the only one to be a citizen of a city that would disappear less than half a century after him. The failure of his own venture was compounded by the downfall of his homeland. That is probably why Hannibal has no place in Plutarch – where his 'parallel' would have been Scipio, who is also missing – yet holds such a singular place in our memory. To put it simply, he occupies the position of a hero who came from another world to write in our own – the classical world from which we are descended – a page of history without any tomorrow.

At least, without any tomorrow as far as Carthage was concerned. Trying to imagine what the western Mediterranean would have become under the Barcid's leadership had he succeeded in his enterprise is an apparently attractive, but useless, intellectual exercise, whereas it is perfectly legitimate and fruitful to try to measure the imprint Hannibal left on the era in which he lived and, paradoxically, on the city that conquered him. Without the spur that he gave to the world of those times, our heritage would not be quite the same.

## Hannibal's 'heritage'

Or, to be more precise, it is useful to try to measure *Hannibal's Legacy* (Toynbee, 1965) and, as the sub-title of this great book specifies, the effects of Hannibal's war on Roman life. We are indebted to Toynbee for having conducted, in two volumes of rare compactness, an analysis that others before him – in particular Gaetano De Sanctis (1923, pp. 260–1) – had merely outlined. One must, however, resist the tendency, which is manifest in the book's conclusions (Vol. II, pp. 486–517), to lay too much emphasis on this heritage, tracing back to Hannibal the original responsibility, because of the pressures that his venture exerted on Roman political structures, for what Toynbee calls *the Roman Hundred Years' Revolution*, which in his view begins with the reforms introduced by Ti. Gracchus in 133. And from there it is only a step to interpreting the 'Roman revolution' (Syme, 1964), which resulted in the institution of the principate with Octavian-Augustus, as Hannibal's revenge from afar. But in company with another expert on the 'century of the Scipios', one may deem it a somewhat excessive step to take (Grimal, 1975, p. 144).

What is true is that the force of the pressure exerted by the Carthaginian on Rome and Italy in so few years, giving the course of events such a pace, caused what have been called *mutations* (Brisson, 1969, pp. 33–59), which are more striking for the speed with which they entered events than for their scope. First, of course, in the military field. Between 218 and 202, the force confronting Hannibal did not fundamentally change its nature. Certainly, after Cannae in 216, as we have seen, it was necessary to fill the gaps by enrolling state-ransomed slaves and even prisoners under sentence of death or condemned debtors (Livy, XXIII, 14, 2). But despite these exceptional measures, the Roman army remained a citizens' army, even an 'elitist' army based on property qualifications, since the 'proletarii' – in the Roman sense, those whose only worldly goods were their offspring – were not allowed to serve in it. What is seen to change in the space of a few years is the very conception of war and the nature of command.

We must bear in mind the heavy defeat of the three successive plebeian consuls of 213, 217 and 216. Sempronius Longus, beaten at the Trebia because he wanted to bring renown *in extremis* to the close of his consulship; Flaminius, dead at Trasimene for running into a trap, spurred on by ill-controlled ardour; Varro, responsible for the disaster of Cannae through trying to force destiny's hand. Over and above their particular circumstances, all three were victims of a rather too chivalrous vision of martial engagements, and were in addition held back by the constraints of magico-religious rituals – the rites of purification surrounding the 'useful season' from March to October – and obsessed by the desire to make a decisive military advantage coincide with the term of their annual magistracy. To these handicaps was added the rule of collegial command with its rigid corollary of the daily alternation of the fasces – above, p. 104 – which was one of the causes of the catastrophe at Cannae. From these setbacks the lesson was swiftly learnt, at least wherever it could be, both by ensuring as often as possible that there was unity of command in armies on campaign and maintaining continuity in strategic action by repeating consulships, several times if necessary, and extending commands by the device of proconsulships or propraetorships. Repeating consulships remained an exceptional case, but it is noteworthy that as well as Q. Fabius Maximus – a really exceptional instance, since the five consulships of this patrician were staggered over a quarter of a century – the two great beneficiaries were the outstanding captains of plebeian origin, Q. Fulvius Flaccus and M. Claudius Marcellus, respectively four and five times consul during the period, who owed these renewals to their talents as generals. In a less politically obvious way, the extension of command by the granting of proconsulships also effectively played the same role, and in a mingling of the two devices, someone like Marcellus, who had started to make a name for himself in 222 against the Gauls in the Cisalpine region, was virtually continuously invested with the highest military responsibilities from 216 until his death in 208. On the Roman side, this is probably the clearest case in that period of a professional soldier's career. The extension of command affecting patricians appears less exceptional, especially when it was exercised overseas; we may remember the continuity in the conduct of the war in Spain shared by P. and Cn. Scipio from 218 to 211. As for Africanus himself, armed with a proconsular *imperium* in Spain as early as 210, and extended to 206, then elected consul in 205, and prorogated as proconsul in his command in Sicily, then Africa, until 201, he exercised full civil and military powers for some ten years running, entirely on his own. And just as the patrician P. Sulpicius Galba had been uninterruptedly the man in Macedonia against Philip V from his consulship in 211 until 206, the patrician T. Quinctius Flamininus was Rome's man in Greece from his consulship in 198 until his mission to Prusias of Bithynia in 183, which tarnished his image. The excess of 'dignity' thus conferred on these men obviously upset the dogma of the interchangeability of rulers, which was fundamental to the constitution of the Roman republic, and contained the seeds of the 'monarchist' inclinations that would surface in Sulla's era (Grimal, 1975, pp. 171–2).

We saw earlier (above, p. 187) that the war against Philip V decided upon in 200 marked the birth of Roman imperialism, in that the Macedonian king was no threat to Rome and no Roman interest was then at stake in Greece. But Rome would have taken no action against Philip had it not been rid of Hannibal at that time, and had it not begun to build its Mediterranean empire by seizing Spain. It is Livy (XXXII, 27, 6) who notes that, 'as the empire was expanding', for the first time six praetors were appointed in the elections for 197. Before the end of the first Punic War two had still sufficed; a few years later two more were necessary to govern Sicily and Sardinia respectively; and another two, therefore, in 197, to administer the two Spains, Citerior and Ulterior. It would take a further three generations before the creation of the province of Gallia Narbonensis around 120 BC – 'Provence', that very necessary hyphen between north Italy and the Iberian peninsula – turned the nascent Roman empire in the West into something other and bigger than the simple result of dismantling Carthage's empire. But the irresistible movement of absorption of the western world which would turn Rome and its political power into the equivalent, relative to the West, of what Greece still was in relation to the Hellenized East, came into being during those years of the end of the second Punic War. And the growing self-awareness that accompanied this territorial expansion also dated from those years. When in the prologue of the *Casina* (v. 71–2), the leader of the theatrical troupe giving Plautus' play around 185 evokes his Apulia by the Latin name *terra nostra*, comparing it with the two political and cultural entities then recognized in an otherwise 'barbarian' world, the Carthaginians and the Greeks, he is probably sketching one of the first pictures of an 'Italian' nationalism that was forged in the ordeals of fifteen years of hard fighting waged from one end of the pensinsula to the other, from the Po Valley to Bruttium, and especially in Apulia, which was the principal theatre for those confrontations. And, moving from the political to the cultural, it is not oversimplifying to say that the successes achieved against Hannibal – and his allies of Hellenic culture in Italy itself: Syracuse and Tarentum – prevented Italy, which had become Roman but was immersed in a world where all culture was Greek, where Greek was the language of diplomacy as it was of business and, of course, literature, from remaining simply another province of Hellenism. It was the breadth of a military and political supremacy which was first acquired at Carthage's expense that gave the Latin language its chance against Greek, although the former was a minority tongue in Italy itself amid a mosaic of dialects. In this regard the destiny of one Ennius, born in 239 not far from Tarentum in Oscan territory, but speaking Greek, is significant; he reached manhood when Hannibal's war was raging through Italy, became the first 'rule-maker' of noble poetry in the Latin tongue and the official eulogist of Roman greatness. The 'Roman-ness' to which we are heirs begins in literature with Ennius' *Annals*.

Last but not least, the occupation of Italian soil by Hannibal's armies and the gigantic depredations committed by them, added to the losses in tax revenues to the Roman treasury, created an unprecedented shock-wave, notably in central and southern Italy, which rocked traditional economic structures and compelled Rome to make rapid adaptations in order to ward off the consequences. To the devastation caused by the enemy army, which lived off the locals, must be added the destruction due to the 'scorched earth' strategy (above, p. 99) carried out by Fabius Maximus in 217 in the Samnite and Campanian regions. To complete the overturning of the Italian rural landscape, there then followed the massive confiscations carried out by Rome which hit city-states and peoples who had sided with Hannibal. Such was the case of Capua's territory, and a large part of Samnium, Lucania, Apulia and Bruttium. In the late third and early second centuries, there was a strong rural exodus in central and southern Italy. While the confiscated lands witnessed the setting-up of vast estates run on slave labour, or large zones of extensive stockbreeding, and even areas left fallow, free peasants and dispossessed small land-owners came to swell the urban plebs, especially in Rome. The agrarian crisis that ensued would make itself felt for a long time, until the end of the second century and even beyond. From this decline emerged the favourable corollary that, during the same period, the Italy whose agriculture became less productive – from then on it would rely increasingly on its new provinces, with Sicily in the forefront, to act as its granary – rapidly began to make up for its deficiencies in the domain of production and trade in manufactured goods. In his *De agri cultura* (135, 1–3), a work written in his old age (*c*.165–160 BC) but whose references are obviously valid for the preceding decades, Cato the Censor gives a list of the industrial products to be found in south-central Italy, and it is interesting to read the names of some of the towns that figure largely in the chronicles of Hannibal's war: Cales, Venafrum, Pompeii, Capua, Nola. In the early second century Campania began to rival the long-industrial Etruria, not only in the field of pottery, where it was queen, its products flooding the entire western half of the Mediterranean basin.

In parallel, accompanying the industrial and commercial boom which would make its fortune, a social class – that of the knights – whose existence had hitherto been mainly civic and based on property qualifications, and whose function had a military origin, captured the domain left open to them by the restrictions placed on senators' entrepreneurial freedom. In 218 or, at the earliest, in 219, a tribune of the plebs, Q. Claudius, had put to the vote a 'plebiscite' banning any senator, or senator's son, from possessing a cargo ship capable of carrying more than 300 amphorae: a tonnage that seemed adequate for the transport and marketing of one property's harvests. Beyond that, dimensions were reached that were more suitable for a commercial undertaking, incompatible with senatorial dignity (Livy, XXI, 63, 3–4). This bill, one imagines, was the subject of a fierce battle in the Senate, where only Flaminius, the plebeian consul who died at Trasimene in 217, had supported him. None the less, it was passed by the comitia. Of course, resorting to 'front-men' enabled senators to get round the law, and we know that the virtuous Cato himself did not hesitate to exercise what was then called the *foenus nauticum* (Plutarch, *Cato Major*, 21, 6). But the legal restriction acted first in the knights' favour, before it became of huge benefit to freedmen two centuries later. It was principally the members of the equestrian class who henceforth grew rich on armaments and trade, subsequently swelling their inherited property by investing fortunes acquired through commerce in *latifundia*, following a process that was general in pre-industrial societies. In the same period, in the aftermath of Cannae, the knights infiltrated the circles of public economy, creating the first company of *publicani*. As a result of massive impoverishment in fiscal income the Roman coffers were empty at that time. In 215, on the appeal of the urban praetor – that year he was Q. Fulvius Flaccus, before the second and then third renewal of his consulship – three 'companies' numbering nineteen members tendered for the supplies destined for the Scipios' army in Spain. As well as exemption from military service as long as their mission lasted, they obtained from the republic the guarantee that it would shoulder any possible losses suffered by the supply fleet at the hand of the enemy or the elements (Livy, XXIII, 49, 1–2). Shortly afterwards, two scandals that erupted in quick succession illustrated both the activity of the knights and the evils of the system. In 213 T. Pomponius Veientanus, a former publican who was notorious for his swindling, as much to the detriment of his own company as of the state, had raised a small army of supporters in Bruttium, in fact a band of looters and pillagers. He was captured in an engagement with Hannibal's lieutenant, Hanno, and, comments Livy (XXV, 1, 4), he was no loss. The following year, more seriously, M. Postumius of Pyrgi was found guilty of clear cases of barratry. In order to claim the guarantee premiums, he declared false, or real but deliberate, shipwrecks of old vessels whose cargoes were fraudulently overstated. On the day of the trial, faced with the disturbance created by the publicans' henchmen, Fulvius, who was consul in 212 for the third time, and had been the instigator of resorting to the publicans during his praetorship in 215, referred the matter to the Senate. Postumius' possessions were confiscated; he was sentenced to exile and his accomplices were similarly exiled or thrown into prison (Livy, XXV, 4). But publicans still had good days ahead of them. Certainly they never represented more than a minor part of the knights (Nicolet, 1974, p. 318); but their influence, in the late third century, was fundamental and the importance of their real role disproportionate to their number.

As we saw earlier (above, p. 122), the successful reorganization of coinage also dates to the heroic years between 215 and 211, which were those of the greatest peril and yet of a sudden burst of energy and survival. I shall not return to it here, save to stress that these emergency reforms were due to the pressure exerted by Hannibal's war on Rome's public finances. Remember, too, that in 210 (above, p. 123) there was a call for national solidarity and private generosity – first of all from senators, then knights – to equip the armed forces, notably the war fleet. At the very end of the century, all had been repaid. But by then that era of financial distress was no more than a bad memory. From 212 onwards, war captures had accumulated: Syracuse, then Capua (211), Cartagena (210), Tarentum (209) and finally and chiefly, in 201, the indemnities imposed on defeated Carthage.

Perhaps, at the turn of the third and second centuries, these exceptional revenues were just sufficient to compensate for the enormous expenses – tens of millions of denarii – of financing the war effort (Marchetti, 1978, pp. 241–74). But in the first years of the second century, wealth continued to flow into Italy from Spain, Greece and Asia Minor. In 195, under the consulship of L. Valerius Flaccus and M. Porcius Cato, a highly symbolic debate took place before the people. Twenty years earlier, in 215, a sumptuary law had been passed – the *lex Oppia*, from the name of the tribune of the plebs who had presented it – strictly limiting feminine luxury. It was in the aftermath of Cannae, and austerity was the order of the day: no more than half an ounce of gold, no richly coloured or brocaded garments, no carriages in the town. When its abrogation was suggested, Cato opposed it in an impassioned speech that will be remembered less for its anti-feminism – which was very real, but commonplace in those days – than for a certain prophetic emphasis on the poisons of prosperity (Livy, XXXIV, 2–4). The law was none the less repealed, in the same year in which, driven from Carthage, Hannibal took the road into exile. And when he died, and long after his death, when the republic seemed in danger and national unity assailed, there were those in Rome who brandished his image, if not to recreate a dynamic of salvation, at least to bring back his memory.

## The legend and the image

Near the place where Hannibal had ended his life, Pliny the Elder (*H.N.*, V, 148) says there was still to be seen in his own time – the middle of the first century AD – the 'tumulus', a simple mound, where his remains were supposed to rest. And according to a learned Byzantine who lived at Constantinople at the time of the Comnenes, in the twelfth century (Tzetzes, *Chil.*, I, 803), much later still the African emperor Septimius Severus, in whose veins ran a little Punic blood, made a compassionate gesture by giving the tumulus a covering of white marble; which indeed he could have done, when between 193 and 195 he had to besiege Byzantium to eliminate his rival Pescennius Niger. It is well known that the tombs of the great army leaders give archaeologists sleepless nights. Early this century, it appears that one of them located Hannibal's tomb where a little river, the Libyssos (today the Dil) flows into the Sea of Marmara (Wiegand, 1902). But we still have to discover those feathery ashes that slipped through Juvenal's fingers....

Is it by chance that, with the Latin satirist of the early second century AD, Hannibal's image becomes refined and settled, rid of its bogeyman trappings? In Juvenal, imprecations give way to mocking irony; the manic ogre who swept through Italy in all directions has become a declamatory theme for the apprentice orator. We are in the reign of Trajan, the ruler who stretched the Empire to frontiers it would never again exceed. Rome is at the centre of the only world it knows, and the only one that matters. It hardly suspects the existence in the Far East of the China of the Han dynasty; it is unaware of the swelling hordes beginning to form in the steppes of central Asia and the great population movements beyond its Danubian *limes*, precursors of the surging human tides to come, of which it has no inkling. How can Rome foresee that three centuries later, at the head of his Visigoths, Alaric will succeed where the Carthaginian failed, entering Rome while the emperor cowers behind the ramparts of Ravenna? When Juvenal writes in the heart of a city-state that is self-confident, without the least enemy for several decades, Hannibal's image has lost much of its sanguinary aura. It is scarcely more than the recollection of a danger that could have proved fatal.

It had not always been so. We may remember (above, p. 44) Livy's 'programme-portrait' frontispiece to the start of his third decade, and we have seen that it was necessary to shade his stereotypes with the less biased and more balanced judgements of Polybius. Especially when the Greek historian makes an effort (IX, 23–5) to relativize the accusations of cupidity and cruelty made against Hannibal and throw light on these complaints by putting them into the context of the situations that gave rise to them. As far as cupidity is concerned, he says (IX, 25) Hannibal had this reputation among his Carthaginian compatriots and he, Polybius, learned it from the Carthaginians themselves and also from the lips of Massinissa, whom he had in fact been able to meet shortly before the Numidian king's death in 148. It seems that for covetousness Hannibal rivalled one of his oldest companions-at-arms, Mago the Samnite, in whose company he had waged war during their youth in Spain, and who was in command in Bruttium between 212 and 203. They reached the point, Polybius feels able to say, where they avoided being side by side at the capture of a town so that they did not have to argue over the booty. The Roman historiographer did not dismiss this cupidity, which must have seemed to him the least of Hannibal's faults; there was the story of the solid gold column in the temple of Juno at Crotona, which subjected him to great temptation (above, p. 000); but at Locri in 205, the town's temples had not been despoiled of their treasures by Hamilcar, the Punic commander, but by Pleminius, one of Scipio's lieutenants (Livy, XXIX, 8, 7–9). As for the cruelty of which the Romans accused him, Polybius says it must be assessed in the light of circumstances, evaluating what was sometimes severity or political 'terrorism', and also taking those who were with him into account. Remember the opinion of the famous Monomachus, according to whom a soldier, if the need arose, should get used to eating human flesh. Hannibal, adds Polybius, had never been able to resort to this extreme solution; but according to Livy, in Varro's short address to the Capuan delegates in the aftermath of Cannae, such cannibalism was presented as a reality in the Carthaginian camps (above, p. 114).

Without further analytical precautions, Roman historiography, beginning with Livy, and subsequent tradition accentuate the trait and repeat sayings about Hannibal that tend to present him as a kind of 'war criminal'. First, the famous *perfidia plus quam Punica*. To grasp the scope of this accusation, one must bear in mind what they called *Fides* meant to the Romans in terms of international law – and morality. *Fides* (with a capital F) was not only a concept but a deity, according to tradition, since Numa Pompilius, the second mythical and thaumaturgical king of Rome (Freyburger, 1986, pp. 259–73). *Fides* was one's sworn word and, in the domain of the *ius gentium*, the sacred and inviolable relationship established between the contracting parties to an agreement or treaty; and thus notably, as a direct consequence, the obligation of a victor to respect the rights and person of the vanquished who placed himself under his allegiance, under his *fides*. But on another level, especially in the conduct of war, *fides* was also respect for the rules, fairness in combat, which in theory excluded recourse to trickery. In Roman eyes, Hannibal was *perfidus* on both scores. In the first sense of the word, he was so by original sin, so to speak, as a Carthaginian, for the crime of belonging to a nation with which Rome had concluded treaties in the late sixth century BC, and it still blamed him for betraying them. And Hannibal from the start had compounded that original sin by attacking Saguntum, then crossing the *Iber* (Ebro) with his army (above, pp. 46–7). From the very start of his venture he had thus become a 'treaty-breaker' (*foedifragus*), an epithet that would cling to him as the Saguntum affair would stick to his skin. But in this area, too, Hannibal left a 'legacy'. Scipio's successors did not share his elegance. In 172, the oldest senators plainly expressed their dispproval of the methods used by the ambassador to Macedonia, Q. Marcius Philippus, a former consul, who had deceived Perseus by granting him a truce and giving him the hope of peace, while at the same time going full-steam ahead with his preparations for war; this new way of thinking (*nova sapientia*), which was rather too smart, was not at all to their liking (Livy, XLII, 47, 4). But twenty-five years earlier, Flamininus had already practised a *Realpolitik* in Greece, solely justified by a concern for immediate effectiveness (Brizzi, 1982, pp. 199–221). As for the other form of *perfidia* on Hannibal's part which so shocked the old Romans, his methods of making war by resorting widely to a whole range of stratagems, ruses, surprise raids and ambushes, it had already gained acceptance, even with his most chivalrous enemy. Remember (above, p. 167) the way in which Scipio, using surprise and trickery, set fire to the camps of Hasdrubal and Syphax, in order to restore the balance of forces in his own favour in the spring of 203.

*Perfidus*, and known as such, to the point where it was enough for a poet like Ovid, in Augustus' era, to apostrophize in the vocative case the *perfide Poene* for everyone to know who was meant without having to name him (*Fasti*, III, 148 and VI, 242), Hannibal in Roman tradition was also, *par excellence*, *crudelis*. Staying in the framework of the wars that affected Italy in the third century, it was a commonplace, echoed by Cicero for example (*Laelius*, 28), to compare the probity and humanity of Pyrrhus with the cruelty of Hannibal. And to back up that accusation it was possible to delve into a fund of anecdotes and sayings whose authenticity no one bothered to check. Thus Seneca, in his own time, did not hesitate to relay one of those snippets that show the Carthaginian in the most odious light; on the eve of a battle, seeing a trench full of human blood, Hannibal exclaimed 'Oh, what a lovely sight!' (*O formosum spectaculum*!: *De ira*, II, 5, 4). This caricature, depicting the Carthaginian as a sadistically destructive roughneck soldier, lets us understand how and why the reminder of Hannibal's war and the evocation of the leader of that war could subsequently become the principal references, in the eyes of those who were greatly affected by the traumatism of the civil wars in the first century BC. For Florus (II, 6, 11), summarizing Livy, neither Hannibal nor Pyrrhus before him had caused as much damage in Italy as the 'Social War', in other words the one that broke out between Rome and its Italian allies, starting with Picenum in 90 BC. Later, when Caesar crossed the Rubicon early in 49 and advanced through Italy in his march on Rome, Cicero (*Ad Att.*, VII, 11, 1) does not hesitate to compare his advance with Hannibal's; and, with epic amplification, in Lucan (*Pharsalia*, I, 303) this crossing of the Rubicon recalls the image of Hannibal's passage over the Alps. In his *Philippics* (notably V, 25–7 and XIV, 9) Cicero sees Antony as another Hannibal, even more destructive of Italy, and whose savagery at Parma outdoes Hannibal's. And a little later, the gentle Horace himself, who had suffered in the civil wars and despaired of ever seeing their end, went as far as to write (*Epodes*, XVI, 8) that this 'Hannibal, execrated by our parents' was in the end less dangerous for Rome than the present bloody dissension.

Heavily present and much diabolized in Roman imaginations at the time of the last convulsive movements in which the Republic ultimately foundered, the figure of Hannibal grows fainter and more indistinct with the beginnings of the principate. Fulfilling a decision already taken by Caesar, Octavian, even before he became Augustus, restored to Carthage the status of capital of the now Roman Africa, after over a century of abandonment (Le Glay, 1985, pp. 235–47). And soon afterwards, from the ashes of the other town was born a new city from which every trace had disappeared of the place where so great a danger to Rome had originated two centuries earlier. Material reconstruction and regained security in Italy, and the extension of the *pax Romana* in the world could foster a belief in the new Golden Age announced by the arrival of the child hymned by Virgil in his Fourth Eclogue. Could Hannibal still be a source of fear? Of course, the stereotypes remained, as we have seen with Seneca and his blood-filled trench. And the famous sayings continued to go the rounds, like the one related in roughly the same period by Pliny the Elder (*H.N.*, VIII, 18), which incidentally illustrates Hannibal's shrewdness as much as his 'cruelty'. The Punic leader forced his prisoners to fight one another, and the survivor had to fight an elephant, with the promise of having his life spared if he overcame the animal. The Roman killed the elephant, but Hannibal, feeling that this story might harm the reputation of his combat elephants, had the man put to death. However, amid these surviving tales, Hannibal's image began to merge into a halo of myth and folklore. In the middle of the first century AD, Petronius' Trimalchio, to enliven his guests, tells them stories in his own way, with a jolly intermingling of times and places. One of them (*Satiricon*, 50, 5) claims to explain the origin of the bronzes of Corinth: it was due to Hannibal who, at the capture of Troy (!) had a quantity of bronze and silver statues piled on an immense pyre – the well-known alloy was the result. The interesting thing is that, in this instance, Petronius' ludicrous hero describes the Carthaginian as cunning (*vafer*) and, chiefly, a 'chameleon' (*stelio*); in my opinion a probable allusion to Hannibal's extraordinary capacity for adaptation, physically evident in the costumes and disguises he assumed, of which our sources give us at least one example (above, p. 90). Later still, Juvenal wavers between two attitudes. The satirist who was little inclined to be taken in by the subject of military glory openly mocks this anti-hero, whose exploits he sums up in some twenty superbly ironic lines (*Sat.*, X, 147–67), which are among the most brilliant left to us by that writer whose pen was dipped in vitriol. Then, becoming a practice topic for apprentice orators, the Carthaginian was a danger no longer, except for the unfortunate teachers whose ears had to bear the brunt (VII, 160–4). But at the same time the inveterate devotee of the past could not help regretting the time when the threat embodied by Hannibal, prancing his horse along the defence walls, kept Rome – and above all Roman women! – in the path of duty (VI, 287–91). Rather than give a translation I will quote the pretty paraphrase of this text by Victor Hugo:

> *Ce qui fit la beauté des Romaines antiques,*
> *C'etaient leurs humbles toits, leurs vertus domestiques*
> *Leurs doigts que l'âpre laine avait faits noirs et durs,*
> *Leurs courts sommeils, leur calme, Annibal près des murs,*
> *Et leurs maris debout sur la porte Colline.*
> (What made the women of ancient Rome beautiful was their humble
> homes, their domestic virtues, their fingers hardened and blackened
> by rough wool, their short hours of sleep, their calm, Hannibal
> at the walls, and their menfolk standing at the Colline Gate.)

Nothing and nobody could cause Trajan's Rome to tremble, at the height of its power yet, three centuries later, the memory was still alive of the one enemy who had come within inches of nipping in the bud the greatest undertaking of political and territorial domination the world has ever known. Suetonius recounts that, not many years earlier, the emperor Domitian ordered the execution of a senator who was more of a crank than a conspirator. His name was Mettius Pompusianus, and he always kept with him a map of the known world, together with the speeches of kings and generals, taken from Livy. Of course he needed to be executed, all the more so because he possessed a horoscope that dangled before him the hope of acceding to the Empire (Arnaud, 1983, pp. 677–99). But he had made matters worse, adds Suetonius, by giving two of his slaves the names Mago and Hannibal, names that evidently still carried, if not a holy terror, at least an emotional charge that ruled out any re-use, whether for amusement or provocation.

## Hannibal in our own times

With the passage of time the prohibition disappeared, but it remained a difficult name to bear, and first of all in Italy itself. For one Annibale, how many are called Cesare, Fabio, Mario! And when there was an exception, what can have been the motive for parents to endow their offspring with a name that is so little Roman, so little Christian? Why was the first organist of St Mark's in Venice in the mid-sixteenth century, a Paduan, called Annibale? And why, a few decades later, did the most gifted of the Carrache bring renown to this name, alongside his elder brother, whose name Agostino, that of another great African, restored the balance? One imagines that in bearing the name Hannibal, whether it was bestowed or chosen – as a pseudonym perhaps – there may have been an element of playfulness or defiance, imposed or freely assumed. Staying in Italy, still in the milieu of painters but a little later, in the eighteenth century, we find a sign of this amusement or defiance in the strange signature which a second-rate artist, who nevertheless frequented the great ones, sometimes put on his work. About 1760 Jean-Robert Ango was part of the circle of the bailiff of Breteuil, who had engaged him as copyist. He developed his talents among the artists of the Académie de France in Rome, and thus accompanied Fragonard to Naples, against the setting of the grand tour of Italian painters organized by the abbé de Saint-Non, from which the *Griffonis* would emerge. (Roland-Michel, 1981). One of his friends was Hubert Robert, whose drawings he sometimes copied or whose counter-proofs he sometimes retouched. A whole group of these proofs carry the note 'Annibale Roberti' in red or black pencil, often with the date, which still intrigues specialists (for example, Cuzin and Boulot, 1990, pp. 253–4). There is obviously a mischievous intent, but what exactly is it? Without being able to rival his friend's drawing abilities, which are lively and sharp, with no second attempts, a sensitivity to the play of light, equal skill in seizing an atmosphere and the structure of a monument or the component elements of a landscape, Ango competed with Hubert Robert, following him from Rome to Campania. But beside this 'Roman', officially resident in the palazzo Mancini, he was merely a 'Hannibal'. By annotating his drawings – or designs, the ambiguity in spelling (*dessins* or *desseins*) in that period lent itself to puns – in this parodical fashion he was being deliberately provocative.

It has been observed that in the neo-classical period – from the sixteenth to the eighteenth centuries – poetic or dramatic fiction was not generous towards Hannibal (Aziza, 1993, p. 8). Probably mainly because in that period the well-read could read in the original what appeared to them to be a true epic, written by Polybius and, above all, by Livy and Silius Italicus. The iconography that developed alongside these texts even before the Renaissance made no small contribution to accentuating their epic nature, sometimes transcending their status of valid historical accounts *hic et nunc*. In these Punic wars in pictures, especially in the iconographic representation of the second, the characters, and first of all Hannibal himself, often appear in guises that transform them into participants in the great conflicts of the time: Saracens versus Franks, and soon Turks against Christians. And although in the great decorative programmes of the official iconography of the Renaissance Antiquity receives greater respect, it is always the important moments of the epic that are portrayed. Think of the cycle of great tapestries, based on Jules Romain's cartoons, executed first in Brussels in the first half of the sixteenth century, then resumed by the Gobelins studios in the next century; the series is devoted to the major exploits of Scipio Africanus, but it culminates in the representation of the *Battle of Zama*, with its elephants, which are forever associated with the Punic leader.

Then, as they say in the theatre, and at least as our sources present him, Hannibal is 'typecast', and the only character that history can hand over to literature is the figure of an epic hero, with a tragic end. His shadow wanders through *Nicomède* by Pierre Corneille; and it is at the centre of *La Mort d'Annibal* by his brother Thomas, published in 1669. Half a century later, stepping out of character, Marivaux thought he too could write a tragedy about him, which did little to increase his renown. The tragic theme of the final episode at Prusias' court was somewhat tenuous. And it is a great pity for the author of the *Fausses Confidences*, and others, that Hannibal's deeds provided no material for any sophisticated banter, or quite simply for the slightest romantic or dramatic development. The only feminine silhouette that passes through the story – and we have seen (above, pp. 168–9) how detailed and strong it is – belongs to a woman from Carthage, whose brief life did not cross his own: Sophonisba. No one can seriously blame Hannibal for lacking in human depth, positive feelings or emotional nobility, as Chateaubriand did, calling him a 'cold, cruel, heartless' being (1969, p. 1173). What did he know? The Carthaginian's enthusiasms, thoughts and dreams remained in the manuscript of Silenos of Kale Akte.

But since I have mentioned Chateaubriand's name, I must add that the author of the *Itinéraire* was the chief witness to the great swing of Hannibal's image in European consciousness at the turn of the eighteenth and nineteenth centuries. In his *Considérations*, published in 1734, drawing a parallel between Carthage and Rome, Montesquieu had already sketched the former's likeness to England and its empire. Chateaubriand's *Essai sur les révolutions* (1791) made the transference more precise: Marlborough was to Albion what Hannibal had been to Carthage. And the revolutionary period, with its constant references to Rome, was unable to alter that view. But a change of mind was in the offing, and was due to the Napoleonic venture. Did Bonaparte, in the early days of his personal 'geste', consciously identify with the Carthaginian? At all events, this identification was acquired early in the official iconography thanks to the greatest French painter of the time. We know the celebrated equestrian portrait of *Bonaparte crossing the Alps*, painted by David in 1801; so that there shall be no mistake, the artist has featured under Bonaparte's name, at the bottom left of his composition, those of Hannibal and Charlemagne. More surprisingly, in Italy itself as early as 1797, the leading light of neo-classicism, Vincenzo Monti, in his *Prometeo*, was singing of 'a second Hannibal, greater than the first', the liberator of Italy. And it comes as no surprise that, on the subject of Hannibal, it is to Napoleon himself that we owe the warmest, most enthusiastic pages of that period, written in an exile which united both in the picture of one and the same destiny: 'This most daring of all men, perhaps the most astonishing; so bold, so assured, so broad of vision in all things; who at the age of twenty-six conceives what is scarcely conceivable and carries out what was deemed impossible; who, giving up all communication with his own land, passes through hostile or unknown peoples whom he must attack and conquer, scales the Pyrenees and the Alps, that were thought insurmountable, and comes down into Italy paying with half his army merely to attain a battlefield and the right to fight; who occupies, overruns and rules this same Italy for sixteen years, on several occasions places the terrible and fearsome Rome within inches of its downfall, and leaves his prey only when Rome profits from the lessons he has taught to go and fight him on his home ground' (1823, vol. II, ch. XI, p. 338). For Hudson Lowe's 'guest', this was a nice way of acknowledging a strategic kinship and paying his debt, in terms of image, to the guest of king Prusias.

Since the middle of the nineteenth century, Hannibal has entered the field of learned history, and has long since ceased to be an ideological pawn or reference. Does he still arouse passions? Malaparte relates (1957, pp. 117–22) that, in the Tuscany of his childhood early this century, people still mocked the Carthaginian, and a play in local dialect was put on in the Prato amphitheatre making fun of Hannibal. Duly noted! This would be countered in a more good-natured echo by an old refrain that people hummed in Paris in the 1930s, when Louis Renault's and André Citroën's second-hand cars were beginning to bring good times to the middle classes:

*J'ai achetée trois cents balles*<br>*Chez Monsieur Annibal,*<br>*Le marchand d'occasion*<br>*D' la rue de Lyon.*

(I got it for 300 francs<br>from Monsieur Annibal,<br>the second-hand dealer<br>in the rue de Lyon.)

Would Hannibal's last use be to boost a common little jingle?

If that were the case, this book, and quite a few others, would not have been written. The renewal of interest in Antiquity in present times especially favours

Hannibal, for two or three features which are his, and his alone. Just as the war he waged against Rome was the first world war, its leader was the first international hero the world had ever known. He was international not only for the breadth of his field of action, which extended to the Orient during his time in exile. Even though he left a trace rather than a heritage, Hannibal is greater than Alexander in that he was not enclosed in a single culture. Perhaps, thanks to Hannibal's exceptional calibre as a leader and his genius as a strategist – which made such an impression on past centuries – our own period has become alive to the polyvalence of a human experience in which so many facets of the ancient Mediterranean are superimposed. And all this during a lifetime that was fairly short, when all is said and done. The most famous Carthaginian is a paradox because, apart from his early childhood, he spent only a few short years in Carthage, and of those years tradition retains only the year of his suffetate for certain. Nevertheless, his acquaintance in his youth with Iberian societies and cultures, then his approach to the Celtic world and, lastly and chiefly, the strong attraction that must have been exerted on him by the Campanian and Samnite lands, the Greek towns of southern Italy, and later the cities of the Hellenized East, never erased his feeling of belonging to a native culture, to a religion that remained original and strict despite external contributions, or his loyalty to his Punic homeland. Rome would have to wait until Hadrian acceded to the empire before it finally found a son who, like Hannibal, would combine both *pietas* and a sense of the universal.

# Chronological highlights

**247** Birth of Hannibal. His father Hamilcar is sent to Sicily, where in 244 he succeeds in taking possession of Eryx (Erice).

**241** A treaty ('the peace of Lutatius') brings to an end the first war between Carthage and Rome. Carthage loses Sicily and has to withdraw from the Aeolian Islands. Start of the Mercenaries' War, which lasts until 238/237. At the close of this war Rome annexes Sardinia.

**237** Hamilcar's departure for Spain, accompanied by the young Hannibal (episode of 'Hannibal's oath'). Hamilcar founds Akra Leuke (Alicante?).

**228** Hasdrubal the Fair, Hamilcar's son-in-law, succeeds his father-in-law in Spain, where he founds a new capital known by its Latin name Carthago Nova (Cartagena). In 226 he receives a Roman embassy with whom he makes an agreement under the terms of which the Carthaginians are banned from 'crossing the river Iber under arms'.

**221** Hannibal takes over as head of the army in Spain from Hasdrubal, who is assassinated in Cartagena.

**219** Hannibal seizes Saguntum after an eight-month siege. In autumn 219 a Roman embassy goes to Carthage; war is declared.

**218** Hannibal leaves Cartagena in the spring. In June he crosses the Ebro, in July the Pyrenees, in mid-August the Rhône north of Avignon. The crossing of the Alps – going up the Maurienne valley at the end of the journey – takes place in autumn 218. First engagement with P. Cornelius Scipio, senior, on the Ticinus at the end of November 218.
Victory on the Trebia, late December 218.

**217** January–April: Hannibal winters in Cisalpine Gaul. He passes the Apennines in late spring and loses the sight of an eye as the result of an infection contracted in the marshes of the Arno.
21 June 217: battle of Trasimene; the consul C. Flaminius Nepos dies on the battlefield.
Summer–autumn 217: Hannibal spends the summer in Picenum and thrusts as far as Apulia. Q. Fabius Maximus, appointed dictator, begins his tactic of delaying action.
Hannibal spends the winter of 217–216 at Gereonium, in Samnite territory.

In Spain, P. and Cn. Scipio consolidate their positions north of the Ebro.

**216** Elected consuls for 216, L. Aemilius Paullus and C. Terentius Varro, take up office in March. Hannibal goes down to Apulia in early summer.
2 August 216: battle of Cannae; between 50,000 and 70,000 die on the battlefield, including the consul Aemilius Paullus.
Hannibal does not march on Rome and chooses to have southern Italy, notably Bruttium, occupied by his brother Mago, while he himself enters Capua, where he spends the winter of 216–215.

**215** Hannibal concludes a treaty of alliance with Philip V of Macedon. Syracuse, where the old Hieron has just died, is ready to swing to a Punic alliance; but an anti-Roman uprising in Sardinia fails. Hannibal takes up his winter quarters at Arpi, in Apulia.

**214** Q. Fabius Maximus, for the fourth time, and M. Claudius Marcellus for the third, are elected consuls. A monetary reform is set in motion, leading to the creation of the denarius. Rome raises eighteen legions and besieges Syracuse.
Hannibal winters at Salapia in Apulia.

**213–212** Marcellus captures Syracuse despite Archimedes' defences.
For his part, Hannibal seizes Tarentum, but the citadel remains in Roman hands.

**211** Hannibal makes an incursion as far as the walls of Rome, but Capua surrenders to the Romans. In Spain, after eroding Carthaginian positions from 216 to 212, the Scipios, opposed by Hannibal's two brothers and a third army, led by Hasdrubal, son of Gisco, succumb in the north of Andalusia.

**210** Following the death of his father and uncle, P. Cornelius Scipio is placed at the head of the army in Spain. He seizes Cartagena.

**209–208** Scipio's victory at Baecula (Bailén). In Italy, Tarentum is recaptured from the Punic forces, but Marcellus dies in an ambush in summer 208.

**207** Coming from Spain, after crossing the Pyrenees and Alps to join his brother, Hasdrubal is defeated on the Metaurus, where he dies.

**206** Scipio's victory at Ilipa, near Seville, puts an end to Carthaginian rule in Spain.

**205** Hannibal's third brother, Mago, coming from Minorca, in the Balearics, lands with his troops on the Ligurian coast, where he hangs on for three years. At Crotona, on the Bruttium coast, Hannibal has the story of his deeds carved on an altar in the temple of Juno Lacinia.

**204** Elected consul in 205, then having his command prorogued in 204, Scipio crosses to Africa and lays siege to Utica, establishing his camp nearby at Castra Cornelia.

**203** Victory of Scipio, allied with Massinissa, against Hasdrubal son of Gisco and Syphax on the Great Plains, in the middle valley of the Medjerda.

Hannibal is recalled from Italy. He lands on the Byzacium coast and sets up his quarters at Hadrumetum (Sousse).

**202** The decisive encounter between Scipio and Hannibal takes place at Zama (or, more precisely, Naraggara) in late summer or autumn 202.

**201** Peace is granted to Carthage on very harsh conditions: it loses its war fleet, is reduced to its own territory in Africa, placed under supervision and has to pay a heavy war indemnity, to be settled in fifty annual payments.

**196** Hannibal is elected suffete in Carthage. He attacks the powers of the order of judges and makes corrupt officials repay their ill-gotten gains. He may be behind the new urban expansion which archaeology shows was taking place in Carthage at that time.

**195** Threatened with being arrested and handed over to the Romans, Hannibal goes into exile. He lands at Tyre and joins Antiochus III at Ephesus.

**193** Hannibal sends an emissary to Carthage on a secret mission that fails. Sent to Rome to arbitrate on a disagreement between Carthage and Massinissa, Scipio handles Carthage carefully.

**192–191** Hannibal accompanies Antiochus on his campaign in Greece; but he is not responsible for the defeat suffered by Antiochus at Thermopylae in the spring of 191.

**190** Hannibal is in command at sea against the Rhodian fleet off Side, in the gulf of Pamphylia, but takes no part in the battle of Magnesia on the Sipylus in the winter of 190–189 which ruins Antiochus' military power and forces Hannibal to new adventures.

**189–188/187** There are signs of Hannibal in Crete, then Armenia, where he draws up the plans for Artaxata, in the upper valley of the Araxes.

**187–183** Hannibal takes refuge with King Prusias of Bithynia, whose fleet he commands against Eumenes of Pergamum on the Sea of Marmara. He builds a new capital for the king at Prusa (Brousse). But in 183, on the point of being handed over by his host to Flamininus, he kills himself by taking poison.

# Bibliography

## Sources

The reader will have noticed that I have been obliged to refer, if not continually, at least very frequently – especially when there was some discrepancy in the sources – to the texts which form the basis of the history presented or the problems expounded.

It is therefore possible to study these texts, chiefly those of Polybius and Livy, our principal sources, and the most accessible and most recent editions in English are given below.

(a) Polybius, *Histories*, translated by W. R. Paton, in six volumes, Loeb Classical Library, London and New York, 1922–27.

(b) Livy, *Livy*, translated by B. O. Foster, Loeb Classical Library, London and New York, 1919–59.

The reader who may wish to refer to the French editions may note the following:

POLYBE, *Histoires*

(a) Collection des Universités de France (Collection 'G. Budé'): texte et traduction, notes explicatives (Paris, Les Belles Lettres)

- Livres I et II, ed. P. Pédech
- Livres III et IV, ed. J. A. de Foucault
- Livre V, ed. P. Pédech
- Livres VI, VII, VIII et IX, ed. R. Weil
- Livres X et XI, ed. E. Foulon and R. Weil
- Livre XII, ed. P. Pédech
- Livres XIII-XVII, ed. E. Foulon and R. Weil

(b) Bibliothèque de la Pléiade (Paris, Gallimard, 1970): traduction (seule) de Denis Roussel, avec notes.

*TITE-LIVE, Histoire romaine*

(a) Collection des Universités de France: texte et traduction, notes explicatives (Paris, Les Belles Lettres)

- Livre XXI, ed. P. Jal
- Livre XXV, ed. F. Nicolet-Croizat
- Livre XXVI, ed. P. Jal
- Livre XXVIII, ed. P. Jal
- Livre XXIX, ed. P. François
- Livre XXXI, ed. A. Hus

– Livre XXXVI, ed. A. Manuelian
– Livre XXXVII, ed. J.-M. Engel
– Livre XXXVIII, ed. R. Adam
– Livre XXXIX, ed. A.-M. Adam
(b) Collection des 'Classiques Garnier' (Paris, Garnier): texte et Eugène Lasserre: Tomes IV, V, VI et VII: livres X à XXXV.
(c) Collection 'GF-Flammarion' (Paris, Flammarion): traduction (seule) d'A. Flobert, et notes: 'La seconde guerre punique, I' (livres XXI à XXV), 'La seconde guerre punique, II' (livres XXVI à XXX).

## Studies

Given below are those authors whose works I have referred to in writing this book, together with some additional works of interest. Publications relating particularly to Hannibal are marked with an asterisk.

Acquaro, Enrico. 'Su i "ritratti Barcidi" delle monete puniche', *Rivista storica dell'Antichità*, **13–14** (1983–4), 83–6.

Adam, Richard, ed. Livy, book XXXVIIII (Paris, Les Belles Lettres, 1982).

Alfaro-Asins, Carmen. *Las monedas de Gadir/Gades* (Madrid, 1988).

Alfieri, Nerro. 'La battaglia del lago Plestino', *Picus*, VI (1986), 7–22.

Alvisi, Giovanna. 'Dal Trasimeno a Capua, le marce di Annibale nel biennio 217–216 A.C.', in *Littérature gréco-romaine et géographie historique. Mélanges offerts à R. Dion* (Paris, 1974).

André, Jean-Marie and Baslez, Marie-Françoise. *Voyager dans l'Antiquité* (Paris, Fayard, 1993).

Arnaud, Pascal. 'L'affaire Mettius Pompusianus, ou le crime de cartographie', *MEFRA*, **95** (1983), 677–99.

Astin, A.E. 'Saguntum and the Origins of the Second Punic War', *Latomus* (1967), 577–96.

Aubet, Maria Eugenia. 'Zum Problematik der orientalisierenden Horizontes auf der iberischen Halbinsel', in *Phoenizier im Westen*, ed. H. G. Niemeyer, Madrider Beitrage, 8 (Mainz, 1982), pp. 309–35.

Austin, N. J. E. and Rankov, N. B., *Exploratio: Military and Political Intelligence in the Roman World from the Second Punic War to the Battle of Adrianople*, London, 1995.

Azan, P. *Annibal dans les Alpes* (Paris, 1902).

Aziza, C. *Carthage, le rêve en flammes* (Paris, 1993).

Badian, E. *Foreign Clientelae, 264–70 BC* (Oxford, 1958).

—— 'Rome and Antiochos the Great: a study in cold war', *Classical Philology* (1959), 81–99.

Bagnall, Nigel. *The Punic Wars* (London, 1990).

Barcelo, P. A. *Karthago und die iberische Halbinsel vor den Barkiden* (Bonn, 1988).

Bar-Kochva, B. *The Seleucid Army: Organization and Tactics in the Great Campaigns* (Cambridge, 1976).

Barruol, G. 'Les civilisations de l'âge du fer en Languedoc', in *La Préhistoire française*, (Paris, 1976), vol. II, pp. 676–86.

Bickerman, E. J. 'An oath of Hannibal', *TAPHA*, **75** (1944), 87–102.

—— 'Hannibal's covenant', *American Journal of Philology*, 73 (1952), 1–23.

Bosch-Gimpera, P., in *Homenaje a J. V. Vives* (Barcelona, 1965), vol. I, pp. 33–59.

Bradford, E. D. S. *Hannibal*, New York, 1981.
Briscoe, John. 'The Second Punic War', in *Cambridge Ancient History*, 2nd edn, ed. J. Boardman *et al.*, vol. 8 (Cambridge, 1989), 44–80.
Brisson, Jean-Paul. 'Les mutations de la seconde guerre punique', in *Problèmes de la guerre à Rome* (under the direction of J.-P. Brisson) (Paris and The Hague, 1969), pp. 35–59.
—— **Carthage or Rome* (Paris, Fayard, 1973).
Brizzi, Giovanni. *I sistemi informativi dei Romani. Principi e realtà nell'età delle conquiste oltremare (218–168 a.C.)* (Wiesbaden, 1982).
—— 'Ancora su Annibale e l'ellenismo. La fondazione di Artaxata e l'iscrizione di Era Lacinia', in *Atti I Congr. intern. di Studi fenici e punici* (Rome, CNR, 1983), pp. 243–59.
—— **Annibale. Strategia e immagine* (Perugia, 1984a).
—— *Studi di storia annibalica* (Faenza, 1984b).
Burton, Paul J. 'The Summoning of the Magna Mater to Rome (205 B.C.)', *Historia* (1996), 36–63.
Cabanes, Pierre. *L'Épire, de la mort de Pyrrhos à la conquête romaine* (Paris, 1976).
Camps, Gabriel. 'Nouvelles observations sur l'architecture et l'âge du Médracen, le mausolée royal de Numidie', *CRAI* (1973), 470–517.
—— *Berbères. Aux marges de l'Histoire* (Toulouse, 1980).
—— *L'Afrique du Nord au féminin* (Paris, Perrin, 1992).
Candiloro, E. 'Politica e cultura in Atene da Pidna alla guerra mitridatica', *Studi classici e orientali*, XIV (1965), pp. 171–6.
Carcopino, Jérôme. *Les Étapes de l'impérialisme romain* (Paris, 1961a).
—— *'Grandeur et faiblesses d'Hannibal', in *Profils de conquérants* (Paris 1961b), pp. 109–237.
Caven, B. *The Punic Wars* (London, 1980).
Chappuis, C. 'Annibal dans les Alpes', in *Annales de l'Université de Grenoble* (1897), pp. 223–356.
Chateaubriand, F. R. *Itinéraire de Paris à Jérusalem*, Paris, 1969.
Christ, Karl. 'Zur Beurteilung Hannibals', in *Hannibal*, ed. K. Christ (Darmstadt, 1974), pp. 361–407.
Chroust, A. H. 'Internationale Verträge in der Antike. Die diplomatischen Verhandlungen zwischen Hannibal und Philipp von Macedonien', in *Hannibal*, ed. K. Christ (Darmstadt, 1974), pp. 275–334.
Cornell, T., Rankov, B., and Sabin, P. *The Second Punic War: A Reappraisal*, Bulletin of the Institute of Classical Studies, Supplement 67 (London, 1996).
Cuzin, Jean-Pierre and Boulot, Catherine, in *J. H. Fragonard e H. Robert a Roma, Villa Medici, 5 dic. 1990–24 feb. 1991* (Rome, 1990).
De Beer, Sir Gavin. **Hannibal: The Struggle for Power in the Mediterranean* (London, Thames & Hudson, 1969).
de Foucalt, J. A., ed. Polybius, *Histoires*, III (Paris, Les Belles Lettres, 1971).
De Hoz, Javier. 'The Phoenician origin of early Hispanic scripts', in *Phoinikeia Grammata, Actes du colloque de Liège, 15–18 nov. 1989* (Namur, 1991), pp. 669–78.
de Lavis-Traffort, M. A. *Le col alpin franchi par Hannibal* (Saint-Jean-de-Maurienne, 1956).
de Saint-Denis, E. *Le vocabulaire des manoeuvres nautiques en latin* (Mâcon, 1935).
—— 'Encore l'itinéraire transalpin d'Hannibal', *Revue des Études latines*, 51 (1973 [1974]), 122–49.
—— 'Nostrum mare', *Revue des Études latines*, 53 (1975) [1976]), 62–84.
De Sanctis, Gaetano. *Storia dei Romani*, vols III, 2; IV, 1, Turin, 1917–23.

Desanges, Jehan. *Recherches sur l'activité des Méditerranéens aux confins de l'Afrique* (coll. 'École française de Rome, 38') (Rome, 1978a).

——'L'Afrique romaine et libyco-berbère', in *Rome et la conquête du monde méditerranéen. II: Genèse d'un empire* (under the direction of C. Nicolet) (coll. 'Nouvelle Clio', 8 bis) (Paris, PHF, 1978b), pp. 627–56.

——ed. Pliny the Elder, *Histoire naturelle*, Book V, 1–46 (Paris, Les Belles Lettres, 1980).

——'Massinissa et Carthage entre la deuxième et la troisième guerre punique: un problème de chronologie', in *Actes du XXX^e Congrès int. d'études phéniciennes et puniques* (Tunis, 11–16 Nov. 1991) Tunis, 1995, I, pp. 252–358.

Desy, Philippe. 'Il grano dell'Apulia e la data della battaglie del Trasimeno', *Parola del Passato*, **245** (1989), 102–15.

Devallet, Georges, and Miniconi, P. ed. Silius Italicus, *La Guerre punique* (Paris, Les Belles Lettres, 1979), vol. I.

Diana, Bettina. 'Annibale e il passaggio degli Appennini', *Aevum*, **61** (1987), 108–12.

Dion, Roger. 'À propos de la marche d'Hannibal sur le versant occidental des Alpes', *Bulletin philologique et historique du CTHS* (1960), 55–6.

——'La voie héracléenne et l'itinéraire transalpin d'Hannibal', in *Mélanges à A. Grenier* (coll. 'Latomus', LVIII) (Brussels, 1962), pp. 132–47.

Ducos, Michèle. 'Les passions, les hommes et l'histoire chez Tite-Live', *Revue des études latines*, **65** (1987), 132–47.

Eckstein, A. M. 'Hannibal at New Carthage: Polybius, 3, 15 and the power of irrationality', *Classical Philology*, **84** (1989), 1–15.

Errington, R. M. 'Rome and Spain before the Second Punic War', *Latomus*, **29**:1 (1970), 25–57.

Fantar, Mhamed Hassine. *Carthage. Approche d'une civilisation* (Tunis, Alif, 1993), vols I and II.

Ferrary, Jean-Louis. *Philhellénisme et impérialisme. Aspects idéologiques de la conquête romaine du monde hellénistique* (BEFAR, 271) (Rome, 1988).

Forres, Emil O. 'Karthago wurde erst 673/663 v. Christ gegründet', in *Festschrift Franz Dornseiff* (Leipzig, 1953), pp. 85–93.

Freyburger, Gérard. *Fides. Étude sémantique et religieuse depuis les origines jusqu'à l'époque augustéenne* (Paris, Les Belles Lettres, 1986).

Granzotto, Gianni. **Annibale* (Milan, Mondadori, 1980).

Gras, Michel. In Michel Gras, Pierre Rouillard and Javier Teixidor, *L'Univers phénicien* (Paris, Arthaud, 1989).

Green, Peter, *Alexander to Actium: The Historical Evolution of the Hellenistic Age*, rev. edn (Berkeley, 1993).

Grimal, Pierre. *Le siècle des Scipions. Rome et l'hellénisme au temps des guerres puniques*, 2nd edn (Paris, Aubier, 1975).

Gruen, Erich, *The Hellenistic World and the Coming of Rome* (Berkeley, 1984).

Gsell, Stéphane. *Histoire ancienne de l'Afrique du Nord* (Paris, Leroux, 1921), vols II and III.

——'Les esclaves ruraux dans l'Afrique romaine', in *Mélanges Gustave Glotz* (Paris, 1932), pp. 395–415.

Guillaume, General A. *Annibal franchit les Alpes, 218 avant J.-C.* (La Tronche-Montfleury, 1967).

Hans-Günther, Linda Marie. 'Hannibal im Exil: seine antirömische Agitation und die römische Gegnerwahrnehmung', in *Studia Phoenicia, X, Punic Wars* (Leuven, 1989), pp. 241–50.

——'L'immagine di Amilcare Barca presso i Romani', in *Atti II Cong. intern. di studi fenici e punici* (Rome, CNR, 1991), pp. 113–16.

Harris, W. V. 'Roman Expansion in the West', in *Cambridge Ancient History*, 2nd edn, ed. J. Boardman *et al.* (Cambridge, 1989) vol. 8, 107–62.

Heurgon, Jacques. *Trois études sur le ver sacrum* (coll. 'Latomus', 26) (Brussels, 1957).

——*Rome et la Méditerranée occidentale jusqu'aux guerres puniques* (coll. 'Nouvelle Clio', 7) (Paris, PUF, 1969).

Hoffmann, Wilhelm. **Hannibal* (Göttingen, 1962).

Holleaux, Maurice. *Rome et la conquête de l'Orient. Philippe V et Antiochos le Grand. Études d'épigraphie et d'histoire grecques, V* (Paris, 1957).

Huss, Werner. *Geschichte der Karthager (Handbuch des Altertumwissenschaft*, III, 8) (Munich, 1985).

——'Hannibal und die Religio', in *Studia Phoenicia, IV, Religio Phoenicia* (Namur, 1986), pp. 223–38.

Jal, Paul, ed. Livy, book XXI (Paris, Les Belles Lettres, 1988).

Jullian, Camille. *Histoire de la Gaule* (Paris, 1920), vol. I.

Kahrstedt, U. in Meltzer, *Geschichte der Karthager* (Berlin, 1913), vol. III.

Kertész, J. 'Die Schlacht bei Cannae und ihr Einfluss auf die Entwicklung der Kriegskunst', in *Wissens. Beiträge der Martin-Luther Univ.* (Halle, 1980), 38, pp. 29–43.

Kienast, D. *Cato der Zensor. Persöhnlichkeit und seine Zeit*, 2nd edn (Darmstadt, 1973).

Kotula, Taddeusz. 'Hannibal-Suffet und seine vermeintlich demokratische Reform in Karthago', *Riv. stor. dell'Antichità*, **XIII–XIV** (1983–4), 87–101.

Kromayer, J. *Antike Schlachtfelder* (Berlin, 1912), III, 1.

Kussmaul, P. 'Der Halbmond von Cannae', *Museum Helveticum*, **XXV** (1978), 249–57.

Lancel, Serge. *Carthage* (Paris, Fayard, 1992).

——*Carthage. A History*, trans. A. Nevill (Blackwell, Oxford, 1995a).

——in V. Krings ed., *La Civilisation phénicienne et punique. Manuel de recherche (Handbuch der Orientalistik, 20)* (Brill, Leiden, New York and Cologne, 1995b), pp. 397–410.

Lazenby, J. F. **Hannibal's War: A Military History of the Second Punic War* (Warminster, 1978).

——*The First Punic War: A Military History* (Stanford, CA, 1996).

Le Glay, Marcel. 'Les premiers temps de la Carthage romaine: pour une revision des dates', in *Histoire et Archéologie de l'Afrique du Nord, II^e coll. intern.* (Paris, CTHS, 1985), pp. 235–47.

Lepelley, Claude. 'Juvenes et circoncellions: les derniers sacrifices humains de l'Afrique antique', *Antiquités africaines*, **15** (1980), 261–71.

Lévêque, Pierre. *Pyrrhos* (Paris, 1957).

Malaparte, G. *Ces sacrés toscans* (Paris, 1957).

Marchetti, Patrick. 'La datation du denier romain et les fouilles de Morgantina', *Revue belge de numismatique* (1971), 81–114.

——'La deuxième guerre punique en Sicile: les années 215–214 et le récit de Tite-Live', *Bulletin de l'Institut belge de Rome*, **42** (1972), 5–26.

——*Histoire économique et monétaire de la deuxième guerre punique* (Brussels, 1978).

Martin, Paul M. *L'idée de la royauté à Rome* (Clermont-Ferrand, Adosa, 1994), vol. II.

Merkelbach, Reinhold. *Griechische Papyri der Hamburger Staats und Universitäts Bibliothek* (Hamburg, 1954).

Meyer, Eduard. 'Hannibals Alpenübergang', *Museum Helveticum*, **15** (1953), 227–41.

——'Noch einmals Hannibals Alpenübergang', *Museum Helveticum*, **21** (1964), 99–101.

Momigliano, Arnaldo. *Alien Wisdom: The Limits of Hellenization* (Cambridge, 1975).
Montgomery, Sir Bernard. *A History of Warfare* (London, 1968).
Morel, J.-P. 'Études de céramique campanienne: l'atelier des petites estampilles', *MEFRA*, **81**:1 (1969), 59–117.
——'Les vases à vernis noir et à figures rouges d'Afrique avant la deuxième guerre punique et le problème des importations de Grande-Grèce', *Antiquités africaines*, **15** (1930), 29–90.
——'La céramique à vernis noir de Byrsa: nouvelles données et éléments de comparaison', in *Actes du colloque sur la céramique antique, CEDAC, Carthage, dossier 1* (1982), pp. 43–61.
——'Les importations de céramiques grecques et italiennes dans le monde punique (V$^{e}$–I$^{er}$ siècle)', *Atti I Congr. intern. di studi fenici e punici*, vol. III (Rome, CNR, 1983), pp. 731–40.
——'La céramique à vernis noir de Carthage, sa diffusion, son influence', in *Cahiers des études anciennes (Québec)*, XVIII (1986), pp. 25–68.
Napoleon I (Bonaparte). *Mémorial de Sainte-Hélène* (Paris, 1823).
Nicolet, Claude. 'À Rome pendant la seconde guerre punique', *Annales E.S.C.*, **18** (1963), 417–36.
——*L'ordre equestre à l'époque républicaine (312–43 av. J.C.)* (Paris, De Boccard, 1974).
——*Rome et la conquête du monde méditerranéen. I: Les structures de l'Italie romaine* (coll. 'Nouvelle Clio', 8) (Paris, PUF, 1977).
——'Les guerres puniques', in *Rome et la conquête du monde méditerranéen. I: Genèse d'un empire*, ed. C. Nicolet (coll. 'Nouvelle Clio', 8 bis) (Paris, PUF, 1978), pp. 594–626.
——*L'inventaire du monde. Geographie et politique aux origines de l'Empire romain* (Paris, Fayard, 1988).
Nicolini, Gérard. *Les bronzes figurés des sanctuaires ibériques* (Paris, 1969).
——*Les Ibères. Art et civilisation* (Paris, Fayard, 1973).
Nizza, D. 'Note sul vero nome del luogo della battaglia di Zama', *Rendiconti dell'Istituto Lombardo, cl. di Lett. e scienze mor. e stor.*, **CXIV** (1980), 85–8.
O'Bryhim, S. 'Hannibal's elephants and the crossing of the Rhône', *Classical Quarterly*, **41** (1991), 121–5.
Paskoff, Roland, Slim, Hédi and Trousset, Pol. 'Le littoral de la Tunisie dans l'Antiquité: cinq années de recherches géo-archéologiques', *CRAI* (1991), 515–46.
Pédech, Paul. *La Méthode historique de Polybe* (Paris, 1964).
Pelletier, Agnès. 'Sagontins et Turdetans à la veille de la deuxième guerre punique', *Revues des études anciennes*, **88** (1986), 307–15.
Picard, Gilbert. 'Le problème du portrait d'Hannibal', *Karthago*, **XII** (1965), 31–41.
——**Hannibal* (Paris, Hachette, 1967).
——'Hannibal hégémon hellénistique', *Riv. Stor. dell' Antichità*, **XIII–XIV** (1983–4), 75–81.
——*La Civilisation de l'Afrique romaine*, 2nd edn. (Paris, Études Augustiniennes, 1990).
Picard, Gilbert and Picard, Colette. *The Life and Death of Carthage*, trans. Dominique Collon (London, 1968).
——*Vie et mort de Carthage* (Paris, Hachette, 1970).
Proctor, Dennis. *Hannibal's March in History* (Oxford, 1971).
Rakob, Friedrich. 'Numidische Königsarchitektur in Nordafrika', in *Die Numider* (Bonn, 1979).
Ramallo, S. *et al.* 'Carthago Nova', *Dialoghi di Archeologia*, **1–2** (1992), 105–18.

Rebuffat, René. 'Unus homo nobis cunctando restituit rem', *Revue des études latines*, **60** (1932 [1983]), 153–65.

Rémy, Bernard. 'Les limites de la cité des Allobroges', *Cahiers d'histoire*, **XV**: 3 (1970), 195–210.

Edward S. G. Robinson. 'Punic coins of Spain and their bearing on the Roman Republic series', in *Essays in Roman Coinage presented to Harold Mattingly* (Oxford, 1956), pp. 34–62.

Roland-Michel, Marianne. 'Un peintre français nommé Ango', *The Burlington Magazine*, **40** (Dec. 1981), 780–6.

Rouillard, Pierre. *Les Grecs et la péninsule ibérique du VIII^e au IV^e siècle avant J.-C.* (Paris, De Boccard, 1991).

Samivel et Norande, S. *Les Grands Passages des Alpes* (Grenoble, Glenat, 1983).

Scullard, Howard H. *Scipio Africanus in the Second Punic War* (Cambridge, 1930).

——*Roman Politics (220–150* BC*)* (Oxford, 1951).

——*Scipio Africanus soldier and politician* (London, Thames & Hudson, 1970).

——'The Carthaginians in Spain', in *Cambridge Ancient History*, 2nd edn, ed. J. Boardman *et al.*, vol. 8 (Cambridge, 1989), 17–43.

Seibert, Jakob. 'Der Alpenübergang Hannibals. Ein gelöstes Problem?', *Gymnasium*, **95**:1 (1986), 21–73.

——*Hannibal* (Darmstadt, 1993).

Shean, John F. 'Hannibal's Mules: The Logistical Limitations of Hannibal's Army and the Battle of Cannae, 216 B.C.', *Historia* (1996), 159–87.

Sumner, G. V. 'Rome, Spain and the outbreak of the second Punic War', *Latomus*, **31**:2 (1972), 469–80.

Susini, G. 'Ricerche sulla battaglia del Trasimeno', *Ann. dell' Accad. etrusca di Cortona*, **XI** (1959–60).

——'L'archeologia della guerra annibalica', in *Studi annibalici. Atti del convegno svoltosi a Cortona-Tuoro sul Trasimeno-Perugia, Oct. 1961* (Cortona, 1964), pp. 132–6.

Syme, Sir Ronald. *Sallust* (Berkeley, 1964).

Sznycer, Maurice. *Les Passages puniques en transcription latine dans le Poenulus de Plaute* (Paris, Klincksieck, 1967).

——'Carthage et la civilisation punique', in *Rome et la conquête du monde méditerranéen. II: Genèse d'un empire* (under the direction of C. Nicolet) (Paris, PUF, 1978, coll. Nouvelle Clio', 8 bis), pp. 545–93.

Thompson, Wesley E. 'The Battle of the Bagradas', *Hermes* **CXIV** (1986), 110–17.

Toynbee, Arnold J. *Hannibal's Legacy. The Hannibalic War's Effects on Roman Life*, 2 vols (Oxford, New York and Toronto, 1965).

Vallet, Georges. 'Un exemple de partialité chez Tite-Live: les premiers combats autour de Gereonium', *Revue des études latines*, **39** (1961) [1962], 182–95.

Veith, George, in Kromayer, J., and Veith, G., *Antike Schlachtfelder*, vol. III (Berlin, 1912).

Veyne, Paul. 'Y a-t-il eu un impérialisme romain?', *MEFRA*, **2** (1975), 793–855.

Villaronga, Leandro. *Las monedas Hispano-Cartaginesas* (Barcelona, 1973).

——*Numismatia antigua de Hispania* (Barcelona, 1979).

Walbank, F. W. *A Historical Commentary on Polybius* (Oxford, Clarendon Press, vol. I: 1957, vol. II: 1967, vol. III: 1979).

——'Polybius and the *Aitiai* of the second Punic War', *LCM*, **8** (1983).

Warmington, B. H. *Carthage*, rev. edn (New York, 1969).

Wiegand, Theodor. 'Zur Lage des Hannibalgrabes', *MDAI, Athen. Abt.*, **XXVII** (1902), 321–6.

Will, Édouard. *Histoire politique du monde hellénistique. II: Des avènements d'Antiochos III et de Philippe V à la fin des Lagides* (Nancy, 1967).

Wuilleumier, Pierre. *Tarente, des origines à la conquête romaine* (Paris, De Boccard, 1939).

# Index

Place-names are indicated in bold type, and the names of people in *italics* (Romans designated by their *tria nomina* have their forename reduced to the initial: A. = Aulus; Ap. = Appius; C. = Gaius; Cn. = Gnaeus; L. = Lucius; M. = Marcus; M' = Manius; P. = Publius; Q. = Quintus; Sex. = Sextus; T. = Titus; Ti. = Tiberius).